An Intertextual Commentary on Romans

An Intertextual Commentary on
ROMANS

VOLUME 2
(ROMANS 5:1—8:39)

Channing L. Crisler

☙PICKWICK *Publications* • Eugene, Oregon

AN INTERTEXTUAL COMMENTARY ON ROMANS
Volume 2 (Romans 5:1—8:39)

Copyright © 2021 Channing Leon Crisler. All rights reserved. Except for brief quotations in critical publications or reviews, no part of this book may be reproduced in any manner without prior written permission from the publisher. Write: Permissions, Wipf and Stock Publishers, 199 W. 8th Ave., Suite 3, Eugene, OR 97401.

Pickwick Publications
An Imprint of Wipf and Stock Publishers
199 W. 8th Ave., Suite 3
Eugene, OR 97401

www.wipfandstock.com

PAPERBACK ISBN: 978-1-7252-6343-7
HARDCOVER ISBN: 978-1-7252-6344-4
EBOOK ISBN: 978-1-7252-6345-1

Cataloguing-in-Publication data:

Names: Crisler, Channing Leon.

Title: An intertextual commentary on Romans : volume 2 (Romans 5:1—8:39) / Channing Leon Crisler.

Description: Eugene, OR: Pickwick Publications, 2021 | Includes bibliographical references and index.

Identifiers: ISBN 978-1-7252-6343-7 (paperback) | ISBN 978-1-7252-6344-4 (hardcover) | ISBN 978-1-7252-6345-1 (ebook)

Subjects: LCSH: Bible. Romans, V-VIII—Commentaries. | Bible. Romans, V-VIII—Criticism, interpretation, etc. | Interxtuality in the Bible. | Bible. New Testament—Relation to the Old Testament.

Classification: BS2665.53 C75 v. 2 2021 (print) | BS2665.53 (ebook)

To My Students

Table of Contents

Acknowledgments | ix

Abbreviations | x

Chapter 1: Introduction | 1

Chapter 2: Romans 5:1–11 | 12

Chapter 3: Romans 5:12–21 | 38

Chapter 4: Romans 6:1–23 | 62

Chapter 5: Romans 7:1–6 | 96

Chapter 6: Romans 7:7–25 | 111

Chapter 7: Romans 8:1–11 | 143

Chapter 8: Romans 8:12–17 | 170

Chapter 9: Romans 8:18–27 | 189

Chapter 10: Romans 8:28–30 | 210

Chapter 11: Romans 8:31–39 | 228

Bibliography | 251

Ancient Documents Index | 261

Acknowledgments

A PROJECT OF THIS size requires help from many individuals and groups. I would like to thank my wife, Kelley, and my children for their support. They always sacrifice as much as, or more than, anyone. I would also like to thank Anderson University (SC) for graciously granting me a quasi-sabbatical in the Spring of 2020 as part of its Faculty Scholars Program. Many staff members at Thrift Library on the campus of Anderson University have helped retrieve countless articles, monographs, commentaries, and other materials. Fred Guyette has been especially helpful in this regard. His ability to find secondary resources in such an organized and efficient way, even in the midst of a global pandemic, is simply legendary. I would also like to thank Chris Spinks at Wipf & Stock for not giving up on this project when it became much longer than originally anticipated. Lastly, I want to thank the various people who have poured into me both in the local church and academy. I cannot list them all here, but I am grateful for people who have instilled in me a love for the sacred text, both old and new, which indeed gives hope (Rom 15:4).

Channing L. Crisler
Domine memento mei

Abbreviations

ABR	Australian Biblical Review
Bib	Biblica
BibInt	Biblical Interpretation
BibSac	Biblica Sacra
BN	Biblische Notizen
CBQ	Catholic Biblical Quarterly
CurBS	Currents in Research: Biblical Studies
ETL	Ephemerides theologicaelovanienses
EvQ	Evangelical Quarterly
EvTh	Evangelische Theologie
ExAud	Ex Auditu
ExpTim	Expository Times
FAT	Forschungenzum Alten Testament
HBTH	Horizons in Biblical Theology
HTR	Harvard Theological Review
Int	Interpretation
JBL	Journal of Biblical Literature
JBQ	Jewish Bible Quarterly
JETS	Journal of the Evangelical Theological Society
JSNT	Journal for the Study of the New Testament
JSOT	Journal for the Study of the Old Testament
JSOTSup	Journal for the Study of the Old Testament Supplements
JTS	Journal of Theological Studies

LEH	Greek-English Lexicon of the Septuagint compiled by J. Lust, E. Eynikel, and K. Hauspie
LXX	Septuagint
NovT	Novum Testamentum
NTS	New Testament Studies
RAC	Reallexikonfür Antike und Christenum
RevScRel	Revue des sciences religieuses
SBL	Society of Biblical Literature
TSK	Theologische Studien und Kritiken
WD	Wort und Dienst
WTJ	Westminster Theological Journal
WUNT	Wissenchaftliche Untersuchungen Neuen Testament
ZNW	Zeitschrfit für die neutestamentliche Wissenschaft und die Kunde der ältern Kirche

1

Introduction

"A SUPERFICIAL GLANCE AT the letter shows that, whereas scriptural references abound in chs. 1–4 and 9–11, they are almost completely absent in the crucial chs. 5–8 and sharply reduced in chs. 12–14, in order to reappear in the conclusion of the letter in ch.15."[1] In this way, J.C. Beker downgrades the intertextual features of Rom 5–8 to "almost completely absent."[2] He appears to measure the impact of Israel's Scriptures in this section of the letter based on the number of citations Paul employs. It is true that these four chapters only contain two citations, a partial citation of Exod 20:17 (Deut 5:21) in Rom 7:7 and the citation of Ps 43:23 LXX in Rom 8:36. However, the number of citations hardly tells the full intertextual story in Rom 5–8. Although it often goes unnoticed, almost every verse in this section of Paul's most famous letter is shaped to varying degrees by Israel's Scriptures.

In volume 2 of this intertextual commentary on Romans, I will focus exclusively on the intertextual subtext of Rom 5:1—8:39.[3] As we shall see, Paul evokes various

---

1. As cited in Hays, *The Conversion of the Imagination*, 181.

2. Beker made these comments as part of a critique of Richard Hays's *Echoes of Scripture in the Letters of Paul*. Hays responded by noting, "In fact, if we look not just for citations but allusions to Old Testament figures and motifs, it is not difficult to show that the chapters Beker singles out contain fundamental features that would be incomprehensible apart from their relation to Old Testament subtexts. In Rom 5 we have Moses and—especially—Adam as key figures whose identity and stories are treated by Paul as *déjà lu*; furthermore, Rom 5:19 echoes Isa 53:11 artfully. In Rom 7 we find a complex analysis of the impact of the commandments of the Mosaic Torah on those who hear it, with Exod 20:17/Deut 5:21 taken as a paradigmatic illustration (Rom 7:7). In Rom 8 we find several pivotal scriptural allusions: the sin offering (8:3), τὸ δικαίωμα τοῦ νόμου (8:4), the fallen creation subjected to decay (8:20–21), the echo of Abraham's offering of Isaac (Gen 22:12, 16: 'did not spare his own son') in Rom 8:32, the citation of Ps 44 in Rom 8:36, and the many echoes of Isa 50 in the surrounding verses" (Hays, *The Conversion of the Imagination*, 181–82).

3. Volume 1 covers Rom 1:1—4:25. Volume 3 covers Rom 9:1—11:36. Volume 4 covers Rom 12:1—16:27.

pre-texts, scriptural motifs, and figures that inform his rhetorical argument in multiple ways. The aim in what follows is to identity these intertextual features, assess their function in Rom 5–8, and articulate the unstated points of resonance produced by the interplay between Paul's text and his intertextual subtext. Even more, this volume informs the overarching aim of the entire commentary which is to explain how various uses of the OT in Romans cohesively support the letter's rhetorical argument and address the needs of his recipients.[4]

As a reminder, or as an introduction for those who have not read volume 1, this commentary is a hybrid work. On the one hand, the main objective is to provide an exhaustive reference work for interpreters and scholars interested in the relationship between Israel's Scriptures and Romans. At the same time, these four volumes have an overarching thesis, which I will articulate more fully in the last chapter of volume 4. The basic argument is that in Romans Paul reads and employs Israel's Scriptures in a holistic way. There is an indissoluble link between his apocalyptic faith in the crucified and risen Christ, the needs of his recipients, and his reliance on Israel's Scriptures as a source of hope for afflicted believers in Rome. Therefore, the various usages of the OT in the letter should be treated in relation to one another and in relation to the situation of the Christians in Rome.

A Prolegomenon to the Commentary on Romans 5–8

It is customary that a commentator will address several preliminary issues such as text critical concerns, historical background, literary structure, and the like.[5] Additionally, the intertextual nature of this commentary requires a special focus upon matters such as Paul's OT *Vorlage*, his scriptural hermeneutic, and the like. Many of these matters received treatment in volume 1; therefore, what I offer here is a summary of that larger conversation. However, special attention needs to be given to these matters as they relate specifically to Rom 5–8.

Introductory Matters Related to Romans

As I noted in volume 1, given the focus of this commentary, two introductory matters are of special interest: (1) the purpose of Romans; and (2) Paul's intertextual audience.[6]

---

4. This resembles the question that Hays poses at the outset of his intertextual analysis of Romans. He asks, "Do the quotations work together in some consistent way to support the letter's argument?" Hays, *Echoes of Scripture in the Letters of Paul*, 34.

5. For an excellent introductory section which treats these items and more, see Jewett, *Romans*, 1–91. See also Longenecker, *Introducing Romans*; Theobald, "Römerbrief," 213–26.

6. I will not address in detail here other commonly discussed matters such as date and provenance. In keeping with several interpreters, I will stipulate that Paul likely wrote this letter in the mid to late 50s. See Carson and Moo, *An Introduction*, 393–94; Kümmel, *Introduction*, 311. He likely wrote Romans from Corinth given the link between the latter city and the individuals identified in Rom 16.

Over the centuries, scholars have suggested several possibilities regarding Paul's original purpose for writing Romans. Suggested purposes generally fit into one of the following categories: (1) to provide a summation of Paul's theology; (2) to prepare for a trip to Jerusalem; (3) to secure support for the Spanish mission; (4) to provide the church in Rome with an apostolic foundation; (5) to combat opponents; (6) to address Jewish and Gentile Christian friction; (7) to address the aftermath of the Claudian edict; (8) to respond to the "situational contexts of Corinth and Galatia;" and (9) there is no discernible purpose.[7]

In what follows, it is my position that Paul wrote to the Christians for two-interrelated purposes. He wrote to both comfort the Christians in Rome and to secure their support for his Spanish mission. Paul accomplishes both of these purposes simultaneously. Regardless of what date we place on the composition, Paul and his recipients had and would experience afflictions of all kinds.[8] Paul expresses a desire to make his way to Rome and impart to the Christians there a gift (χάρισμα). Although the nature of the χάρισμα is often disputed, based on the wider contets of the letter, it is the gift of comfort through an explanation of the gospel which he offers in the letter. As I will highlight at various points in what follows, suffering is a primary motif in the letter.[9] Paul addresses suffering that stems from the following sources: ongoing problems with sin (Rom 7:7–25); futility, death, and forces that raise doubts about God's love for his children (Rom 8:12–39); Israel's unbelief (Rom 9:1–5); ecclesiastical unrest (14:1–15:6); possible afflictions that await Paul in Jerusalem (Rom 15:30–33); and the unrelenting work of Satan (Rom 16:17–20). Hovering over all of these afflictions is the harsh reality that the Christians in Rome live in a world that is under God's wrath (Rom 1:18). Given all of these emphases, suffering is the most "situational" element of the letter. Simply put, the *Sitz im Leben* of both Paul and the Romans is one of suffering. Therefore, Paul writes and plans a visit by which they will be mutually strengthed in faith (Rom 1:12). After all, their suffering raises the prospect that the gospel could be a shameful and disappointing message (Rom 1:16–17). This is all the more reason for Paul to reasurre the Romans that the gospel has not and will not disappoint them with respect to what God promises in it, namely the revelation of his righteousness in the crucified and risen Christ.

As Paul reassures the Romans, his reassurance also functions as an explanation of the gospel that he preaches and for which he needs their missional support. In this

---

For further discussion of provenance, see Hultgren, *Romans*, 2–4.

7. I am helped here by Thomas Vollmer's recent review of proposed purposes for Romans. See Vollmer, *The Spirit Helps Our Weakness*, 41–95. See also the discussion on purpose in Longenecker, *Introducing Romans*, 92–166.

8. Dates of composition generally range from the mid to late 50's. See Carson and Moo, *An Introduction*, 393–94; Kümmel, *Introduction*, 311.

9. I have written about this extensively elsewhere. See Crisler, *Reading Romans as Lament*. See also Wu, *Suffering in Romans*.

way, the purpose of Romans is two-fold and unfolds at the same time.[10] On the one hand, Paul reassures the Romans in their mutual suffering (Rom 8:17) by reassuring them of God's righteousness in Christ. On the other hand, he also lays out his gospel with the hope that the Romans will support his effort to reach Spain (Rom 15:24).

These interrelated purposes are the historical catalyst for Paul's letter, and his use of Israel's Scriptures coincide with these purposes. Paul often evokes OT pre-texts that address the suffering which characterizes his experience with Christ and that of his recipients. He even indicates in his sweeping statement about Israel's Scriptures that they give hope to the afflicted, "For as much as was written beforehand, it was written for our instruction, in order that through the encouragement of the scriptures (διὰ τῆς παρακλήσεως τῶν γραφῶν) we might have hope (τὴν ἐλπίδα)" (Rom 15:4). The referent of ἐλπίς here is the fulfillment of God's prior promises from Israel's Scriptures which are now realized through the crucified and risen Davidic messiah (Rom 1:2–4). At the same time, Paul frames his desire for missional support from the Romans with Israel's Scriptures. His desire to preach the gospel where it has not been proclaimed stems from Isaianic prophecy. Paul explains, "But in this way I aspire to preach the gospel where Christ has not been named, in order that I might not build upon another's foundation, but just as it is written, 'To whom it has not been proclaimed about they will see, and those who have not heard will understand'" (Rom 15:20–21; Isa 52:15). He then pivots in Rom 15:23–24 to his request for missional support in Spain. In this way, Paul's interreleated purposes for writing Romans largely shape his use of the OT in the letter.

A second introductory matter in need of brief attention is what I will refer to here as Paul's "intertextual audience." Some interpreters have raised questions about the ability of Paul's recipients to detect and understand his use of Israel's Scriptures, particularly the kinds of finer intertextual nuances proposed by some scholars.[11] I will stipulate from the outset that Paul's original Roman audience likely had varying degrees of familiarity with Israel's Scriptures. Those with less familiarity would obviously not understand the OT citations or detect the allusions and or echoes to the same degree that those with greater familiarity would. It is even possible that the former group made up the majority of Paul's original recipients. Nevertheless, while Paul was likely aware of his diverse "intertextual audience," it did not necessarily stifle his robust engagement with Israel's Scriptures.

---

10. In other words, it is not necessary to speak about a plurality of purposes as if those purposes are not intertwined with one another.

11. Stanley's work is especially noteworthy on this point. He suggests three classifications of audiences as it relates to scriptural acumen: (1) informed audience; (2) competent audience; and (3) minimal audience. See Stanley, "'Pearls before Swine?'" 122–44; Stanley, "Paul's Use of Scripture," 125–55.

Introduction

Intertextual Terminology

Once again, what follows is primarily a reference work that provides scholars and students of Romans with an exhaustive analysis of how Paul uses the OT in his letter.[12] The study of how the NT uses the OT, or how the OT impacts the NT, has a jargon of its own.[13] It will be helpful to clarify how I am using common terms from this field of study.

In this study, the adjective "intertextual" describes a variety of interactions between Israel's Scriptures and Romans.[14] These interactions are not the creation of the interpreter as many practioners, or critics, of intertextual readings assert.[15] Rather, Paul intends these interactions even when many of his Roman recipients might not detect them. Simply put, intertextuality here is synonymous with Paul's scripturally informed presuppositions about the gospel he preaches.[16]

The term *pre-text* refers to any citation, allusion, or echo proper from the OT while *text* refers to Romans.[17] The qualifications of an OT *citation* for this work are as follows: (1) the inclusion of an introductory formula such as καθὼς γέγραπται ("just as it is written"); (2) the use of a interpretive gloss such as τοῦτ᾽ἔστιν ("that is"); (3) a syntactical or stylistic interruption within the flow of Paul's argument; and (4) substantial verbal overlap with an identifiable scriptural pre-text.[18] An *allusion* in this work refers to instances in which Paul explicitly mentions a figure, event, or the like from Israel's Scriptures without citing a specific pre-text.[19] I realize that many scholars use the terms allusion and echo interchangeably. However, for the sake of clarity, I make a formal distinction between the two.[20]

---

12. Admittedly, as many readers will surely recognize, the attempt to be exhaustive does not preclude the fact that I have surely failed to detect certain allusions and echoes in the letter. Nevertheless, I have attempted to be as thorough as I can.

13. For some recent overview of the topic, see Bates, "The Old Testament in the New Testament," 83–102; Docherty, "Do you Understand what you are Reading?" 112–25.

14. I will use the terms Israel's Scriptures and OT interchangeably. Use of the latter is for the sake of convenience. It is of course the case that Paul never referred to this body of writing as the "Old Testament." He simply referred to is as Scripture (γραφή). On this point, see Hays, *Echoes of Scripture*, x.

15. See the discussion in Thiselton, *New Horizons in Hermeneutics*, 38–42.

16. Thiselton, *New Horizons in Hermeneutics*, 38.

17. I am helped here by Bates's terminology. Bates defines pre-text as "a specific textual source that the NT author utilized." Bates, *The Hermeneutics of the Apostolic Proclamation*, 54.

18. As Kujanpää notes, an example of a syntactical or stylistic interruption would be a "an abrupt change of personal pronouns or verb forms." For a helpful discussion of all these criteria, see Kujanpää, *The Rhetorical Functions*, 19–20.

19. Paul's discussion of Ἀδάμ in Rom 5:12–19 is an example of allusion as I am defining the term in this work.

20. As John Sutherland notes, allusion is a "visible, controlled, and knowing form of connection" between two texts. Sutherland, *How Literature Works*, 100.

An *echo*, or what I sometimes refer to in this work as an *echo proper*, is an aural metaphor borrowed from the world of literary criticism.[21] The term normally refers to the literal repetition of sound in a piece of writing. In this sense, Cuddon defines echo as "The repetition of the same sound, or a combination of sounds, fairly close together, so that they 'echo' each other. A common device in verse to strengthen meaning and structure, and also to provide tune and melody."[22] When applied metaphorically, Cuddon's definition of echo refers to the repetition of lines from a pre-text in a subsequent text so that the former is "echoed" in the latter and "strengthens" the meaning of the latter. The echo from a pre-text strengthens the meaning of a text in at least three ways: (1) an echo can provide the source of a text's language, imagery, and or narrative substructure; (2) an echo provides a wider context in which the text can be interpreted; and (3) the interplay between an echoed pre-text and the text produces unstated points of resonance that further illuminate the meaning of the text.[23] Of course, Hays is largely responsible for making "echo" a well-known term in the study of the NT.[24] Much of my analysis of echoes is indebted to him.

While discussing these various intertextual features, I will often describe the text of Romans as "echoing," "evoking," "extending/expanding," and or "reconfiguring/re-contextualizing" Israel's Scriptures. I described "echo" above. By "evoking," a term borrowed from Steve Moyise, I simply mean that the text of Romans recalls or brings to mind an OT pre-text.[25] "Extending, or expanding," along with "reconfiguring," are efficient ways of referring to the various ways Paul moves a pre-text beyond its OT context and repurposes that pre-text to meet his rhetorical needs in Romans. Similarly, "re-contextualization" refers to the "re-use" of the OT in Romans which, as we shall see, can be a complicated and variegated exercise.[26]

---

21. An "echo proper" refer to an intertextual feature that is distinct from a citation or allusion. The distinction is necessary, because I will sometimes describe citations or allusions as "echoing" the OT pre-text.

22. Cuddon, "Echo," 247.

23. Point (3) pertains to metalepsis which is an intertextual pheonemon that applies to citations and allusions as well. I will return to this discussion below.

24. See Hays, *Echoes of Scripture in the Letters of Paul*, 14–33; Hays, *Echoes of Scripture in the Gospels*, 1–14; Hays borrowed the aural metaphor of "echo" from John Hollander. See Hollander, *The Figure of Echo*.

25. See Moyise, *Evoking Scripture*.

26. As Eric Waaler notes, "Re-use of the Old Testament in the New Testament is best described as re-contextualization of text. This is a complicated process involving many factors, and hence, it is a multidimensional approach to itertextuality." Waaler, "Multidimensional Intertextuality," 222. Beale provides a kind of taxonomy for the variety of ways a NT writer uses the OT which some might find helpful. See Beale, *Handbook on the NT Use of the OT*, 55–93.

INTRODUCTION

Paul's OT Hermeneutic in Romans 5–8

If we are to understand the interplay between OT pre-texts and Rom 5–8, it is necessary to consider Paul's overarching attitude and approach to Israel's Scriptures.[27] It is important to keep in mind that Israel's Scriptures are not merely "used" by Paul. Rather, his use of the sacred text demonstrates the profound impact they have on him.[28] With that said, Paul is at different times a scriptural apologist, theologian, redactor, poet, narrator, and pastor. These facets of his scriptural hermeneutic are on display in Rom 5–8.

Paul is a scriptural apologist in the sense that he appeals to Israel's Scriptures as an authoritative source. The apostle often finds himself embroiled in disputes that are hermeneutical in nature. Consequently, he sometimes appeals to Israel's Scriptures to articulate and buttress his arguments.[29] These disputes are real and imagined. The latter refers to Paul's use of ancient diatribe where he appeals to the sacred text in his argument with an imaginary interlocutor.[30] Within Rom 5–8, 5:12–21 is at least diatribe like.[31] Paul does not cite an OT text to win a point against his interlocutor, but he does appeal to his reading of the Gen 3 narrative which helps him make the case that Christ outdoes Adam.

Paul also engages Israel's Scriptures as a scriptural "theologian." The title "theologian" is admittedly anachronistic.[32] I do not wish to portray Paul as a "theologian" in a modern sense. However, it is the case that Paul interprets the story of Jesus in relation to Israel's Scriptures. The sacred text shapes the way he understands and thereby explains several issues such as God's work in Christ, the person and work of Christ, the identity of God's people, the τέλος of all things in Christ, obedience to God, and a host of other items. In this sense, Paul engages Israel's Scriptures as a scriptural "theologian." Rom 5–8 features numerous examples of this hermeneutical approach to Israel's Scriptures. For example, in Rom 5:12–19, Paul roots the origin of sin and death in the primeval account of Adam which he then uses to narrate God's work in Jesus. Rom 6 evokes the water-death-life motif from seminal moments in Israel's

---

27. Regarding Paul's attitude towards Israel's Scriptures, I agree with Ellis's assessment. Ellis suggests that for Paul, "The Scriptures are holy and prophetic; they constitute the very oracles of God (), and they 'we written . . . for our learning.'" Ellis, *Paul's Use of the Old Testament*, 20.

28. The nomenclature of the "New Testament use of the Old Testament" will likely never change. However, such phrases tend to eclipse what really transpires when a NT writer engages Israel's Scriptures. In the case of Paul, this engagement is far from the kind of utilitarian and convenient experience conveyed by the phrase "use of the OT." As I noted in volume 1, Paul sees himself as a gifted "charismatic" interpreter. On this point, see Michel, *Paul und Seine Bibel*, 134.

29. On this point, see Harris, *Testimonies*, 2:30.

30. See, e.g., the use of Isa 52:5 in Rom 2:24.

31. Stan Porter suggests that Rom 5:12–21 is a diatribe. Porter, "The Argument of Romans 5," 655–77.

32. In Christian circles, the descriptor θεολόγος does not occur until the second century as a description of John. BDAG 449.

Scriptures to narrate the Romans' baptism with Christ. Paul patterns the experience of the the enigmatic "I" in Rom 7:7–25 after figures from the Psalms of Lament to retrospectively describe the tortuous experience of sin within the body. He takes up the OT motif of lament in Rom 8:18–27 to tether the suffering of creation, the children of God, and the Holy Spirit.

In Rom 5–8, we also find Paul approaching Israel's Scriptures like a "poet" who consciously and unconsciously weaves the language, imagery, and storyline of the OT into his rhetorical argument.[33] For example, in Rom 7:1–6, Paul reconfigures marriage stipulations from Deut 24 to craft a marriage analogy which explains how the Romans have died to their former husband, the law, through the death and resurrection of their new husband, Jesus Christ.

Paul also acts as a scriptural "pastor" in Rom 5–8, though I acknowledge the term can be misleading if it is associated with "pastors" in the modern, especially Protestant, sense.[34] Here it simply refers to the apostolic responsibility, both in a doctrinal and ethical sense, that Paul felt for his recipients who were often afflicted by ongoing problems with sin, false teachers, death, and the like. This pastoral care is evident in his citation of Ps 43:23 LXX in Rom 8:36. Based on the wider contexts of the pre-text and text, his use of this pre-text acknowledges that affliction in the Christian experience may resemble divine condemnation. However, in truth, the affliction is inexplicable just as the speaker in the wider context of Ps 43 LXX acknowledges.

Paul's OT hermeneutic in Rom 5–8 is explicitly typological. Paul even employs the noun τύπος in Rom 5:14.[35] As I discussed in volume 1, Goppelt identifies two typological strands in Paul's thought "Christ the second Adam who brings the new creation" and "the church as the 'children of Abraham' and as the 'spiritual Israel.'"[36] The former strand is obviously on full display in Rom 5:12–19. As I will discuss further in a later chapter, Paul combines his typological exegesis of Jesus with Greco-Roman syncrisis.[37] Paul depicts a clear escalation, the defining characteristic of typology according to Goppelt, between the actions of Adam and Christ as it relates to the respective outcomes of those actions. As we shall see, Paul's typological engagement with

---

33. As I noted in the larger discussion of Paul as scriptural "poet" in volume 1, the description of Paul's OT hermeneutic stems in large part from Hays's analysis. See Hays, *Echoes of Scripture in the Letters of Paul*, 33.

34. As noted in volume 1, Paul as scriptural "pastor" refers to the way he uses Israel's Scriptures to defend his apostleship and to comfort his recipients in their affliction. The term "pastor," like "minister," can be misleading. In the Pauline corpus, the term ποιμήν only occurs in Eph 4:11. See BDAG 843. Paul never applies the term to himself. In volume 4, I will discuss how Paul likely viewed himself as both a priest (λειτουργός) and prophet (προφήτης) in the vein of those who preceded him from Israel's past. See the use of λειτουργός in Rom 15:16. See also Rom 15:18–21 which indicates Paul's missional strategy is shaped by the prophecy of Isaiah.

35. Cf. use of τύπος in 1 Cor 10:6.

36. Goppelt, *Typos*, 129, 136.

37. As Parsons and Martin note, "At a key turning point in the argument of Romans, Paul engages in a syncrisis of Adamic sin and Christ's grace/gift." Parsons and Martin, *Ancient Rhetoric*, 259.

the Gen 2–3 narrative supports part of the narrative substructure beyond Rom 5. Additionally, Paul engages in other typological treatments of OT figures in Rom 6–8 such as evoking Abraham as a type of Yahweh and Christ as a type of Isaac in Rom 8:31–34.

Paul's Hermeneutical Framework

None of Paul's hermeneutical diversity in Rom 5–8, which I have just outlined, occurs in a disparate or vacuous way. He works within a hermeneutical framework shaped by his apocalyptic-typological view of history, his experience with Jewish exegesis and Greco-Roman rhetorical devices, the early Christian kerygma, his apocalyptic encounter with the risen Jesus, and suffering. As we shall see, in Romans, suffering often influences the kind of OT pre-texts that Paul selects and how he uses them. Paul's statement about Israel's Scriptures in Rom 15:4 is informative on this point, "For as much as was written beforehand, it was written for our instruction, in order that through the endurance and encouragement of the scriptures (τῶν γραφῶν) we might have hope." It is telling that in one of the rare instances where Paul talks directly about the nature and purpose of Israel's Scriptures he stresses that they bring hope to those in Rome. Hope assumes hurt which Paul speaks at length about in the letter. He constantly draws from Israel's Scriptures to address that hurt. Therefore, in the search to locate Paul's OT hermeneutic as it relates to Romans, one should look with an especially keen eye at the suffering of Paul and his recipients.

That suffering takes center stage in Rom 5–8. Paul signals the importance of this motif through an *inclusio* marked by his discussion of θλῖψις in Rom 5:1–5 and his discussion of the tripartie "groaning" (στενά–root), or lamenting, by creation, the children of God, and the Holy Spirit in Rom 8:18–27. Between these two literary poles, Paul describes to the Romans how their experience with Christ is defined by a tension between suffering and hope. Paul abbreviates this tension in Rom 8:17, "But if we are children, we are also heirs; heirs of God, and coheirs of Christ, if indeed with suffer with him (συμπάσχομεν) in order that we might also be glorified with him (συνδοξασθῶμεν)." Not coincidentally, as we shall see, the intertextual subtext of Rom 5–8 contains several OT pre-texts that echo the same kind of tension. This comports with my intertextual analysis of Paul's *propositio*. Paul uses OT pre-texts from the outset of his letter that address the tension between the promise of the gospel and the suffering of the righteous.[38]

The Intertextual Approach to Romans 5–8

The overall approach implemented throughout this commentary consists of three steps which will be repeated in the analysis fo Rom 5–8.

---

38. See the intertextual analysis of Rom 1:16–17 in volume 1.

First, I list all OT pre-texts (citations, allusions, and echoes proper) identified in each pericope as identified by Hans Hübner, NA 28th ed., Richard B. Hays, and Mark. A Seifrid. It does not follow that I will analyze all the pre-texts listed in these four sources. However, the lists provide the reader an opportunity to explore pre-texts that I may not specifically discuss.

Second, the "intertextual analysis" for each pericope varies based on the kind of pre-text under consideration. Treatments of citations in Romans includes the following: (1) a comparison of the citation in Romans, the MT, and the LXX; (2) a summary of the wider OT context of the citation; and (3) an analysis of the "contextual consistency" between the pre-text and text.

The analysis of allusions and echoes proper includes identifying and testing the proposed pre-texts. The intertextual tests which I employ are a modification of Hays's proposed tests for intertextual echoes.[39] Five tests are implemented, though not pedantically and not every test is administered in every single instance. First, I test the *volume* of the echo to determine if it is strong, moderate, or low. Strong volume requires that the pre-text and text parallel contain at least three semantic parallels.[40] In some instances, if the parallel involves a rarely used term, the volume may still qualify as strong even if it does not meet the three parallels threshold.[41] Two parallel terms qualifies as moderate volume, and one parallel is labelled as low volume. Second, I test the *contextual consistency* of the echo. Do the proposed pre-text and text share common themes, images, historical referents, and or theological concepts? Third, I will sometimes test the *motif consistency* between pre-text and text. This is similar to *contextual consistency*; however, motif consistency allows for the possibility that the pre-text and text, though using different language and historical referents, overlap with respect to their dominant patterns or ideas. For example, the pre-text and text may both feature an emphasis on divine judgment but express that emphasis through different linguistic and conceptual means. A fourth test involves the *recurrence* of a pre-text. Does Paul explicitly or allude to the pre-text elsewhere in Romans or in another letter? Fifth, I test proposed pre-texts in relation to the *history of interpretation*. Have previous interpreters identified this pre-text? How have they treated its significance? This final test cannot be carried out in an exhaustive way. The secondary literature on Paul's use of the OT in Romans is gargantuan. In fact, some readers may

---

39. As is well-known, Hays lays out seven tests: (1) availability; (2) volume; (3) recurrence; (4) thematic coherence; (5) historical plausibility; (6) history of interpretation; and (7) satisfaction. See Hays, *Echoes of Scripture in the Letters of Paul*, 29–31.

40. Three points of contact is not a random number within the criteria. Rather, it is based upon the recommendation of Armin Lange and Matthias Weigold in their examination of biblical quotations and allusions in Second Temple literature. They explain, "Allusions are employments of anterior texts in which the anterior text is still linguistically recognizable in the posterior text but not morphologically idenitical with it. We recognize any parallel of at least three words to another as an *implicit allusion*." Lange and Weigold, *Biblical Quotations and Allusions*, 25.

41. As Lange and Weigold notes, "In some cases a parallel of two rare and one common word can mark an allusion by one text to another." *Biblical Quotations and Allusions*, 32.

be disappointed by the absence of certain articles and or monographs in the pages ahead. I have attempted to be thorough in the integration of previous scholarship, but I have not been able to include everything.

The third and final step is to asses the interpretive impact of the intertextual analysis on Paul's argument in Romans. How does reading Paul's argument in light of its intertextual subtext impact our understanding of his argument? Here I will attempt to articulate the points of resonance generated by the interplay between the OT pre-text and text of Romans. These points will then be verified and clarified based on how they fit with the immediate and larger rhetorical contexts of the letter.

Even with the implementation of this approach, readers will not always agree with the proposed pre-texts or with how I articulate the impact of these pre-texts on Paul's argument. Nevertheless, it is my hope that this close intertextual reading of Paul's most famous letter may shed a least a little more exegetical light on the meaning of his text.

Exegetical Disclaimer

As a final disclaimer, the reader needs to keep in mind that this is a reference work designed with a narrow focus which will hopefully pay wider dividends. Readers expecting to find items such as lengthy engagement with Paul's Greco-Roman milieiu will be disappointed.[42] Such engagement is undoubtedly fruitful and necessary for exegesis. Therefore, it would be prudent for interpreters using this reference work to pair it with other commenatries on Romans which is always a wise practice anyway.

---

42. I hope at some point to write an intertextual commentary that focuses solely on Greco-Roman echoes, both literary and material cultural echoes, in Romans. Such material simply cannot be included in what is already a very large project.

2

Romans 5:1–11

"In the whole Bible there is hardly another chapter which can equal this triumphant text."[1] Thus Luther begins his analysis of Rom 5 in his commentary on the letter. However, a cursory reading indicates a less than "triumphant" use of Israel's Scriptures once Paul finishes his protracted discussion of Abraham in Rom 4:23–25. Rom 5:1–11 contains no formal citation. Many interpreters sense little to no engagement with Israel's Scriptures as Paul's makes his critical "turn to Christ."[2] Not even Hays's *Echoes of Scripture in the Letters of Paul* engages a single pre-text in Rom 5.[3] In short, while the intertextual subtext of Rom 5:1–11 has not been entirely neglected, it does not always receive the attention that it deserves. The following chapter aims to help reverse this trend.

As we shall see, Rom 5:1–11 is part of that "vast sea" of intertextual engagements which characterizes the entire letter.[4] Intertextual analysis of this section yields significant exegetical insights that shed light on Paul's rhetorical argument. Paul evokes

---

1. Luther, *Commentary on Romans*, 88.

2. This phrase is borrowed from Seifrid who observes that Paul makes a critical "turn to Christ" in Rom 5:1. In comparison to Rom 1:1—4:25, 5:1—8:39 contains far more uses of Χριστός and extended reflection on the person of Jesus. I will have more to say about this below. See Seifrid, "Paul's Turn to Christ in Romans," 15.

3. Hays's intertextual analysis contains a large lacuna between Rom 5–7. See, e.g., the Scripture index in *Echoes of Scriptures in the Letters of Paul*, 233. In fairness, as part of his retort to Beker's critique of his work, Hays explains "One implication of my work is that we cannot confine our investigation of Pauline intertextuality to passages in which there is an explicit quotation (καθὼς γέγραπται) of a source. In fact, if we look not just for citations but for allusions to Old Testament figures and motifs, it is not difficult to show that the chapters Beker singles out contain fundamental features that would be incomprehensible apart from their relation to Old Testament subtexts. In Rom 5 we have Moses and—especially—Adam as key figures whose identity and stories are treated by as Paul déjà lu; furthermore, Rom 5:19 echoes Isa 53:11 artfully." Hays, *The Conversion of the Imagination*, 181. However, even this observation is cursory and does not pertain to intertextual subtext of Rom 5:1–11.

4. In discussing Paul's use of Hab 2:4 in Rom 1:17, John Chrysostom observes "First he uses a short phrase that opens a vast sea of stories, if one is able to understand his meaning." Burns, *Romans*, 25.

a wide range of pre-texts from Israel's Scriptures that shape how he describes the tension between Christian suffering and hope, a tension which holds Rom 5–8 together.[5] Justification by faith results in peace with God and access to him through the Lord Jesus Christ (Rom 5:1–2). One can now boast in the hope of the glory of God. Yet, none of this precludes the reality of suffering for the Christians in Rome. Instead, as Paul will explain, suffering is in fact the constant *Sitz im Leben* for those who are justified by faith in Christ. Israel's Scriptures provide Paul with the language and framework he needs to explain to his recipients how the afflictions of those who are justified by faith comport with the hope of the justified.

Romans 5:1–5

(5:1–5) Therefore, having been justified by faith we have peace with God through our Lord Jesus Christ through whom we also have access by faith into this grace in which we stand, and we boast in the hope of the glory of God. And not only this, but we also boast in tribulations, knowing that tribulation produces endurance, and endurance produces character, and character produces hope. And hope does not disappoint, because the love of God has been poured out in our hearts through the Holy Spirit who was given to us.

Interpreters have long noted that the post-positive conjunction οὖν in Rom 5:1 is one of the most important points in the entire letter. What is at stake here exegetically is nothing less than how one understands the relationship between Rom 1–4 and 5–8.[6] However, a problem arises at this point. Cranfield explains, "The point at which the new main division begins is disputed. Some see the first eleven verses, others the whole of chapter 5, as belonging to what precedes, while others see the significant break as occurring between chapters 4 and 5."[7] Longenecker observes, "Many commentators have understood 1:16—4:25 as continuing on through 5:11; others as continuing on through 5:21. Most scholars today, however, view 5:1—8:39 as a discrete and distinctive section of material."[8] Following Longenecker, I will stipulate that Rom 5:1—8:39 is distinct from what precedes and follows it in the letter but not in an entirely disjunctive manner. Rom 5:1–11 both teases out the implications of what preceded it in 1:16—4:25 while also transitioning the argument to a "new movement."[9]

---

5. On this point, see Still, "Placing Pain in a Pauline Frame," 73–86.

6. As Hultgren notes, "The opening verses of 5:1–11 produce a 'rhetorical bridge' from what has been said previously to what he will be saying in this and the three chapters to follow." Hultgren, *Romans*, 202. See also the discussion in Thiselton, *Discovering Romans*, 123–24.

7. Cranfield, *Romans*, 1:253.

8. Longenecker goes on to list seven reasons for seeing Rom 5:1—8:39 as a "distinctive section of material." See Longenecker, *Romans*, 539–41.

9. See Matera, *Romans*, 124.

As noted above, one distinctive feature here is what Seifrid refers to as "the turn to Christ."[10] While we cannot rely upon Paul's semantic activity alone, it is the case that explicit references to Jesus Christ (Χριστός) are extremely limited in Rom 1:1—4:25.[11] To be sure, Christ is axiomatic and pivotal to Rom 1:1—4:25. However, Paul's full-throated and sustained reflection on the person of Christ does not commence until Rom 5:1. Along these lines, the intertextual subtext of Rom 5:1—8:39 has a distinct christological bent. In Rom 5:1–11 specifically, Paul frames God's work in Christ as the eschatological hope one has in the face of suffering as promised in Israel's Scriptures.

Suggested Pre-Texts in Romans 5:1–5

Hübner lists the following pre-texts: Ps LXX 71:13; Isa 32:17, 18; Ezek 34:25; 37:26; (Rom 5:1); Ps LXX 5:12; 9:19; 70:5 (Rom 5:2–3); and Ps LXX 21:5; 24:2–3; 70:1; 118:116; Joel 3:1–2; Isa 32:15–17 (Rom 5:5).[12]

Nestle-Aland 28th edition lists the following pre-texts in its margin: Isa 32:17 (Rom 5:1) and Ps 22:6; 25:20; Isa 28:16 (Rom 5:5).[13]

As noted above, Hays's intertextual analysis of Romans tapers off after his analysis of Rom 4:23–25. In the entirety of his seminal work, Hays does not analyze any pre-text in Rom 5:1—7:25.[14] However, in responding to critiques of *Echoes of Scripture in the Letter of Paul*, Hays takes J. Christian Beker to task for suggesting that intertextual echoes are "almost completely absent" in Rom 5–8.[15] Hays retorts, "Does Beker really want to maintain the references to Scripture are 'almost completely absent' in these chapters? Such a position can be maintained only by focusing narrowly on direct quotations and ignoring the Scripture-laden language that Paul employs in his own discourse."[16] I agree with Hays in principle as the following analysis demonstrates. However, in practice, Hays offers little intertextual engagement with Rom 5–8 in

---

10. Seifrid notes, "Without question, Paul's opening affirmation in Rom 5 takes up his preceding description of Abraham's faith. Yet within that description of Abraham's faith an abrupt turn appears that anticipates a decisive change in Paul's argument. It is that turn—a turn to Christ—that I wish to explore." Seifrid, "Paul's Turn to Christ in Romans," 15.

11. The proper name Ἰησοῦς occurs ten times in Rom 1:1—4:25. See Rom 1:1, 4, 6, 7, 8; 2:16; 3:22, 24, 26; and 4:24. Five of these ten occurrences are in the letter opening (Rom 1:1–15). By comparison, Ἰησοῦς occurs fourteen times in Rom 5:1—8:39. See Rom 5:1, 11, 15, 17, 21; 6:3, 11, 23; 7:25; 8:1, 2, 11, 34, 39. Χριστός occurs eight times in Rom 1:1—4:25. See Rom 1:1, 4, 6, 7, 8; 2:16; 3:22, and 24. Five of the eight occurrences are in the letter opening (Rom 1:1–15). By comparison, Χριστός occurs twenty-four times in Rom 5:1—8:39.

12. He also lists Hübner, *Vetus Testamentum in Novo*, 2:78–83.

13. NA 28th ed. 489–90.

14. As I will discuss in a later chapter, he picks up his intertextual analysis again beginning with Rom 8:18. See Hays, *Echoes of Scripture in the Letters of Paul*, 158.

15. See Hays, *Conversion of the Imagination*, 182.

16. Hays, *Conversion of the Imagination*, 182.

comparison to the attention he gives Rom 1–4 and 9–11. Similarly, Seifrid does not discuss specific pre-texts in his analysis of Rom 5:1–5.[17]

Intertextual Analysis of Romans 5:1–5

Paul's "turn to Christ" at the beginning of Rom 5 echoes several pre-texts. Many of the pre-texts discussed in what follows are part of the intertextual subtext which I discussed in the analysis of Rom 1:1—4:25.[18] Additionally, as we shall see, Paul draws from several scriptural motifs that coalesce around the eschatological promise of righteousness and peace through God's anointed one.

Romans 5:1 and Echoes of δικαιοσύνη and εἰρήνη Pre-texts

To begin, the phrase "Therefore, having been justified by faith (Δικαιωθέντες οὖν ἐκ πίστεως)" in Rom 5:1 must be understood in relation to Rom 4:1–25 where Paul's discussion is largely informed by his reading of Gen 15, 17, and Ps 31 LXX. From this perspective, the phrase Δικαιωθέντες ἐκ πίστεως is intertextually informed in several ways. For example, Δικαιωθέντες evokes Gen 15:6, a programmatic pre-text for Paul.[19] As noted in the previous volume, Gen 15:6 is the prism through which Paul views Abraham's entire life before God and thereby Jewish and Gentile Christians who follow in his footsteps of faith (Rom 4:12). Abraham believed in a God who could raise the dead, and God reckoned that faith as righteousness. This faith encases the promise that Abraham's descendants would inherit the world and that Abraham would be the father of many nations (Rom 4:13, 17–18). However, from an even wider intertextual perspective, Δικαιωθέντες ἐκ πίστεως evokes Paul's scripturally informed assertion that God justifies the ungodly who believe in a God who raises the dead. As Rom 4:1–8 make clear, Paul includes both Abraham and David with the ungodly. The "blessing" (μακαρισμός) of God reckoning righteousness to the ungodly apart from works includes the blessing of forgiveness (Rom 4:6–8).

Second, Paul's conclusion that the justified have "peace" (εἰρήνη) with God evokes Isaiah's prophecy of a king who would reign in righteousness and bring peace:

---

17. See Seifrid, *Romans*, 628.

18. See volume 1. One finds very few studies dedicated to the intertextual features of Rom 5:1–5. Most intertextual analysis at this point occurs within the larger analysis of the passage in commentaries and monographs. Among these analyses, Shun's stands out. He discusses at length the impact of Isa 32:17; 54:8; and other Isaianic pre-texts on Rom 5:1–11. See Shun, *Paul's Use of Isaiah*, 193–202. Additionally, Sandnes briefly discusses the overlap between the hope language used to describe Abraham in Rom 4:18–22 and the hope language in Rom 5:2–3. See Sandnes, "Abraham, the Friend of God," 124–28.

19. See Rom 4:3, 9, 22, 23.

> Therefore, having been justified by faith (Δικαιωθέντες ἐκ πίστεως) we have peace (ἔχομεν πρὸς τὸν θεὸν) with God through our Lord Jesus Christ (Rom 5:1).

> And the works of righteousness (τὰ ἔργα τῆς δικαιοσύνης) will be peace (εἰρήνη), and righteousness (ἡ δικαιοσύνη) will take hold of rest, and those who have trusted (πεποιθότες) forever (Isa 32:17).

The *volume* of the echo from Isa 32:17 is moderate based on the semantic parallels involving δικαιόω, δικαιοσύνη, and εἰρήνη.[20]

Contextual consistency occurs at the point of a ruling figure (βασιλεύς/κύριος) whose righteous work results in peace. In the wider context of Isa 32, the prophet describes a righteous king (δίκαιος βασιλεύς) and princes who would reign with justice (Isa 32:1).[21] They provide protection for Israel, beyond the exile, from ungodly fools and schemers (Isa 32:2–8). However, the prophecy also shifts back to a warning of coming judgment marked by fruitlessness and defeat (Isa 32:9–14). The prophecy then shifts yet again to a vision of hope beyond exile where the Spirit comes from on high (ἐπέλθη ἐφ᾽ ὑμᾶς πνεῦμα ἀφ᾽ ὑψηλοῦ), the fields are fruitful, and where the work of righteousness results in peace (Isa 32:15–20). Similar motifs occur in the wider context of Rom 5:1–5 and beyond. For example, just as Isaiah prophesied that the time beyond judgment would be marked by the Spirit coming upon people (ἐπέλθη ἐφ᾽ ὑμᾶς πνεῦμα ἀφ᾽ ὑψηλοῦ), Paul notes in Rom 5:5 "for the love of God has been poured out in your hearts through the Holy Spirit who was given to us (διὰ πνεύματος ἁγίου τοῦ δοθέντος ἡμῖν)." Additionally, just as Isaiah envisioned a shift from a deserted land to a fruitful one, Paul speaks in this section of the letter about the groaning and birth pains of creation (ἡ κτίσις) ready to be liberated from ruin through the resurrection of the dead (Rom 8:18–24). The children of God have the "firstfruits of the Spirit" (τὴν ἀπαρχὴν τοῦ πνεύματος) in anticipation of that liberation (Rom 8:23).

Within the *history of interpretation*, Matera detects the parallel between Isa 32:17 and Rom 5:1 observing "The book of Isaiah draws a similar relation between peace and righteousness: 'The effect of righteousness will be peace, and the result of righteousness, quietness and trust forever (Isa. 32:17). This experience of peace, which the justified enjoy, comes through our Lord Jesus Christ."[22] Additionally, Shun notes "Here Paul's language is reminiscent of one of the most important Isaianic passages pertinent to this motif, namely, Isa 32:17. In view of Paul's use of Isaiah in Romans and such a distinctive logical connection between δικαιοσύνη and εἰρήνη, there is no reason to reject the suggestion that Paul's theological reflection on the effect of

---

20. Conceptual overlap occurs with πείθω in Isa 32:17 and πίστις in Rom 5:1.

21. Cf. emphasis on εἰρήνη in Isa 9:5; 26:3, 12; 27:5; 45:7; 48:18; 52:7; 53:5; 54:10; 57:2, 19; 59:8; 60:17; 66:12.

22. Matera, *Romans*, 131.

justification may have been inspired and directed by this Isaianic motif as a whole or Isa. 32:17 in particular."²³

Third, an echo that resembles Isa 32:17 emanates from Ps 71 LXX, a royal psalm, where we find the same combination of a kingly figure and the arrival of peace in righteousness.²⁴ This combination is clear from the opening lines of the psalm:

> O God, give your judgment to the king (τῷ βασιλεῖ) and your righteousness (τὴν δικαιοσύνην) to the son of the king (τῷ υἱῷ τοῦ βασιλέως) to judge your people with righteousness (ἐν δικαιοσύνῃ) and your poor with justice. Let the mountains and the hills bring up peace (εἰρήνην) to your people in righteousness (ἐν δικαιοσύνῃ) (Ps 71:1-3 LXX).

The *volume* of the echo is moderate based on the overlap between δικαιοσύνη, δικαιόω, and εἰρήνη. Conceptually, God brings peace through the king (βασιλεύς) in the psalm and through the Lord (κύριος) in Rom 5:1.

We find substantial *contextual consistency* between the pre-text and text. The kingly figure dominates Ps 71 LXX, and God's work through him corresponds to Paul's description of what God does in Christ. Ps 71:1-17 LXX contains a rich and protracted description of the βασιλεύς. He saves/ransoms (ῥύομαι/σῴζω/λυτρόω) the needy from enemies and unrighteousness:

> For he delivered (ἐρρύσατο) the poor from the hand of the powerful and the needy, to whom there was no help; he spared the poor and needy; and he will save (σώσει) the souls of the needy. From usury and unrighteousness (ἀδικίας) he will ransom (λυτρώσεται) their souls, and their name will be precious before him (Ps 71:12-14 LXX).²⁵

The saving reign is eternal, "And he will continue as long as the sun and before the moon forever" (Ps 71:5 LXX). His reign is cosmic in scope, "And all the kings (πάντες οἱ βασιλεῖς) will bow down to him, and all the nations (πάντα τὰ ἔθνη) will serve him" (Ps 71:11 LXX).²⁶ Righteousness defines his reign, "Righteousness (δικαιοσύνη) will rise up in his days, and a multitude of peace (πλῆθος εἰρήνης) until the moon should be removed" (Ps 71:7 LXX). Overall, as the psalmist indicates towards the end of the description, God fulfills the promise to Abraham through this figure "Let his name be blessed forever, before the sun his name will remain; and all the tribes of the earth will be blessed in him (εὐλογηθήσονται ἐν αὐτῷ πᾶσαι αἱ φυλαὶ τῆς γῆς), and all the nations will bless him" (Ps 71:17 LXX). The phrase εὐλογηθήσονται ἐν αὐτῷ πᾶσαι αἱ φυλαὶ τῆς γῆς alludes to Gen 12:3 "And I will bless those who bless you, and

---

23. Shun, *Paul's Use of Isaiah*, 193. Shun also lists Isa 48:17-18; 54:1-14; and 60:8-17 as informative for the combination of δικαιοσύνη and εἰρήνη. Jewett finds Shun's suggestion of Isa 32:17 as a pre-text unconvincing, but he offers no explanation for his critique. See Jewett, *Romans*, 349n33.

24. Anderson, *Out of the Depths*, 240.

25. See also Ps 71:1-4 LXX.

26. See also Ps 71:8-9, 15 LXX.

I will curse those who curse you; and all the tribes of the earth will be blessed in you (ἐνευλογηθήσονται ἐν σοὶ πᾶσαι αἱ φυλαὶ τῆς γῆς).²⁷

Several elements of the psalmist's description of the king are found in Paul's description of Christ both here in Rom 5 and the wider context of the section (Rom 5:1—8:39). It is helpful to enumerate these elements:

> God's righteousness in Christ results in peace (Ps 71:3, 7 LXX; Rom 5:1).
>
> Christ delivers the afflicted from sin (Ps 71:12-14 LXX; Rom 5:6-10; 6:18, 7:24-25).
>
> Christ's reign is cosmic in scope (Ps 71:8-11, 15 LXX; Rom 5:21; 8:31-39).
>
> Christ's reign is defined by righteousness (Ps 71:7 LXX; Rom 5:1, 17, 21).
>
> Christ's reign fulfills God's promise to Abraham (Ps 71:17 LXX; Rom 4:1-25).

Of course, Paul reconfigures the psalmist's description of the king around the Lord Jesus Christ. We will consider below the points of resonance that emerge from the interplay between pre-text and text. The resemblance between these descriptions is quite remarkable, and it may indicate that echoes of a Davidic figure play a larger role in Rom 5–8 than is often appreciated. In any case, within the *history of interpretation*, a few interpreters have at least noted Ps 71 LXX as a possible pre-text in Rom 5:1.²⁸

Fourth, Rom 5:1 may also contain an echo from Ps 84 LXX where the psalmist requests that God's wrath would cease while at the same time trusting that God will bring righteousness and peace to his people. That statement of trust includes the following, "Mercy and truth met, righteousness (δικαιοσύνη) and peace (εἰρήνη) kissed" (Ps 84:11 LXX). The *volume* of the echo is moderate based on the shared terms δικαιοσύνη/Δικαιωθέντες and εἰρήνη.

The *contextual consistency* here resides with the psalmist's juxtaposition between divine wrath and peace/righteousness which is consistent with Paul's juxtaposition of the same concepts from Rom 1:18 to 5:1-10. In typical psalmic fashion, the psalmist begins by recounting how God had brought an end to his wrath against Israel in the past "You ceased all your wrath (τὴν ὀργήν σου), you turned from the wrath of your anger (ἀπὸ ὀργῆς θυμοῦ σου)" (Ps 84:4 LXX). This is quickly followed by the request, "Do not be angry (μὴ ὀργισθῇς) forever with us or extend your wrath (τὴν ὀργήν σου) from generation to generation" (Ps 84:6 LXX).²⁹ The psalmist follows this recollection with a request for mercy and salvation (Ps 84:7-8 LXX). He then expresses trust that God will hear the requests, "I will hear what the Lord God will speak with

---

27. The syntactical and semantic overlap is obvious. Even the word order matches. The overlap is not quite as tight in the MT of Gen 12:3 and Ps 72:17. See also Gen 18:18.

28. See, e.g., Dunn, *Romans*, 1:247.

29. See also Ps 84:5 LXX.

me, for he will speak peace (εἰρήνην) over his people and over his holy ones and over those who turn their heart to him" (Ps 84:9 LXX). The psalmist trusts that God's salvation is near to those who fear him (Ps 84:10 LXX). It is at this point that we find the explicit combination of righteousness and peace, "Mercy and truth have met, righteousness (δικαιοσύνη) and peace (εἰρήνη) have kissed" (Ps 84:11 LXX).[30]

The larger context of Rom 5:1–10 includes the same juxtaposition of wrath and peace/righteousness. With respect to the former, Paul concludes in Rom 5:9 "Therefore, how much more now having been justified (δικαιωθέντες) by his blood we will be saved from wrath (ἀπὸ τῆς ὀργῆς)."[31] As I will discuss further below, Paul reconfigures the juxtaposition between wrath and peace/righteousness around the crucified and risen Jesus.[32]

Overall, the link between peace (εἰρήνη) and righteousness (δικαιωθέντες) in Rom 5:1 evokes an OT motif that links these two concepts. As Dunn notes, peace and righteousness are "overlapping or complementary concepts" in Israel's Scriptures.[33] Besides the echoes discucssed above, one can find examples of the overlap in additional prophetic and poetic material:

> Let those who want my righteousness (δικαιοσύνην μου) be glad and rejoice, and let them say continually, "Let the Lord be magnified," those who want the peace (εἰρήνην) of his servant (Ps 34:27 LXX).[34]

> And if you had listened to my commandments, your peace (ἡ εἰρήνη σου) would be like a river and your righteousness (ἡ δικαιοσύνη σου) like a wave of the sea (Isa 48:18).[35]

The point here is not that Paul has these specific pre-texts in mind. It is simply that the consistent combination in Israel's Scriptures of peace and righteousness likely shape the way Paul understands the relationship between the concepts. If the experience of righteousness and peace marked the "future age" in Second Temple Jewish thought based on readings of Israel's Scriptures, Paul's combination of the concepts in Rom 5:1 implies that age has dawned in Christ.[36] We will return to this line of thought below.

---

30. The statement of trust continues until the end of the psalm. See Ps LXX 84:12–14.
31. Cf. ἀπὸ τῆς ὀργῆς in Rom 5:10 and ἀπὸ ὀργῆς θυμοῦ σου in Ps 84:4 LXX.
32. Fitzmyer notes the echo of Ps 85:11 (84:11 LXX) in Rom 5:1. See Fitzmyer, *Romans*, 395.
33. Dunn, *Romans*, 1:247.
34. See also Pss LXX 71:3; 85:10.
35. See also Isa 9:7; 32:17; 60:17.
36. As Dunn suggests, "Since in prophetic hope the full flowering of God's covenanted peace belonged to the future new age, Paul's assertion amounts to a claim that Israel's eschatological hope is now already in process of fulfillment." Dunn, *Romans*, 1:247. See Isa 9:6–7; 54:10; Ezek 34:25–31; 37:26; Mic 5:4; Hag 2:9; Zech 8:12. See also 1 En. 5:7, 9; 10:17; 11:2.

Romans 5:2 and Echoes of Access to God's Presence

Romans 5:2 contains two intertextual echoes which emanate from the phrases "through whom we also have access (τὴν προσαγωγήν) by faith into this grace in which we stand (ἑστήκαμεν)" and "we boast in the hope of the glory of God (τῆς δόξης τοῦ θεοῦ)."

Although προσαγωγή does not occur in the LXX, the contextual use of the term in Rom 5:1 evokes the OT motif that one must be "qualified and unblemished" to approach and stand (ἵστημι) before God.[37] The verbal cognate προσάγω occurs frequently in contexts that underscore this "qualified and unblemished" approach. For example, Aaron and his priestly sons are brought to the tent of meeting in a certain manner "And you shall bring (תקריב/προσάξεις) Aaron and his sons to the doors of the tent of meeting and you shall wash (λούσεις) them with water" (Exod 29:4).[38] We find a surge of this language in Leviticus where προσάγω is often employed as part of the divine instruction for how Israelites and priests must approach God.[39] The people were commanded to bring specified animals to the priest for sin, guilt, burnt, and other offerings. Priests were commanded to bring offerings on behalf of the people and for themselves before God. Given Paul's allusion to it in Rom 3:21–26, he may once again have in view Lev 16 and the day of atonement.[40] This day is highlighted by the priest's unique approach (προσάγω) to God:

> And Aaron shall bring (προσάξει) a bull which is for his sin and he will make atonement for himself and for his house (Lev 16:6).[41]

> And Aaron shall bring a goat, upon which the lot to the Lord has come upon it, and he shall offer it for a sin offering (Lev 16:9).[42]

The priest brought sacrifices before God in the innermost part of the tabernacle and into the wilderness.

This qualified and unique "approach" (προσάγω) to God, especially on the day of atonement, is *contextually consistent* with Paul's statement in Rom 5:2 and the larger context of the letter. The approach/access (προσαγωγή) to God is "through" (διά) the Lord Jesus Christ. While he does not unpack Jesus' intermediary work here, we know

---

37. As Jewett puts it, "Only those qualified and unblemished can approach God in this way (e.g., Exod 29:4, 8; Lev 21:18–19; Num 8:9–10), a theme extensively developed by the Essenes, who believed that their community alone enjoyed access to God (e.g., 1QH 12:20–26)." Jewett, *Romans*, 349–50.

38. See also the use of προσάγω in Exod 29:8, 10; 40:12.

39. See the use of προσάγω in Lev 1:2, 3, 10; 3:1, 3, 7, 12; 4:3, 4, 14; 5:8; 6:7; 7:8, 14, 16, 25, 35; 8:13, 14, 18, 22, 24; 10:19; 14:2, 12; 16:1, 6, 9, 11, 20, 22, 24; 23:8, 18, 25, 27; 23:36. See also the use of προσάγω in Num 5:16; 6:12, 14, 7:3; 8:9, 10; 15:27, 33; 16:5, 9, 10, 17; 18:2; 25:6; 27:5; 28:3, 9, 11, 19, 27; 29:13, 36.

40. See the discussion in volume 1.

41. See also Lev 16:11.

42. See also Lev 16:20.

from Rom 3:21–26 that Paul describes Jesus as the "mercy seat" (ἱλαστήριον).⁴³ In this way, Christ expiates and propitiates the sin of both Jew and Gentile before God. Their access to God is grounded in Christ who is the "mercy seat" put forward by God. Moreover, as we shall see in subsequent chapters, Paul describes Jesus as having an ongoing intercessory role which is grounded in the salvific work at the cross. This is clear in the latter part of the *inclusio* for this section of the letter (Rom 5:1—8:39), "Who is the one who condemns? Christ Jesus is the one who died, but rather who was raised, who also is at the right hand of God (ἐν δεξιᾷ τοῦ θεοῦ), who also intercedes (ἐντυγχάνει) for us" (Rom 8:34). The reference to the "right hand of God (ἐν δεξιᾷ τοῦ θεοῦ)" indicates an allusion to Ps 110 (109 LXX) which I will discuss later. It is sufficient to note at this point that this psalm has both royal and priestly characteristics, characteristics which are evoked here in Rom 5:1–2.⁴⁴

The phrase "in which we stand (ἑστήκαμεν)" in Rom 5:2 also evokes pre-texts related to priests and the congregations of Israel standing before God.⁴⁵ For example, the description of Aaron's priestly inauguration includes "And they took it, as Moses commanded, before the tent of meeting, and all the congregation came near and they stood before the Lord (יעמדו/ἔστησαν)" (Lev 9:5). Part of the general description of Levites includes, "And now do not cease, because the Lord has chosen you to stand (στῆναι) before him to serve and to be those who serve and make incense offerings" (2 Chr 29:11). In addition to priests "standing" before God, Jewett points to the "famous passage" from Ps 23 LXX which includes he question "Who will ascend to the mountain of the Lord and who will stand (στήσεται) in his holy place? The one who is innocent in hands and pure in heart, who has not taken his soul up to vanity and has not sworn against his neighbor in deceit" (Ps 23:3–4 LXX).⁴⁶ Overall, for Paul, as with the OT pre-texts, the "standing" refers to access before God's glory and ultimately judgment before him.⁴⁷ These are both concerns that Paul raises in Rom 5:1–10.

The second echo in Rom 5:2 stems from Paul's phrase "we boast in the hope of the glory of God (τῆς δόξης τοῦ θεοῦ)." The phrase τῆς δόξης τοῦ θεοῦ also occurs in Rom 3:23 which I analyzed in the previous volume.⁴⁸ There I noted that the phrase echoes three interrelated OT motifs: (1) removal from God's glorious presence; (2) depravation of God's glory; and (3) the departure of God's glory. Removal from God's glorious presence is best demonstrated in Gen 3:22–25 with the removal of Adam and Eve from the garden. Consequently, they are removed from God's glorious presence

---

43. See the discussion in volume 1.

44. Cf. the use of Ps 109 LXX in Hebrews which also underscores the royal and priestly work of the messianic figure in the psalm. See Heb 1:3, 13; 5:6; 6:20; 7:3; 8:1; 10:12.

45. See Jewett, *Romans*, 350.

46. Jewett, *Romans*, 350.

47. As Hultgren notes, "The experience of being in the presence of the glory of God becomes a future hope in portions of the OT and postbiblical Judaism." Hultgren points to Ps 102:15–16, Isa 24:23; 1QpHab 10:14; 1QM 4:6, 8. See Hultgren, *Romans*, 206.

48. See volume 1.

which gives them life. Depravation of God's glory is exemplified in 1 Sam 4:1–17 where the ark of the covenant is lost in battle and a humiliating defeat ensues. Ezek 10–11 describes the departure of God's glory from the temple due to Israel's sin. Contrastively, through the access to God's glory that Christ provides, Jewish and Gentile Christians in Rome can boast in the "glory of God." They are no longer removed from his life giving and protective glory.[49] Instead, Paul reconfigures the boast in the "hope of the glory of God" around Christ and the resurrection of children of God.[50] We will return to this reconfiguration below.

Romans 5:3–4 and Echoes of the Afflictions of the Righteous

In Rom 5:3–4, Paul expands upon the boast of those who are in Christ, and it evokes the OT motif of the afflictions of the righteous. Those who have peace and access to God through Christ not only "boast (καυχώμεθα) in the hope of the glory of God." They also boast in tribulations, "And not only this, but we also boast in tribulations (καυχώμεθα ἐν ταῖς θλίψεσιν)" (Rom 5:3a). Paul immediately explains that he and his recipients can boast in tribulations, because they know the result of them "Because we know (εἰδότες) that tribulation (ἡ θλῖψις) produces endurance (ὑπομονήν), and endurance character (δοκιμήν), and character hope (ἐλπίδα)." The scenario that Paul lays out here evokes the afflictions of certain OT figures, particularly the "righteous" (δίκαιος) who are afflicted.

Paul's specifically evokes the description and paradigm of righteous lamenters in the Psalms of Lament.[51] As the psalmist plainly states, "The afflictions of the righteous (αἱ θλίψεις τῶν δικαίων) are many, and he will deliver them from all of them" (Ps 33:20 LXX). Their afflictions come from a variety of sources including political opponents, disease, guilt for sin, death, divine hiddenness, and divine wrath.[52] Echoes of OT lament throughout Romans indicate a high level of engagement with these psalms by Paul. For example, in the previous volume, I discussed Paul's use of Psalms of Lament in Rom 3:10–18 and 3:19–20.[53] In the latter, he evokes Ps 142 LXX, an individual lament, where the petitioner seeks a right standing before God to acquire deliverance

---

49. As Gathercole puts it, "This 'glory of God' is precisely that which has been forfeited, as described by Paul in Romans 3:23, and which is featured in the Life of Adam and Eve 20.2. So, the divine glory that humanity had possessed is now lacking but will finally be restored." Gathercole, *Where is Boasting*, 256.

50. The use of ἐλπίς in Rom 5:2 and 8:24 forms an inclusio in this section which indicates the "hope of the glory of God" is ultimately experienced through resurrection from the dead like the risen Jesus.

51. For a discussion of righteous figures, their afflictions, and vindication in Second Temple Judaism, see Nickelsburg, *Resurrection, Immortality, and Eternal Life*, 19–178.

52. On the afflictions of righteous lamenters in the Psalms, see Crisler, *Reading Romans as Lament*, 45–65; idem, *Echoes of Lament and the Christology of Luke*, 50–85; Miller, *They Cried to the Lord*; Westermann, *Praise and Lament in the Psalms*.

53. See volume 1.

from enemies.[54] This right standing leads to the psalmist's boast towards the end of the psalm, "On account of your name you will bring my soul out from tribulation (ἐκ θλίψεως); and in your mercy you will destroy my enemies and you will ruin all those who afflict (τοὺς θλίβοντας) my soul; because I am your servant" (Ps 142:11–12 LXX).[55] As we move forward in our analysis of the entire letter, we will see several echoes from the Psalms of Lament. This includes Paul's allusion to Ps 21 LXX in Rom 5:5 which I will discuss below.

In Romans 5:3–4, Paul evokes a paradigm from the Psalms of Lament in which the righteous are involved in a patterned experience involving promise, suffering, a cry of distress, deliverance, and praise.[56] In short, lamenters hold to a prior promise of deliverance from God that is challenged by their suffering. Their suffering elicits a cry of distress which God answers through some form of deliverance, ordinarily through a reiteration of the promise, an oracle, or a vision.[57] The deliverance shifts the cry to praise. As we shall see, this same paradigm, or patterned experience, is reflected in Paul's argument at various points in Romans. In keeping with his hermeneutical practice, Paul reconfigures this paradigm around God's work in Christ. Roman Christians boast in the hope of the glory of God, but, like OT lamenters, their boast does not eliminate pain or silence laments. Here in Rom 5:3 Paul evokes the boast (καυχώμεθα) of righteous lamenters who have experienced deliverance. As the psalmist commands, "Rejoice in the Lord and be glad, O righteous ones (δίκαιοι), and boast (καυχᾶσθε), all those who are upright in heart" (Ps 32:11 LXX).[58]

A second echo in Rom 5:3–4 stems from the three characteristics that Paul claims are produced (κατεργάζεται) by tribulations, namely "endurance (ὑπομονή)" which produces "character (δοκιμή)" which in turn produces "hope (ἐλπίς)"[59] Once again, the ultimate object of Paul's hope is to experience God's glory in bodily resurrection from the dead.[60] It is a hope bound up with endurance. Not coincidentally, endurance characterizes the righteous who are afflicted in the OT:

> And now what is my endurance (ὑπομονή)? Is it not the Lord? And my support is from you (Ps 38:8 LXX).

---

54. See Ps LXX 142:2–10.

55. Cf. the tribulation (θλῖψις) of the righteous in Pss LXX 4:2; 9:10, 22; 19:2; 21:12; 24:17, 22; 31:7; 33:7, 18, 20; 36:39; 43:25; 45:2; 49:15; 53:9; 54:4; 58:17; 59:13; 65:11, 14; 70:20; 76:3; 77:49; 80:8; 85:7; 90:15; 106:39; 107:13; 114:3; 117:5; 118:143; 137:7; 141:3; 142:11.

56. The pattern is flexible as OT scholars note. See Villaneuva, *Uncertainty of a Hearing*; Westermann, "The Role of Lament in the Theology of the Old Testament," 20–38.

57. Cf. Habakkuk's experience which I discussed at length in a previous chapter due to Paul's citation of Hab 2:4 in Rom 1:17.

58. Cf. the use of καυχάομαι in Pss LXX 5:12; 149:5.

59. Cf. the use of κατεργάζομαι in Rom 1:27; 2:9; 4:15; 7:8, 13, 15, 17, 18, 20; 15:18.

60. Rom 8:18–27.

> Nevertheless, be subject to God, O my soul, because my endurance (ἡ ὑπομονή μου) is from him (Ps 61:6 LXX).

> For you are my endurance (ἡ ὑπομονή μου), O Lord; the Lord is my hope (ἡ ἐλπίς μου) from my youth (Ps 70:5 LXX).

In the wider contexts of these pre-texts, the psalmist situates "endurance" (ὑπομονή) within great distress. Moreover, as is clear in Ps 70:5 LXX, ὑπομονή and ἐλπίς are closely related. One needs to endure, or persevere, in their hope of what God promised. When these figures are afflicted, they find their endurance (ὑπομονή) from the Lord. They persevere in their hope that God will deliver them. Paul reconfigures this experience of endurance around faith and hope in Christ. Such endurance then produces character (δοκιμή) (Rom 5:4).

In Rom 5:4, δοκιμή bears the sense of character produced in Gentile and Jewish believers through enduring various afflictions.[61] Such a quality continues to echo figures who are afflicted in the Psalms. While the term δοκιμή does not occur in the LXX Psalms, the verb δοικμάζω often appears in descriptions of these figures:

> For you tested (ἐδοκίμασας) us, O God, you tried us by fire, as silver is tried by fire (Ps 65:10 LXX).

> O Lord, you tested me (ἐδοκίμασάς με) and you knew me; you understood my thoughts from afar (Ps 138:1 LXX).[62]

These statements indicate that God tests the righteous through various afflictions that they experience. This testing takes place at both the individual and community level in ancient Israel. With respect to the latter, the psalmist looks at Israel's afflictions in the wilderness generation and concludes God "tested" them. Ps 80 LXX uses the divine voice to make this point, "In tribulation you called me, and I delivered you. I heard you in the secret place of the storm, I examined you (ἐδοκίμασά σε) at the water of strife" (Ps 80:8 LXX).[63] Similarly, the reader can infer from Rom 5:1–5 that God ultimately stands behind the afflictions which produce character. Paul picks up this motif at various points in this section of the letter as I will discuss later.[64] In the immediate context, Paul notes that the character which God produces through afflictions produces hope (Rom 5:4).

---

61. BDAG 256. See the use of δοκιμή in 2 Cor 2:9; 8:2; 9:13; 13:3; Phil 2:22.

62. Petitioners also ask God to "test", or "examine" (δοκίμασόν με) them. See, e.g., Pss LXX 25:2; 138:23.

63. Ps 81:8 MT locates the place of examination at the "water of Meribah" (מי מריבה). See Exod 17:7; Num 20:13, 24; 27:14; Deut 33:8.

64. See, e.g., Rom 6:12–23; 8:28–30.

Romans 5:5 and Echoes of Disappointment

This brings us to Rom 5:5 where we find two more echoes which further explain Paul's interrelated boast in "the hope of the glory of God" and the boast "in tribulations."

First, the phrase "hope does not disappoint (ἡ ἐλπὶς οὐ καταισχύνει)" echoes Ps 22 (21 LXX), a classic psalm of lament which played a significant role in early Christology.[65] As part of the opening complaint and request in the psalm, the lamenter recalls God's prior deliverance of his people "They cried to you and they were saved, they hoped in you (ἤλπισαν) and they were not disappointed (οὐ κατῃσχύνθησαν)" (Ps 21:6 LXX). The *volume* of the echo is moderate to high. Both the pre-text and text combine ἤλπισαν/ἐλπίς with οὐ κατῃσχύνθησαν/ οὐ καταισχύνει.

We also find *contextual consistency* given the wider contexts of both the pre-text and text. The former is an individual psalm of lament that moves in typical lament fashion.[66] It has seven clear movements: (1) *complaint* against God's abandonment (21:2–3); (2) *statement of trust* based on God's answer to those who hoped in him and cried to him in the past (21:4–6); (3) *complaint* against enemies (21:7–11); (4) *request* for God's nearness (21:12); (5) *complaint* against enemies (21:13–19); (6) *request* for deliverance (21:20–22); and (7) *shift* to trust and praise (21:23–32). The lamenter's tribulation here (θλῖψις, Ps 21:12 LXX) has two interrelated sources: divine abandonment and mocking enemies. God has abandoned the lamenter in the face of enemies. Therefore, a cry is elicited "My God, my God, pay attention to me; why have you abandoned me?" (Ps 21:2a LXX).

Other complaints are launched directly against enemies, "Many bulls have encircled me, strong bulls have surrounded me; they opened their mouth against me like a lion who snatches and roars" (Ps 21:13–14 LXX). This distress elicits requests for God's nearness and deliverance (Ps 21:12, 20–22). However, the distress does not lead the lamenter to abandon their hope and their trust in God. Again, within the distress, he recalls how God had answered his ancestors "They cried to you and they were saved, they hoped in you (ἤλπισαν) and they were not disappointed (οὐ κατῃσχύνθησαν)" (Ps 21:6 LXX). The same hopefulness is reflected in the closing praise, "And my seed will serve him; the coming generation will be recounted to the Lord, and they will proclaim his righteousness (τὴν δικαιοσύνην αὐτοῦ) to the people who will be brought forth, that the Lord has done it" (Ps 21:31–32 LXX). Given the lamenter's circumstances, the referent of "righteousness" (δικαιοσύνη) is the way God answers and delivers the lamenter.

---

65. As Dodd noted in his seminal work, "The psalm (i.e., Ps 22) as a whole was clearly regarded as a source of testimonies to the passion of Christ and His ultimate triumph, and probably from an early date, since it is woven into the texture of the Passion-narrative, and used in writings almost certainly independent of one another." Dodd, *According to the Scriptures*, 97–98. See also Watts, "The Psalms in Mark's Gospel," 41–44.

66. Anderson, *Out of the Depths*, 240–44.

The context of Rom 5:1–5 echoes many of these wider features from Ps 21 LXX. For example, Paul and his recipients, like the lamenter, experience tribulation (Ps 21:12 LXX; Rom 5:3). As this section of the letter unfolds, the nature of those tribulations come into sharper focus. They include an ongoing battle with sin (Rom 6–7), distress caused by created forces that marshall themselves against God's children (Rom 8:18–39), divine absence/separation (Rom 8:35–39), and uncertainty regarding whether these afflictions are the result of divine wrath (Rom 5:6–10; 8:1–4). Additionally, tribulations notwithstanding, the hope of those in Christ does not ultimately disappoint (Ps 21:6 LXX; Rom 5:5). Even as the lamenter endured in the hope that God's promise of deliverance would not disappoint in the end, Paul makes a similar point in Rom 5:5. In this way, Paul returns to a key element from his thesis statement in Rom 1:16, "I am not ashamed/disappointed in the gospel."[67] We will return to this below. Finally, both the lamenter and Paul hope in God's righteousness (δικαιοσύνη/ Δικαιωθέντες) (Ps 31:32 LXX; Rom 5:1). The lamenter hoped in the promise that God would be near and deliver him. Paul hopes in the promise that Christ has brought him near to God (προσαγωγή) and delivered him.

With respect to the *history of interpretation*, various interpreters have noted the echo of Ps 21 LXX in Rom 5:5. For example, in his analysis of Rom 5:5, Barrett observes "The language is based upon Ps. xxii. 5; xxv. 3, 20."[68] Moreover, as Barrett points out, Ps 24 LXX also contains the language that we find in Rom 5:5:

> For all those who wait on you certainly shall not be ashamed/disappointed (οὐ μὴ καταισχυνθῶσιν); let all those who do lawlessness in vanity be ashamed (Ps 24:3 LXX).

> Keep my life and deliver me; may I not be ashamed/disappointed (μὴ καταισχυνθείην), because I have hoped (ἤλπισα) in you (Ps 24:20 LXX).[69]

Paul does more than merely borrow language from Psalms LXX 21 and 24. The lamenter's experience frames Paul's description of those who "boast in the hope of the glory of God."

It is also worth noting that the motif of disappointment/shame is present in Isa 28:16 which Paul cites later in the letter.[70] As the prophet announces judgment against corrupt leaders in Israel, he gives a glimmer of hope beyond judgment "For this reason,

---

67. See the discussion in volume 1.

68. He goes on to explain, "Paul means that our hope (of the glory of God (v.2)) will not be disappointed, and that we shall therefore not have to bear the shame of having followed a false hope." Barrett, *The Epistle to the Romans*, 104. On the link between Ps 21 LXX and Rom 5:5, see also Hultgren, *Romans*, 207–208; Jewett, *Romans*, 355; Stuhlmacher, *Romans*, 80.

69. Similarly, Longenecker notes "In using the phrase οὐ καταισχύνει ('it does not put to shame [or 'disappoint']'), Paul picks upon on the expression of two psalms attributed to David." He points to Pss LXX 21:5–6 and 24:20. Longenecker, *Romans*, 561.

70. See Rom 9:33; 10:11. For analysis, see volume 3.

in this way the Lord says 'Behold I will lay in the foundations of Zion a costly stone, choice, a cornerstone, a precious stone for its foundations, and the one who believes (ὁ πιστεύων) in it certainly shall not be disappointed (οὐ μὴ καταισχυνθῇ)" (Isa 28:16). The *volume* of the pre-text is moderate to high based on the overlap between οὐ μὴ καταισχυνθῇ in Isa 28:16 and οὐ καταισχύνει in Rom 5:5. Isaiah promises a deliverance beyond judgment that will not shame or disappoint those who believe it, because it ultimately proves "illusory."[71] For Paul, God fulfills this promise in Christ who will not be an eschatological disappointment or embarrassment to those who trust in him.

The second pre-text in Rom 5:5 is related to Paul's description of the Spirit, "For the love of God (ἡ ἀγάπη τοῦ θεοῦ) has been poured out in our hearts (ἐκκέχυται) through the Holy Spirit (πνεύματος ἁγίου) who was given to us." Paul grounds (γάρ) his confidence that the believer's hope will not lead to shame or disappointment in the way God loves the believer through the gift of the Spirit poured out in their hearts. The imagery of God pouring out (ἐκχέω) the Spirit in the heart evokes the prophecy of Joel, "And it will be after these things I will pour out (ἐκχεῶ) from my Spirit (ἀπὸ τοῦ πνεύματός μου) upon all flesh, and your sons and daughters will prophesy, and your elders will dream dreams, and your young men will see visions" (Joel 3:1).[72] The *volume* here is moderate to high given the correspondence of the terms ἐκχέω and πνεῦμα.[73]

Contextual consistency occurs at the point of a shared motif, namely the role of the Spirit in the hope of salvation beyond judgment. Joel warned about the coming "day of the Lord" in which God would judge his people through foreign invaders. For example, in Joel 3:4, we find "The sun will be turned to darkness and the moon to blood before the great and glorious day of the Lord (ἡμέραν κυρίου) comes."[74] All those who called on God's name for deliverance would be saved (Joel 3:5). The Spirit's arrival would mark the "day of the Lord" and salvation for those who cried out to be saved from divine judgment. Similarly, the "hope of the glory of God" that Paul has in view indicates an eschatological setting which is marked by the Spirit's arrival. Both Rom 5:1–5 and 6–10 underscore that Paul has in view the final "day of the Lord." As Paul puts it in the next paragraph, "Therefore, how much more having been justified now by his blood we will be saved (σωθησόμεθα) from the wrath (ἀπὸ τῆς ὀργῆς). For if while being enemies we were reconciled to God through the death of his son,

---

71. As Cranfield notes, "The hope which is thus strengthened and confirmed does not put those who cherish it to shame by proving illusory." Cranfield lists Isa 28:16, along with Pss LXX 21 and 24, as pre-texts that inform Rom 5:5. However, his assessment of their impact is very limited. He merely notes, "The language is reminiscent of the OT." Cranfield, *Romans*, 1:162.

72. See also Isa 32:15 LXX which, although it does not contain the verb ἐκχέω, refers to the Spirit coming upon God's people. Interestingly, Isa 32:15 MT contains a verb in the niphal stem that bears the sense "pour out" (ערה).

73. The *volume* would be substantially high if Rom 5:5 contained a reference to the Spirit being poured out "on flesh" (ἐπὶ πᾶσαν σάρκα) rather than "in our hearts (ἐν ταῖς καρδίαις)."

74. See "day of the Lord" (יום יהוה/ἡμέρα κυρίου) references in Joel 1:15; 2:1, 11; 4:14 (3:14).

how much having been reconciled we will be saved (σωθησόμεθα) by his life" (Rom 5:9–10).[75] For Paul, God has already shown that their hope of salvation on the day of the Lord will not disappoint, because God has already poured out his love now through the gift of the Spirit. The divine love they experience now through the Spirit indicates that their hope of divine love on the last day will not disappoint.[76]

Interpretive Impact of Pre-texts in Romans 5:1–5

While Paul does not cite the OT at this pivotal transition point in the letter, these five verses clearly have a rich and informative intertextual subtext. Several points of resonance are generated here. Four unstated points of resonance emerge from the interplay between pre-texts discussed above and Rom 5:1–5.

First, the phrase Δικαιωθέντες ἐκ πίστεως evokes three OT figures whom Paul discussed in Rom 1:16—4:25: (1) Habakkuk (Rom 1:16–17); (2) Abraham (Rom 4:1–25); and (3) David (Rom 4:6–8). In all three figures, God reckoned their faith in his promise as righteousness. The story of each figure informs Paul's understanding of what it means for Jews and Gentiles to be justified by faith. Habakkuk believed in the promise of deliverance by means of judgment and beyond judgment. Abraham believed in the promise of a God who raises the dead. As Sandes points out, "Abraham's faith is described as hope in a situation where a promise finds itself contradicted by reality and has a correspondence in the justified believers in Rom 5."[77] David believed the promise that his sins are covered and forgiven. Paul reconfigures their stories around God's promise in Christ. Jews and Gentiles alike trust that in Christ there is deliverance by means of and beyond judgment, because God has raised his crucified son from the dead. Therefore, in Christ, sins are forgiven, there is protection through and beyond divine wrath, and there is life from the dead. Paul will unpack many of these motifs throughout Rom 5:1—8:39.

Second, through the Lord Jesus Christ, God fulfills the Messianic promise of a king who would rule in righteousness and bring peace to God's people. Paul reconfigures OT pre-texts such as Isa 32, Ps LXX 71, and 84 around Christ. The reign of righteousness is far greater than Israel's golden age with David or post-exilic hopes that the nation would experience something like that golden age again. The Lord Jesus provides righteousness, that is a right standing, before God for both Jew and Gentile. The result is not merely peace in the promised land but an eschatological and eternal peace with God.

---

75. See also the eschatological setting signaled in Rom 1:31; 2:1–16; 6:5; 8:11, 18–25; 13:11–14; 14:10–11; 15.

76. However, as I will discuss in my analysis of Rom 5:6–10, God's love for the believer is measured by the death of Christ. As Schlatter puts it, "For Paul, however, the love of God is gauged not by spiritual experience but by the death of Christ who died for the powerless and the godless." Schlatter, *Romans*, 122.

77. Sandes, "Abraham, The Friend of God," 128.

This brings us to Rom 5:2. Justification by faith results in peace (εἰρήνην ἔχομεν) with God through the Lord Jesus Christ *and* access to God (τὴν προσαγωγὴν ἐσχήκαμεν) through the Lord Jesus Christ. Specifically, it is access "by faith into this grace in which we stand (ἐστήκαμεν) and we boast in the hope of the glory of God (ἐπ' ἐλπίδι τῆς δόξης τοῦ θεοῦ)." Two points of resonance emerge between the pre-texts and Rom 5:2. First, the Lord Jesus Christ is the qualified and unblemished sacrifice who provides access (προσαγωγή) to God. The echoes of pre-texts such as Exod 29:4 and Lev 16:6 (προσάγω/προσαγωγή) indicate that Paul has in view an "access" supplied through the sacrifice of Jesus whose death both expiated sin and propitiated divine wrath.[78] As we shall see, this section of the letter confirms these points of resonance.[79] Second, the Lord Jesus Christ provides a "standing" (ἐστήκαμεν) wherein Jewish and Gentile Christians are given (εἰς τὴν χάριν ταύτην) the "glory of God" in the sense that God protects them and they receive a favorable judgment. Echoes of pre-texts such as Lev 9:5, 2 Chr 29:11, and Ps LXX 23:3–4 indicate that a "standing" with God involves protection and judgment. Paul reconfigures this standing, which provides both protection and a favorable judgment, around faith in the Lord Jesus Christ. Such a standing elicits a "boast" in the hope of the glory of God (καυχώμεθα ἐπ' ἐλπίδι τῆς δόξης τοῦ θεοῦ).

In Rom 5:3–4, Paul mentions a second "boast" in the afflictions experienced by both Jewish and Gentile believers (καυχώμεθα ἐν ταῖς θλίψεσιν). The main point of resonance here is that Jews and Gentiles are living out the patterned existence of righteous lamenters described in the OT, especially the Psalms.[80] Paul highlights three characteristics from these figures: (1) their endurance in tribulations; (2) their divinely approved character; and (3) their threat of disappointment/shame in God's promise. He reconfigures these characteristics around faith in the Lord Jesus Christ. Paul and his recipients can boast in tribulations, because God produces endurance through the afflictions of the righteous. Moreover, he produces the kind of character that he eschatologically approves. That character in turn produces hope within believers that they will experience God's glory, ultimately in their resurrection from the dead. One of the main benefits of reading Rom 5:3–4 against the backdrop of what righteous lamenters experienced in the OT is that it casts the believer's experience in a

---

78. Cf. Rom 3:25 and Paul's use of ἱλαστήριον. See the discussion of the former in volume 1.
79. See, e.g., Rom 5:6–10; 8:1–4, 31–34.
80. See once again Pss LXX 32:11; 38:8.

realistic light.⁸¹ The hope Paul describes in Rom 5:1—8:39 is a painful and sometimes confusing experience.⁸²

Finally, with respect to the pre-texts in Rom 5:5, the hope of sharing in God's glory on the last day will not disappoint those who suffer in the vein of righteous sufferers from Israel's Scriptures. That is because God has already poured out his eschatological love now through the gift of the Holy Spirit who will raise them from the dead just as he did Christ (Rom 8:9–11). This experience evokes prophetic promises of an eschaton marked by the gift of the Spirit such as that described in Joel 2–3.⁸³

Romans 5:6–10

(5:6–10) For while we were still weak according to the time Christ died for the ungodly. For one will rarely die for a righteous person; though perhaps for a good person one might dare to die. But God demonstrates his own love to us, that while were still sinners Christ died for us. Therefore, how much more having been justified now by his blood we will be saved through him from the wrath. For if while being enemies we were reconciled to God through his death, how much more having been reconciled we will be saved by his life; but not only this, but also boasting in God through our Lord Jesus Chris through whom we received the reconciliation.

Here Paul further explains (γάρ) the inference that he drew from Rom 1:18—4:25 and laid out in Rom 5:1–5.⁸⁴ The justification of Jew and Gentile by faith in the Lord Jesus Christ results in peace with God and access to the gift of a "standing," or access, before him. They can boast in the hope that they will experience God's glory in their resurrection from the dead. They can also boast in their tribulations given what God does with them, namely he produces endurance which produces the character that he approves which produces hope that they will experience God's glory in their resurrection from the dead. Despite tribulations, and even because of tribulations, their hope will not become a disappoint to them on the last day. That is because God's love that is to be experienced on the last day when God raises the dead has already been given through the Spirit. Paul now grounds this inference of peace, access, hope and love

---

81. Stuhlmacher appreciates the way Paul evokes righteous sufferers from the OT and Jewish tradition to explain Christian suffering. He points to the following pre-texts: Pss 18, 56; Jer 36–45; Sir 2; Wis 2:12–20; 1 En. 103:9–1–4:5. He concludes, "Paul applies both traditions to Christians. As the 'suffering righteous,' they follow the path of perseverance and are inspired in it by their hope in the future reign of Christ and by their hope of being allowed to participate in the glory of God." Stulmacher, *Romans*, 79.

82. See Rom 7:7–25; 8:18–39.

83. Cf. Acts 2:17; 10:45.

84. Wolter refers to Rom 5:1–11 as the "Gegenstück" (counterpart; antithesis) to Rom 1:18–3:20. Wolter, *Der Brief an die Römer*, 1:338.

in a more elaborate explanation of God's love and reconciliation given through the crucified and risen Christ.

Not surprisingly, Paul's explanation contains multiple intertextual echoes. They can be categorized as follows: (1) God's love for ungodly Israel in Hosea; (2) the description of ungodly enemies in the Psalms; (3) sacrificial death in the OT; (4) an echo of Prov 11:31; and (5) eschatological wrath in the OT.

Suggested Pre-Texts in Romans 5:6–10

Hübner lists the following pre-texts: Hos 3:1; 11:1–9 (Rom 5:8).[85] Neither Nestle-Aland 28th ed., Hays, nor Seifrid identify any OT pre-texts for Rom 5:6–10.[86]

Intertextual Analysis of Romans 5:6–10

Paul underscores three different times the condition of himself and recipients at the time (κατὰ καιρόν) Christ died for them: (1) "while we were still weak (ὄντων ἡμῶν ἀσθενῶν) Christ died for the ungodly (ἀσεβῶν)" (Rom 5:6); (2) "while we were still sinners (ἁμαρτωλῶν ὄντων)" (Rom 5:8); and (3) "while being enemies (ἐχθροὶ ὄντες)" (Rom 5:10). God demonstrates (συνίστησιν) his love while Jews and Gentiles are weak, ungodly, and sinners.[87] In short, God demonstrates love to his enemies.

Romans 5:6–10 and Echoes of Ungodly Enemies

Paul's description of God's love for these enemies faintly evokes the love that God demonstrated to his people in Hosea. I cannot point to the *volume* of any specific echoes from Hosea. Instead, the broad contours of God's love for his people in the prophecy are reflected in Paul's description. In this way, there is *contextual consistency*. As God commands Hosea, "Still go and love (ἀγάπησον) the wife who loves evil things and adultery, just as God loves (ἀγαπᾷ) the sons of Israel and they look away to foreign gods and they love cakes with dried grapes" (Hos 3:1). Similarly, Christ dies for Jews and Gentiles while they are still unfaithful and sinful due to God's love for them. We can also point to the *recurrence* of Hosea in the letter. Paul cites Hos 2:1 and 2:25 in Rom 9:25–26 which I will discuss in the next volume.

Romans 5:6–10 also evokes the description of ungodly enemies in the Psalms. Once again, he underscores the condition of himself and recipients at the time (κατὰ καιρόν) Christ died for them: (1) "while were still weak (ὄντων ἡμῶν ἀσθενῶν) Christ died for the ungodly (ἀσεβῶν)" (Rom 5:6); (2) "while we were still sinners

---

85. Hübner, *Vetus Testamentum in Novo*, 2:84.
86. NA 28th ed. lists 1 En. 5:9 as a parallel text for Rom 5:9.
87. Cf. the use of συνίστημι in Rom 3:5.

(ἁμαρτωλῶν ὄντων)" (Rom 5:8); and (3) "while being enemies (ἐχθροὶ ὄντες)" (Rom 5:10). I will put aside the reference to being "weak" for the moment, because it does not echo the description of enemies in the Psalms. However, the terms ἁμαρτωλός, ἀσεβής, and ἐχθρός occur frequently in the Psalms.[88] The common characteristics of these figures include: (1) deceptive and flattering speech; (2) plotting to harm others; (3) violent; (4) deny God's judgment against them; and (5) refuse to call on the Lord for deliverance.[89] Many of these characteristics are reflected in the Psalms that Paul cites in the catena of Rom 3:10–18.[90] For example, the psalmist describes the speech of enemies noting "Their throat is an open grave, the poison of asps is under their lips" (Ps 5:10; Rom 3:13). Their deadly speech and plotting elicits the lamenter's cry, "O Lord, guide me in your righteousness because of my enemies (ἐχθρῶν), make your way straight before me" (Ps 5:9). Both in the catena and here in Rom 5:6–10, Paul aligns Jewish and Gentile believers with the ungodly and sinful enemies of the Psalms. In the theology of the Psalms, God crushes these enemies.[91] However, in Paul's reconfiguration of these figures, God loves them and Christ dies for them. He treats Christ as the enemy on behalf of the enemies whom he loves.

Romans 5:6–10 and Echoes of Sacrificial Death

Paul's persistent combination of ἀποθνῄσκω and ὑπέρ, in concert with the references to blood (αἷμα) and death (θάνατος), echoes OT language of sacrificial death. This combination occurs four times in Rom 5:6–8: (1) "he died for the ungodly (ὑπὲρ ἀσεβῶν ἀπέθανεν);" (2) "For one will rarely die for a righteous person (ὑπὲρ δικαίου τις ἀποθανεῖν);" (3) "for a good person one might dare to die (ὑπὲρ γὰρ τοῦ ἀγαθοῦ τάχα τις καὶ τολμᾷ ἀποθανεῖν);" and (4) while we were still sinners Christ died for us (Χριστὸς ὑπὲρ ἡμῶν ἀπέθανεν)." Interpreters often find these phrases in Rom 5:6–8 difficult to understand. Longenecker observes, "The material of these verses is, at first glance, exceedingly difficult to understand, not only linguistically and structurally but

---

88. See ἁμαρτωλός in Pss LXX 1:1, 5; 3:8; 7:10; 9:17, 18, 24, 25, 36; 10:2, 6; 27:3; 31:10; 33:22; 35:12; 36:10, 12, 14, 16, 17, 20, 21, 32, 34, 40; 38:2; 49:16; 54:4; 57:4, 11; 67:3; 70:4; 72:3, 12; 74:9, 11; 81:2, 4; 83:11; 90:8; 91:8; 93:3, 13; 96:10; 100:8; 103:35; 105:18; 108:2, 6; 110:10; 118:53, 61, 95, 110, 119, 155; 124:3; 128:3, 4; 138:19; 139:5, 9; 140:5, 10; 144:20; 145:9; 146:6. See ἀσεβής in Pss LXX 1:1, 4, 5, 6; 9:6, 23, 34; 10:5; 11:9; 16:9, 13; 25:5, 9; 30:18; 36:28, 35, 38; 50:15; 57:11. See ἐχθρός in Pss LXX 5:9; 6:8, 11; 7:5, 6, 7; 8:3; 9:4, 7, 14, 26; 12:3, 5; 16:9, 13; 17:1, 4, 18, 20, 38, 41, 49; 20:9; 24:2, 19; 26:2, 6, 11; 29:2; 30:9, 12, 16; 36:20; 37:17, 20; 40:3, 6, 8, 12; 41:10; 42:2; 43:6, 11, 17; 44:6; 53:7, 9; 54:4, 13; 55:3, 10; 58:2, 11; 60:4; 63:2; 65:3; 67:2, 22, 24; 68:5, 19; 70:10; 71:9; 73:3, 10, 18; 77:53, 61, 66; 79:7; 80:15, 16; 82:3; 88:11, 23, 24, 43, 52; 91:10, 12; 96:3; 101:9; 104:24; 105:10, 42; 106:2; 107:14; 109:1, 2; 111:8; 117:7; 118:98, 139; 126:5; 131:18; 135:24; 137:7; 138:21, 22; 142:3, 9, 12.

89. See also the discussion about enemies in Kraus, *Psalms*; Westermann, *Praise and Lament in the Psalms*.

90. See the analysis of this catena in volume 1.

91. E.g., "But you, O God, will bring them down into a bit of ruin, men of blood and of treachery certainly shall not live out half of their days. But I will hope in you, O Lord" (Ps 54:24 LXX).

also theologically."[92] Some suggest that Paul employs an early Christian confession.[93] One also finds the suggestion that phrases such as ὑπὲρ ἀσεβῶν ἀπέθανεν indicate a conscious use of Second Temple martyr terminology.[94]

Without denying these possibilities altogether, my interest lies with how the OT shapes Paul's language at this point. It is hard to imagine that the OT suddenly ceases to influence Paul description of Jesus' death. It is the case that we do not find specific ἀποθνῄσκω and ὑπέρ combinations in Israel's Scriptures that match the context of Rom 5:6–10.[95] Nevertheless, Paul's contextual use of ἀποθνῄσκω and ὑπέρ indicate that he identifies Jesus as both the representative and substitute for ungodly enemies.[96] While LXX translators do not employ this combination, it does not follow that the OT lacks altogether the concept of sacrificial deaths that are both substitutionary and representative in nature. Moreover, as noted already, Paul mentions blood (αἷμα) and death (θάνατος) which are clearly informed by OT sacrificial language. This brings us to Paul's combination of two kinds of OT pre-texts.

Paul's language once again evokes Isa 53.[97] Although the latter text does not contain the combination of ἀποθνῄσκω and ὑπέρ, the suffering servant suffers and dies on behalf of/in place of others:

> He bears our sins and he suffers pain for us (περὶ ἡμῶν), and we reckoned him to be in trouble and in misfortune and in affliction. And he was wounded because of our lawlessness (διὰ τὰς ἀνομίας ἡμῶν) and he was weakened because of our sins (διὰ τὰς ἁμαρτίας ἡμῶν); the chastisement of our peace was upon him, by whose wound we have been healed. We have all gone astray like sheep, everyone has gone astray in his own way; and the Lord handed him over for our sins (ταῖς ἁμαρτίαις ἡμῶν) (Isa 53:4–6).

Israel's sin is clearly the cause of the servant's suffering and death. The implication is that Israel did not have to suffer and die, because he experienced that pain for them. In this way, the servant dies in place of (substitution) and on behalf of (representation) Israel. Paul identifies this suffering servant as the Lord Jesus Christ. The *contextual consistency* between the pre-text and text is substantial. In the pre-text, the suffering servant dies for sinful Israel (Isa 53:6, 8, 11–12). The servant's death is in accordance

---

92. Longenecker, *Romans*, 562.

93. E.g., Jewett notes, "The chiastic argument of vv.6–8 employs traditional creedal formulations interspersed with rhetorical comments." Jewett, *Romans*, 357.

94. See, e.g., 2 Macc 7:9; 8:21; 4 Macc 1:8, 10; Josephus, *Ant.* 13:5–6. On this point, see Dunn, *Romans*, 1:255; Williams, *Maccabean Martyr Traditions*, 85–119.

95. The closest match may be Deut 24:16, "Fathers will not die (ἀποθανοῦνται) for their children (ὑπὲρ τέκνων), and sons will not die (ἀποθανοῦνται) for their fathers (ὑπὲρ πατέρων); each one will die for his own sin."

96. As Schreiner notes, "The idea behind ὑπέρ is that Christ died both as our representative and as our substitute." Schreiner, *Romans*, 260. See also Käsemann, *Romans*, 138. Cf. Paul's use of ὑπέρ in 2 Cor 5:14–15, 21; Gal 3:13.

97. Cf. the echo of Isa 53 in Rom 4:25. For a discussion, see volume 1.

with God's will, "And the Lord wills (βούλεται) to purge him from the wound" (Isa 53:10a).⁹⁸ Similarly, Paul portrays Christ as dying for sinful enemies. In Christ's death, God "demonstrates (συνίστησιν)" his love to these enemies.⁹⁹

Romans 5:6–10 also evokes sacrificial language from Lev 16. This is especially clear in Rom 5:9, "Therefore, much more having been justified by his blood (ἐν τῷ αἵματι αὐτοῦ) we will be saved through him from the wrath." The prepositional phrase ἐν τῷ αἵματι αὐτοῦ is an almost exact match with the phrase in Rom 3:25, "whom God put forward as the mercy seat (ἱλαστήριον) through faith in his blood (ἐν τῷ αὐτοῦ αἵματι) for a demonstration of his righteousness in the present time because of the passing over of sins committed beforehand."¹⁰⁰ As I noted in the previous volume, Paul's use of "mercy seat" (ἱλαστήριον) evokes Lev 16 and the blood sacrifices required on the day of atonement. Given the correspondence of the phrases "by his blood (ἐν τῷ αὐτοῦ αἵματι /ἐν τῷ αἵματι αὐτοῦ)" in Rom 3:25 and 5:9, the latter is likewise associated with the "mercy seat" (ἱλαστήριον) from Lev 16 even though it is not specifically mentioned. In short, Paul reconfigures the blood sprinkled *at* and *on* the mercy seat in God's presence in relation to the blood of the crucified Christ. Such a sacrifice is the means by which God justifies his ungodly enemies (δικαιωθέντες νῦν ἐν τῷ αἵματι).

Romans 5:7 and the Echo of Proverbs 11:31

Paul's reference to a "righteous person (δίκαιος)" in Rom 5:7 contains an echo from Proverbs:

> For one will scarcely (μόλις) die for a righteous person (δικαίου); though perhaps for a good person one might dare to die (Rom 5:7).

> If the righteous person (ὁ δίκαιος) is scarcely (μόλις) saved, where will the ungodly person (ὁ ἀσεβής) and sinner (ἁμαρτωλός) appear (Prov 11:31)?

The *volume* of the echo is high based on the shared use of δίκαιος and μόλις. The only LXX use of the adverb μόλις is found here in Prov 11:31.¹⁰¹ Additionally, Rom 5:6 and 5:8 contains uses of ἀσεβής and ἁμαρτωλός respectively. The *contextual consistency* is difficult to articulate. For this reason, some interpreters suggest that Paul simply draws the key terms from Prov 11:31.¹⁰² However, as Wolter suggests, Paul is using the

---

98. Cf. Isa 53:10a MT, "But the Lord was pleased (חפץ) to crush him."

99. Cf. use of συνίστημι in Rom 3:5.

100. The only difference between the phrases in Rom 3:25 and 5:9 is the placement of the possessive pronoun αὐτοῦ.

101. See μόλις in 3 Macc 1:23; 5:15; Wis 9:16; Sir 21:20; 26:29; 29:6; 32:7; Acts 14:18; 27:7, 8, 16; 1 Pet 4:18.

102. E.g., Jewett notes the parallel terms in Prov 11:31 and Rom 5:7. However, he concludes "While

"derselbe Logik" ("the same logic") as Prov 11:31.[103] It is a kind of soteriological logic that Paul expands from earthly deliverance in Proverbs to eschatological salvation in Rom 5:6–10. The logic in Proverbs is that if the righteous are scarcely saved on the earth, it is even more unlikely that the wicked and the sinner are saved.[104] Similarly, the sense in Rom 5:7 is that if someone will scarcely die for a righteous person, it is even more unlikely that someone dies for an ungodly person.

Romans 5:9–11 and Echoes of Divine Wrath

Paul's reference to "wrath" (ὀργή) and the future tense expression "we will be saved" (σωθησόμεθα) evoke the expectation of eschatological wrath in Israel's Scriptures (Rom 5:9–11). We have already seen several texts in Romans where Paul's reference to wrath and judgment evoke an OT motif that warns about a final judgment of all people.[105] Therefore, I will not retest the echoes of this motif. I would simply note that the same motif is echoed here. For example, pre-texts from Zephaniah inform this motif:

> And their silver and their gold certainly shall not be able to deliver them in the day of the wrath of the Lord (ἐν ἡμέρᾳ ὀργῆς κυρίου), and all the earth (πᾶσα ἡ γῆ) will be consumed by the fire of his zeal, because he will make a hasty end upon all those who dwell in the earth (Zeph 1:18).[106]

> Seek the Lord, all you humble of the earth; do justice and seek righteousness and answer accordingly, in order that you might be sheltered in the day of the wrath of the Lord (ἐν ἡμέρᾳ ὀργῆς κυρίου) (Zeph 2:3).

The wrath here is both eschatological and cosmic in scope. Paul reconfigures this eschatological wrath around present (νῦν) justification (δικαιόω) and reconciliation (καταλλάσσω) in Christ. Simply put, present justification and reconciliation in the crucified and risen Christ assures those who are in Christ that they will be saved from God's wrath on the last day.[107] Attempts to downplay the eschatological backdrop of divine wrath in Rom 5:9–11 are historically and exegetically suspect.[108]

---

this parallel demonstrates the likely source of several key terms, it is unrelated to the decisive idea of one person's dying for another." Jewett, *Romans*, 360.

103. Wolter, *Der Brief an die Römer*, 329.

104. Prov 11:31 MT includes the location בארץ.

105. See, e.g., Rom 1:18; 2:1–16; 3:1–8; 4:15. See the intertextual analysis of these texts in volume 1.

106. See also ἡμέρα ὀργῆς in Zeph 1:15.

107. As Hultgren notes, "Salvation is primarily in the future, and it means deliverance from divine wrath at the final judgment." Hultgren, *Romans*, 212.

108. E.g., Dodd attempts to distance God from wrath in Paul's thought by treating it as an "objective principle" at work in the world rather than a divine action. He explains, "As we have seen, this term stands for the process by which sin brings its own retribution, a process conceived as reaching its

Interpretive Impact of Pre-Texts in Romans 5:6–11

These six verses have a richer intertextual subtext than some interpreters realize.[109] Several points of resonance emerge from the interplay between various pre-texts and the text.

To begin, in an even greater demonstration of God's love than what unfaithful and ungodly Israel received in Hosea's prophecy, God demonstrates his love in the death of Christ for ungodly Jews and Gentiles. Paul aligns all Jews and Gentiles with ungodly enemies in the Psalms, but he does so to quantify the depth of God's love for them in the death of Christ. He prefaces his remarks on God's love by applying the soteriological logic of Prov 11:31 to Christ's death for the ungodly (Rom 5:7). Christ's death for the ungodly is as rare as the earthly deliverance of the ungodly.

Second, God's love is bound up with Jesus' sacrificial death which escalates the efficacy of the blood sacrifices offered on the day of atonement. While the latter sacrifices served as an annual expiation and propitiation for ancient Israel before God, Jesus' death secures present justification and reconciliation which assures believers of eschatological salvation from God's wrath on the cosmic-wide day of judgment which prophets such as Zephaniah warned about.

Finally, we need to consider how the reference to reconciliation (καταλλάσσω, καταλλαγή) informs both the intertextual subtext and argumentation of this section. Paul explains that present reconciliation is the basis for salvation from God's wrath on the last day noting, "For if while being enemies we were reconciled (κατηλλάγημεν) to God through the death of his son how much more having been reconciled (καταλλαγέντες) we will be saved by his life; but not only this, but also boasting in God through our Lord Jesus Christ through whom now we have received the reconciliation (τὴν καταλλαγήν)" (Rom 5:10–11).[110] One issue that arises here is the close relationship between justification and reconciliation in this context. As Stuhlmacher notes, "For Paul justification and reconciliation belong inextricably together."[111] How, though, does Paul link them together? Some interpreters "read 'reconciliation' as a

---

consummation at the Last Judgment. From this process the divine love, which has already acquitted us of our past sins, will surely saves us. We may observe that if Wrath stood for an act and attitude of God, there would be no need for this 'much more" for justification means that God is not in a wrathful attitude towards us. But, since Wrath is an objective principle and process in the moral order, we still need at all points the help of Christ to overcome sin and destroy its baneful effects." Dodd, *Romans*, 98. This special pleading by Dodd is undercut by Paul's clear syntactical link between θεός and ὀργή in Rom 1:18 and the wider context of 5:6–11. Moreover, where in Second Temple thought does final judgment consist of facing an "objective principle" of wrath?

109. To reiterate, Hays's seminal work has a gaping lacuna with respect to the intertextual analysis of Rom 5:1–8:17.

110. In this context, καταλλάσσω/καταλλαγή bears the sense of God exchanging hostilities against the ungodly with a "friendly relationship." BDAG 521. Cf. Paul's use of this terminology in Rom 11:15; 1 Cor 7:11; 2 Cor 5:18–20.

111. Stuhlmacher, *Paul's Letter to the Romans*, 82.

broadening of 'justification' to include the new life of obedience."[112] However, as Seifrid notes, "It (reconciliation) describes the present reality of a right relation with God, but does not carry the overtones of eschatological redemption that 'justification' does."[113] Paul asserts that Jewish and Gentile Christians are presently reconciled and at peace with God; however, their afflictions (Rom 5:3) challenge that assertion.

This is where the wider intertextual subtext of Rom 5:1–11 sheds light on Paul's reconciliation metaphor. While it is true that καταλλάσσω/καταλλαγή language is sparse in the LXX, it does not follow that the metaphor is intertextually uninformed.[114] As noted in the previous section, Rom 5:3–5 evokes the figure of a righteous sufferer or lamenter. Such figures are often befuddled by God's absence which leaves their enemies unchecked. Lamenters are left to wonder where they stand before God given their suffering. A similar dynamic informs the experience of believers in Rom 5:1—8:39. This entire section of the letter is framed by suffering but not merely as a theme.[115] Rather, Paul reassures his recipients about their reconciliation with God through the crucified and risen Jesus. He uses the paradigm of righteous lamenters to explain the relationship between the afflictions of the believer and one's standing before God. Afflictions do not signal a lack of peace before the Romans and God. Rather, they characterize righteous figures in the divine economy from Abraham, to Habakkuk, to David, and climactically to those who are reconciled to God through Christ.

---

112. Seifrid, *Christ Our Righteousness*, 70n88.

113. Seifrid, *Christ Our Righteousness*, 70n88.

114. The verb καταλλάσσω only appears in Jer 31:39. See also 2 Macc 1:5; 7:33; 8:29. The noun καταλλαγή only occurs in Isa 9:4. See also 2 Macc 5:20.

115. Once again, several interpreters have noted how Rom 5:1–11 and 8:31–39 form an inclusio. Therefore, the material wedged between these two poles should be read in relation to the affliction (θλῖψις) that Paul suggests defines the believer's reconciled existence before God. See, e.g., Still, "Placing Pain in a Pauline Frame," 73–86.

3

Romans 5:12–21

ALTHOUGH PAUL DOES NOT cite a single verse from Gen 2–3, his allusion to this pretext and his hermeneutical engagement with it stand at the heart of Rom 5:12–21. Paul draws from his rhetorical education, specifically the literary device of *syncrisis*, to show the superior accomplishments of Christ in comparison to Adam.[1] In his encomium of Christ and invective against Adam, Paul draws a stark contrast between the two figures.[2] It is a contrast that relies upon specific details from the Genesis narrative as we shall see. We shall also see that, though the intertextual subtext is dominated by Gen 2–3, a few other pre-texts are evoked here as well.[3]

Romans 5:12–14

(5:12–14) For this reason just as through one man sin entered the world and through sin death, also in this way death spread to all men, under which circumstance all sinned; for until the law sin was in the world, but sin is not reckoned where there is no law, but death reigned from Adam until Moses and over those who did not sin in the likeness of the transgression of Adam who is a type of the one to come.

---

1. On Paul's use of *syncrisis* here, see Forbes, "Paul and Rhetorical Comparison," 154–55. Parsons and Martin, *Ancient Rhetoric*, 259–61.

2. Regarding the rhetorical classification of encomium and invective, Parson and Martin note "the stark contrast between two subjects is generally the point." *Ancient Rhetoric*, 233.

3. For intertextual studies of Rom 5:12–21, see Bray, "Adam and Christ," 4–8; Byrne, "The Type," 19–30; Caneday, "Already Reigning in Life," 27–43; Hofius, "The Adam-Christ Antithesis," 165–205; Kister, "Romans 5:12–21 Against the Background of Torah-Theology," 391–424; Leithart, "Adam, Moses, and Jesus," 257–73; Porter, "The Pauline Concept of Original Sin," 3–30; Kister, "Romans 5:12–21 Against the Background of Torah-Theology," 391–424; Kline, "Gospel Until the Law," 433–46; Westerholm, "Righteousness, Cosmic and Microcosmic," 21–38. See also de Jesús, *The Figure of Adam in Romans*, 5.

Before I engage in the intertextual analysis of these three verses, it is necessary to address a few exegetical difficulties that have plagued interpreters for quite some time now.

The use of the phrase Διὰ τοῦτο indicates a clear shift in the argument between Rom 5:11 and 5:12. The immediate question that arises is does Διὰ τοῦτο point backwards or forwards? To put it another way, how is 5:12–21 related to what Paul wrote in 5:1–11 and how is it related to what he will lay out in 6:1–8:39? Interpreters have proposed various solutions over the centuries.[4] It is peculiar that Paul enters an almost diatribe-like discussion of Adam at this point in the letter.[5] Consequently, many interpreters have concluded that Rom 5:12–21 is a separate pericope.[6] However, when we recall that Paul makes a significant "turn to Christ" in Rom 5:1, the purpose of discussing Adam at this point becomes clearer.[7] Rom 1:18–4:25 largely discusses the revelation of God's righteousness (δικαιοσύνη, 1:17) and wrath (ὀργή, 1:18) from the perspective of the standing that Jews and Gentiles have before God (θεός).[8] Apart from faith in Christ, they are all under God's wrath and the power of sin.[9] Peace with God comes through the Lord Jesus Christ as Jewish and Gentiles believers stand justified and reconciled before God in Christ; therefore, their tribulations (θλῖψις) are not the result of being under divine wrath. Instead, God uses tribulation to produce even greater hope in the peace that they have in Christ and hope in the glory of God, that is resurrection from the dead (Rom 5:1–11). In Rom 5:12–14, Paul sets this robust motif of hope against the widest possible backdrop, namely "human history" defined "in terms of divine judgment in Adam and grace in Christ."[10]

Another well-known exegetical difficulty arises in Rom 5:12. Two small particles have caused a disproportionate amount of troubles, "For this reason just as through one man sin entered the world and through sin death, also in this way death spread to all men, because/when/on which (ἐφ' ᾧ) all sinned." The particles in question are ἐφ' ᾧ, and how their translation contributed to later theological discussions about

---

4. For a summary of these solutions, see Longenecker, *Romans*, 580.

5. Although I do not adopt the view entirely here, Stan Porter suggests that Rom 5:12–21 is in fact a Greek diatribe. See Porter, "The Argument of Romans 5," 655–77.

6. See, e.g., Erickson, "The Damned and the Jusitifed in Romans 5.12–21," 287–88; Reid, *Augustinian and Pauline Rhetoric in Romans Five*, 117.

7. Once again, see Seifrid, "The Turn to Christ in Romans," 15–24.

8. As Seifrid puts it, "Up to this point in the letter he has presented justification as a matter of the standing of the individual before God." Seifrid, *Christ Our Righteousness*, 70. This is not to suggest that χριστός play no role at all in Rom 1:18–4:25. See, e.g., the references to χριστός in Rom 2:16; 3:22, 24. See also Rom 4:25. However, the references to θεός in Rom 1:18—4:25 are far greater. See the use of θεός in Rom 1:18, 19, 21, 23, 24, 25, 26, 28, 32; 2:2, 3, 4, 5, 11, 13, 16, 17, 23, 24, 29; 3:2, 3, 4, 5, 6, 7, 11, 18, 19, 21, 22, 23, 25, 26, 29, 30; 4:2, 3, 6, 17, 20.

9. Rom 1:18; 2:1–11; 3:9, 19–20; 4:15.

10. Seifrid, *Christ Our Righteousness*, 70. Additionally, Schreiner suggests that Rom 5:1–11 and 5:12–21 are "joined by the theme of hope." Schreiner, *Romans*, 271.

original sin.[11] If the dative particle ᾧ is masculine, its antecedent could be an "implied law," death, or one man (Adam).[12] The translation would either be "on the basis of what (law) all sinned," "because of which (death) all sinned," or "in whom (Adam) all sinned."[13] If the dative particle ᾧ is neuter, then the phrase ἐφ᾽ ᾧ has a "conjunctive sense" such as "because" or "so that."[14] The translation would either be "because all sinned" or "so that all sinned." While these suggestions have various strengths and weaknesses, I will proceed with the position that ἐφ᾽ ᾧ bears the sense of "under which circumstance."[15] In other words, given the entrance of sin in the world and the spread of death in all people, under these circumstances, all sinned.

With these exegetical difficulties in tow, we turn our attention to the intertextual subtext of Rom 5:12–14. The explicit allusion to Adam (Ἀδάμ, 5:14) and the Gen 2–3 narrative will guide the discussion. Six salient points emerge from Paul's interaction with the Adamic narrative.

Suggested Pre-Texts in Romans 5:12–14

Hübner lists the following pre-texts: Gen 2:17; 3:19; Hos 6:17 (Rom 5:12).[16] Nestle-Aland 28th ed. lists the following: Gen 2:17; 3:19 (Rom 5:12).[17]

Seifrid assumes Gen 3 as the main pre-text here. Overall, with respect to Rom 5:12–14, he suggests "Adam serves as a promissory pattern for Christ (*typos* [5:14]), whose death transcends and overcomes Adam's disobedience."[18] He also gives a fair amount of attention to Second Temple interpretations of Adam's fall concluding, "In contrast with all such reflections, Paul here underscores the responsibility of the one human being for the entrance of sin into the 'world' of human beings."[19]

---

11. Jewett, *Romans*, 375. Rom 5:12–14 has proved to have a significant impact on other theological concerns as well. For instance, as Peter Leithart notes, "The basic structure of covenant theology rests on the Adam-Christ analogy that Paul develops most full here." Leithart, "Adam, Moses, and Jesus," 257.

12. Leithart, "Adam, Moses, and Jesus," 257. For a discussion of identifying the antecedent of ᾧ as an implied law, see Danker, "Romans v.12," 424–39. For a discussion of identifying the antecedent as death, see Stauffer, *New Testament Theology*, 270.

13. See Fitzmyer, *Romans*, 413–16.

14. Jewett, *Romans*, 375.

15. On this interpretation, see Seifrid, *Christ Our Righteousness*, 70n91. Seifrid follows Zahn on this point.

16. Hübner, *Vetus Testamentum in Novo*, 2:88–89.

17. NA 28th ed. also lists the following parallel texts: 2 Bar. 54:15; 4 Ezra 3:21; Wis 2:24.

18. Seifrid, *Romans*, 628.

19. Seifrid, *Romans*, 629. Seifrid especially engages the apocalypses of 4 Ezra and 2 Baruch. See, e.g., 4 Ezra 3:20–27; 4:30–32; 2 Bar. 19:8; 23:4; 48:42–43.

Intertextual Analysis of Romans 5:12–14

The intertextual subtext of these three verses rests largely on Gen 2:16–17, the larger narrative of Gen 3, and the scriptural space between the figures of Adam and Moses. Additionally, the phrase τύπος τοῦ μέλλοντος in Rom 5:14 provides hermeneutical guidance for 5:15–19. As Goppelt notes in his classic study of New Testament typology, "For Paul, Adam is not simply an illustrative figure. He views Adam through Christ as a true type in redemptive history, as a prophetic personality placed in Scripture by God. This is the only way he can draw certain conclusions from the relationship of Adam to Christ as conclusions that are founded on a typology."[20] As we shall see, the interplay between these intertextual pre-texts and Paul's text generate unstated points of resonance that shed interpretive light on a notoriously difficult passage.

Romans 5:12 and the Allusion to the Divine Warning of Death

While Paul has all of Gen 2–3 in view at this point in the letter, Rom 5:12 specifically evokes two verses from the larger pre-text:

> For this reason, just as through one man sin entered the world and through sin death (ὁ θάνατος), also in this way death (ὁ θάνατος) spread to all men, under which circumstance all sinned (Rom 5:12).

> And the Lord God commanded Adam saying, "From every tree which is in the garden you may certainly eat, but from the tree of knowing good and evil, you certainly shall not eat from it; but in which day you eat from it, you will surely die (θανάτῳ ἀποθανεῖσθε)" (Gen 2:16–17).

> By the sweat of your brow you will eat your bread until you return to the earth (ἀποστρέψαι σε εἰς τὴν γῆν), from which you were taken; because you are earth and you will return to the earth (εἰς γῆν ἀπελεύσῃ) (Gen 3:19).

Genesis 2:16–17 and 3:19 are the two passages in Gen 2–3 that contain explicit references to death; therefore, in his discussion of Adam, Paul has these two passages in view. He also has in view the larger context wherein God doles out judgment to the serpent, Eve, Adam, and the earth itself (Gen 3:14–19). The fulcrum of these judgments is the removal of Adam and Eve from the garden. Separation from God in the garden results in separation from Adam and Eve's source of life. Simply put, it leads to their deaths.[21] The Genesis narrator presents a thoroughgoing picture of death which Paul then expands to "the world" (εἰς τὸν κόσμον) and "all men" (εἰς πάντας ἀνθρώπους) (Rom 5:12). In short, Paul retrospectively narrates the Genesis warnings about death, and he underscores the cosmic toll accrued by ignoring the warnings.

---

20. Goppelt, *Typos*, 130.
21. See Gen 3:22–24.

The toll is death via separation from God as well as the entrance of sin and death as malevolent powers.[22]

Romans 5:12 and the Allusion to the Entrance of the Serpent

Paul's reference to the entrance (εἰσῆλθεν) of sin (ἁμαρτία) in Rom 5:12 evokes Adam's specific sin and the work of the serpent as it is described in Gen 2–3. Contextually, both Adam and Eve sin.[23] The serpent deceives Eve by questioning God's warning (Gen 2:16–17) and enticing her to covet what God forbid, namely partaking of the tree of the knowledge of good and evil (Gen 3:1–7).[24] In evoking this narrative from Gen 3, Paul does not explicitly mention the serpent (ὄφις, Gen 3:1).[25] However, he personifies sin in such a way that it resembles the actions of the serpent.[26] For example, Paul notes that "sin entered the world" (ἡ ἁμαρτία εἰς τὸν κόσμον), like the serpent's appearance in the garden. Sin is not merely an action that Adam took.[27] Similar personifications occur throughout this section of the letter which further supports the notion that, at the very least, Paul sees a very close relationship between sin as a power that entered the world in the Adamic episode and the serpent whom Adam encountered in the garden. For example, in Rom 5:21, Paul notes that sin "reigned" (ἐβασίλευσεν) in death.[28] An even clearer link between sin and the serpent occurs in Paul's description of the tortured "I" (ἐγώ) in Rom 7, "For sin (ἁμαρτία), having seized an opportunity through the commandment deceived (ἐξηπάτησεν) me and through it killed me" (Rom 7:11).[29] We will consider below the implications of the interplay between the serpent in Gen 3 and sin in Rom 5:12–14.

---

22. As de Boer puts it, "Paul's cosmological language about Sin and Death as malevolent powers respresents an attempt to account for anthropological realities and experiences. Behind human sinning and human dying, Paul discerns cosmological powers at work which he calls Sin and Death." de Boer, "Paul's Mythologizing Program," 13–14.

23. Cf. Paul's explicit reference to Eve (Εὕα) in 2 Cor 11:3. See also 1 Tim 2:13.

24. Coveting is implied in Gen 3:6. Paul cites the prohibition against coveting in Rom 7:7 which he ties to the Adamic narrative as I will discuss in a later chapter.

25. See Paul's use of ὄφις as a reference to Satan in 2 Cor 11:3.

26. The only overt reference to Satan in the letter occurs in Rom 16:20, "But the God of peace will soon crush Satan (τὸν σατανᾶν) under your feet."

27. To be sure, Gen 3:1 does not explicitly describe the serpent as entering the garden. The narrator does not indicate how the serpent made its way into the garden.

28. See also Paul's description of ἁμαρτία in Rom 6:6, 7, 12, 14, 16, 17, 18, 20, 22, 23; 7:5, 7, 8, 9, 11, 13, 14, 20, 23, 25. Cranfield observes, "A tendency to personify sin is perhaps to be discerned here, as in 6:12ff and 7:8ff, but here (as v.13b shows) it is not sustained." Cranfield, *Romans*, 1:274. For a thorough discussion of the personification of sin in Romans, see Dodson, *The Powers of Personification*.

29. As I will discuss in a later chapter, ἐξηπάτησεν in Rom 7:11 has ἁμαρτία as its subject; however, in Gen 3:13, Eve notes that the serpent deceived (ὁ ὄφις ἠπάτησεν με) her.

Romans 5:12 and the Allusion to the Entrance of Death

Paul's reference to the entrance (εἰσῆλθεν) of death (θάνατος) into the world (εἰς τὸν κόσμον) and the spread (διῆλθεν) of death (θάνατος) to all people (εἰς πάντας ἀνθρώπους) in Rom 5:12 evokes God's judgment in the garden and its eventual realization in the life of Adam and his descendants.[30] Like his portrayal of sin, Paul ultimately personifies death as a power and enemy in keeping with its personification in Israel's Scriptures.

We begin with God's judgment of death in Gen 3. Neither Adam nor Eve die in the immediate aftermath of their transgression. However, the divine judgment of death is swift "By the sweat of your brow you will eat your bread until you return to the earth (ἀποστρέψαι σε εἰς τὴν γῆν), from which you were taken; because you are earth and you will return to the earth (ἐις γῆν ἀπελεύσῃ) (Gen 3:19)." As the primeval narrative unfolds, this judgment of death is manifested in at least four ways: (1) Cain's murder of Abel (Gen 4:1–17); (2) a toledoth list which record the deaths (וימת/ἀπέθανεν) of Adamic descendants (Gen 5:1–32); (3) the flood narrative (Gen 6:1–8:22); and (4) a toledoth list which records the deaths (וימת/ἀπέθανεν) of Shem's descendants (Gen 11:10–32).[31] Within the toledoth list of Adamic descendants, Adam's death is listed first "And all the days of Adam, which he lived, were 930, and he died (ἀπέθανεν)" (Gen 5:5). The perpetuation of death in the primeval narrative stems from both Adam's transgression and God's sentence of death. These are the circumstances under which Adam's descendants lived, sinned, and died. For Paul, the cosmic and anthropological spread of sin and death, since Adam, kills both heart and body.[32] He detects a clear link between the sin and death of Adam and the sin and death of all those who come after him.[33] The Adamic experience is recapitulated in humanity generation after generation. He clearly portrays sin as power that works closely with death. However, Paul's statement in Rom 5:12 does not allow us to go beyond this observation.[34]

---

30. Rom 5:12 contains two uses of θάνατος. The first use is not accompanied by the verb εἰσῆλθεν or the prepositional phrase εἰς τὸν κόσμον. However, given the occurrence of both items at the beginning of 5:12, they are assumed for the first use of θάνατος later in the verse. As Cranfield notes, "The further words καὶ διὰ τῆς ἁμαρτίας ὁ θάνατος indicate that sin's entry meant also the entry of death, which followed sin like a shadow." Cranfield, *Romans*, 1:274.

31. The expression וימת/ἀπέθανεν occurs over twenty times in Gen 5:1—11:32.

32. See Eph 2:1–3.

33. de Boer notes that in Second Temple literature the figure of Adam has a "double function." In his analysis of 2 Baruch and 4 Ezra, he notes "The figure of Adam functions as both a corporate personality who determines all subsequent human destiny and as the paradigmatic human being who sets the pattern for his descendants." de Boer, "Paul's Mythologizing Program," 12. See, e.g., 2 Bar. 23:4; 56:6; 4 Ezra 3:7; 7:118–20; 8:60.

34. As Dunn puts it, "All that Paul seems to want to say is that this epoch of human history is characterized and determined by the fatal interplay of sin and death—as evidenced by the fact that everyone sins and everyone dies—a partnership first established in power at the beginning of the epoch, through the one man Adam." Dunn, *Romans*, 1:290.

Beyond the judgment of death in Gen 3, some OT writers subsequently portray sin as a power and or enemy. For example, the LXX Psalms personify death in several ways: "gates of death" (Ps 9:14; 106:18); "birth pains of death" (Ps 17:5; 114:3); "snares of death" (17:6); "shadow of death" (22:4; 43:20; 106:10, 14); death as "shepherd" (Ps 48:15); "terrors of death" (Ps 54:5); .[35] Additionally, Isa 25 contains one of the most notable examples, "Death (θάνατος) having prevailed swallowed up (κατέπιεν), and again God has taken away every tear from every face; he took away the reproach of the people from all the earth, for the mouth of the Lord spoke."[36] Paul conflates part of this Isaianic pre-text with Hos 13:14 in 1 Cor 15:54–55, "Death has been swallowed up in victory, where O death, is your victory? Where, O death, is your sting?" The citation shows his familiarity with the scriptural personification of death. The same personification of death is reflected in Rom 5:12–14; however, Paul situates the personification within his typological reading of the Adamic narrative. God's judgment against Adam is death. Death then becomes the enemy to which Adam and his seed are handed over.[37] Moreover, Christ's work simultaneously oveturns the divine judgment of death and death's power as an enemy.[38]

Romans 5:13–14 and the Period Between Adam and Moses

With the synonymous phrases "until the law (ἄχρι νόμου)" and "from Adam until Moses (ἀπὸ Ἀδὰμ μέχρι Μωϋσέως)" in Rom 5:13–14, Paul evokes a large swath of OT narrative (Gen 3:1—Exod 19:25) to explain the operation of sin and death during the period in which the Mosaic Law had not yet been given to Israel. Paul follows up his comments about the Adamic perpetuation of sin and death in v. 12 by explaining, "For (γάρ) until the law sin was in the world, but sin is not reckoned when there is no law, but death reigned from Adam until Moses, even over those who did not sin in the likeness of the transgression of Adam who is a type of the one to come" (Rom 5:13–14). Before discussing the swath of OT narrative that Paul evokes, we must address the problematic link between v. 12 and vv. 13–14.

Paul's explanatory clause (γάρ) in v. 13 is "problematic," because it is not immediately clear why he shifts his attention to the absence of the law in the period from Adam until Moses.[39] As Moo observes, "Paul apparently thinks that something

---

35. Though the personification is less vivid, see also Pss LXX 54:16; 55:14; 67:21; 77:50; 87:7; 88:49; 114:8.

36. In Isa 25:8 MT, God is the subject of the verb and death is the object: "He swallowed (בלע) death (המות) forever. In any case, death is still personified as an enemy.

37. As the psalmist prays, "The Lord certainly disciplined me, and he did not hand me over (παρέδωκεν) to death (τῷ θανάτῳ)" (Ps 117:18 LXX).

38. This is in keeping with the way Yahweh relates to ancient Israel. He hands the nation over to foreign enemies, but he then judges and defeats those enemies on behalf of his people.

39. Regarding the function of γάρ in Rom 5:13, Casson labels the occurrence as "problematic" in her taxonomy of the various functions of γάρ in Romans. Casson, *Textual Signpots*, 290.

he said in v. 12 requires immediate elaboration in a kind of 'aside.' But what is the purpose of this 'aside,' which takes up vv. 13-14?"⁴⁰ Interpreters put forward various solutions; however, the most likely explanation is that Paul feels inclined to explain how all people sin and suffer Adam's judgment of death when not all people have the Mosaic Law or even a specific commandment such as the one Adam received in Gen 2:16-17.⁴¹

Paul's explanation in vv. 13-14 needs to be read against the backdrop of the large swath of OT narrative that he evokes with the synonymous phrases "until the law" and "from Adam until Moses." From a literary perspective, Gen 3:1—Exod 19:25 covers this period. Paul describes the period "until the law (ἄχρι νόμου)" as a period in which "sin was in the world" (ἁμαρτία ἦν ἐν κόσμῳ) (Rom 5:13). Additionally, the time "from Adam until the Moses" was a time in which "death reigned" (ἐβασίλευσεν ὁ θάνατος) (Rom 5:14). This foreboding description of sin and death reigning in the world is supported by several episodes recorded in Gen 3:1—Exod 19:25. For example, as noted above, the primeval narrative contains two key instances of sin resulting in death: (1) Cain's murder of Abel (Gen 4:1-17); and (2) the flood brought on by humanity's pervasive sinfulness in which God "wiped out" (ἀπαλείψω, Gen 6:7) all flesh except those in Noah's ark (Gen 6:1—8:22). Gen 12-50 likewise reports instances where sin resulted in death such as the attempted murder of Joseph by his brothers and the violation of Dinah which resulted in Simeon and Levi deceiving and slaying Hamor and Shechem along with those in their city (Gen 34:1-31). The Exodus narrative, prior to the reception of the Mosaic Law, also recounts Pharaoh's attempted infanticide of Hebrew male babies (Exod 1-2).

Readers of this swath of narrative (Gen 3:1—Exod 19:25) are right to conclude that sin and death churned on in the world before Moses received the law at Sinai. Paul in fact describes the entire period as death's "reign" (Rom 5:14). Sin and death reigned even when God did not reckon (ἐλλογέω) sin based on violation of the Mosaic Law or even when people did not "sin (μὴ ὄντος νόμου) in the likeness of the transgression of Adam (τῆς παραβάσεως)" (Rom 5:14).⁴² Once again, if we ask why Paul feels inclined to mention this now, it is likely because he wants to underscore the point that reconciliation with God in Christ (Rom 5:10-11) required a defeat of the reign of sin and death which has plagued all of history regardless of a divine command (Gen 2:17) or law (Exod 20).

---

40. Moo, *Romans*, 329. Similarly, as Longenecker notes, "Many have viewed what is written in 5:13-14 as a series of rather tortuous, perhaps even incoherent, statements, and all sorts of interpretations have been given." Longenecker, *Romans*, 592.

41. For this solution, see Matera, *Romans*, 137; Seifrid, *Christ Our Righteousness*, 70n91. For a discussion of possible solutions, see Moo, *Romans*, 329-32.

42. The only other use of ἐλλογέω occurs in Phlm 18. See BDAG, 319. Watson suggests that the reference here could be "to the tradition that a heavenly record is kept of all sinful actions, ready to be produced in evidence on the day of judgment." Watson, *Paul and the Hermeneutics of Faith*, 512. See also Friedrich, "Röm 5, 13," 525-28.

Romans 5:14 and Adamic Typology

When Paul modifies Adam with the relative clause "who is a type (τύπος) of the one who is to come (τοῦ μέλλοντος)," he signals his hermeneutical approach to the Adamic narrative and evokes a Messianic designation. With respect to the former, Paul indicates that he applies typological exegesis to his reading of Gen 2–3.[43] Ellis summarizes Paul's typological approach observing, "His typology is drawn chiefly from three OT periods: the Creation, the Age of the Patriarchs, and the Exodus."[44] With respect to Paul's "creation typology" in Rom 5, Ellis explains "From the Creation narratives Paul draws a typological relation between Adam and Christ in which the whole scope of cosmic redemption appears to be encompassed: Ἐν Χριστῷ a man enters a new resurrection creation (καινὴ κτίσις) whose head and sovereign is the Lord Christ; and from Rom. 8 it appears the whole cosmic order is to be in this new redeemed creation."[45] Indeed, as I will discuss below, Paul links the "whole scope of redemption" to the figures of Adam and Christ. An "escalation" occurs between these two figures, and "escalation" best defines Paul's hermeneutical approach here.[46] While the actions of both figures have cosmic and historical implications for all of humanity, Christ's actions result in life and justification for all who believe rather than their death and condemnation in Adam.

With respect to the substantival participle τοῦ μέλλοντος, Paul tethers his Christ–Adam typology to Messianic expectations in Israel's Scriptures. Some interpreters reject the notion that the phrase bears a Messianic sense. As Cranfield notes, "The expression τοῦ μέλλοντος ('of him who was to come,' not 'of him who is to come') may remind us of ὁ ἐρχόμενος in Mt 11.3 = Lk 7.20; but its use here is explicable simply on the basis of the contents of this paragraph by itself."[47] Additionally, Jewett notes that the phrase τοῦ μέλλοντος "has occasioned much debate over Christ as the 'second' or 'last' Adam."[48] It is true that Paul does not employ the phrases "first Adam" (ὁ πρῶτος ἄνθρωπος Ἀδάμ) and "last Adam" (ὁ ἔσχατος Ἀδάμ) as he does in

---

43. The literal sense of τύπος is a mark left on something due to pressure such as a hole that appears in the ground when a stone is removed. Figurative meanings can include "a kind, class, or thing that suggests a model or pattern" or "an archetype serving as a model." BDAG 1020. Cf. Paul's use of τύπος in 1 Cor 10:6. Cf. also Paul's use of τυπικῶς in 1 Cor 10:11.

44. Ellis, *Paul's Use of the Old Testament*, 129.

45. Ellis, *Paul's Use of the Old Testament*, 129.

46. For Goppelt, the two defining characteristics of typology in the NT are: (1) correspondence between type and anti-type; and (2) escalation between type and anti-type. See Goppelt, *Typos*, 1–20.

47. Cranfield, *Romans*, 1:283. See also Sanday and Hedlam, *Romans*, 136. Contrastively, Schlatter notes "Ho mellon is synonymous with ho erchomenos. Paul here uses the pre-Christian name for Christ because he puts himself in the situation of the races that have long passed, which were strictly under the dominion of the first human being and for whom Christ was only the One to come." Schlatter, *Romans*, 129.

48. Jewett, *Romans*, 378. See Black, "The Pauline Doctrine of the Second Adam," 170–79; Brandenburger, *Adam und Christus*, 9–14.

1 Cor 15.⁴⁹ However, it does not follow that such a framework is out of Paul's purview in Rom 5:14. The syncritical description of Adam and Christ in Rom 5:15–19 assumes the protological and eschatological implications of their actions. Moreover, the use of τοῦ μέλλοντος implies that for Paul "Adam prefigured the Messiah in certain respects."⁵⁰ Messianic qualities are inherent to Genesis 3 itself. Judgment against the serpent includes the promise that Adam's seed will crush the head of the serpent, "And I will set enmity between you and between the woman and between your seed and her seed (τοῦ σπέρματος αὐτῆς); he will bruise/keep (ישופך/τηρήσει) your head, and you will bruise/keep (תשופתך/τηρήσεις) his heel" (Gen 3:15).

Against this intertextual backdrop, "the one who is to come" in Rom 5:14 can be identified as the Adamic descendant whom God promised would bring an end to the rule of the serpent, or sin and death. Thus, the phrase bears a Messianic sense.⁵¹ The Messianic sense of τοῦ μέλλοντος holds even if it means that Paul is outside of the Second Temple mainstream in his description of Adam.⁵² As Hultgren notes in his comments on Paul's use of τύπος, "Paul uses the term in reference to OT persons, events, and institutions that announce the forthcoming, eschatological intervention of God."⁵³ Throughout Israel's Scriptures, these eschatological persons, events, and institutions are tethered to a Messianic figure. Paul identifies that figure as Jesus Χριστός whom Adam typified.

Romans 5:12–14 and Echoes of Corporate Solidarity

Romans 5:12–14 evokes the OT motif of corporate solidarity.⁵⁴ This is especially clear in v. 12, "For this reason just as through one man sin entered the world and through sin death, also in this way death spread to all men, under which circumstance all sinned." Ellis explains corporate solidarity from Paul's first-century perspective noting "A second principle of deep consequence for Pauline exegesis is the Jewish concept of 'corporate solidarity.' For example, Israel the patriarch, Israel the nation, the king of Israel, and Messiah stand in such relationship to each other that one may be viewed as the 'embodiment' of the other."⁵⁵ Similarly, Dodd observes:

49. See 1 Cor 15:45.
50. Wright, *Romans*, 527.
51. Some interpreters have identified the referent of τοῦ μέλλοντος as Moses. See, e.g., Scroggs, *The Last Adam*, 80–81.
52. Jewett notes, "The historical-religious background of this comparison between Adam and Christ remains problematic. Despite claims that Paul's view develops primarily on Judaic soil, there is no credible evidence that Jewish thinkers ever viewed the Messiah as a kind of second Adam." Jewett, *Romans*, 378. Nevertheless, Paul's Adamic description of Christ in Rom 5:12–19 at least hints at Messianic connotations.
53. Hultgren, *Romans*, 226.
54. As I will discuss below, OT corporate solidarity is also evoked in Rom 5:15–21.
55. Ellis adds that the concept is "particularly important for Paul's understanding of such matters

What lies behind it is the ancient conception of solidarity. The moral unit was the community (clan, tribe, or city), rather than the individual. If an Achan broke *taboo* (Josh. vii.) his whole clan fell under the curse. Thus the whole humanity could be thought of as the tribe of Adam, and Adam's sin was the sin of the race.[56]

Both Dodd and Ellis locate the concept of corporate solidarity in Israel's Scriptures. Paul knew the scriptural tradition of corporate solidarity defined by figures whose actions impacted the entire nation. For example, Achan's sin drew God's ire so that Ai defeated Israel's army.[57] The narrator clearly imputes Achan's sin to the entire nation:

> And the sons of Israel (οἱ υἱοὶ Ισραηλ) trespassed greatly (ἐπλημμέλησαν) and they stole (ἐνοσφίσαντο) from the thing devoted to the ban (ἀπὸ τοῦ ἀναθέματος); and Achan (Αχαρ), the son Carmi, the son of Zabdi, son of Zerah, of the tribe of Judah, took (ἔλαβεν) from the thing devoted to the ban (ἀπὸ τοῦ ἀναθέματος); and the anger of the Lord burned (ἐθυμώθη ὀργῇ κύριος) against the sons of Israel (Jos 7:1).

Even though Achan stole what had been devoted to the ban, God's anger was kindled against the entire nation.[58] Paul expands this concept of corporate solidarity to the whole world (εἰς τὸν κόσμον) with the result that all sin and die. To put it another way, they all face God's wrath as Achan and the sons of Israel did. However, one difference in Paul's expansion of the concept is that all really do sin and all really do thereby face the judgment of death.

Interpretive Impact of Pre-Texts in Romans 5:12–14

The intertextual subtext in these three verses generate multiple points of resonance that inform Paul's argument in multiple ways.

First, Paul personifies sin as a power in a way that overlaps with the serpent from the Adamic narrative. While Paul observes that "all sinned" (πάντες ἥμαρτον), he also notes that "sin entered the world (ἡ ἁμαρτία εἰς τὸν κόσμον) through one man (δι᾽ ἑνὸς ἀνθρώπου)" (Rom 5:12). If we read this statement in relation to Gen 3:1–7, it follows that sin entered the world through one man, and woman, who succumbed

---

as original sin, the seed of Abraham, 'Israel,' and the body of Christ." Ellis, *Paul's Use of the Old Testament*, 136. Throughout the history of interpretation, some theologians, most notably Johannes Cocceius, have referred to this concept as "federalism." With specific reference to Rom 5:13–14, see, e.g., Kline "Gospel Until the Law," 433–46.

56. Dodd, *The Epistle of Paul to the Romans*, 100.

57. Thirty-six men perished in the initial battle with Ai, and the hearts of the Israelites "melted." See Josh 7:4–5.

58. Though, to be sure, it is only Achan and his family that are ultimately stoned to death. See Josh 7:16–26. However, prior to the stoning, all of Israel is defeated in Ai. See Josh 7:4–5.

to the serpent's temptation. Sin entered the world when they listened to the voice of the serpent rather than God's voice and when, by the encouragement of the serpent, they coveted what God said they could not have. Paul does not explicitly qualify sin in this way, but he evokes these qualifications through his engagement with the Adamic narrative. Adam and those who follow in his train are culpable for their transgression and the penalty of death which ensues. However, they all face sin as a crafty power much like Adam and Eve faced a crafty serpent (Gen 3:1).[59] Paul's description of sin in Rom 6–7 has more points of contact with the serpent from the Adamic narrative as we shall see.

Second, Paul also personifies death (θάνατος) as a power which originated with the sentence of death doled out in Gen 3 and which subsequent OT writers portrayed as an enemy. As I noted above, the wider narratives of Genesis and Exodus indicate widespread death from Gen 3 and forward. While these narratives do not personify death as a power, or enemy, other OT writers do.[60] In this way, Paul's personification of death is scripturally informed, and he continues that personification far beyond Rom 5:12–14. As we shall see, in Rom 5:1—8:39, θάνατος receives a great deal of attention.[61] Many of Paul's descriptions echo the personification of death in Israel's Scriptures which Paul reconfigures in relation to Christ. We can already see in Rom 5:12–14 that θάνατος is an enemy to which God hands over both the Adamic seed and Christ himself.

Third, Paul evokes the period between Gen 3:1—Exod 19:25 to make the point that sin and death have historically plagued human beings irrespective of an explicit command (Gen 2:17) or even the Mosaic Law (Exod 20). Sin is not reckoned without the Mosaic Law, but it is still at work. Consequently, death still reigned (ἐβασίλευσεν ὁ θάνατος, Rom 5:14) prior to the arrival and work of Christ.

Finally, Paul interprets Adam as a typological figure whose actions and experiences bear essential christological import. To fully explain reconciliation with God in Christ, Paul juxtaposes Christ with Adam. We will return to the specific points of this juxtaposition below. Here we need to note that through the phrase "the one who is to come" (τοῦ μέλλοντος) Paul evokes the Messianic character of Adam that is inherent to the Genesis narrative. As I noted above, Christ fulfills the promise that a descendant of Adam would come to crush the serpent, or, as Paul sees it, to crush sin and thereby death. It is Messiah Jesus whose work undoes the deleterious effects of humanity's corprorate solidarity with Adam. Just as the death of Achan removed condemnation against the Israelite camp stemming from his disobedience, the death

---

59. As Dunn puts it, "'Sin' is not initially defined, but clearly it is the power which human beings experience drawing them into disobedience and transgression." Dunn, *Romans*, 1:288.

60. For Paul, the most notable pre-texts are Isa 25:8 and Hos 13:14 given the composite citation of both pre-texts in 1 Cor 15:54–55.

61. Rom 5:1—8:39 contains the vast majority of references to θάνατος in the letter. See the uses of θάνατος in Rom 1:32; 5:10, 12, 14, 17, 21; 6:3, 4, 5, 9, 16, 21, 23; 7:5, 10, 13, 24; 8:2, 38. See also the use of θανατόω in Rom 7:4; 8:13, 36.

of Jesus removes condemnation against human beings stemming from their participation in Adam's disobedience.

Romans 5:15–21

(5:15–21) But not as the transgression, in this way also is the gift; for if by the transgression of the one many died, how much more the grace of God and the gift by the grace which is of the one man Jesus Christ abounded to the many. And not as through the one who sinned is the gift; for the judgment from the one resulted in condemnation, but the gift from many transgressions resulted in justification. For if by the transgression of the one death reigned through the one how much more those who receive the abundance of grace and of the gift of righteousness will reign in life through the one Jesus Christ. So then, as through one transgression the result was condemnation, in this way also through one righteous deed the result was justification of life for all men; for just as through the disobedience of the one man many were made sinners, in this way also through the obedience of one many will be made righteous. But the law entered in order that the transgression might increase; but where sin increased grace increased all the more, in order that just as sin reigned in death, in this way also grace might reign through righteousness resulting in eternal life through Jesus Christ our Lord.

The conjunction ἀλλά in Rom 5:15 signals Paul's intent to forcefully contrast Adam with the one whom he typifies (τύπος), namely "the one who is to come," or the Lord Jesus Christ.[62] We will discuss the features of this contrast verse by verse while we consider Paul's ongoing intertextual engagement with Gen 2–3 and a few other OT pre-texts.

Suggested Pre-Texts in Romans 5:15–21

Hübner lists two pre-texts: Dan 7:22, 27 θ (Rom 5:17).[63] Nestle-Aland 28th ed. lists only one pre-text: Isa 53:11 (Rom 5:15, 19). Once again, Hays does not discuss any pre-texts from Rom 4:25—8:18. Seifrid offers a great deal of reflection on the

---

62. As Longenecker, notes, "Paul takes pains throughout 5:15–17 to point out that there is no comparison between what Adam has brought about in human history and what Jesus Christ has effected on behalf of all humanity. That is why he begins 5:15 with the very strong negative ἀλλά which functions to draw attention to the facts that (1) there is a very great difference between Adam, 'the first man' of 5:12a, and Jesus Christ, 'the one to come' of 5:14c, and (2) 'the gift of grace brought by 'the one to come' is far greater than the 'trespass' of the 'first man.'" Longenecker, *Romans*, 593–94.

63. Hübner, *Vetus Testamentum in Novo*, 2:90.

intertextual subtext of Rom 5:12–21. He summarizes his reflection by noting, "Paul's contrast between Adam and Christ serves to define and describe the grace of God."[64]

Intertextual Analysis of Romans 5:15–21

We should keep in mind that Paul alerts us to how he engages Gen 2–3 in Rom 5:15–21, namely typologically. In Rom 5:14, Paul describes Adam as a τύπος τοῦ μέλλοντος.[65] Therefore, the overarching approach to the comparison of Adam and Christ is typological in nature. It follows that one should look for the way in which Paul escalates the relationship between the two figures, because escalation is the defining characteristic of typology. While the bulk of Paul's intertextual engagement here revolves around Gen 2–3, he also evokes wider strands from Israel's Scriptures as I will discuss below.

Romans 5:15–16 and Typological Allusions to Genesis 2–3

Paul begins the contrast in v. 15 by juxtaposing τὸ παράπτωμα with τὸ χάρισμα.[66] The intertextual referent of Adam's παράπτωμα is the violation of the prohibition in Gen 2:17, "But from the tree of knowing good and evil, you shall not eat from it." As I noted above, this transgression unfolds through the serpent's temptation to doubt the motivation behind the divine prohibition and to covet the fruit of the tree. Paul immediately explains how this transgression is not like the gift, "For (γάρ) if by the transgression of the one many died, how much more the grace of God (ἡ χάρις τοῦ θεοῦ) and the gift (ἡ δωρεά) by the grace (ἐν χάριτι) which is of the one man Jesus Christ abounded to the many." This explanation, particularly the phrase εἰ γὰρ τῷ τοῦ ἑνὸς παραπτώματι οἱ πολλοὶ ἀπέθανον, again evokes the warning in Gen 2:17, "you will surely die (θανάτῳ ἀποθανεῖσθε)," as well as larger strands of the Genesis narrative wherein the narrator consistently notes the onset of death in creation.[67] Even more, given Paul's explanation that "many died" (οἱ πολλοὶ ἀπέθανον) by Adam's transgressions, he evokes even wider strands of Israel's Scriptures which are chock-full of death on an individual, regional, and global scale.

For Paul, death by Adam's transgression is death in the fullest sense. It is spiritual and physical. Death is ultimately separation from God and the life which he provides.[68] In this way, Paul evokes the end of Gen 3 in which Adam and Eve are removed from

---

64. Seifrid, *Romans*, 629.
65. Cf. the use of τυπικῶς in 1 Cor 10:11 where Paul treats the wilderness generation of Israel in a typological manner.
66. The choice of χάρισμα rather than χάρις could be due to the assonance (μα) that the former term creates with παράπτωμα. See Jewett, *Romans*, 379–80.
67. The primeval narrative chronicles the onset of death. See, e.g., Gen 4:1–17; 5:1–32; 6:1–8:22.
68. On this point, see Schreiner, *Romans*, 284.

the garden and thereby the life God provides.⁶⁹ "Many" were impacted in this way.⁷⁰ The rest of Israel's Scriptures bear this out as even Israel itself, though enjoying the divine presence in a way unexperienced by those outside the nation, never retrieves the access to the life once enjoyed by Adam and Eve.

By juxtaposing the fatal, far-reaching, and separating effect of Adam's transgression (παράπτωμα) with the divine gift (χάρισμα), the latter should be understood as the gracious antithesis of those effects. It is the gift of access to God which results in life in the fullest sense. Paul piles up gift language in the second half of v. 15, "how much more the grace of God (ἡ χάρις τοῦ θεοῦ) and the gift (ἡ δωρεά) by the grace (ἐν χάριτι) which is of the one man Jesus Christ abounded to the many." The heavy use of gift language (χάρισμα, χάρις, δωρεά), along with the verb "abounded" (ἐπερίσσευσεν), underscores the lavishness of divine grace through the "one man (τοῦ ἑνὸς ἀνθρώπου)" Jesus Christ which counteracts the transgression of the one man Adam.⁷¹ Simply put, the transgression results in death in the fullest sense, but the gift results in life in the fullest, namely life before God.

In v. 16, Paul continues to contrast the results of Adam's sin with God's gift "And not as through the one who sinned (ἁμαρτήσαντος) is the gift (τὸ δώρημα); for the judgment (κρίμα) from the one (ἐξ ἑνός) resulted in condemnation (εἰς κατάκριμα), but the gift (χάρισμα) from many transgressions (ἐκ πολλῶν παραπτωμάτων) resulted in justification (εἰς δικαίωμα)." Three contrasts occur here: (1) the one who sinned is contrasted with the gift; (2) judgment from one transgression is contrasted with the gift from many transgressions; and (3) the result of condemnation is contrasted with the result of justification. Intertextually, these contrasts evoke various features of the Adamic narrative: (1) the transgression of the command in Gen 2:17; (2) the divine judgment (κρίμα) in Gen 3:14–19; (3) and the removal of Adam and Eve from the garden in Gen 3:22–24. These contrasts also evoke the wider effects of the Adamic narrative as they are seen throughout Israel's Scriptures and human history. Paul points to these wider effects in his references to condemnation (κατάκριμα) and many transgressions (ἐκ πολλῶν παραπτωμάτων).

Within this evocation of the Adamic narrative and its sweeping effects, Paul accentuates the divergent results of Adam's sin (ἁμαρτήσαντος) and the divine gift (τὸ δώρημα). Adam received a judgment (κρίμα) from one sin (ἐξ ἑνός). The referent of κρίμα in v. 16 is the judgment God doled out in Gen 3 which is encapsulated in the removal of Adam and Eve from the garden and thereby from the creator's source of life (Gen 3:22–24). The result of this one judgment (κρίμα) against Adam

---

69. Gen 3:22–24.

70. As Jewett notes, "many" (πολλοί) is equivalent to "all" who died in Rom 5:12 and 5:18. Jewett, *Romans*, 380. See also Cranfield, *Romans*, 1:285.

71. As Barclay observes, "We find here an extraordinary concentration of gift-terminology, whose variation seems to be more rhetorical than substantial (the -μα endings creating neat verbal antitheses); within 5:15–21 words from the χαρ- and δωρ- roots occur no fewer than ten times, eight within verses 15–17 alone." Barclay, *Paul and the Gift*, 495.

was condemnation (κατάκριμα) for all. Given the echo of Gen 3:22–24 within Paul's argument, the referent of κατάκριμα is a cosmic wide and continuous removal of all people from the creator and the life he provides.[72] Paul contrasts the judgment (κρίμα) that came from Adam's one sin (ἐξ ἑνός), as well as the condemnation (κατάκριμα) which ensued, with the gift (τὸ δώρημα) that came from many sins (ἐκ πολλῶν παραπτωμάτων) and the justification (δικαίωμα) it produced.[73] It is surprising that Paul contrasts judgment (κρίμα) from one transgression with the gift (χάρισμα) from many transgressions. One would assume that the parallel of judgment from one transgression would be condemnation from many transgressions. As Cranfield puts it, "That one single misdeed should be answered by judgment, this is perfectly understandable: that the accumulated sins and guilt of all the ages should be answered by God's free gift, this is the miracle of miracles, utterly beyond human comprehension."[74]

It should also be noted that Paul interprets the Adamic narrative, and all that succeeded it, in a forensic fashion. This is clear from Paul's use of κρίμα to describe Adam's removal from the garden and the juxtaposition of κατάκριμα and δικαίωμα. In this way, Paul portrays God as passing judgments in the garden and beyond. As I have noted already, Gen 3:14–24 describes God's judgment against the serpent, Eve, Adam, and the earth. Paul expands this one judgment to condemnation for all. In a sweeping hermeneutical observation, Paul looks at the Adamic narrative, the larger swath of Israel's Scriptures, and human history to conclude that all are under divine condemnation. The essence of that condemnation is separation from the life-giving presence of God first experienced by Adam and then by all his descendants. Paul contrasts divine judgment and condemnation with divine justification in Christ. While God condemns in Adam, he justifies in Christ. Condemnation in Adam consists of separation from God and death. Justification in Christ consists of access to God and thereby life.

Romans 5:17–19 and Typological Allusions to Genesis 2–3

Paul continues the typological contrast between Adam and Christ by juxtaposing the "reign" (βασιλεύω) of death and life.[75] He explains, "For (γάρ) if by the transgression of the one death reigned (ὁ θάνατος ἐβασίλευσεν) through the one how much more those who receive the abundance of grace and of the gift of righteousness will reign in life (ἐν ζωῇ βασιλεύσουσιν) through the one Jesus Christ."[76] Intertextually, the

---

72. We will return to the intertextually informed referent of κατάκριμα in our discussion of Rom 8:1.
73. Cf. the use of δικαίωμα in Rom 1:32; 2:26; 8:4.
74. Cranfield, *Romans*, 1:286.
75. Cf. the use of βασιλεύω in Rom 6:12.
76. Casson labels the γάρ in Rom 5:17 as "somewhat complex." Casson, *Textual Signposts*, 290.

"transgression of the one" again evokes Adam's multilayered transgression of God's command in the garden. By eating from the tree of the knowledge of good and evil, Adam trusts the voice of the serpent rather than God's voice and covets what God prohibits (Gen 2:17; 3:1–7). Paul concludes that by this transgression death reigned (ὁ θάνατος ἐβασίλευσεν). As noted in v. 14, "death reigned" (ἐβασίλευσεν ὁ θάνατος) from Adam until Moses. However, in v. 17, the phrase ὁ θάνατος ἐβασίλευσεν does not refer to the period from Adam until Moses. It either refers to the starting point of death's reign by the transgression of Adam in Gen 3, or the entire reign of death, in all locales and periods, by the transgression of Adam.[77]

It is against this intertextual backdrop that Paul contrasts the pervasive reign of death with the much greater (πολλῷ μᾶλλον) reign of life in Christ. Paul identifies those who will reign in life through Christ as "those who receive (οἱ λαμβάνοντες) the abundance of grace (τὴν περισσείαν τῆς χάριτος) and of the gift of righteousness (τῆς δωρεᾶς τῆς δικαιοσύνης)." This is a pregnant description full of theological abbreviations. The substantival participle οἱ λαμβάνοντες raises the question as to whether this is an active or passive reception of grace.[78] To put it another way, does Paul have in view how one takes hold of the gift with respect to the human will? Or does he only have in view the fact that people receive the gift with no real consideration of how the human will is involved?[79] Although Paul does not elaborate here, one can assume that faith plays a role in receiving the gift.[80] He repeatedly emphasizes the soteriological role of faith in the letter; therefore, it is axiomatic to the reception of grace in 5:17.[81] With respect to the phrase τὴν περισσείαν τῆς χάριτος, Paul again underscores the sufficiency and extravagance of the gift that believers receive. The phrase τῆς δωρεᾶς τῆς δικαιοσύνης refers to the right standing that God gives to the believer.[82] Believers receive the gift of a right standing with God in Christ in contrast to the death and condemnation they have in Adam.

In Rom 5:18–19, Paul infers (Ἄρα οὖν) from the preceding verses that disobedience and obedience stand at the heart of the typological relationship between Adam and Christ. He concludes, "So then, as through one transgression (διὰ τοῦ ἑνὸς παραπτώματος) the result was condemnation (κατάκριμα), in this way also through one righteous deed (διὰ ἑνὸς δικαιώματος) the result was justification of life (δικαίωσιν ζωῆς) for all men; for just as through the disobedience (τῆς παρακοῆς) of the one man many were made sinners, in this way also through the obedience

---

77. The *aktionsart* of the aorist ἐβασίλευσεν in Rom 5:17 could either be ingresssive ("death began to reign"), or constative ("death reigned"). See Dunn, *Romans*, 1:281; Moo, *Romans*, 339n117.

78. Cf. Paul's use of λαμβάνω in Rom 1:5; 4:11; 5:11; 7:8, 11, 15; 13:2.

79. On these questions, see Schreiner, *Romans*, 291.

80. The verb πιστεύω does not occur in Rom 5:1–21. The noun πίστις occurs in Rom 5:1–2.

81. E.g., πίστις occurs 40 times in the letter. The verb πιστεύω occurs 21 times.

82. The genitive τῆς δικαιοσύνης in the construction τῆς δωρεᾶς τῆς δικαιοσύνης is a descriptive genitive (i.e., the gift which is righteousness).

(τῆς ὑπακοῆς) of one many will be made righteous." Paul's second comparative statement in v. 19 expands upon the first in v. 18.[83] Intertextually, Paul once again defines Adam's transgression (παράπτωμα) described in Gen 2:17 and 3:1–7 as trusting the serpent's voice rather than God's voice, and defines Adam's coveting as "disobedience" (ὑπακοή).[84] This disobedience resulted in condemnation (εἰς κατάκριμα) for all people (εἰς πάντας ἀνθρώπους).[85] In this way, in Paul's reading of the Adamic narrative, κατάκριμα consisted of fatal sentences against Adam, and the sentence of death commenced with their expulsion from the garden which separated them from life in God. The way Paul explains the whole ordeal in v. 19 is that through Adam's disobedience "many were made sinners" (ἁμαρτωλοὶ κατεστάθησαν οἱ πολλοί). They "were made" (κατεστάθησαν) sinners through Adam's disobedience in a forensic and experiential sense.[86] Through Adam's disobedience people were "inaugurated," or "instated," into a state of sin where they recapitulate the Adamic transgression.[87]

Paul then contrasts Adam's transgression/disobedience and its results with Christ's act of righteousness/obedience and its results. He notes in v. 18, "In this way also through one act of righteousness (δι' ἑνὸς δικαιώματος) the result was justification of life (δικαίσων ζωῆς) for all men." Christ's death is the referent of δι' ἑνὸς δικαιώματος. This is the antithesis of Adam's one transgression (δι' ἑνὸς παραπτώματος). When viewed in relation to this Adamic contrast, Jesus' death becomes an act of righteounseess in the sense that the crucified Christ neither transgressed the divine command, nor listened to the serpent's voice, nor coveted what God forbid. While Adam's transgression resulted in condemnation for all, Jesus' act of righteousness resulted in what Paul abbreviates as the "righteousness of life" (δικαίωσιν ζωῆς). Given Paul's typological contrast, the sense of δικαίωσιν ζωῆς is best understood in relation to its parallel abbreviation κατάκριμα. As noted already, the latter phrase in both the Adamic narrative and Paul's argument refers to the sentence of death enacted by separation from God's life giving presence. It follows then that δικαίωσιν ζωῆς refers to a sentence of life enacted by access to God's life giving presence in Christ. This is life before God presently and eschatologically as Paul's wider argument in Rom 5:1—8:39 bears out.[88]

---

83. See Longenecker, *Romans*, 597.

84. See the use of ὑπακοή in Rom 1:5; 6:16; 15:18; 16:19, 26.

85. Cf. εἰς πάντας ἀνθρώπους in Rom 5:12 and the spread of death to all people.

86. For a discussion of κατεστάθησαν and its interpretive options, see Jewett, *Romans*, 386; Moo, *Romans*, 344–45.

87. "Inaugurated" is how Moo describes κατεστάθησαν in Rom 5:19. He explains, "It often means 'appoint,' and probably refers here to the fact that people are 'inaugurated 'into' the state of sin/righteousness. Paul is insisting that people were really 'made' sinners through Adam's act of disobedience just as they are really 'made righteous' through Christ's obedience." Moo, *Romans*, 345. Seifrid describes the use of κατεστάθησαν as "instated" explaining, "This is also the case in verse 19, where he promises that 'the many will be instated (*katastathesontai*) as 'righteous ones' as the result of the obedience of 'the one.'" Seifrid, *Christ Our Righteousness*, 71.

88. E.g., Rom 6:4 points to a "newness of life" that is experienced presently. By contrast, Rom 6:5 points to eschatological through resurrection from the dead. See also Rom 8:11, 24.

In Rom 5:19, Paul expands on Christ's act of righteousness and the righteousness of life that ensued by referring to the former as "obedience" and the latter as being "made righteous." Paul writes, "for just as through the disobedience of the one man many were made sinners, in this way also through the obedience of one (διὰ τῆς ὑπακοῆς τοῦ ἑνός) many will be made righteous (δίκαιοι κατασαθήσονται οἱ πολλοί)." Christ's death is the referent of διὰ τῆς ὑπακοῆς τοῦ ἑνός. Given Paul's typological contrast, Christ's obedience (ὑπακοή) in this context is best understood in relation to its Adamic counterpart, namely disobedience (παρακοή). As I have noted several times, the latter refers to Adam violating the command not to eat from the tree, trusting the serpent's voice rather than God's, and coveting what God forbids. However, by specifically referring to this transgression as "disobedience" (παρακοή), Paul underscores the fact that Adam did not listen to God's command.[89] Therefore, given the typological contrast, Paul understands Christ's "obedience" (ὑπακοή) as listening to and keeping what God commanded. The result of his obedience is that "many will be made righteous (δίκαιοι κατασαθήσονται οἱ πολλοί)." From a typological perspective, when we compare the two passive uses of καθίστημι, the many will be made righteous through Christ's obedience eschatologically in the same way that protologically many were made sinners through Adam's disobedience. This means from an eschatological perspective many will be "inaugurated," or "instated," into a righteous state through Christ's obedience.[90]

Romans 5:19 and the Echo of Isaiah's Suffering Servant

The result of Christ's obedience, namely that "many will be made righteous (δίκαιοι κατασαθήσονται οἱ πολλοί)," has a thicker intertextual subtext than Gen 3. It also echoes the obedience of Isaiah's suffering servant:

> Due to the anguish of his soul he will see it and be satisfied; by his knowledge my righteous servant will justify many (יצדיק צדיק עבדי לרבים), and he will bear their sin (Isa 53:11 MT).

---

89. BDAG 1028.

90. We should take κατασαθήσονται as a real future. As Seifrid notes, "The topics which control Paul's argument in this section, namely the beginning and end of human history, strongly suggest that we should render his verb as a 'real' future, a reading which is confirmed by its immediate parallels." Seifrid, *Christ Our Righteousness*, 71. Of course, interpreters are divided on the issue. As Murray notes, "The future tense in 'will be constituted righteous' must not be taken as referring to an act that is reserved for the consummation. This would violate the nature of justification as a free gift received by believers here and now in its completeness and perfection." Murray, *Romans*, 206. See also Sanday and Hedlam, *Romans*, 142. However, Paul's genuine future reference does not necessarily mitigagte a present experience of justification. Yet, if Paul is drawing a genuine contrast between the beginning and the end with Adam and Christ. It follows that, at least in Rom 5:19, Paul has in view future and final justification. He has shown an ability to make this distinction in the letter already. See, e.g., Rom 2:13.

And the Lord wants to take away from the pain of his soul, to show to him light and to form him with understanding, to justify the righteous one who serves many well (δικαιῶσαι δίκαιον εὖ δουλεύοντα πολλοῖς), and he will take away their sins (Isa 53:11 LXX).

In this instance, the MT pre-text may be closer to Rom 5:19 than the LXX. The servant is the subject of the justifying action in the MT just as Jesus is the implied agent of the passive expression δίκαιοι κατεστάθησαν οἱ πολλοί. In any case, the *volume* is low to moderate.[91] The pre-text does not employ καθίστημι; however, we do find overlap with δίκαιος. There is *contextual consistency*, because both in the pre-text and text "sinners" are served by having their sins removed and their statuses before God changed. Within the *history of interpretation*, several interpreters note the possibility that Rom 5:19 evokes Isa 53.[92] However, they do not always explore the implications of the echo for understanding Paul's argument. One exception is Shiu-Lun Shum who argues that by evoking Isa 53:11 in v. 19 "what Paul draws on from the Suffering Servant song is not simply (Second) Isaiah's language, but the prophet's concept of a *one-many-solidarity-relationship*."[93] We will return to these implications below.

Romans 5:20–21 and Echoes of the Law's Entrance

Paul drops the typological comparison with Adam in Rom 5:20–21, and he shifts his intertextual attention to the entrance of the Mosaic Law. He observes, "But the law entered in order that the transgression might increase; but where sin increased grace increased all the more, in order that just as sin reigned in death, in this way also grace might reign through righteousness resulting in eternal life through Jesus Christ our Lord." Paul has made his case that sin and death reigned in the world and in people without the Mosaic Law.[94] Now he makes the point that the Law in fact perpetuated the reign of sin, though in a way that ultimately served God's gracious purposes. Paul's point here evokes a few OT pre-texts.

The phrase "the law entered" (νόμος παρεισῆλθεν) evokes Exod 20 as a pre-text which, at least for Paul, recounts a key moment in God's dealings with Israel and thereby the world. Moses' reception of the tablets at Sinai marked a kind of "entrance" of the law into Israel and the world. Paul interprets this moment from the perspective of God's gracious intent. Verses 20 and 21 have two purposes clauses (ἵνα) that clearly spell out this intent: (1) the law entered to increase the transgression of the law; and (2) the law-induced increase of transgression resulted in the increase of grace to

---

91. However, it is interesting that Isa 53:11–12 contains three uses of πολύς. Paul uses the same substantival adjective several times in Rom 5:15–21. See Rom 5:15, 16, 17, and 19.

92. See, e.g., Fitzmyer, *Romans* 421; Jewett, *Romans*, 387; Wright, *Romans*, 529.

93. Shum, *Paul's Use of Isaiah*, 199.

94. In this way, Paul returns to the expression ἀπὸ Ἀδὰμ μέχρι Μωϋσέως (Rom 5:14) and focuses upon the period from Moses onward.

establish the reign of grace over the reign of sin in death.⁹⁵ These purposes clauses point to the personification of four entitites: sin, law, death, and grace. By making νόμος the subject of παρεισῆλθεν, Paul personifies the law as he has sin (ἁμαρτία) and death (θάνατος) in Rom 5:12–19.⁹⁶ Rom 5:20 hints at this dynamic, because the entrance of the law (νόμος παρεισῆλθεν) is parallel with sin abounding (ἐπλεόνασεν ἡ ἁμαρτία).⁹⁷ Therefore, sin, death, and the law are three actors who, as Longenecker puts it, have "'strutted their stuff' on the stage of human history in opposition to God and his will."⁹⁸ Of course, as Paul will explain later in Rom 7:7–25, it does not follow that the Mosaic law is evil.

Personifications notwithstanding, God introduced the law at Sinai for his gracious purposes towards Adam's seed. He introduced the law into Israel, and thereby into the world, to increase (πλεονάζω) the transgression. The law increases transgression in multiple senses. As Cranfield observes "It was first of all necessary that sin should increase somewhere among men in the sense of becoming clearly manifest."⁹⁹ God made sin manifest in the world by giving the law to a nation, Israel, who then transgressed it. The increase of transgression also increased sin in the sense that people consciously and willfully sinned against God with the entrance of the law. Even more, sin increased through the entrance of the law in the sense that people would seek to conceal their transgression, justify it, or even exploit the law for their own profit. Israel's Scriptures bear out this multi-layered increase of sin through the law. Interestingly, their experiences with the Law echo Adam and Eve's experience with a single command (Gen 2:17). They consciously and willfully disobeyed God. Adam and Eve attempted to conceal their transgression by hiding in the garden.¹⁰⁰ They also attempted to justify their transgression as Adam blamed Eve and Eve blamed the serpent.¹⁰¹ In this way, Israel recapitulated the experience of Adam and Eve on a larger and more protracted scale.

Nevertheless, the increase of sin in Israel through the entrance of the Law only served God's gracious purposes. Every step of the way, where sin increased through the Law, grace increased all the more (ὑπερεπερίσσευσεν ἡ χάρις) for the purpose of establishing the reign of grace (ἡ χάρις βασιλεύσῃ). Here Paul juxtaposes two reigns: (1) the reign of sin in death (ἡ ἁμαρτία ἐν τῷ θανάτῳ); and (2) the reign of grace through righteousnesss (διὰ δικαιοσύνης) resulting in eternal life through our Lord

---

95. Paul does not exhaust the law's purpose with his statement in Rom 5:20. On this point, see Cranfield, *Romans*, 1:292.

96. Cf. the personification of νόμος in Rom 3:19; 4:15; Gal 3:24.

97. One should also note the parallel semantics/syntax of "sin entered the world" (ἡ ἁμαρτία εἰς τὸν κόσμον) in Rom 5:12 and the "law entered" (νόμος παρεισῆλθεν) in Rom 5:20. The latter phrase does not contain the prepositional phrase εἰς τὸν κόσμον.

98. Longenecker, *Romans*, 598.

99. Cranfield, *Romans*, 1:293.

100. See Gen 3:8–10.

101. See Gen 3:12–13.

Jesus Christ (διὰ Ἰησοῦ Χριστοῦ τοῦ κυρίου ἡμῶν). The syntax of the phrase ἐν τῷ θανάτῳ most likely functions as a dative of sphere.[102] Sin reigned in the domain, or sphere, of death. The sphere of death's reign includes the world and all people as Paul made clear in Rom 5:12. Contrastively, grace reigns within that sphere of death where sin reigns. Grace reigns through the means, or agency, of righteousness (διὰ δικαιοσύνης). The prepostional phrase διὰ δικαιοσύνης is theologically loaded given all that Paul says about righteousness in Romans. Contextually, Paul refers to righteousness, that is a right standing with God in the crucified and risen Christ, as a gift (Rom 5:17). Here in 5:21 the point is that grace reigns through the gift of righteousness in Christ which results in eternal life.

Interpretive Impact of Pre-Texts in Romans 5:15–21

Given Paul's overt allusions to the Adamic narrative and the entrance of the Mosaic Law at Sinai, we have already considered some of the main exegetical effects of OT pre-texts on this portion of the letter. What I offer here are some larger points of resonance related to typological protology and Paul's wider theology which still have implications for our understanding of these verses. By typological protology, I am referring to the principle that the "first things" in Adam foreshadow and typify the "last things" in Christ. What began with Adam ends with Christ. The reign of sin and death began with Adam, but it ends with Christ. If sin and death began to reign through Adam, that reign ends in Christ while grace and life begin to reign through him.

God ends in Jesus Christ the one man (τοῦ ἑνὸς ἀνθρώπου Ἰησοῦ Χριστοῦ, Rom 5:15) what began with Adam the one man (δι' ἑνὸς ἀνθρώπου, Rom 5:12) through antithetical actions and results. In Rom 5:15–17, Paul sets Adam's transgression, which resulted in death, against God's grace in the crucified and risen Christ which resulted in life. He describes the result of Adam's sin in three interrelated ways: (1) "many died" (5:15); (2) "condemnation" (5:16); and (3) "death reigned" (5:17). As noted above, Paul has in view the prohibition from Gen 2:17 and the forensic scene that unfolds in Gen 3:1–24. Adam broke the command (Gen 2:17) by listening to the serpent rather than God and by coveting what God prohibited. Therefore, God doled out judgment that included pain, enmity, and death brought on by removal from God's life-giving presence in the garden. All subsequent human beings share in the same condemnation.[103] In this way, death reigns as an enemy to whom God handed over Adam and his seed. Antithetically, God gives life in Christ. In vv. 15–17, Paul does not yet explicitly refer

---

102. Moo notes the syntactical possibilities of ἐν τῷ θανάτῳ, "This 'in' might indicate accompaniment–'sin reigned with death'–instrument–'sin reigned through death'–or sphere–'sin reigned in the 'dominion' of death.'" Moo, *Romans*, 349. See also Schreiner, *Romans*, 296.

103. As Watson observes, "No-one else in Genesis is given a commandment to observe on pain of death. Adam is the historical point of entry of sin and death into the world, and he can therefore serve as a type of Christ on the basis of the universal scope of his action." Watson, *Paul and the Hermeneutics of Faith*, 512.

to Christ's obedience. Instead, he sets Adam's transgression (παράπτωμα/ἁμαρτάνω) against God's gift (χάρισμα/χάρις/δωρεά). God meets the Adamic transgression with a christological gift. The results of this gift are laid out in three interrelated ways: (1) grace, not death, abounds in the one man Jesus Christ (5:15); (2) justification not condemnation (5:16); and (3) a reign in life rather than the reign of death.

The antithetical actions and results continue in vv. 18–19 where Paul explicitly juxtaposes Adam's disobedience with Christ's obedience. Adam's transgression (παράπτωμα) results in condemnation (εἰς κατάκριμα) to all while Christ's righteous deed (δικαίωμα) results in the justification which produces life (εἰς δικαίωσιν ζωῆς) before God for all. Intertextually, Adam's disobedience (παρακοή) consists of succumbing to the serpent's temptation, coveting, and transgressing the divine command from Gen 2:17. Conversely, Christ's obedience (ὑπακοή) is not succumbing to the serpent's temptation, not coveting, and not transgressing the divine command which is typified in Gen 2:17. Just as the serpent tempted Adam and Eve to question and transgress the command not to eat of the tree, so he tempted Christ. Though he does not explicitly state it here, the serpent tempted Christ to transgress the divine command which was to die upon a tree.[104] The disobedience of Adam resulted in many being made, that is "inaugurated" or "instated" (κατεστάθησαν), sinners. The obedience of Christ will result in many being made, that is "inaugurated" or "instated" (κατεστάθησαν), as righteous. In this way, God ends in Jesus Christ the one man (τοῦ ἑνὸς ἀνθρώπου Ἰησοῦ Χριστοῦ, Rom 5:15) what began with Adam the one man (δι' ἑνὸς ἀνθρώπου, Rom 5:12) through antithetical actions and results.

We must also consider the christological interplay in these verses which is quite remarkable. From the typological perspective that Paul's insists on (Rom 5:14), a few salient points emerge. For example, by applying the phrase δι' ἑνὸς ἀνθρώπου to both Adam and Christ Paul implies the necessity of the latter's incarnation. God's eschatological, and antithetical, actions and results must take place in the flesh of Christ just as the protological ones transpired in the flesh of Adam. Paul will return to the significance of God doing his work in the "flesh" of Christ. As he puts it in Rom 8:3, "He condemned sin in the flesh (ἐν τῇ σαρκί)." Additionally, the interplay between Gen 2–3 and Rom 5:15–21 generates the unstated point that Adam did not listen to God's voice regarding the "tree" but Christ did. Christ's obedience at this point evokes the suffering servant in Isa 53. As noted above, Isa 53:11 indicates that the servant would make others righteous. Paul suggests that through his obedience Christ will make many righteous (Rom 5:19). What we find then is that Paul's typological comparison is a poly-figural reading of Adam and Christ. Paul brings in other figures from Israel's Scriptures to describe both Adam and Christ. These additional figures include Mesianic figures such as the suffering servant from Isa 53.

Finally, based on the interplay between Israel's experience with the law, which is chronicled in the OT and briefly mentioned in Rom 5:20–21, the point arises that God

---

104. Cf. the use of ὑπακοή in Rom 5:19 with the use of the same term in Phil 2:8. See also Heb 5:8.

established the reign of grace in a suprising way. Simply put, he increased sin through giving the Mosaic Law so that he could at the same time increase grace on a greater scale and thereby establish the reign of grace (Rom 5:20). The more that sin used the law to increase transgressions and perpetuate its reign the more God was gracious to perpetuate the reign of grace through the righteousness revealed in Christ. Sin's reign resulted in death, but the reign of grace results in eternal life through Jesus Christ the Lord. This entrie juxtaposition of two "reigns" is built upon the interrelated subtexts of Gen 2–3 and Israel's experience with the Mosaic Law. Although Paul never cites the OT in this elaborate typological description, as is so often the case, his entire effort depends upon allusions to and echoes of Israel's Scriptures.

4

Romans 6:1–23

INTERPRETERS GENERALLY DETECT VERY little intertextual engagement in Rom 6. Articles, monographs, and commentaries dedicated to Paul's use of the OT in these verses are quite thin.[1] However, as this chapter will demonstrate, Paul's engagement with Israel's Scriptures is alive and well at this point in the letter. The absence of citations in these verses does not indicate that Israel's Scriptures altogether cease to shape Paul's thought and language. Instead, Paul makes extensive use of scriptural motifs.

Romans 6:1–11

(6:1–11) What then shall we say? Shall we remain in sin, in order that grace might abound? May it never be. We who died to sin, how will we still live in it? Or do you not know that as many of us who were baptized in Christ Jesus, were baptized into his death? Therefore, we have been buried with him through baptism resulting in death, in order that just as Christ was raised from the dead through the glory of the father, in this way also we might walk in newness of life. For if we have become sharers in the likeness of his death, but we will also share in the likeness of his resurrection; knowing this, that our old man was crucified with him, in order that the body of sin might be nullified, so that we no longer serve sin. For the one who has died has been justified from sin. But if we died with Christ, we believe that we will also live with him. Knowing that Christ having been raised from the dead no longer dies, death no longer lords over him. For that which he died, he died to sin once

---

1. One of the most notable exceptions is Wright's intertextual reading of Rom 6:1–11. He suggests that Paul evokes a "new-exodus" motif to explain baptism with Messiah Jesus. Wright notes of the text, "It cries out to be interpreted in terms of the exodus. And when we find that the key event through which slavery is abandoned and freedom is gained consists of passing through the water, reenacting the death of Jesus, which was already interpreted in terms of Passover imagery, the case can be closed. Exodus is not a distant echo here. It is a main theme." Wright, *Romans*, 534.

for all; but that which he lives, he lives to God. In this way also you consider yourselves to be dead to sin but alive to God in Christ Jesus.

As is well-known, Paul's argument at this point pivots upon a false inference. If it is the case that grace increased as sin increased, should one conclude that it is best to remain in the power of sin? As Paul puts it bluntly, "What then? Shall we remain in sin, in order that grace might increase (πλεονάσῃ)?"[2] (Rom 6:1). Paul quickly dismisess this false inference with his well-known interjection "may it never be" (μὴ γένοιτο).[3] He then proceeds to explain why such an understanding of divine grace is faulty.

As we shall see, Paul's explanation has an intertextual subtext that is not always appreciated by interpreters. To be sure, we find no OT citations or allusions here. What we do find are echoes of a water-death-life motif from Israel's Scriptures that shaped the nation's understanding of itself and its God. This motif, coupled with a few other pre-texts, provides interplay which produces the kind of resonance we have come to expect in the letter.

Suggested Pre-Texts in Romans 6:1–11

Hübner lists the following pre-texts: 2 Kgs 3:3; 10:31; Hos 10:9 (Rom 6:1); Deut 28:9; Ps 85:11 LXX; Dan 12:2 θ (Rom 6:4); and Ps 21:30 LXX (Rom 6:10).[4] Nestle-Aland 28th ed. does not list any pre-texts. To reiterate, Hays does not list any pre-texts from Rom 5:1 to 8:18. Seifrid likewise does not discuss any pre-texts related to Rom 6:1–23.[5]

Intertextual Analysis of Romans 6:1–11

The main pre-text in this section is the water-death-life motif from Israel's Scriptures. As I will discuss in what follows, Israel's Scriptures contain several episodes in which God brings death and life out of water. Paul evokes this motif through his description of a baptism and burial with Christ. Although Rom 6:1–11 is not just about baptism, the imagery here is significant to Paul's argument. It is imagery informed by this OT motif.[6]

---

2. The verb πλεονάζω is a hook word linking Rom 5:20–21 with its use of the verb to 6:1.

3. Cf. use of μὴ γένοιτο in Rom 3:4, 6, 31; 6:15; 7:7, 13; 9:14; 11:1, 11. The only occurrences of the interjection outside of Romans are found in 1 Cor 6:15, Gal 2:17; 3:21, and 6:14.

4. Hübner, *Vetus Testamentum in Novo*, 2.

5. See Seifrid, *Romans*, 631.

6. Although Paul's baptism imagery receives a great deal of exegetical attention, some interpreters stress that the imagery is not the main point of Rom 6:1–11. See, e.g., Jewett, *Romans*, 400.

Romans 6:1–4 and Echoes of A Water-Death-Life Motif

Romans 6:3–4 portray baptism as a death with Christ Jesus, "Or do you not know that as many of us were baptized in Christ Jesus (ἐβαπτίσθημεν εἰς Χριστὸν Ἰησοῦν), we were baptized into his death (εἰς τὸν θάνατον αὐτοῦ ἐβαπτίσθημεν)? Therefore, we have been buried with him through baptism (συνετάφημεν αὐτῷ διὰ τοῦ βαπτίσματος) resulting in death, in order that just as Christ was raised from the dead through the glory of the father, in this way also we might walk in newness of life." Paul links a person's baptism to Christ's death and resurrection.[7] The specific nature of the link has caused not a little controversy within the *history of interpretation*.[8] However, my focus for the moment is the analysis of the text's intertextual subtext which needs to begin with the water-death-life motif from Israel's Scriptures. Rom 6:1–11 echo certain features of this motif.

First, the text echoes the Exodus narrative and especially Israel's trek through the Red Sea. The pre-texts here include both the book of Exodus and subsequent reflection on this event in other portions of Israel's Scriptures. The *volume* of the echo is moderate based on the contextual use of the terms βαπτίζω/βάπτισμα, ἐπιμένω, and the phrase διὰ τῆς δόξης τοῦ πατρός. Although βαπτίζω rarely occurs in the LXX, Paul can use the term as a reference to Israel's trek through the Red Sea.[9] This is clear in 1 Cor 10:1–13 where Paul likens the experience of Christians in Corinth to Israel's experience in the Exodus and in the wilderness. As part of this explicit typological (τυπικῶς συνέβαινεν, 1 Cor 10:11) comparison, Paul begins "For I do no want you to be ignorant, brothers, that our fathers were under a cloud and all went through the sea (διὰ τῆς θαλάσσης) and all were baptized (ἐβαπτίσθησαν) into Moses (εἰς τὸν Μωϋσῆν) in the cloud and in the sea (ἐν τῇ θαλάσσῃ)" (1 Cor 10:1–2).[10] Paul describes the trek through the Red Sea as a baptism into Moses and a baptism that took place in the sea. Given that Paul links βαπτίζω to the Red Sea episode in 1 Cor 10, it follows that a similar link is echoed in Rom 6.

Additionally, the use of ἐπιμένω in Rom 6:1, "Shall we remain (ἐπιμένωμεν) in sin?", may also echo the events of the Exodus. Specifically, it could evoke Israel's

---

7. Paul's use of βαπτίζω and βάπτισμα in this context refers to "the Christian sacrament of initiation after Jesus' death." BDAG 164. However, it does not follow that such a referent exhausts Paul's use of the terminology in Rom 6:3–4. As I will discuss later, even the Christian sacrament itself within the earliest church is informed by the water motif from Israel's Scriptures.

8. E.g., Bousset's seminal work, *Kyrios Christos*, popularized the idea that Christian baptism originated from ancient Near eastern cults of Mithra and or Isis. See Bousset, *Kyrios Christos*. However, Longenecker notes "That thesis is thoroughly discounted today." Longenecker, *Romans*, 612. See also Wagner, *Pauline Baptism and the Pagan Mysteries*; Wedderburn, *Baptism and Resurrection*. Of course, a far greater debate stemming from the interpretation of Rom 6:3–4 invovles various Roman Catholic and Protestant interpretations.

9. The verb βαπτίζω only occurs in 2 Kgs 15:14 and Isa 21:4. See also Jdt 12:7; Sir 34:25. The noun βάπτισμα never occurs in the LXX.

10. For other uses of βαπτίζω in the Pauline corpus, see 1 Cor 1:13, 14, 15, 16, 17; 12:13, 15:29, and Gal 3:27. The only other use of βάπτισμα occurs in Eph 4:5.

hurried flight from Egypt in which they did not even have time to allow their bread to leaven. The Exodus narrator describes this moment noting, "And they baked the dough, which they brought out from Egypt, unleavened cakes; for it was not leavened; for the Egyptians threw them out, and they were not able to remain (ἐπιμεῖναι) nor did they prepare provision for themselves for the way" (Exod 12:39). Paul reconfigures the language of not remaining (ἐπιμένω) in Egypt due to God's swift deliverance around not remaining in sin because of God's deliverance in Christ.[11]

Finally, Paul's use of the phrase διὰ τῆς δόξης τοῦ πατρός evokes the Exodus narrative as well. He describes the resurrection of Christ from the dead as something that transpired "through the glory of the father." Similarly, in describing God's deliverance of Israel through the Red Sea, the song of Moses underscores divine glory (δόξα/δοξάζω) to describe the event:

> Let us sing to the Lord, for he is highly glorified (ἐνδόξως δεδόξασται); he threw the horse and rider into the sea (Exod 15:1).[12]

> Your right hand, O Lord, you have been glorified (δεδόξασται) in strength; your right hand, O Lord, scattered enemies. And in the multitude of your glory (τῆς δόξης σου) you crused the opponents; you sent out your wrath, and you consumed them like a reed (Exod 15:6–7).

> Who is like you among the God, O Lord? Who is like you, glorifed (δεδοξασμένος) among holy ones, wonderful in glories (δόξαις), doing wonders? (Exod 15:11).

The song describes the parting of the sea and the drowning of Israel's enemies as a revelation of divine glory, or power.[13] Paul likewise describes the resurrection of Christ from the dead as something that took place "through the glory of the Father." It is glory in the sense that it reveals divine power.[14]

The *contextual consistency* between this pre-text and text occurs in a few different ways. For example, both the Exodus motif and Rom 6 stress a location from which God has delivered his people. Yahweh brought his people out of Egyptian bondage through the waters of the Red Sea. In Rom 6:1, Paul signals that in Christ God has brought believers out of bondage to sin through the waters of baptism. The dative

---

11. Exod 12:39 contains the only use of ἐπιμένω in the LXX. For other uses of the verb in the Pauline corpus, see Rom 11:22, 23; 1 Cor 16:7, 8; Gal 1:18; Phil 1:24; Col 1:23; 1 Tim 4:16. Interpreters often note the use of ἐπιμένω + the dative case in texts such as Philo, *Leg. All.* 3:94; *Spec. Leg.* 4:48; Test Jos 13:4; Josephus, *Ant.* 14:135; 15:281. See, e.g., Wolter, *Der Brief an die Römer*, 1:368. However, they often ignore the use of the verb in Exod 12:39.

12. See also Exod 15:21.

13. Cf. other descrptions of the Red Sea event in Pss LXX 65:6; 73:13; 76:20–21; 77:12–13; 77:52–53; 105:7–12, 21–22; 135:11–15; Isa 43:16; 50:2; 51:10.

14. On this point, see Cranfield, *Romans*, 1:304.

τῇ ἁμαρτίᾳ in Rom 6:1 is locative in its syntactical force.[15] For Paul, believers cannot remain in the domain of sin any more than ancient Israelites could remain in Egypt. This locative force in 6:1 fits with Paul's larger personification of sin as an enslaving power.[16] He enhances this peronsification in Rom 6 as I will discuss below.[17] Additionally, the means of deliverance in pre-text and text are consistent with one another. God performs many judgments against Egypt to deliver Israel from bondage. The death of the firstborn and the deliverance through the sea are the crowning judgments of Israel's deliverance. Similarly, for Paul, God delivers his people from sin through their participation in the death and resurrection of Jesus. Paul uses baptism language, with its intertextual connotations, to describe how the Romans participate in this experience.

Within the *history of interpretation*, many interpreters do not consider the Exodus subtext in their interpretation of Rom 6:1–11. The discussion here often revolves around the source of Paul's baptismal language. Once again, some have suggested a Greco-Roman parallel such as initiation rites into mysterious religions or a Jewish source such as proselyte baptism.[18] While some uncertainty remains, it is reasonable to conclude that early Christian tradition shaped Paul's understanding of baptism.[19] However, that tradition itself is likely shaped, at least in part, by a Jewish background that Paul knew quite well. Part of the background evoked here in Rom 6 could be a link between the Red Sea episode, Jewish proselyte baptism, and Christian baptism. As Ellis explains:

> In 1 Cor. 10.1ff and Rom. 6.3 Christian baptism is explained in terms of the Exodus imagery. In the former passage the Red Sea crossing and envelopment in the *Shekinah* cloud are taken as typical of the Christian's experience. A parallel to Jewish proselyte baptism seems implicit in Rom. 6.3. In Judaism this baptism was essential to identify the proselyte with Israel; and this identification, as the *Pesach* ritual stresss, signified an identification with Israel's Exodus from Egypt, i.e. with 'baptism' in the Red Sea and *Shekinah* cloud. So Christian baptism identifies one with the new Exodus—Christ's death and resurrection.[20]

---

15. On the locative force of τῇ ἁμαρτίᾳ in Rom 6:1, see Murray, *Romans*, 213; Wright, *Romans*, 537.

16. See, e.g., Rom 3:9; 5:12–14; 7:7–25.

17. See, e.g., Rom 6:6, 7, 9, 12, 14, 18.

18. For a summary of possible Greco-Roman sources such as the cult of Isis or Dionysius, see Dunn, *Romans*, 1:308–11. See also Wagner, *Pauline Baptism and the Pagan Mysteries*. With respect to Jewish sources as a possible source for Paul's baptism language, see the discussion in Longenecker, *Romans*, 613.

19. Longenecker, *Romans*, 613.

20. Ellis, *Paul's Use of the Old Testament*, 133.

Ellis interprets the intertextual subtext of Rom 6:3–4 in relation to the Red Sea imagery which was inherent to proselyte baptism and which Paul explicitly evokes in 1 Cor 10:1–13. Additionally, patristic literature consistently makes a typological link between the Red Sea and Christiam baptism.[21] I will consider the points of resonance generated by this interplay below.

Besides the Red Sea episode, the OT water-death-life motif is also represented in the parting of the Jordan River. OT writers interpret the latter in relation to the former. In fact, when Joshua leads the Israelites across the Jordan River, twelve stones are erected at Gilgal memorializing the way that God dried up the Jordan as he had the Red Sea. Joshua instructs parents to explain the meaning of the twelve stones to their children by linking the event at the Jordan to the event at the Red Sea:

> Whenever your sons should ask you saying, "What are these stones?" Proclaim to your sons that "Israel went through the Jordan on dry land after the Lord our God dried up the water of the Jordan from before them until when they passed through, just as the Lord our God did with the Red Sea, which the Lord our God dried up before us until we passed by, in order that all the nations of the earth might know that the power of the Lord is mighty, and in order that you might worship the Lord your God in every time" (Josh 4:21–24).

While Israel's God brought the nation through the Red Sea to deliver them from bondage, he brought them through the Jordan River to bring them into the land which he had promised to Abraham's descendants.[22] Admittedly, echoes of the Jordan River pret-ext are not as loud as those emanating from the Red Sea episode. Nevertheless, one finds *contextual consistency* between pre-text and text based on the shared motif of water-death-life.[23]

In both the Red Sea and Jordan River episodes, God brings Israel out of the water into life. This dynamic is reflected in Rom 6:1–11. God brings the believer into the waters of baptism to die with Christ, and he brings them out of the water to live with him. Passage through the Red Sea resulted in life beyond slavery. Passage throught the Jordan River resulted in the inheritance of the promised land. Passage through baptism with Christ is associated with deliverance from sin and death as well as inheritance of life, ultimately resurrection from the dead (Rom 6:5). In this way, the "newness of life" that typifies baptism with Christ evokes the water-death-life motif represented in both the parting of the Red Sea and the parting of the Jordan River which are already intertwined in Israel's Scriptures.

The water-life-death motif is of course reflected in the flood narrative of Gen 6–8. God brings death to his sinful creation through water (Gen 6:5–7; 7:1–24). Yet,

---

21. On this point, see Jensen, *Living Water*, 38.

22. Cf. Gen 12:1–3.

23. Within the *history of interpretation*, the Jordan River episode is not widely suggested as a pre-text for Rom 6:1–11.

through the same waters, he brings life to Noah and to those with him in the ark (Gen 8:1–22). No semantic or syntactical correspondence links this flood episode to Rom 6:1–11. However, the episode is *contextually consistent* with the Romans text. Baptism with Christ involves both sharing in the deadly waters of judgment and being delivered with Christ out of those waters.[24] Moreover, we know that early Christians made an explicit connection between the flood narrative and baptism. 1 Peter provides a prime example, though the link between the flood and baptism is part of one of the most exegetically difficult passages in the NT (1 Pet 3:18–22).[25] Peter mentions that Noah prepared an ark in which eight people were delivered from the flood (1 Pet 3:20). He then qualifies Noah's deliverance noting "and corresponding to that (ἀντίτυπον), baptism (βάπτισμα) now saves (σῴζει) you, not the removal of dirt from the flesh but an appeal to God for a good conscience, through the resurrection (δι᾽ ἀναστάσεως) of Jesus Christ" (1 Pet 3:21). In this way, we find clear links in early Christian thought between the flood narrative, baptism, salvation, and Jesus' resurrection. Obviously, Paul does not explicitly mention the flood narrative in Rom 6:1–11. However, it is a typological interpretation of baptism already present in early Christianity, and it is consistent with features of Paul's argument here.

Israel's Scriptures also contain several individual episodes that reflect the water-life-death motif. For example, Moses' name sake (משה/Μωϋσῆς) reflects how God drew him out of the waters of death into life.[26] Jonah's three-day entombment in the flesh takes up the basic contours of the motif. The waters act as divine judgment against the disobedient prophet, but his rescue from those waters brings life.[27] The Psalms use the motif in a figurative way. For example, the psalmist praises the way God rescued him from deadly waters "He sent from on high and took me, he drew me out of many waters (ἐξ ὑδάτων πολλῶν)" (Ps 17:17 LXX).[28] Similarly, Isaiah takes up the motif, especially as it is reflected in the Red Sea episode, to describe God's future deliverance of his people. For example, the divine promise is "And if you should go through the water (διαβαίνῃς δι᾽ ὕδατος), I am with you (μετὰ σοῦ εἰμι), and rivers will not wash over you; and if you should go through fire, you certainly shall not be burnt, the flame will not burn you" (Isa 43:2).[29] In short, the water-death-life motif reflected in these pre-texts is consistent with Paul's baptism imagery in Rom 6. Baptism is like a watery entombment with Christ where the believer dies. Yet, God brings the believer through those deadly waters with Christ to resurrected life.

---

24. As Seifrid puts it, "Baptism into Christ entails baptism into his death and thereby participation in his resurrection." Seifrid, *Christ Our Righteousness*, 72.

25. For a recent exploration of this passage and the so-called descent of Christ, see Emerson, *He Descended to the Dead*.

26. See Exod 2:1–10.

27. See Jonah's prayer in Jonah 2:1–10.

28. See also Pss LXX 31:6; 68:2, 15; 123:4; 143:7.

29. See also Isa 43:16; 50:2; 51:10; 54:9; 63:12.

Romans 6:1–4 and the Echoes of Newness and Walking

Beyond the water-death-life motif, Rom 6:4 also echoes the combination of two OT metaphors: (1) the promise of newness; and (2) walking with or before God as a metaphor for right living.

In drawing an inference from baptism into Christ' death (6:3), Paul concludes "Therefore, we have been buried with him through baptism into death, in order that just as Christ was raised from the dead through the glory of the Father, in this way we might also walk in newness of life (ἐν καινότητι ζωῆς περιπατήσωμεν)." The phrase ἐν καινότητι ζωῆς evokes promises of "newness" sometimes referenced in prophetic material.[30] For example, Isaiah spoke of "new things" (חדשות/καινά) which God would do including: (1) make Israel a light to the nations (Isa 42:6–10); (2) make a way in the wilderness for his people (Isa 43:19); (3) create new/hidden things (Isa 48:6); and (4) create a new heavens and earth (Isa 65:17; 66:22). Jeremiah spoke of a "new covenant" (διαθήκη καινή) in days to come:

> "Behold days are coming," says the Lord, "And I will make a new covenant (διαθήκην καινήν) with the house of Israel and the house of Judah, not according to the covenant, which I made with their fathers in the day when I took them by their hand to bring them out from the land of Egypt, because they did not remain in my covenant, and I disregard them," says the Lord; for this is the covenant, which I will make with the house of Israel after those days," says the Lord, "I will certainly give my laws in their mind and I will them upon their hearts; and I will be their God, and they will be my people; they certainly shall not teach each one his fellow-citizen and each one his brother saying 'Know the Lord;' because all will know me from little from their little and unto their great, because I will forgive their unrighteous deeds and I certainly shall not still remember their sins" (Jer 38:31–34 LXX).[31]

The newness of the covenant consists of forgiveness and a heart that walks in God's ways.

These references to newness in Isaiah and Jeremiah may inform Paul's expression "newness of life." Although the *volume* of these pre-texts is low, they certainly pass the tests of *recurrence* and *contextual consistency*.[32] With respect to the latter, the newness envisioned by both prophets is consistent with Paul's description of a new life in Rom 6:1–11. This new life is charactized by freedom from sin (Rom 6:7) and life with God (Rom 6:11) just as Isaiah and Jeremiah envisioned. Such newness is not limited to a change in obedience. Rather, it includes an entire new existence in a new aeon/creation, just as Isaiah envisioned, through the resurrected Christ. We will return below

---

30. The noun καινότης only occurs in 1 Kgs 8:53 (8:12 MT) and Ezek 47:12.

31. Cf. Jer 31:31–34 MT.

32. For recurrence of these pre-texts in the Pauline corpus, see, e.g., Rom 11:27; 1 Cor 11:25; 2 Cor 3:3.

to the way that Paul reconfigures the prophetic promise of newness around participation in the crucified and risen Christ. For the moment, it is enough to point out that Paul does not invent "newness of life" out of thin air. Instead, he reconfigures an existing OT motif around Christ. That existing motif emanates from specific pre-texts.

Paul weds this OT motif of "newness" to the OT metaphor of walking—"in order that we might walk (περιπατήσωμεν) in newness of life" (Rom 6:4).[33] As Dunn notes, the figurative use of the "walk of life" is "characteristically Jewish."[34] The metaphor (הלך) occurs frequently in the Hebrew Bible; however, in the LXX, translators frequently use the verb πορεύω to translate הלך rather than περιπατέω.[35] It seems then that the NT use of the metaphor, including Paul's use, reflects the Hebrew idiom rather than the LXX.[36] The walking metaphor is applied to prominent figures from Israel's history such as Enoch, Noah, Abraham, and Jacob.[37] Walking with and before God also plays a prominent role in the Mosaic Law. If Israel walks in God's commands, the result will be blessing and life. As indicated in Leviticus, "You shall do my judgments and you shall keep my statutes to walk (ללכת) in them, I am the Lord your God." If they do not walk in the commands, the result will be curse and death. Therefore, you shall keep my statutes and my judgments which, if a man will do them, then he will live (וחי) by them, I am the Lord" (Lev 18:4–5).[38] Contrastively, if Israel does not "walk" in the divine commands, the result will be curse and death. As indicated in Leviticus, "Then if you walk (תלכו) in hostility with me, and you are not willing to obey me, then I will increase the plague on you seven times according to your sins" (Lev 26:21).[39] In short, "walking" or "not walking" in God's commands is the difference between life and death. As the psalmist puts it, "Blessed is everyone who fears the Lord, the one who walks (ההלך) in his ways" (Ps 128:1).[40]

Paul combines this Hebrew metaphor of "walking" with the metaphor of "newness" (ἐν καινότητι ζωῆς) and reconfigures it around baptism with the crucified and risen Christ. In this way, life and death with Christ holds the key to walking before God in the new life that he promised. Walking in this promised new life also includes

---

33. Cf. Paul's use of περιπατέω in Rom 8:4; 13:13; 14:15; 1 Cor 3:3; 7:17; 2 Cor 4:2; 5:7; 10:2–3; 12:18; Gal 5:16.

34. Dunn, *Romans*, 1:315.

35. For the infrequent use of περιπατέω in the LXX, see e.g, Prov 6:28; 8:20; and Eccl 11:9.

36. As Dunn notes, "The divergence between Jewish and Greek idiom at this point is indicated by the *in*frequency with which περιπατέω is used to translate the regular הלך, halak of the OT (only in 2 Kgs 20:3; Prov 8:20; and Eccl 11:9). NT usage therefore reflects knowledge of the Hebrew idiom rather than of the LXX." Dunn, *Romans*, 1:315–16.

37. See the use of הלך to describe these figures in Gen 5:22–24; 6:9; 17:1; and 28:20.

38. See Paul's citation of Lev 18:5 in Rom 10:5 and Gal 3:12. For other statements linking "walking" in the commands to life, see, e.g., Deut 5:33; 8:6–7; 10:12–13; 26:17–19; 30:16.

39. See also Lev 26:22–46

40. See also the metaphor of walking linked to life and the penalty of not walking in Pss 1:1; 15:2; 26:1, 11; 78:10; 81:13; 82:5; 84:11; 85:14; 86:11; 89:31; 101:2, 6; 116:9; 119:1, 3.

the gift of the Spirit as indicated in Paul's other use of "newness" (καινότης) in Rom 7:6. We will return to Paul's reconfiguration of these metaphors below.

Romans 6:6-7 and Additional Intertextual Echoes

We now turn our attention to the phrase ὁ παλαιὸς ἡμῶν ἄνθρωπος in Rom 6:6 which echoes Gen 2-3. While asserting that beleivers share in the likeness of Christ's death and resurrection, Paul notes "Knowing this, that our old man (ὁ παλαιὸς ἡμῶν ἄνθρωπος) was crucified with him, in order that the body of sin might be nullified, so that we no longer serve sin." Obviously, ὁ παλαιὸς ἡμῶν ἄνθρωπος does not occur in Gen 2-3. However, based on Rom 5:15-19, the expression is best understood in relation to the way Paul juxtaposes Adam and Christ. "Our old man" encapsulates fallen humanity in Adam and since Adam. As Fitzmyer puts it, the phrase refers to "the self we once were, the self that belongs to the old aeon, the self dominated by sin and exposed to wrath. Paul uses the adj. *palaios* to characterize the condition of human life prior to baptism and conversion, i.e., humanity in its Adamic condition."[41] Paul then reconfigures this Adamic condition around its end in Christ. Specifically, it is a condition of being "crucified with" (συνεσταυρώθη) Christ.

Paul adds in Rom 6:6 that the purpose (ἵνα) of this crucifixion with Chirst is to "nulillfy (καταργηθῇ) the body of sin (τὸ σῶμα τῆς ἁμαρτίας)" with the results that we no longer serve sin. The phrase "body of sin" (τὸ σῶμα τῆς ἁμαρτίας) does not refer strictly to the physical body but the "whole" person (physically, volitionally, emotionally) controlled by sin.[42] Once again Paul personifies sin as a power whose control is set aside through crucifixion with Christ. As we shall see in the next chapter, Paul describes sin's work in the body along the lines of enemies from the Psalms of Lament (Rom 7:7-25). At this point, I would simply note that lamenters sometimes complain about the toll that sin takes on their minds and bodies. As one lamenter complains, "There is no healing in my flesh (ἐν τῇ σαρκί) because of your wrath, and there is no peace in my bones (τοῖς ὀστέοις) because of my sins" (Ps 37:4 LXX).[43]

As Paul explains how sin is nullified with the crucified Christ, his statement in v. 7 echoes a specific way that God delivers afflicted individuals in Israel's Scriptures. Paul explains, "For the one who has died has been justified/vindicated (δεδικαίωται) from sin (ἀπὸ τῆς ἁμαρτίας)" (Rom 6:7). Interpreters often render δεδικαίωται as "has been freed."[44] Some offer this rendering while acknowledging Paul's play on words. Others

---

41. Fitzmyer, *Romans*, 436. For an Adamic echo in Rom 6:6, see also Dunn, *Romans*, 1:318; Jewett, *Romans*, 403.

42. See Cranfield, *Romans*, 1:309.

43. As we shall in the analysis of Rom 7:7-25, Ps 37 LXX plays a prominent role in Paul's description of the afflicted "I."

44. See BDAG 249.

deny any forensic force of δεδικαίωται here.⁴⁵ Part of the difficulty here is determining the forensic force of the verb in comparsion to Paul's use of the δικ- root elsewhere.⁴⁶ Jewett ultimately concludes, "It appears that no fully satisfactory solution is currently available."⁴⁷ However, we may find help from intertextual echoes related to God's justifying/vindicating work on behalf of the needy against their enemies. For example, when Judah recognizes that he has acted unjustly towards Tamar and oppressed her, he declares "Tamar has been justified/vindicated (Δεδικαίωται) rather than I, because I did not give her to Selom (Shelah) my son" (Gen 38:26).⁴⁸ Additionally, the psalmist requests "Judge the orphan and the needy, justify/vindicate (δικαιώσατε) the lowly and the poor" (Ps 81:3 LXX).⁴⁹ In Isaiah, the suffering servant praises God for his vindicating action towards him "For the one who justifies/vindicates (ὁ δικαιώσας) me is near; who is the one who judges me? Let him rise together with me; and who is the one who judges me? Let him come near to me" (Isa 50:8).

In short, the OT contains instances in which God takes the side of those who are afflicted by their enemies. He justifies/vindicates them which requires that he free them from their enemies. Paul use of δεδικαίωται echoes this divine action and reconfigures it around the beliver's death and resurrection with Christ. In this scenario, God vindicates the one who died with Jesus (ὁ ἀποθανών) from the enemy of sin who enslaved and oppressed them. The use of δικαιόω retains its forensic force and assumes that in Christ God has freed, or "justified," the believer from sin.⁵⁰ We will return to this reconfiguration below.

Interpretive Impact of Pre-Texts in Romans 6:1–11

It is now clear that Rom 6:1–11 contains a richer intertextual subtext than many interpreters recognize. We identified at least three kinds of pre-texts: (1) the water-life-death motif; (2) the combination of promised newness and walking with God; and (3) justification/vindication from enemies. The interplay between these pre-texts and Paul's argument produce multiple points of resonance that inform our reading of these verses.

---

45. E.g., Hultgren notes, "To render the verb 'has been justified from sin' does not work here." Hultgren, *Romans*, 241.

46. E.g., Schreiner suggests, "The verb δεδικαίωται is not merely forensic in verse 7, as is clear from the way the entire proposition in verse 7 relates to verse 6." Schreiner, *Romans*, 319.

47. Jewett, *Romans*, 405.

48. Ezek 21:18 contains the only other occurrence of the exact form δεδικαίωται in the LXX.

49. See also the request δικαιώσατε in Isa 1:17. Cf. Pss Sol 2:15; 3:5; 4:8; 8:7.

50. As Sanday and Headlam noted long ago, the sense of δεδικαίωται is still forensic: "'is declared righteous, acquitted from guilt.' The idea is that of a master claiming legal possession of a slave: proof being put in that the slave is dead, the verdict must needs be that the claims of law are satisfied and that he is no longer answerable; Sin loses its suit." Sanday and Headlam, *Romans*, 159.

First, those who are baptized with Christ are entombed in the waters of judgment with him and raised with him from those same waters to walk in the life that God promised. Paul evokes the water-death-life motif from Israel's Scriptures, but he reconfigures it around baptism-death-life with Christ. Just as God judged sinful humanity in the waters of the flood and defeated Israel's enemies in the waters of the Red Sea, he judges and delivers the believer in Christ's death. Even more, just as God brought Israel through the water of the Jordan River to inherit the promised land, God brings the beliver thorugh the waters of baptism with Jesus to inherit resurrection life. This is what death and burial with Christ in baptism entails. Therefore, the believer cannot remain in the domain of sin anymore than ancient Israel remained in Egypt after God brought them out of bondage through the waters of the Red Sea and into the promised land through the waters of the Jordan River.

Second, the purpose of death and resurrection with Christ in baptism is so that believers might walk with God and before God in the life that he promised in Israel's Scriptures. As noted above, Paul combines the OT metaphor of "walking" with the promise of "newness" (Rom 6:4). The "walking" metaphor of the Hebrew Bible has two dimensions: (1) walking in God's commands results in blessing and life; and (2) not walking in God's commands results in curse and death. Paul reconfigures this two-dimeonsional metaphor so that blessing and life is determined by death and resurrection with Christ rather than obedience to the Mosaic Law.[51] The referent of "life" in Rom 6:4 is largely determined by the multifaceted promise of newness in Isaiah and Jeremiah. In Isaiah, the promise of newness includes God making his people a light to the nations, making a way for his people in the wilderness, doing new and hidden things, and ultimately creating a new heavens and earth. In Jeremiah, God promises a "new" covenant with his people which is marked by forgiveness and a heartfelt obedience to God. In short, this is "eschatological" life in resurrected life with Christ.[52] Of course, as the wider context of the section in Romans makes clear, this is no overrealized eschatological experience. Tribulations abound for those raised to walk in newness of life, because they live in a world subjected to futility and teeming with inimical forces all while longing for the hope of a redeemed body in which sin no longer dwells.[53]

Third, Paul grounds the hope that believers will share in the likeness of Christ's resurrection in the crucifixion of the "old Adamic man" with Christ. To be sure, Rom 6:6 does not qualify the phrase "our old man" with "Adamic." Nevertheless, as noted

---

51. This is not to suggest that the believer's obedience to ethical demands are optional in Paul's thought. To the contrary, the rhetorical thrust of Rom 6:1–23 is that baptism with Christ is a kind of death to immorality. As Paul puts in Rom 6:11, "In this way consider yourselves dead to sin but alive to God in Christ."

52. As Seifrid puts it, "The obedience of believers is a 'walking in the newness which is [eschatological] life.' The resurrection of Christ is distributed to us here and now in the form of service to God." Seifrid, *Christ Our Righteousness*, 72.

53. See Rom 7:7–25; 8:18–39.

above, the phrase should be read against the intertextual backdrop of Gen 2–3. The old Adamic man, along with the entire cosmos, is enslaved to sin and death. Those powers are defeated in Christ's crucifixion in which believers share. The entire human being ("body of sin;" τὸ σῶμα τῆς ἁμαρτίας) who was ruled by sin is freed from that enslavement through sharing in Christ's crucifixion.

Fourth, the one who died through crucifixion with Christ has been vindicated from the enemy of sin in the same way God vindicated figures oppressed by enemies in Israel's Scriptures (Rom 6:7). The verb δεδικαίωται retains its forensic force when it is read against this intertextual backdrop. Those who die with Christ are freed and shown to be in the right against the power of sin.

To summarize up to this point, Romsans 6:1–11 is Paul's response to the false inference that believers should remain in the domain of sin since God's grace abounds where sin abounds (Rom 5:20–21). The thrust of Paul's response revolves around the believer's participation in Christ's death and resurrection. Simply put, believers cannot remain in the domain of sin (τῇ ἁμαρτίᾳ, Rom 6:1), because their death with the buried and crucified Christ in baptism frees them and vindicates them from the enemy of sin. Instead of remaining in sin, they are already experiencing a forestaste of eschatological life through the risen Christ. The thrust of Paul's argument is enhanced when read against the intertextual backdrop that I outlined above.

Romans 6:12–14

> (6:12–14) Therefore, do not let sin reign in your mortal body so as to obey its desires, nor present your members as instruments of unrighteousness to sin, but present yourselves to God as those alive from the dead and your members as instruments of righteousness to God. For sin will not lord over you; for you are not under the law but under grace.

The inferential conjunction (οὖν) and shift to the imperative mood in v. 12, "let sin not reign (βασιλευέτω)," marks a transition in Paul's argument. He issues multiple admonitions that his Roman recipients must not serve sin. He grounds the admonitions in the fact that sin no longer rules over them since they are under grace and not law. These three verses contain a few OT pre-texts which need to be considered: (1) the personification of sin based on descriptions of OT enemies; and (2) sin's use of the Mosaic Law.

Suggested Pre-Texts in Romans 6:12–14

Hübner lists one pre-text: Ps 111:10 LXX (Rom 6:12).[54] Neither Nestle-Aland 28th ed., Hays, or Seifrid discuss any pre-texts for these three verses.

---

54. Hübner, Hübner, *Vetus Testamentum in Novo*, 2:94.

Intertextual Analysis of Romans 6:12–14

We have noted at several points already that Paul personifies sin as a power, and his personfication echoes Israel's Scriptures of various enemies, mainly geo-political ones.[55] In Rom 5:12–14, Paul describes both sin and death as entities that "entered" (εἰσῆλθεν) the world spreading to all people. Once again, his allusions to Adam and the Gen 3 narrative imply a close, though unspecified, connection between the serpent in the garden and the sin that entered the world. In Rom 6:1–11, Paul continues this personification in various ways: (1) sin is a location/dominion (τῇ ἁμαρτίᾳ, 6:1); (2) sin rules over the "body" (τὸ σῶμα τῆς ἁμαρτίας, 6:6); (3) one needs to be justified/vindicated from sin (δεδικαίωται ἀπὸ τῆς ἁμαρτίας, 6:7); and (4) deliverance from sin's power requires death (6:2, 10–11). In short, as noted above, the intertextual subtext of this personification indicates that sin is somehow tied to the serpent, a place of enslavement like ancient Egypt, and an enemy such as Pharaoh and or enemies described in the Psalms. The personification of sin in vv. 12–14, like its personification prior to this point in the letter, continues to echo Israel's Scriptures.

To begin, in v. 12, Paul describes sin as having "desires" (ἐπιθυμία) which evokes the prohibition against coveting in the garden and the Mosaic Law. Paul admonishes the Romans, "Therefore, do not let sin reign in your mortal body so as to obey its desires (εἰς τὸ ὑπακούειν ταῖς ἐπιθυμίαις αὐτοῦ)."[56] Although Paul does not pause at this point to explain how sin operates with its own desires, it is crystal clear in Rom 7 "What then shall we say? Is the law sin? May it never be; but I would not have known sin except through the law; for I was not knowing coveting (ἐπιθυμίαν) except the law was saying, 'You shall not covet (οὐκ ἐπιθυμήσεις).' But sin having seized the opportunity through the commandment produced in me all coveting (πᾶσαν ἐπιθυμίαν); for without the law sin is dead" (Rom 7:7–8). Simply put, sin uses the divine prohibition against coveting to produce coveting in the one who hears the prohibition.

Of course, as I will discuss further in the next chapter, the prohibition against coveting has a thick intertextual referent which is first echoed here in Rom 6:12. Both Gen 3 and Exod 20 contain prohibitions against coveting. In the former pre-text, the prohibition against coveting is implied in Gen 2:16–17 which the serpent then takes advantage of in Gen 3:1–7. Coveting is in full swing with Eve's assessment of the tree, "And the woman saw (εἶδεν) that the tree was good for eating and pleasing to look at with the eyes (ἀρεστὸν τοῖς ὀφθαλμοῖς) and it is beautiful to consider (ὡραῖον ἐστιν τοῦ κατανοῆσαι), and having taken from its fruit she ate; and she gave it to her husband with her, and he ate" (Gen 3:6). The narrator's emphasis on what Eve

---

55. The first explicit indication is found in Rom 3:9, "For we already charged that both Jews and Greek are all under sin (ὑφ' ἁμαρτίαν)." Once again, for extensive analysis of the personification of sin in Romans, see Dodson, *The Powers of Personification*.

56. Jewett notes that the phrase εἰς τὸ ὑπακούειν ταῖς ἐπιθυμίαις αὐτοῦ in Rom 6:12 is a hapax legomenon in the NT which reflects "Paul's distinctive view of sin's domination of the old age." Jewett, *Romans*, 409.

saw and desired anticipates the prohibition against coveting in the Mosaic Law. For example, the prohibition in Exod 20:17 assumes that coveting is tied to seeing what others have "You shall not covet (תחמד/ἐπιθυμήσεις) your neighbor's wife. You shall not covet (תחמד/ἐπιθυμήσεις) your neighbor's house nor his field nor his servant nor his female servant nor his ox nor his donkey nor any of his cattle nor any possesions of your neighbor."⁵⁷ Both versions of the prohibition are echoed in Paul's reference to to sin's desires/lusts. The *volume* is low to moderate based on the same shared use of ἐπιθυμία/ἐπιθυμέω.

These two pre-texts are *conxtextually consistent* with Paul's argument here and larger sections of the letter. Rom 5:12–7:25 contains several references to both the Adamic narrative and the Mosaic Law.⁵⁸ Paul reconfigures these pre-texts around a personified enemy of sin who, like the serpent, uses the prohibition against coveting to enslave those who hear it. These two pre-texts also pass the test of *recurrence* as both are alluded to or cited elsewhere in the letter. With respect to the *history of interpretation*, Fitzmyer notes "Here again *hamartia* is the personified active force that came into human history with Adam, has reigned over human beings up to the time of Jesus' coming, and seeks to continue to regin, by enticing Christians too."⁵⁹

A second echo stems from the way Paul characterizes sin as something to which one can present their members as "instruments of unrighteousness (ὅπλα ἀδικίας)" (Rom 6:13). Paul continues his admonition, "Nor present your members (τὰ μέλη ὑμῶν) as instruments of unrighteousness (ὅπλα ἀδικίας) to sin (τῇ ἁμαρτίᾳ), but present yourselves to God as those alive from the dead and your members (τὰ μέλη ὑμῶν) as instruments of righteousness (ὅπλα δικαιοσύνης) to God (τῷ θεῷ)." Paul likens limbs/parts of a body (μέλη) as either instruments used for the purpose of unrighteousness (ὅπλα ἀδικίας) or for the purpose of righetousenss (ὅπλα δικαιοσύνης).⁶⁰ He juxtaposes two entities to which these "instruments" can be presented (παρίστημι), "to sin (τῇ ἁμαρτίᾳ)" or "to God (τῷ θεῷ)." It is in this juxtaposition that one finds an echo of an OT idiom in which earthly and heavenly servants present themselves before God for service.

The main indicator of this echo is the phrase "present yourselves to God (παραστήσατε ἑαυτοὺς τῷ θεῷ)." This kind of command occurs in the Mosaic Law, particularly as it relates to the tribe of Levi. For example, Levitical priests are commanded to present themselves for service before God "In that time the Lord separated the tribe of Levi to bear the ark of the covenant of the Lord, to stand (παρεστάναι) before the Lord (ἔναντι κυρίου) to serve (λειτουργεῖν) and to pray (ἐπεύχεσθαι) in his

57. Cf. Exod 20:17 and Deut 5:21.

58. See, e.g., Rom 5:15–19; 7:1–16; 7:7–25.

59. Fitzmyer, *Romans*, 446. Surprisingly, many interpreters do not consider the link between the Adamic narrative, the Mosaic prohibition against coveting, and Paul's description of sin in Rom 6:12.

60. The genitives in the expressions ὅπλα ἀδικίας and ὅπλα δικαιοσύνης indicate purpose. On this point, see Schreiner, *Romans*, 324.

name until this day" (Deut 10:8).[61] Additionally, in his apocalyptic vision, Zechariah sees four chariots/winds presenting themselves to God for service "These are the four winds of heaven, they are going out to stand before the Lord (παραστῆναι τῷ κυρίῳ) of all the earth" (Zech 6:5).[62] Similarly, the heavenly counsel in Job describes the sons of God/angels as presenting themselves before God in service to him, "And behold the angels of God came to stand before the Lord (παραστῆναι ἐνώπιον τοῦ κυρίου), and the devil was with them" (Job 1:6).[63] Eljiah describes himself as someone who presents himself to God for service, "And Elijah the prophet, the Thesbite of Thesbae of Galaad said to Achaab 'As the Lord God of hosts, the God of Israel lives, before whom I stand (παρέστην ἐνώπιον αὐτοῦ), there will not these years dew and rain except by the word of my mouth'" (1 Kgs 17:1).[64]

The *volume* of this idiom is moderate to high based on the combination of the verb παρίστημι and the dative τῷ θεῷ.[65] That Paul evokes this OT idiom is also indicated by the *contextual consistency* between pre-texts and text.[66] When the idiom occurs in the OT, it often appears in contexts where either earthly or heavenly figures are presenting themselves before Israel's God to serve and worship him. Idolatry functions as the antithesis of presenting one's self to God for service. Prohibitions in the Mosaic Law make this clear such as, "You shall not make for yourselves gods made by human hands nor idols nor shall you erect a pillar nor shall you set up a stone as an object which one fixes their eye on in your land so that you worship it (προσκυνῆσαι αὐτῷ); I am the Lord your God" (Lev 26:1).[67] Worshipping and serving other gods kindled God's wrath against ancient Israel. As the Deuteronomic warning expresses it, "You shall not worship them (οὐ προσκυνήσεις) nor serve them (οὐδὲ μὴ λατρεύσῃς), for I am the Lord your God, a zealous God giving back the sins of the fathers upon children unto the third and fourth generation to those who hate me" (Deut 5:9).[68] Similarly, in our Romans text, Paul exhorts his recipients to present their "members" as instruments of righteousness to God (τῷ θεῷ) rather than present them to sin (ἁμαρτίᾳ).[69] Presenting one's self is tantamount to an act of worship. As Paul puts it later in the letter, "Therefore, I encourage you, brothers, through the mercies of God to present (παραστῆσαι) your bodies as a living sacrifice, holy and acceptable

---

61. See also the use of παρίστημι in relation to Levitical priests in Deut 17:12; 18:5; 21:5.

62. See also Zech 4:14.

63. Job 1:6 MT contains "sons of God" (בני האלהים) rather than angels. See also the use of παρίστημι in Job 2:1.

64. See also the use of παρίστημι in 1 Kgs 18:15; 2 Kgs 3:14; 5:16.

65. In the LXX, the dative τῷ θεῷ is often preceded by other verbs of service such as λατρεύω.

66. See also the use of παρίστημι in Ps LXX 5:4.

67. See also Exod 20:5; 23:24; 32:8; 34:14; Num 25:2; Deut 4:19; 5:9; 8:19; 11:16; 17:3; 29:26; 30:17.

68. See also Josh 23:16.

69. Haacker notes that μέλη (Glieder) should remind one of Rom 3:10–18 where those under the power of sin use body "members" such as mouths and feet to deceive and kill. Paul uses various Psalms of Lament to make this point. See Haacker, *Der Brief des Paulus an die Römer*, 160.

to God (τῷ θεῷ), as your spiritual act of service" (Rom 12:2).[70] Paul reconfigures this OT idiom so that those who are "alive from the dead" in Christ must and can present themselves to God. Paul explains that their ability to do so stems from the fact that sin does not "lord over" (οὐ κυριεύσει) the believer, because they are not "under law (ὑπὸ νόμον)" but "under grace (ὑπὸ χάριν)." (Rom 6:14).

This brings us to the third pre-text in Rom 6:12–14 signalled by the way Paul juxtaposes the prepositional phrases "under law" (ὑπὸ νόμον) and "under grace" (ὑπὸ νόμον).[71] The former phrase is theological shorthand for a situation prior to the eschatological dawn in Christ.[72] "Under the Law" is a situation characterized by sin's use of the Mosaic Law to enslave and kill. Obviously, Paul does not mention specific commands here; however, he has in view more than ceremonial laws or "identity markers" such as circumcision.[73] This is clear from OT commands that Paul explicitly evokes in the letter. For example, when Paul expands on his description of how sin uses the law in Rom 7, he uses the prohibition against coveting as an example "For I would not have known sin except the law was saying 'You shall not covet' (οὐκ ἐπιθυμήσεις)" (Rom 7:7). Additionally, in the typological comparison of Adam and Christ in Rom 5:15–19, Paul alludes to God's prohibition against eating from the tree of the knowledge of good and evil (Gen 2:16–17; Rom 5:17). In this way, "under the law" spans the time of Adam, Moses, and up to the death and resurrection of Christ. It does not follow that grace (χάρις) entirely lacked a role prior to God's work in Christ. Paul has already explained that God graciously justified Abraham.[74] Nevertheless, in Christ, an eschatological shift has taken place.[75] It is a shift from being ruled (κυριεύω) by the power of sin which uses the law to deceive and kill its slaves to being ruled by a God who graciously forgives and justifies in Christ with the result that believers are enslaved to righteousness. Such is the essence of being "under the law" or "under grace."

Finally, Rom 6:14 evokes the OT motif of God handing people over to enemies. This echo is closely related to the phrases "under the law" and "under grace." When Paul explains why his recipients should present themselves to God for service, he asserts "For sin will not lord over you (ὑμῶν οὐ κυριεύσει)" (Rom 6:14a). This personification

---

70. See once the combination of παρίστημι and τῷ θεῷ.

71. On the importance of theological abbreviation ὑπὸ νόμον in Paul's thought, see Betz, *Galatians*.

72. See Witherington, *Paul's Letter to the Romans*, 164.

73. As is well-known, Dunn often interprets Paul's references to the Mosaic Law as bearing a social stamp, though, despite some depictions of Dunn, not exclusively so. As McKnight and Oropeza have recently noted in summarizing Dunn's interpretation of "works of the law," "Dunn has repeatedly clarified that 'works of the law' has a broader meaning than the boundary markers." McKnight and Oropeza, *Perspectives on Paul*, 8.

74. See, e.g., Rom 4:4, 16.

75. Barrett helpfully reminds us that Paul's exhortations are thoroughly eschatological in nature. Barrett observes, "The death and resurrection of Jesus were eschatological events—the messianic affliction and the manifestation of God's glory. The practice, and efficacy, of baptism were rooted in these eschatological events; baptism is not simply a religious rite, but springs out of the fact that an hour has struck on the world clock." Barrett, *Romans*, 129.

of sin echoes a Psalm that Paul has already drawn from in Rom 1:23, namely Ps 105 LXX.[76] Specifically, the phrase "sin will not lord over you (ὑμῶν οὐ κυριεύσει)" echoes Ps 105:41 LXX "And he handed them over into the hands of enemies, and those who hate them lorded over them (ἐκυρίευσαν αὐτῶν)." The *volume* of the echo is low, because the only link is the shared use of κυριεύω.[77]

However, the *contextual consistency* is higher. Both the psalmist and Paul identify God as the one who places rebellious people under the power of their enemies. Paul reconfigures this divine activity by placing sin, along with its use of the law, in the slot occupied by the foreign nation to which God handed Israel over in Ps 105 LXX. This reconfiguration fits with what Paul has already articulated in the letter. In Rom 1:18–3:20, Paul laid out how God righteously placed Jew and Gentile "under sin" (ὑφ᾽ ἁμαρτίαν, Rom 3:9). Moreover, in Rom 5:12–19, Paul broadens the reader's perspective on this divine activity when he juxtaposes Adam and Christ. God places the former figure under the power of sin and death so that these two enemies rule over (βασιλεύω/κυριεύω) Adam and all who come after him, both Jew and Gentile.[78] Yet, due to baptism with the crucified and risen Jesus, the Romans are no longer under these powers. That is why Paul can exhort, "Let sin not reign (μὴ βασιλευέτω ἡ ἁμαρτία) in your mortal bodies" (Rom 6:12). It is also why he can command the Romans to present themselves to God rather than to sin for service.

Interpretive Impact of Pre-Texts in Romans 6:12–14

When we consider the interplay between the pre-texts and text, three points of resonance emerge which impact the interpretation of Paul's argument in specific ways.

First, sin is a power at work in the mortal body (ἐν τῷ θνητῷ σώματι) of believers which uses the same covetous desires (ἐπιθύμια) marshalled against Adam and Israel. However, Paul reconfigures past obedience to sin's desires by denying its ruling power. The believer's death and resurrection with Christ in baptism frees them from covetous desires which sin used against Adam, ancient Israel, and all of those who are "under the law." That is why Paul can exhort the Romans, "Let sin not rule in your mortal body so that you obey its desires" (Rom 6:12).

Second, "to present" (παρίστημι) one's self to God is to serve and worship him rather than to continue in the kind of idolatrous worship that God condemned in Israel's Scriptures. Presenting one's self to someone, or something, is a combined act of service and worship in keeping with the OT idiom reviewed above. This point is consistent with the question that Paul poses in Rom 6:16 "Do you not know that to whom you present yourselves (παριστάνετε ἑαυτούς) as slaves for obedience, you are slaves to whom you obey, either of sin resulting in death or of obediene resulting

---

76. See the analysis in volume 1.
77. Cf. use of κυριεύω in Rom 6:9; 7:1; 14:9.
78. See the use of βασιλεύω in Rom 5:14, 17, 21.

in righteousness?" The service (δοῦλος) that Paul has in view in Rom 6:12–14 and 6:15–23 is not detached from worship. Rather, given the OT idiom of presenting one's self to God and or an idol, combined with Paul's larger doxological concerns expressed in pericopes such as Rom 1:18–32 and 12:1–2, service to God (τῷ θεῷ) or to sin (τῇ ἁμαρτίᾳ) is an act of devotion and worship to one or the other.[79]

Third, the lordship of sin over all people since the time of Adam has ended, because God has placed believers under his gracious reign in Christ rather than keep them under the rule of sin which uses the law against them and which they cannot keep.[80] This is how one should unpack the theological abbreviations "under grace" (ὑπὸ χάριν) and "under law" (ὑπὸ νόμον) in Rom 6:14. The Romans could and should present themselves and their members to God as instruments of righteousness, because the crucified and risen Christ graciously rules over them rather than the tyrannical and deadly rule of sin which uses the law against them.

Romans 6:15–23

(6:15–23) What then? Shall we sin, because we are not under the law but under grace? May it never be. Do you not know that to whom you present yourselves as slaves for obedience, you are slaves to whom you obey, whether of sin resulting in death or of obedience resulting in righteousness? But thanks be to God that although you were slaves of sin, you have become obedient from the heart to the pattern of teaching to which you were handed over. And having been freed from sin you were enslaved to righteousness. I speak humanly because of the weakness of your flesh. For just as you presented your members as slaves to uncleanliness and to lawlessness resulting in lawlessness, in this way now present your members as slaves to righteousness resulting in sanctification. For when you were slaves of sin, you were free with respect to righteousness. Therefore, what fruit were you having then? About which things you are now ashamed, for the outcome of those things is death. But now having been freed from sin and having been enslaved to God you have your fruit resulting in sanctification, and the outcome is eternal life. For the wages of sin is death, but the gift of God is eternal life in Christ Jesus our Lord.

Paul once again anticipates a false inference based on his previous statement.[81] This time the erroneous conclusion is that believers should go on sinning since they are "under grace" and not "under the law." Paul responds to this false inference through a protracted use of a slavery (δοῦλος) metaphor. He underscoes the divergent outcomes of one's obedience to sin or to God. Obedience to the latter is predicated on

---

79. The noun δοῦλος occurs six times in Rom 6:15–23.

80. With respect to the relationshiop between being "under sin" and "under the law," Seifrid observes "Freedom from sin has its basis in freedm from the law." Seifrid, *Christ Our Righteousness*, 115.

81. Cf. Rom 5:20–6:1.

what God gives in Christ (Rom 6:23). As Paul argues against another false inference, he draws from Israel's Scriptures in a variety of ways. Therefore, we must consider the interplay between Paul's text and the pre-texts from Israel's Scriptures which inform the argument here in various ways.

Suggested Pre-Texts in Romans 6:15-23

Hübner lists the following pre-texts: Rom 6:16 (Josh 22:20; 2 Kgs 14:6; 2 Chr 25:4; Prov 24:9; Jer 38:39 (31:30 MT); 6:19 (Lev 11:44, 45; 19:2); 6:21-22 (Deut 30:15-20).[82]

Neither Nestle-Aland 28th ed., Hays, or Seifrid engage any specific OT pre-texts related to Rom 6:15-23.[83]

Intertextual Analysis of Romans 6:15-23

It needs to be noted from the outset that in Rom 6:15-16 Paul's use of "present yourselves as servants (παριστάνετε ἑαυτοὺς δούλους)," the phrase "under the law (ὑπὸ νόμον)," and the phrase "under grace (ὑπὸ χάριν)" overlap with 6:12-14 and its intertextual subtext which I discussed above. Therefore, I will not rehash that discussion here. In any case, as Paul's argument unfolds in these verses, other echoes emerge which shed interpretive light on the arugment.

Romans 6:15-16 and Echoes of Death

To begin, when Paul explains that death is the outcome for being a slave of sin, he evokes an OT motif which identifies sin as the cause of death.[84] As he responds to the false inference that believers should sin given the fact that they are under the reign of grace rather than the law, Paul rhetorically asks "Do you not know that to whom you present yourselves as slaves for obedience, you are slaves to whom you obey, whether of sin resulting in death (ἁμαρτίας εἰς θάνατον) or of obedience resulting in righteousness?" (Rom 6:16). The phrase "of sin resulting in death" (ἁμαρτίας εἰς θάνατον) evokes pre-texts that make an explicit connection between sin and death.

Given Paul's discussion of Adam in Rom 5:12-19, one pre-text evoked here is the command and accompanying warning from Gen 2:17 "But from the tree of knowing

---

82. Hübner, *Vetus Testamentum in Novo*, 2:94-97.

83. Even in his response to Beker's suggestion that Rom 5-8 contains a dearth of intertextual interaction, Hays does not identify any echoes in Rom 6. See Hays, *Conversion of the Imagination*, 181-82.

84. Interpreters often look to Greco-Roman discussions of slavery to locate the source of Paul's imagery. My intertextual analysis of Pau's slavery language is not an attempt to deny the historical points of contact that many interpreters identify. See, e.g., Witherington, *Romans*, 170. Rather, as I have noted elsewhere in this study, in the spirit of Hengel's "cross-fertilization" description of the first-century world, Paul's slavery language is shaped both by imperial slavery and Israel's Scriptures. See Hengel, *Judaism and Hellenism*.

good and evil, you shall not eat from it; and in whatever day you should eat from it, you will surely die (θανάτῳ ἀποθανεῖσθε)." Similarly, the Mosaic Law warns "Fathers will not die for their children, and sons will not die for their fathers; each one will die in his own sin (τῇ ἑαυτοῦ ἁμαρτίᾳ ἀποθανεῖται)" (Deut 24:16). This warning is echoed in the Achan narrative (Josh 7:). When Achan's sin is recalled in the latter chapters of Joshua, the description makes death the result of sin "Behold, did not Achar (Achan) the son of Zara commit a transgression from the accursed thing and wrath came upon all the congregation of Israel? And this was not one lone person; and this one did not die alone in his own sin (ἀπέθανεν τῇ ἑαυτοῦ ἁμαρτίᾳ) did he?" (Josh 22:20).[85]

While these pre-texts are not specifically echoed in Rom 6:15–23, they likely shaped the way that Paul articulates the link between sin and death. He combines this OT motif of sin as the cause of death with the metaphor of slavery.

Romans 6:15–23 and Echoes of Slavery

This brings us to the second intertextual consideration in Rom 6:15–23, namely the referent of the slavery (δοῦλος) metaphor. One question that arises at this point is whether the referent of the metaphor is first-cenutry imperial slavery or slavery as it is described in Jewish literature.[86] With respect to the former, Witherington suggests

> In his use of slavery language here he is drawing on the fact that people in the Roman Empire did indeed often volunteer to become slaves because in many cases it gave themselves and their families a more secure living than they would have otherwise. There may indeed have been those in Paul's audience in Rome who had actually done this, for Rome was the slave capital of the empire, a place where more domestic slave labor was used than probably anywhere else in the Mediterranean crescent.[87]

Like Witherington, other interpreters note the voluntary nature of many instances of first-century slavery, and they identify it as the referent of Paul's metaphor.[88] Other

---

85. See also the echo of Deut 24:16 in 2 Kgs 14:6 and 2 Chr 25:4. See also the causal link between sin and death in Prov 24:9; Jer 38:30 (31:30 MT); and Ezek 3:20.

86. See a helpful sketch of the Jewish literature background in Goodrich, "From Slaves of Sin to Slaves of God," 509–30. He reviews proposals by Horsley, Byron, and Holland. Goodrich ultimately concludes that Paul's metaphor is "an extension of a Jewish theological motif" which was "significantly influenced by Greco-Roman notions of domestic slavery."

87. Witherington, *Paul's Letter to the Romans*, 170.

88. Jewett likewise underscores this dynamic observing, "Severe economic necessity was the usual motive of selling oneself, although there were cases of selling oneself or one's family members into particular forms of slavery such as imperial service or service to a distinguished patron in the hope of economic and social advancement. This social reality is the basis of the comparison Paul draws with service to sin: those who voluntarily place themselves into the position of slavery in fact become actual 'slaves to what you obey.'" Jewett, *Romans*, 416. Additionally, drawing on the work of Dale Martin, Thiselton explains "Since Paul now uses the metaphor of being 'obedient' slaves of Christ, it is worth noting again the important research on slavery in Martin. Slavery could involve

interpreters acknowledge that Israel's Scriptures may in fact inform the metaphor. For example, Schreiner suggests "The liberation of the Roman Christians from the power of sin fulfills God's promises of liberation made to Israel in the OT. Israel would no longer be in exile when their sins were forgiven and they were free from bondage to other nations. Believers in Christ have now experienced the freedom and joy promised in the OT."[89] I will return to the referent of the metaphor after considering the larger intertextual subtext of Paul's argument. It is sufficient to note here that it is not necessary to limit Paul to one historical antecedent in his use of slavery language.

After making it clear in v. 16 that one either slavishly obeys (δοῦλοί ἐστε ᾧ ὑπακούετε) sin resulting in death or obedience resulting in righteousness, Paul breaks out into spontaneous doxology "But thanks be to God that although you were slaves of sin, you have become obedient from the heart to the pattern of teaching to which you were handed over. And having been freed from sin you were enslaved to righteousness" (Rom 6:16–17). Paul's doxology contains three echoes.

First, Paul's statement "you have become obedient from the heart (ὑπηκούσατε ἐκ καρδίας)" echoes the kind of obedience demanded and promised in Israel's Scriptures. One of the most prominent examples occurs in Deut 30:

> And it will be when all these things come upon you, blessing and curse, which I have set before your face, and you will receive them in your heart (εἰς τὴν καρδίαν σου) among all the nations, wherever the Lord might scatter you there, and you shall return to the Lord your God and obey his voice (ὑπακούσῃ τῆς φωνῆς αὐτοῦ) according to all things, as much as I command you today, from all your heart (ἐξ ὅλης τῆς καρδίας σου) and from all your soul (ἐξ ὅλης τῆς ψυχῆς σου), also the Lord will heal your sins (τὰς ἁμαρτίας σου) and he will have mercy on you and again he will gather from all the nations, to which the Lord has scattered you there. If your dispersion should be from one end of heaven unto the end of heaven, from there the Lord your God will give you, and from there the Lord your God will receive you; and the Lord your God will bring you into the land, which your fathers inherited, and you will inherit it; and he will do good to you and he will make you more numerous than your fathers. And the Lord will circumcise/clean (ומל/περικαθαριεῖ) your heart (τὴν καρδίαν σου) and the heart of your seed (τὴν καρδίαν τοῦ σπέρματός σου) to love (ἀγαπᾶν) the Lord your God from all your heart (ἐξ ὅλης τῆς καρδίας σου) and from all of your soul (ἐξ ὅλης τῆς ψυχῆς σου), in order that you might live (Deut 30:1–6).

---

oppressive miserty. Torture and corporal punishment could occur." Thieslton also acknowledges that slavery could be voluntary. Thiselton, Discovering *Romans*, 150. See also Haacker, *Der Brief des Paulus die Römer*, 161–62; Martin, *Slavery as Salvation*, 15–22, 50–85, 122–24, and 145–49. Schottroff, "Schreckensherrschaft," 500–507.

89. Schreiner, *Romans*, 334.

The *volume* of this echo is moderate to high based on the overlap between ὑπακούω and the prepositional phrase ἐκ καρδίας/ἐξ ὅλης τῆς καρδίας.⁹⁰

We find *contextual consistency* not only at the point of obedience from the heart but also at the point of exiled/enslaved people. Deut 30 envisions a time in Israel's history when the nation would be exiled and enslaved outside the promised land. Their return would be marked by an obedience and love for God that was "from the whole heart (ἐξ ὅλης τῆς καρδίας)."⁹¹ God enables the obedience by circumcising/cleansing their hearts (Deut 30:6). Paul likewise compares his Roman recipients to those who "were slaves of sin (ἦτε δοῦλοι τῆς ἁμαρτίας)" but have since "been freed from sin (ἐλευθερωθέντες ἀπὸ τῆς ἁμαρτίας)." Their liberation, like that of exiled Israel, resulted in obedience from the heart. Moreover, in keeping with the Deuteronomic pre-text, Paul underscores the divine causation behind the obedience through his used of the passive "you were handed over (παρεδόθητε)" and "having been freed (ἐλευθερωθέντες)."⁹² This suggested pre-text also passes the test of *recurrence*, because Paul cites Deut 30:12–13 in Rom 10:7–8. Even more, we have already seen Paul's use of Deuteronomic obedience "from the heart" in Rom 2:5, 15, and 29.⁹³ Paul is once again stressing a kind of "deeply felt and deeply motivated" internal action.⁹⁴ Surprisingly, within the *history of interpretation*, many interpreters do not recognize this pre-text as part of Paul's argument.⁹⁵ Nevertheless, there are some exceptions.⁹⁶

Given the echo of Deut 30 in Rom 6:17–18, it follows the Paul is evoking an exile motif to explain that Christians in Rome have been freed from slavery to sin and handed over to an obedience from the heart. Paul not only draws this motif from Pentateuchal texts such as Deut 30 but prophetic pre-texts such as Isaiah and Jeremiah. The prophetic material certainly contains exilic references taken up to articulate the promise of a future deliverance. One Isaianic pre-text that may inform Paul's metaphor stems from Isa 59, "And the deliverer (ὁ ῥυόμενος) will come on account of Zion and he will turn ungodliness (ἀσεβείας) from Jacob."⁹⁷ This messianic figure (ὁ ῥυόμενος) delivers Israel specifically from ungodliness/sin.⁹⁸ Similarly, in Jer 24:1–10,

---

90. The obvious difference between Deut 30:2, 6, 10 and Rom 6:16 is the absence of ὅλης in the latter.

91. The phrase ἐξ ὅλης τῆς ψυχῆς σου is the rendering of the phrase בכל לבבך in Deut 30:2, 6, and 10. See the phrase also Deut 4:29; 6:5; 10:12; 26:16.

92. See Schreiner, *Romans*, 334.

93. See the analysis in volume 1.

94. Dunn, *Romans*, 1:343.

95. See, e.g., the absence of this pre-text in the discussions by Cranfield, *Romans*, 1:323–24; Matera, *Romans*, 154–58; Hultgren, *Paul's Letter to the Romans*, 261–63.

96. See Byron, *Slavery Metaphors*; Holland, *Contours of Pauline Theology*, 82; Wright, *Justification*, 230; Wright, "New Exodus, New Inheritance: The Narrative Substructure of Romans 3–8," 26–35.

97. Cf. the difference with Isa 59:20 MT. We will discuss this difference later when consider the citation of Isa 59:20 in Rom 11:26–27.

98. See the description of Israel's sin in Isa 59:1–15. Cf. Matt 1:21.

the prophet sees a vision of good and bad figs. The good figs are those whom God promised to bring out of exile, an act which would result in heartfelt obedience "And I will give to them a heart so that they know me that I am the Lord, and they will be my people, and I will be their God, because they will turn to me from their whole heart (ἐξ ὅλης τῆς καρδίας αὐτῶν)." (Jer 24:7).[99] For Paul, the prophetic promises that God would deliver his people from sin and give them obedience "from the heart" is realized in Christ. It is realized through the obedience from the heart which is faith in Christ.[100]

A second echo in the doxology (Rom 6:17–18) emanates from Paul's expression "to the pattern of teaching (τύπον διδαχῆς) to which you were handed over (παρεδόθητε)" (Rom 6:17).[101] Before I discuss the intertextual element of the phrase, it is necessary to address the exegetical difficulties associated with "pattern of teaching" (τύπον διδαχῆς). The phrase τύπον διδαχῆς has caused not a little consternation among interpreters.[102] Some interpreters locate the referent in baptismal catechesis.[103] Others stress that the phrase refers to "the way of life demanded by the gospel."[104] As Murray suggests, "There is stress upon the ethical implications of gospel teaching."[105] It is important to remember that in the immediate context Paul contrasts being under the powers of sin/law (ὑπὸ νόμον) and grace (ὑπὸ χάριν) (Rom 6:14–15).[106] One either serves sin or obedience which results in righteousness (Rom 6:16). This contrast continues in v. 17 which means the phrase "form of teaching (τύπον διδαχῆς)" should be read in relation to Paul's wider contrast of the competing powers of sin

---

99. See also Ps 129:8 LXX, "And he will ransom (λυτρώσεται) Israel from all its iniquities (ἐκ πασῶν τῶν ἀνομιῶν αὐτοῦ)."

100. Cf. the use of εἰς ὑπακοὴν πίστεως in Rom 1:5. See the use of ὑπακοή in Rom 15:18; 16:19, 26. See also the use of ὑπακούω in Rom 10:16.

101. Gagnon renders the phrase "you obeyed from the heart the imprint stamped by teaching, to which (imprint) you were handed over." In this rendering of τύπον διδαχῆς, the genitive functions as a subjective genitive, though Gagnon refers to it as a genitive of source. In any case, the point is that the teaching stamps the heart. See Gagnon, "Heart of Wax," 687.

102. Longenecker summarizes four possible meanings: (1) a "Jewish form of teaching;" (2) a "'rule' or 'pattern' of early Christian teaching;" (3) a form of Christian teaching "different from other forms of Christain teaching;" and (4) Christ himself as the model for Christian living. Longenecker, *Romans*, 623–24. Jewett ultimately concludes that the phrase is an interpolation. Jewett, *Romans*, 419.

103. E.g., Matera suggests, "'The pattern of teaching' to which they were delivered refers to the teaching of the gospel that they received at baptism, a baptismal catechesis summarized in 10:9–10." Matera, *Romans*, 155. See also Byrne, *Romans*, 206; Stuhlmacher, *Romans*, 95.

104. Cranfield explains, "What is being said in v. 17b is that the persons addressed have obeyed from the heart (not merely formally but with inward commitment) that teaching (concerning the way of life demanded by the gospel—that teaching which is the mould by which their lives are to be shaped), to which they were delivered up (in their baptism?) as slaves to a new master." Cranfield, *Romans*, 1:324.

105. Murray, Romans, 232.

106. As noted above, in Rom 6:14–15, Paul describes the Romans as those who are "under grace (ὑπὸ χάριν)" rather than "under the law (ὑπὸ νόμον)." The latter phrase refers to being under the power of sin which uses the law to deceive and kill.

and grace. In this way, "form of teaching" is related to being "under grace" which is theological shorthand for God's saving work in the crucified and risen Christ who rules over sin and death.[107] Therefore, "form of teaching (τύπον διδαχῆς)" and "gospel (εὐαγγέλιον)" are synonymous here.[108] Nevertheless, since choice implies meaning, we must consider why Paul employs the phrase "form of teaching" rather than "gospel." The short answer is that Paul likens the gospel to an authority for living.[109] The combination of τύπον διδαχῆς and παρεδόθητε signals authority. God handed over the Christians in Rome to a "form/type of teaching" which imprinted itself on their hearts.[110] He freed them in Christ from sin (ἐλευθερωθέντες ἀπὸ τῆς ἁμαρτίας) and enslaved (ἐδουλώθητε) them to righteousness (Rom 6:18).

Romans 6:15–23 and Echoes of Being "Handed Over"

We can now turn our attention to a third intertextual element embedded in Paul's doxology (Rom 6:17–18). This element stems from the interrelated actions of being "handed over" (παρεδόθητε) to a pattern of teaching and being "freed" (ἐλευθερωθέντες) from sin. Many interpreters observe that Paul's use of παραδίδωμι in this context resembles the handing down of traditional teaching.[111] However, Paul does not portray the action here in typical fashion so that the traditional teaching is entrusted to the Romans.[112] Instead, the Romans are handed over to the teaching. One should not miss the way that Paul's previous uses of παραδίδωμι in the letter informs its meaning here. We have already discussed in previous chapters how Paul's use of θεός + παραδίδωμι in Rom 1:24, 26, 28, and 4:25 evokes an OT motif in which God hands over his enemies to other powers. There is no need to rehash the entire motif here.[113] Simply put, God handed over both ancient Israel and Israel's enemies to defeat and or slavery based upon their rebellion against him. This was in keeping with warnings and assurances in the Mosaic Law such as, "And I will bring upon you a sword avenging the cause of the covenant, and you will flee to your cities; and I will send out death to you, and you will be handed over (παραδοθήσεσθε) into the hands

---

107. In addition to the immediate context, the wider context of Romans and Paul's wider thought resist reducing the referent of "form of teaching" to moral behavior. As Käsemann rightly notes, "Christian obedience involves more than moral behavior. It is always oriented to faith by hearing, to which one is committed in baptism and which one simultaneously accepts from the heart and therefore radically and willingly." Käsemann, *Commentary on Romans*, 182.

108. Stuhlmacher suggests "form of teaching" in Rom 6:17 is "a matter above all of the 'gospel' akin to Pauline articulations in 1 Cor 15:1–11." See Stuhlmacher, *Paul's Letter to the Romans*, 95.

109. As Stuhlmacher puts it, "The gospel appears here in the function of a living authority which is decisive for life." Stuhlmacher, *Paul's Letter to the Romans*, 95.

110. Calvin notes, "It seems indeed to me to denote the formed image or impress of that righteousness which Christ engraves on our hearts." Calvin, *Romans*, 237.

111. Cf. the use of παραδίδωμι in 1 Cor 11:23; 15:3. See the discussion in Fitzmyer, *Romans*, 450.

112. See Hultgren, *Paul's Letter to the Romans*, 262.

113. See the analysis in volume 1.

of enemies (εἰς χεῖρας ἐχθρῶν)" (Lev 26:25).[114] Paul reconfigures this motif in Rom 1:24–32 to include all of humanity and not just ancient Israel or a foreign power from the anciet world. In short, God handed over idolatrous humanity to the power of sin. He also reconfigures the motif around the work of God in Christ whom God handed over to death for sinners (Rom 4:25; 8:32).

Along these lines, Rom 6:17–18 is yet another reconfiguration of this OT motif. Here the "handing over" is positively conceived. Rather than being handed over to the power of sin due to their idolatry and lawlessness, the Romans are handed over to a "form of teaching" (Rom 6:17). Just as God freed ancient Israel from its enemies after they had been handed over to them, God freed the Romans from sin. He then enslaved them to righteousness (Rom 6:18). Therefore, the Romans are under the "power" of a benevolent teaching and righteousness rather than the malevolent powers of sin and death.

To reiterate, none of this is to suggest that the referent of Paul's slavery metaphor (Rom 6:12–23) is unrelated to imperial slavery in the first-century. Paul makes it clear in v. 19 that by employing the slavery metaphor he is speaking "humanly (ἀνθρώπινον)." This is Paul's acknowledgment that he is drawing from a well-known feature of his Greco-Roman milieu; however, this milieu alone "may be inadequate" for understanding the slavery language.[115] Ultimately, the interpreter should not be forced to exclusively locate the referent of the metaphor in either Paul's reading of Israel's Scriptures or his Greco-Roman milieu. It is not as if Paul drew from two hermetically sealed conceptual wells. To borrow an expression from Hengel, there is "cross-fertilization" here.[116] As Cranfield notes in his reflection on the overall language and style of Romans, "Many of the words with strong LXX associations were necessarily characteristic terms of Greek-speaking Christianity from the very beginning, and, as used in Romans, have not only their OT background but also their background in the common usage of the Greek-speaking church."[117]

There are additional intertextual features to consider in Rom 6:19–23. In v. 19, Paul onces again takes up the language of presenting one's self to one of two rulers "I speak humanly because of the weakness of your flesh. For just as you presented (παρεστήσατε) your members as slaves to uncleanliness and to lawlessness resulting in lawlessness, in this way now present (παραστήσατε) your members as slaves to righteousness resulting in sanctification." As I discussed above, this presentation (παρίστημι) language echoes a combined act of service and worship in keeping with

114. For assurances that Israel's enemies would be handed over, see Deut 7:2, 23, 24.

115. Hultgren, *Paul's Letter to the Romans*, 262. Similarly, Witherington suggests "It is possible that he is indirectly making clear that he is not in fact an advocate of slavery or enslaving oneself to to some other human being in the literal sense. He is simply speaking metaphorically about slavery to sin or righteousness." Witherington, *Paul's Letter to the Romans*, 172.

116. I am playing on Hengel's famous dictum in his seminal study of the reciprocal impact of Second Temple Judiasm and Hellenistic thought. See Hengel, *Judaism and Hellenism*.

117. Cranfield, *Romans*, 1:25.

OT idiom. Priests, prophets, and angels present themselves to Israel's God in service and worship.[118] Similarly, the Romans are to present themselves "to righteousness (τῇ δικαιοσύνῃ)" which results in sanctification (εἰς ἁγιασμόν) rather than "to uncleanliness/to lawlessness (τῇ ἀκαθαρσίᾳ/τῇ ἀνομίᾳ)" which results in lawlessness (εἰς τὴν ἀνομίαν). The dative phrases τῇ δικαιοσύνῃ and τῇ ἀκαθαρσίᾳ/τῇ ἀνομίᾳ are metonymies for God and the power of sin respectively. From the outset of this argument, Paul identifies God (τῷ θεῷ) and sin (τῇ ἁμαρτίᾳ) as the rulers to whom one presents themselves (Rom 6:13).[119] Subsequent iterations of this bifurcation expand on different facets of these rulers. Presenting one's self "to righteousness (τῇ δικαιοσύνῃ)" in v. 19 represents serving the God who gives righteousness in Christ and its accompanying "fruit" (6:22). The result is sanctification. Contrastively, prior to being freed from sin and enslaved to righteousness, the Romans presented themselves to uncleanliness (τῇ ἀκαθαρσίᾳ) and lawlessness (τῇ ἀνομίᾳ). Uncleanliness is a facet of sin's power which renders one impure before God. Lawlesness is a closely related facet of sin wherein one transgresses divine commands. The result of presenting one's self to these powers is in fact a state of lawlessness.

Romans 6:15-23 and Echoes of Being Presented to God

Paul's third iteration of presenting one's self (παρίστημι) to God or sin in v. 19 echoes Israel's Scriptures in three ways.[120] First, Paul's conception of "uncleanness (ἀκαθαρσία)" as a condition of moral corruption is at least partially informed by OT pre-texts such as purity regulations laid out in the Mosaic Law and uncleanliness language employed in a variety of OT genres to describe sin.[121] The former occurs most frequently in Leviticus which contains copious restrictions to avoid contact with unclean things such as specified animals, carcasses, vessels, homes, and people.[122] Contact with unclean things made a person unclean in relation to the community and before God. Consequently, given the fact that neither unclean things nor unclean people could have contact with God, those in a state of uncleanliness were removed until the impurity was removed. Within Paul's Second Temple milieu, this kind of concern with uncleanliness became a characteristic way of describing the ritual and

---

118. Once again, see, e.g., the use of παρίστημι in Deut 10:8; 1 Kgs 17:1; Job 1:6; Zech 6:5.

119. For other personifications of ἁμαρτία in the letter, see Rom 3:9; 5:12, 13, 20, 21; 6:1, 2, 6, 22, 12, 14, 16, 17, 18, 20, 22, 23; 7:5, 7, 8, 9, 11, 13, 14, 17, 20, 23, 25; 8:2, 3, 10; 11:27.

120. Cf. Rom 6:13, 16.

121. In addition to Israel's Scriptures, we must also allow for the influence of Second Temple Jewish perceptions of cleanliness/uncleanliness on Paul's thought. Cf. other uses of ἀκαθαρσία in Rom 1:24; 2 Cor 12:21; Gal 5:19; Eph 4:19; 5:3; Col 3:5; 1 Thess 2:3; 4:7. See also the use of ἀκάθαρτος in 1 Cor 7:14; 2 Cor 6:17; Eph 5:5. See BDAG 34.

122. See the use of ἀκαθαρσία (טמאה) in Lev 5:3; 7:20, 21; 15:3, 24, 25, 26, 30, 31; 16:16, 19; 18:19; 19:23; 20:21, 25; 22:3, 4, 5. Leviticus also contains uses of ἀκάθαρτος (טמא).

ethical impurity of Gentiles.¹²³ Ethicial impurity is Paul's concern in Rom 6:19, but it includes both Jews and Gentiles.¹²⁴

Paul's concern with ethical impurity reflects the way OT writers employed Levitical descriptions of ritual uncleanliness to describe sin in ancient Israel. For example, Isaiah's prayer of penitence likens the nation's sin to a rag defiled by a menstruating woman "And all of us have become like those who are unclean (ἀκάθαρτοι), all our righteousness is like a filthy rag (ῥάκος ἀποκαθημένης); and we have fallen off as leaves because of our lawlessness (τὰς ἀνομίας), in this way the wind will carry us away" (Isa 64:5).¹²⁵ Interestingly, this Isaianic pre-text combines ἀκάθαρτος and ἀνομία just as Paul combines ἀκαθαρσία and ἀνομία in Rom 6:19.

Along these same lines, Wolter suggests that Paul's combination of ἀκαθαρσία and ἀνομία reflects the same manner (*derselben Weise*) in which Ezekiel described the uncleanliness and lawlessness of Jerusalem.¹²⁶ Ezek 36:16–38 stands out here. The prophet relays God's promise to renew Israel after its exile. The promise of renewal is juxtaposed with the nation's uncleanliness and lawlessness:

> O son of man, the house of Israel dwelled upon their land and they defiled it with their way and with their idols and with their uncleanliness (ἐν ταῖς ἀκαθαρσίαις αὐτῶν); their way was before me according to the uncleanliness of a woman indisposed by menstrual impurity (κατὰ τὴν ἀκαθαρσίαν τῆς ἀποκαθημένης) (Ezek 36:17).

> And you will remember your evil ways and your habits which were not good and you shall be offended before them because of your transgressions (ἐν ταῖς ἀνομίαις ὑμῶν) and because of your abominations (ἐπὶ τοῖς βδελύγμασιν ὑμῶν). "I will not do it because of you," says the Lord God, "It will be known to you; be ashamed (αἰσχύνθητε) and humiliated (ἐντράπητε) from your ways, O house of Israel." Thus says the Lord, "In the day, in which I will cleanse (καθαριῶ) you from all your transgressions (ἐκ πασῶν τῶν ἀνομιῶν ὑμῶν), I will settle the cities, and the deserted places will be built up" (Ezek 36:31–33).

---

123. On this point, see Jewett, *Romans*, 420. As Sanday and Hedlam note, "ἀκαθαρσία and ἀνομία fitly describe the characteristic features of Pagan life." Sandy and Hedlam, *Romans*, 169. However, since Paul places both Jew and Gentile under the power of sin, the paired terms apply to both Jew and Gentile life outside of Christ.

124. Paul makes it clear in Rom 1:18–32 and 2:17–24 that Jews and Gentiles are both ethically impure. As we shall see, Paul's combination of ἀκαθαρσία and ἀνομία is reflected in Israel's Scriptures to describe the nation's condition at various junctures such as the Babylonian invasion/captivity. As Wolter rightly notes, the combination of these two terms is not strictly a "typical Jewish perspective for Greeks (jüdischer Perspektive für Heiden typisch sind)." Wolter, *Der Brief an die Römer*, 400.

125. Cf. the use of ἀποκάθημαι to describe the uncleanliness of a menstruating woman in Lev 15:3; 20:1. See also Lev 1:17; Ezek 22:10; 36:17.

126. Wolter points to the descriptions of Jerusalem in Ezek 9:9; 22:5; 36:17; and 39:24. Wolter, *Der Brief an die Römer*, 400.

The *volume* between the Ezek 36:16–38 and Rom 6:19–23 is strong. They not only overlap with the terms ἀκαθαρσία and ἀνομία but also with αἰσχύνω/ἐπαισχύνομαι (Ezek 36:32; Rom 6:21), καρπός (Ezek 36:30; Rom 6:22), and ἁγιάζω/ἁγιασμός (Ezek 36:23).

The *contextual consistency* is strong as well. Israel's condition and God's actions in the pre-text are consistent with Paul's description of the Romans and God's actions towards them. In the former, Israel was defiled (ἀκαθαρσία) by their idolatry, and they were lawless (ἀνομία) before God. Therefore, they experienced divine wrath in the form of exile "I poured out my anger (ἐξέχεα τὸν θυμόν μου) upon them, and I dispersed them among the nations and I scattered them in countries; according to their way and according to their sin I judged (ἔκρινα) them" (Ezek 36:18–19). Even in exile they profaned the divine name (Ezek 36:20). Nevertheless, God spared them, promised to sanctify his name by transforming them, gather them in, and cleanse them (Ezek 36:21–25). This cleansing would remove their uncleanliness and include the gift of a new heart:

> I will sprinkle clean water upon you (ῥανῶ ἐφ' ὑμᾶς ὕδωρ καθαρόν), and you will be cleansed (καθαρισθήσεσθε) from all your impurities (ἀπὸ πασῶν τῶν ἀκαθαρσιῶν) and from all your idols, and I will cleanse you. And I will give to you a new heart and I will give a new spirit in you and I will remove the heart made of stone from your flesh and I will give to you a fleshly heart. And I will give my spirit in you and I will do it in order that you might go in my righteous requirements and you will keep my judgments and you shall do it (Ezek 36:25–27).

Ezekiel also describes this cleansing and gift in an explicitly soteriological fashion, "And I will save (σώσω) you from all your defilements (ἐκ πασῶν τῶν ἀκαθαρσιῶν) and I will call for the grain and I will not give a famine upon you" (Ezek 36:29).[127] Salvation from ethical defilements such as idolatry, sexual immorality, and social injustice would have clear results. It would result in fruitfulness rather than famine, "And I will multiply the fruit of the tree (τὸν καρπὸν τοῦ ξύλου) and the produce of the field, in order that you might not the reproach of famine among the nations" (Ezek 36:30).[128] Salvation from defilement would also result in shame for past transgressions, "And you will remember your evil ways and your habits which were not good and you shall be offended (προσοχθιεῖτε) before them because of your transgressions (ἐν ταῖς ἀνομίαις ὑμῶν) and because of your abominations (ἐπὶ τοῖς βδελύγμασιν ὑμῶν). "I will not do it because of you," says the Lord God, "It will be known to you; be ashamed (αἰσχύνθητε) and humiliated (ἐντράπητε) from your ways, O house of Israel." In all of this, there was a promise that Israel would be lead like sheep. Their restoration would

---

127. See also Ezek 36:33.
128. See also Ezek 36:34–35.

make known to all the nations (γνώσονται τὰ ἔθνη) that Israel's God had rebuilt what had been desolated (Ezek 36:36-38).

This pre-text is consistent with Rom 6:19-23 in various ways. To begin, prior to their faith in Christ, the Romans, like ancient Israel, were guilty of uncleanliness and lawlessness which provoked God to anger and resulted in being placed under the power of enemies. Paul describes this scenario as Jews and Gentiles presenting (παρίστημι) their members to uncleanliness and lawlessness. From Paul's wider perspective, due to their sin, God handed them over to the power of sin so that they were enslaved to uncleanliness and lawlessness. Rather than living in geopolitical exile, they were subjected to a state of lawlessness (εἰς τὴν ἀνομίαν, Rom 6:19).[129] Next, just as God mercifully delivered ancient Israel from Babylonian exile, Paul describes the Romans as "having been freed from sin (ἐλευθερωθέντες ἀπὸ τῆς ἁμαρτίας)" (Rom 6:22).[130] Paul's wider thought makes clear that God freed the Romans from the power of sin through the crucified and risen Christ based only on his grace and mercy.[131] Third, Paul notes that the Romans are ashamed (ἐπαισχύνεσθε, Rom 6:21) of their past lawlessness which is consistent with the command to post-exilic Israel that they were to be ashamed of their past lawlessness (αἰσχύνθητε, Ezek 36:32). Fourth, just as Ezekiel's prophecy envisioned a time of fruitfulness after Israel's deliverance (Ezek 36:30), Paul informs the Romans "But not having been freed from sin and having been enslaved to God you have your fruit (τὸν καρπὸν ὑμῶν) resulting in sanctification, and the end is eternal life" (Rom 6:22). Finally, while Ezekiel envisioned a time beyond exile when Israel would receive a new heart (καρδίαν καινήν, Ezek 36:26) and God's Spirit (πνεῦμα μου, Ezek 36:27), Paul links freedom from sin and enslavement to God with sanctification (εἰς ἁγιασμόν, Rom 6:19, 22). The phrase εἰς ἁγιασμόν in this context refers to a "state of being holy, not a process."[132] Paul's wider thought on the subject explicitly refers to God's Spirit (πνεῦμα) just as Ezekiel does (Ezek 36:27).[133] For example, in Rom 15:16, Paul describes believing Gentiles as those who are "sanctified by the Holy Spirit (ἡγιασμένη ἐν πνεύματι ἁγίῳ)."

Romans 6:15-23 and Echoes of Eternal Life

The final intertextual consideration in Rom 6:19-23 invovles Paul's two references to "eternal life (ζωὴ αἰώνιος)."[134] He explains, "But now having been freed from sin and

---

129. The phrase εἰς τὴν ἀνομίαν in Rom 6:19 refers to a state or condition of lawlessness. See Schreiner, *Romans*, 337.

130. See also ἐλευθερωθέντες ἀπὸ τῆς ἁμαρτίας in Rom 6:18.

131. See, e.g., Rom 3:24; 5:9-10.

132. Hultgren, *Paul's Letter to the Romans*, 264.

133. See, e.g., Rom 2:29; 5:5; 7:6; 8:2, 4, 5, 6, 9, 10, 11, 13, 14, 15, 16, 23, 26, 27; 12:11; 14:17; 15:13, 19, 30.

134. Cf. Rom 2:7; 5:21; Gal 6:8; 1 Tim 1:16; 6:12; Titus 1:2; 3:7.

having been enslaved to God you have your fruit resulting in sanctification, and its outcome, eternal life (ζωὴν αἰώνιον). For the wages of sin is death, but the gift of God is eternal life (ζωὴ αἰώνιος) in Christ Jesus our Lord" (Rom 6:22–23). Paul's understanding of eternal life did not develop out of thin air. One can assume that, in conjunction with his Second Temple and early Christian milieu, Israel's Scriptures played a fundamental role in shaping his thought on the matter. Once again, this requires us to consider the kinds of pre-texts that would have shaped Paul's thinking even if they are not explicitly used in Rom 6:22–23. To be sure, Paul employs the phrase in Rom 2:7 and 5:21, but, due to its prominence in 6:22–23, I have delayed full reflection on the intertextual background of "eternal life" until now.

However, we face some difficulties here. While the GNT contains several references to "eternal life," the phrase ζωὴ αἰώνιος rarely occurs in the LXX.[135] In fact, we find only one occurrence in Daniel "And many of those who sleep in the dust of the earth will rise, some to eternal life (לחיי עולם/εἰς ζωὴν αἰώνιον), some to reproach, and some to dispersion and eternal shame" (Dan 12:2).[136] The use of ζωὴ αἰώνιος in Daniel likely informs Paul's understanding of eternal life. The *volume* of the echo proper is moderate to strong given that both the pre-text and text contain the exact same expression ζωὴν αἰωνιον.

We also find *contextual consistency* between the pre-text and text. In the former, Daniel is informed about a coming day (ἡ ἡμέρα), or end (συντέλεια), which would result in unprecedented distress for many in the world but salvation for those whose names are "written in the book" (Dan 12:1). Those who "sleep (καθεύδω)" in the earth will either be raised to "eternal life" (εἰς ζωὴν αἰωνιον) or "eternal shame" (αἰσχύνην αἰώνιον) (Dan 12:2). Those raised to eternal life are further described in Dan 12:3, "And those who understand will shine like the stars of heaven and those who grow strong with respect to my words like the stars of heaven forever and ever."[137] Daniel is then commanded to seal the book "until the time of the end (ἕως καιροῦ συντελείας)" (Dan 12:4). In Dan 12:5–13, Daniel sees two figures on the banks of the river. The dialogue between the figures raises questions about the timing of these events (Dan 12:5–7). Daniel asks about the interpretation/end (λύσις/τὰ ἔσχατα τούτων) of the things revealed to him (Dan 12:8).[138] The response to Daniel includes a command for the prophet to "run," seal up the words "until the end (ἕως καιροῦ πέρας)," and one

---

135. See the use of ζωὴ αἰώνιος in Matt 19:16, 29; 25:46; Mark 10:17, 30; Luke 10:25; 18:18, 30; John 3:15, 16, 36; 4:14, 36; 5:24, 39; 6:27, 40, 47, 54, 68; 10:28; 12:25, 50; 17:2, 3; Acts 13:46, 48; Rom 2:7; 5:21; 6:22, 23; Gal 6:8; 1 Tim 1:16; 6:12; Titus 3:7; 1 John 1:2; 2:25; 3:15; 5:11, 13, 20; Jude 1:21.

136. Dan 12:2 θ reads, "And many of those who sleep in the dust of the earth will be raised, some to eternal life (εἰς ζωὴν αἰώνιον) and some to eternal reproach and eternal shame."

137. Dan 12:3 θ reads, "And those who understand will shine like the brightness of the firmament and those from the many righteous like stars forever and ever." Dan 12:3 MT reads, "And those who are wise will shine like the shining of the expanse, and those lead many to righteousness, like the stars forever and ever."

138. Cf. Dan 12:8 LXX, θ, MT.

last comment on two groups of people and the timing of what awaits them. Many will be "tested and sanctified (ἁγιασθῶσι πολλοί)" while sinners will sin (ἁμάρτωσιν οἱ ἁμαρτωλοί) (Dan 12:10).

Romans 6:19–23 reflects multiple features from the larger context of Dan 12. For example, both the pre-text and text contain τέλος language. The former repeatedly reflects on the συντέλεια which includes resurrection to eternal life or shame while Paul juxtaposes the τέλος of being enslaved to death with the τέλος of being enslaved to God. Just as Daniel distinguishes two eschatological groups, those who are sanctified (ἁγιασθῶσι πολλοί) and those who sin (Dan 12:10), Paul distinguishes those who are enslaved to sin from those who are freed from sin and enslaved to God bearing fruit which results in sanctification (εἰς ἁγιασμόν). Based on this intertextual subtext, Paul's reference to eternal life is thoroughly eschatological and defined by resurrection from the dead. Of course, as I will discuss further below, Paul reworks Daniel's eschatological expectation around the risen Lord Jesus Christ.

Within the *history of interpretation*, Longenecker reflects on Paul's use of ζωὴ αἰώνιος within a Second Temple milieu observing "Based on Dan 12:2, the expression evidently came to be used by Jews during the period of Second Temple Judaism for the final destination of the righteous."[139] Longenecker's point allows for the dual influences of Dan 12:2 and the Second milieu on Paul's use of ζωὴ αἰώνιος.

Interpretive Impact of Pre-Texts in Romans 6:15–23

It is obvious that Rom 6:15–23 has a more substantial intertextual subtext than is often appreciated by interpreters. The interplay between the OT pre-texts and this portion of the letter produce unstated points of resonance which shed further light on the way Paul responds to the false inference about God's grace in Christ. Five specific points emerge.

First, the cause and effect link between sin and death in Israel's Scriptures shapes Paul's perception of eschatological death which he reworks around the Lord Jesus Christ. As noted above, Israel's Scriptures connects sin and death in the Adamic narrative (Gen 2:17), in the Mosaic Law (Deut 24:16), and in subsequent moments of Israel's history (Josh 22:20). Simply put, sin results in death. Paul expands this motif so that it defines the fatal "end" (τέλος) for all. This is clear in Rom 6:21, "Therefore, what fruit were you having then? About which things you are now ashamed, for the end of those things (τέλος ἐκείνων) is death (θάνατος)." Paul juxtaposes this fatal outcome with an alternative τέλος, namely eternal life. He explains, "But now having been freed from sin and enslaved to God you have your fruit resulting in sanctification, and the end (τὸ τέλος), eternal life (ζωὴ αἰώνιον)" (Rom 6:22). These contrasting eschatological outcomes revolve around God's work and grace in Christ. In Christ, God frees the

---

139. Longenecker, *Romans*, 257. Cf. 2 Macc 7:9; 1QS 4:7; 4 Macc 5:13.

Romans from sin, enslaves them to righteousness, and gives (τὸ χάρισμα τοῦ θεοῦ, Rom 6:23) them eternal life.[140]

Second, Paul sees deliverance from sin in Christ and obedience from the heart as a return from exile in accordance with Israel's Scriptures. The slavery (δοῦλος) metaphor evokes OT pre-texts in which a return from exile involved obedience from the heart; therefore, the metaphor is neither abstract nor derived exclusively from Paul's Greco-Roman milieu. Pre-texts such as Deut 30:1–6 and Jer 24:1–10 promise that a return from exile will be marked by obedience from the heart. For Paul, that return takes place in the crucified and risen Christ. As he puts it in his doxology, "But thanks be to God that although you were slaves of sin, you have become obedient from the heart (ὑπηκούσατε ἐκ καρδίας) to the pattern of teaching to which you were handed over, but having been freed from sin (ἐλευθερωθέντες ἀπὸ τῆς ἁμαρτίας) you were enslaved to righteousness" (Rom 6:17).

Third, Paul positively charges the OT motif of God "handing over" (παραδίδωμι) his enemies by describing the Romans as those whom God handed over to a "form of teaching (τύπον διδαχῆς)." Paul has already taken up this OT motif in Rom 1:24–32 and 4:25 to describe how God dealt with sinful humanity. God handed humanity over (παρέδωκεν) to the power of sin and handed Jesus (παρεδόθη) over for their transgressions. Here Paul describes the Romans as being handed over (παρεδόθητε) to the authority of a teaching. As I noted above, the phrase τύπον διδαχῆς is a theological abbreviation which portrays the gospel as an authoritative teaching to which the Romans have been handed over and by which the Romans live. Paul specifically has in view those aspects of the gospel that teach how, in the crucified and risen Christ, God frees believers from the power of sin and enslaves them to himself.

Fourth, Paul portrays the Romans as those who are experiencing the promise of renewal as it is laid out in Ezek 36:16–38. In short, the Ezekiel pre-text portrays ancient Israel as facing God's wrath in exile for their moral "impurity (ἀκαθαρσία)" such as their idolatry, sexual immorality, and social injustice as well as their "lawlessness (ἀνομία)." Ezekiel promises that God would save Israel from exile, return them to the land, cleanse them of their moral impurity, give them a new heart and his very Spirit, command them to be ashamed of their past transgressions, and make their land fruitful. Most of these elements are reflected in Rom 6:19–23; however, Paul reworks the promise of restoration in Ezekiel around God's work in Christ. God frees Jews and Gentiles who are under his wrath from the exile/power of sin through the person and work of Christ. He sanctifies them by enslaving them to righteousness in Christ. He gives them the Holy Spirit and makes them, rather than the land, fruitful.

Finally, Paul identifies the eternal life envisioned by Daniel at the end (συντέλεια/τέλος) as the eschatological gift of God "in Christ Jesus our Lord (ἐν Χριστῷ Ἰησοῦ τῷ κυρίῳ ἡμῶν)" (Rom 6:23). Just as Daniel's vision juxtaposes people at the end of all things as the sanctified (ἁγιασθῶσι πολλοί) and sinners (ἁμαρτωλοί), Paul juxtaposes

---

140. Cf. use of χάρισμα in Rom 1:11; 5:15, 16; 11:29; 12:6.

the Romans as those who were enslaved to sin with an outcome (τέλος) of eschatological death and those who are now (νῦν) freed from sin and enslaved to God with an outcome of eternal life (ζωὴ αἰώνιος). If the latter phrase is informed by Dan 12:2, the ultimate nature of that eternal life is resurrection from the dead. Daniel spoke of people being raised from the earth, "And many of those who are sleeping in the dust of the earth will rise (ἀναστήσονται)." Consequently, for Paul, eternal life is not ultimately an endless existence of the soul. Rather, "life in the age to come" is experienced in a resurrected body. This would be in keeping with the nature of Christ's resurrection which Paul asserts the Romans will share in.[141] After all, resurrected life in the age to come is "in Christ Jesus our Lord (ἐν Χριστῷ Ἰησοῦ τῷ κυρίῳ ἡμῶν)" (Rom 6:23).

---

141. See Rom 6:5; 8:11, 23.

5

Romans 7:1–6

PAUL'S ARGUMENT FROM 6:23 pivots to 7:1 on the rhetorical question, "Or (ἤ) do you not know, brothers, for I speak to those who know the law, that the law lords over a man as long as he lives?" Paul signals his intent to continue his explanation that the Romans should not continue in sin, because, based on their participation in Christ's death and resurrection, they are not "under the law" but "under grace." He shifts his explanatory analogy from slavery in 6:15–23 to marriage in 7:1–6.[1] As we shall see, just as OT pre-texts inform the former analogy, they inform the latter as well.

The main exegetical difficulty with the latter analogy is identifying the referents of the married woman, the husband who has not yet died, and the "other" husband. Some interpreters have suggested that identifying the referent is moot, because Paul's real concern is the principle to be extracted from the scenario. As Schlatter puts it, "From the marriage law Paul only extrapolates the principle that for him was of paramount significance and was linked closely with his interpretation of the cross of Jesus, namely, that death alone effectively and ultimately cancels the bond decreed by the law."[2] Others suggest that the point of Paul's symbolism was "not to construct a point-for-point correspondence" in the marriage illustration.[3]

While I agree that Paul is working with a principle from Israel's Scriptures to make his point, it does not necessarily follow that the figures in the analogy lack clear referents. This is clear in Rom 7:4 where Paul referenes "another" (ἑτέρῳ) husband whom he then identifies as "the one who was raised from the dead (τῷ ἐκ νεκρῶν ἐγερθέντι)." If "another" husband refers to the risen Jesus, it follows that the wife (γυνή) and husband (ἀνήρ) in 7:2–3 also have specific referents. Moreover, Paul's analogies

---

1. Gale suggests that Paul uses seven analogies in Romans. He points to Rom 4:4, 5:7, 6:1–14, 6:15–23; 7:1–6, 9:20–24, and 11:16–24. See Gale, *The Use of Analogy*, 18.

2. Schlatter, *Romans*, 153.

3. Schreiner, *Romans*, 348. As Moo puts it, "Probably, then, Paul does not intend us to find significance in the details of vv. 2–3." Moo, *The Epistle to the Romans*, 413.

generally have specific referents.⁴ Therefore, I will proceed with the understanding that the wife refers to a Jew and or Gentile believer both prior to and after faith in Christ. The first husband refers to the law and sin's use of it, namely the production of sinful desires (τὰ παθήματα τῶν ἁμαρτιῶν) (Rom 7:5).⁵ With this understanding in tow, we can proceed to consider how the intertextual subtext in Rom 7:1-6 informs Paul's thought.

Romans 7:1-6

(7:1-6) Or do you not know, brothers, for I am speaking to those who know the law, that the law dominates a man as long as he lives? For the married woman is bound by law to her living husband; but if the husband should die, she is released from the law of the husband. So then if she should belong to another man while her husband is living she will be called an adulteress; but if her husband dies, she is free from the law, so that she is not an adulteress if she belongs to another man.⁶ Therefore, my brothers, also you died to the law through the body of Christ, that you might belong to another, to the one who has been raised from the dead, in order that we might bear fruit to God. For when we were in the flesh, the sinful desires, which were through the law, were at work in our members, to bear fruit to death; but now we have been released from the law having died to that by which we were being bound, so that we serve in the newness of the Spirit and not in the oldness of the letter.

Romans 7:1-6 echoes multiple pre-texts from Israel's Scriptures. As we shall see, Deut 24:1-4 plays a significant role in Paul's marriage analogy. However, other pre-texts are in play as well. The points of resonance produced here help to unravel some of the hermeneutical condundrums which emerge from the marriage analogy.

Suggested Pre-Texts in Romans 7:1-6

Hübner lists the following pre-texts: Deut 6:6-9 (Rom 7:1); Exod 20:13; Deut 5:17; Prov 6:23-24 (Rom 7:2); Prov 6:24, 29; Hos 3:1, 3 (Rom 7:3); and Gen 3:3 (Rom 7:5).⁷

---

4. E.g., the olive tree analogy in Rom 11:17-24 has specific referents as the branches grafted into the cultivated olive tree symbolize Gentiles and the branches regrafted into the tree symbolize Jews.

5. As Calvin puts it, "The law was, as it were our husband, under whose yoke we were kept until it became dead to us." Calvin, *Romans*, 246.

6. I have translated γένηται, γενομένην, and γενέσθαι as "belong to." For this rendering, see BDAG 199.

7. Hübner, *Vetus Testamentum in Novo*, 2:98-100.

Neither Nestle-Aland 28th ed. nor Hays note any pre-texts for Rom 7:1–6. Seifrid moves his analysis straight to Rom 7:7–25; therefore, he does not consider OT pre-texts in 7:1–6.[8]

Intertextual Analysis of Rom 7:1–6

Νομός is clearly the *leitwort* in this pericope, and it something that both Paul's Jewish and Gentile recipients understand, at least to some degree, given the fact that he addresses them as "those who know the law (γινώσκουσιν νόμον)" (Rom 7:1). Paul employs the noun νόμος eight times in these six verses.[9] In every instance, the referent of νόμος is tied to the Mosaic Law. He uses the Mosaic law as both a specific reference to instructions about marriage/divorce and a broad reference to a prior way of life. The entirety of the analogy underscores Paul's point that only through death is one freed from the law. We will proceed according to the order that the echoes arise in the text.

Romans 7:1 and the Statement of a General Legal Principle

In Rom 7:1, Paul personifies the law as a ruler that dominates a person noting "the law domaintes a man (κυριεύει τοῦ ἀνθρώπου) as long as he lives." This personification is best understood in relation to the personification of death in Rom 6:9 where θάνατος is the subject of κυριεύω and Rom 6:14 where Paul makes ἁμαρτία the subject of κυριεύω, "For sin (ἁμαρτία) will not dominate over you (ὑμῶν οὐ κυριεύσει); for you are not under the law but under grace." The substitution of "law" for "death" and "sin" as the subject of κυριεύω implies a relationship between the three subjects which Paul will further work out in Rom 7:7–25.[10] For now, it is enough to note that Paul insists that the law is "holy (ἅγιος, 7:12)" and "spiritual (πνευματικός, 7:14)." Nevertheless, as Rom 7:1 and Paul's wider thought indicate, the law has an inherent limitation with respect to its reign (κυριεύω) over a person and its power (δύναμαι) to make a person righteous and alive before God.[11]

---

8. However, in his work *Christ our Righteousness*, Seifrid briefly mentions that the marriage metaphor in Rom 7:1–6, especially as it concerns the believer's union with Christ, echoes Gen 2:24. Seifrid, *Christ Our Righteousness*, 115n74.

9. Rom 7:7–25 contains fifteen uses of νόμος which echo the OT in various ways as I will discuss below.

10. As Dunn puts it, "The formulation is surprising, until we realize that the same verb (κυριεύειν) was used in 6:9 and 14 of death and sin. The implication is clear: having recalled in 6:22–23 the thematic statement of the rule of sin and death in 5:21, Paul naturally turns to draw in the third element in that rule, namely, 'law.'" Dunn, *Romans*, 1:359.

11. With respect to the law's limitied power, Paul clearly states in Galatians "Therefore, is the law against the promises of God? May it never be. For if a law which is able to make alive (δυνάμενος ζῳοποιῆσαι) was given, righteousness would certainly be from the law" (Gal 3:21).

One intertextual concern in Rom 7:1 stems from Paul's qualification of the law's reign over a person, namely that the reign is "as long as he lives (ἐφ' ὅσον χρόνον ζῇ)." While the referent of νόμος is clearly the Mosaic Law, the principle that the law's reign over a person terminates with one's death is not something explicitly stated in Israel's Scriptures.[12] Many interpreters point out that Paul's statement about the law in v. 1 reflects debates within later Rabbinic Judaism.[13] Others point out that Paul's qualification of the Mosaic Law is straightforward and could apply to any kind of law.[14] In this way, as Sanday and Headlam note, Paul simply states a "general principle."[15] The latter point is well-taken.

Romans 7:2 and the Echo of Proverbs 6:29

In Rom 7:2, Paul uses the phrase "unmarried woman (ὕπανδρος γυνή)" which echoes Prov 6:29 "In this way is the one who enters to a married woman (γυναῖκα ὕπανδρον), she will not be innocent nor any one who touches her."[16] The *volume* of the echo is moderate to high based on the shared use of ὕπανδρος γυνή (והער תשא). This is only one of two LXX uses.[17]

This pre-text and text also share *contextual consistency*.[18] In Prov 6:20–35, a father exhorts his son to heed parental instruction.[19] Much of that instruction is dominated by warnings about the dangers of adultery. The father likens his son's potential sexual encounter with a married woman (ὕπανδρος γυνή) to being burned or walking on hot coals (Prov 6:27–28). The consequence of the encounter will be a foolish, destructive, and disgraceful loss of life which incurs the jealousy of the adulteress's husband (Prov 6:29–35).

At first glance, it may appear that Prov 6:20–35 shares little in common with Rom 7:1–6 except for the shared use of ὕπανδρος γυνή. However, both the pre-text and text agree that participating in adultery is dangerous to those involved. The danger is

---

12. As Fitzmyer notes, "Paul's statement as such, however, is not found in the OT." Fitzmyer, *Romans*, 457.

13. See, e.g., Hultgren, *Romans*, 269. Stuhlmacher notes that Rabbis developed their thoughts about the termination of the law's power over a person upon death from Ps 88:6 MT. He points to b. Sabb. 30a. See Stuhlmacher, *Romans*, 102.

14. E.g., Sanday and Hedlam note that Paul's qualification of the law in Rom 7:1 reflects "a general principle of all Law; an obvious axiom of political justice—that death clears all scores, and that a dead man can no longer be prosecuted or punished." Sanday and Hedlam, *Romans*, 172.

15. Murray, *The Epistle to the Romans*, 240.

16. Num 5:20 contains the closely related phrase ὑπ' ἀνδρὸς οὖσα. Num 5:11–31 lays out what was to be done to an adulterous wife in ancient Israel.

17. The phrase ὕπανδρος γυνή also occurs in Prov 6:24. See also the use of ὕπανδρος γυνή in Sir 9:9; 41:23.

18. With respect to the test of *recurrence*, Paul has already shown engagement with the book of Proverbs through his citation of Prov 24:12 in Rom 2:6. For a discussion of this citation, see volume 1.

19. See Prov 6:20.

axiomatic to Paul's observation that a woman will be called an adulteress (μοιχαλίς) if she "belongs (γίνομαι)" to another man while her husband is still living. One wants to avoid such a label. To be sure, Paul reconfigures the danger described in Prov 6:20–35 to fit his own marital metaphor. Paul locates the danger for the wife (i.e., believer) in remaining with the husband (i.e., the Mosaic Law). She needs to "belong" to another husband (i.e., Christ), but such a transition cannot take place without death.[20] Otherwise, it would be adultery which is rife with danger as the Proverbs pre-text indicates. We will return to this line of thought below.

Romans 7:2–3 and the Echo of Deuteronomy 24:1–4

Romans 7:2–3 evoke laws concerning marriage and divorce as they are articulated in Deut 24:

> And if anyone should take a wife and live together with her, and it will be if she should not find favor before him, because he found a shameful mark in her, he will write for her a certificate of divorce and he will give it into her hands and he will send her out from his house, and having gone away if she should belong to another man (γένηται ἀνδρὶ ἑτέρῳ), and the last husband should hate her and he will write for a certificate of divorce and he will give it into her hands and he will send her out from his house, or if the last husband should die (ἀποθάνῃ ὁ ἀνὴρ ὁ ἔσχατος), who took her to himself as a wife, the former husband who sent her out having returned will not be able to take her for himself as a wife after she was hated, because it is an abomination before the Lord your God; and you shall not defile the land, which the Lord your God gives to you in inheritance (Deut 24:1–4).

The *volume* of the echo is strong based on the exact semantic and syntactical overlap involving the phrases γένηται ἀνδρὶ ἑτέρῳ (Deut 24:2; Rom 7:3) and ἀποθάνῃ ὁ ἀνὴρ ὁ ἔσχατος/ἀποθάνῃ ὁ ἀνήρ (Deut 24:3; Rom 7:3).[21]

Contextual consistency stems from what the "woman" can and cannot do with respect to her two husbands. The pre-text mentions a "former husband (ὁ ἀνὴρ ὁ πρότερος)" and a "last husband (ὁ ἀνὴρ ὁ ἔσχατος)." If the "former husband" finds his wife unfit based on the discovery of a "shameful mark" (i.e., adultery), the Mosaic Law permitted him to write a certificate of divorce and send her out of the home (Deut 24:1). The womam could then remarry (Deut 24:2). If the "last husband" "hated" her, perhaps due to the discovery of adultery, he could also write a certificate of divorce and send her out of the home (Deut 24:3). The woman could not return to the "former husband," because such a return would be an "abomination" (βδέλυγμα) to God

---

20. As Jewett puts it, Paul applies the "principle of release through death for believers who have died to the law in experiencing the shift in lordship through Christ." Jewett, *Romans*, 428–29.

21. There are three occurrences of the phrase γένηται ἀνδρὶ ἑτέρῳ in the LXX. See Deut 24:2; Hos 3:3; Jer 3:1. Of the three occurrences, the best contextual match is Deut 24:1–4. See also Tob 6:13.

(Deut 24:4). This prohibition also applied if the last husband died (ἀποθάνῃ ὁ ἀνὴρ ὁ ἔσχατος, Deut 24:3).

Some of these features are taken up in Rom 7:2–3 but not without considerable reworking on Paul's part.[22] For example, Paul takes up the figure of the married woman in the pre-text to describe the condition of his Roman recipients both before and after their "marriage" to the risen Christ (εἰς τὸ γενέσθαι ὑμᾶς ἑτέρῳ, Rom 7:4). Before their marriage to Christ, the Roman recipients were "bound by law (δέδεται νόμῳ)" to the Mosaic Law (Rom 7:1). They could not be married to Christ without death. Marriage to another husband without the death of the living husband would be adultery as both the pre-text and text make clear. In the pre-text, the death of the "last husband" is required for the woman to be married to another (ἀποθάνῃ ὁ ἀνὴρ ὁ ἔσχατος, Deut 24:3). She could not return to her "first husband," because it is an abomination to God (Deut 24:4). Paul reconfigures these details so that Christ fills the slot of a husband who dies and frees the wife from marriage to another.[23] He does not die so that the Roman recipients can return to their first husband which is the Mosaic Law. According to the pre-text, that would be an abomination to God. Instead, he dies to free them from that marriage, and he is raised so that they might be wed to him. The recipients shared in Christ's death to the law, "and you died to the law (ἐθανατώθητε τῷ νόμῳ) through the body of Christ," for the interrelated purposes of being wed to him and bearing fruit to God (Rom 7:4). After all, in their previous marriage to the law, they were bearing fruit to death (Rom 7:5).

Within the *history of interpretation*, interpreters have viewed Paul's engagement with Deut 24:1–4 in different ways. Some, although acknowledging some points of contact between the pre-text and text, have very little to say about it.[24] Others do not mention their semantic, syntactical, and contextual overlap at all.[25] Many interpreters fail to see the overlap between ἀποθάνῃ ὁ ἀνήρ in Rom 7:3 and ἀποθάνῃ ὁ ἀνὴρ ὁ ἔσχατος in Deut 24:3. This is surprising given the fact that Deut 24:3 contains the only occurrence of ἀποθάνῃ ὁ ἀνήρ in the entire LXX. A few interpreters at least acknowledge a possible echo.[26] Additionally, if it is the case that Deut 24:1–4 shapes Paul's thought here, it follows that he evokes a marital metaphor to describe the union between Christ and the Romans. This is not merely "transference to another master"

---

22. Some have suggested that in Rom 7:1–6, Paul is appealing to an "apostolic marriage law" wherein a woman could not divorce her husband (1 Cor 7:10). See, e.g., Tomson, "What Did Paul Mean," 573–81.

23. Cf. the phrase ἐὰν ἀποθάνῃ ὁ ἀνήρ in Rom 7:3 to the phrase ἀποθάνῃ ὁ ἀνὴρ ὁ ἔσχατος in Deut 24:3.

24. See, e.g., Dunn, *Romans*, 1:342; Moo, *The Epistle to the Romans*, 413. Some do not even mention Deut 24:1–4 at all.

25. See, e.g., Longenecker, *The Epistle to the Romans*, 630–34; Witherington, *Paul's Letter to the Romans*, 175–77.

26. See, e.g., Hultgren, *Paul's Letter to the Romans*, 269; Jewett, *Romans*, 431.

but a union likened to marriage.²⁷ Paul's Corinthian correspondence indicates that he sometimes uses a marital metaphor to describe the relationship between Christ and believers.²⁸ We will return to this intertextual metaphor below as we consider its interpretive impact.

Romans 7:2-3 and An Echo of David's Marriage

Another intertextual consideration in Rom 7:2-3 stems from one of the few narrative examples of Mosaic regulations regarding marriage/remarriage. 1 Sam 25:39-42 briefly recounts David's marriage to Abigail after her husband Nabal died. After Nabal insulted David and his entourage of young men by refusing to assist them with food and water, David intended to attack Nabal (1 Sam 25:1-13). However, Nabal's wife Abigail went secretly to David's camp and prevented their impending attack by offering them the assistance that her husband refused to give (1 Sam 25:14-31). David grants her petition, acknowledges the effectiveness of her intercession, and sends her back home to her husband (1 Sam 25:32-35). Upon returning home, Nabal dies when, after his drunken stupor, Abigail informs him that she offered the assistance to David which he foolishly refused to give (1 Sam 25:36-38). David receives news of Nabal's death and sends messengers to Abigail who announce, "David sent us to you to take you for himself for a wife (εἰς γυναῖκα)" (1 Sam 25:40). This brief account reflects adherence to Mosaic regulations regarding marriage, namely that the wife cannot marry another unless her living husband dies.²⁹

Although there are no indications that Paul has this specific pre-text in view in Rom 7:2-3, it is a narrative illustration from Israel's Scriptures of the legal principle that he uses to explain to his recipients that they have died to the law through the death and resurrection of Jesus to whom they are now bound. Haacker refers to this narrative account as a "description of the legal position (*die beschriebene Rechtslage*)" of the biblical tradition from which Paul draws.³⁰

Romans 7:1-6 and Echoes of Yahweh's Marriage to Israel

When Paul asserts that the Romans have been married to Christ (εἰς τὸ γενέσθαι ὑμᾶς ἑτέρῳ), it not only echoes Deut 24:1-4 but also the OT marital metaphor which

---

27. Cranfield objects to the presence of a marital metaphor noting, "The expression is less naturally explained as reflecting the preceding illustration, the union with Christ being presented in terms of marriage to a second husband, than (with Thomas Aquinas, Lipsius, Cornely et al.) as simply signifying the transference to another master." Cranfield, *Romans*, 1:336.

28. See, e.g., 1 Cor 6:12-20; Eph 5:21-33.

29. Cf. Deut 24:1-4.

30. See Haacker, *Der Brief des Paulus an die Römer*, 168. Haacker also points to historical examples of the legal position within Second Temple Judaism. See, e.g., Josephus, *Ant.* 18:109-36; Tacitus, *Annals* 11:12-38.

depicts Yahweh as married to Israel.³¹ Israel's Scriptures sometimes use the metaphor of marriage to describe the relationship between Israel and her God. Hosea contains one of the most well-known examples of this metaphor, "And it will be in that day, says the Lord, she will call me 'my husband (ὁ ἀνήρ μου),' and she will not still call me 'Baalim'" (Hos 2:16).³² Similarly, in Isaiah, we find "And as a young man lives together with a virgin, in this way your sons will live with you; and it will be as the bridegroom (νυμφίος) rejoices over the bride (νύμφῃ), in this way the Lord (οὕτως κύριος) will rejoice over you" (Isa 62:5).³³ Both prophets look beyond Israel's judgment and liken the nation's restoration to a marriage.

Paul may be evoking this OT marriage metaphor, but he reworks it around the person of Christ. He places Christ in Yhwh's role as "husband." Even more, he expands the "bride" to include both Jew and Gentile. This marital metaphor is consistent with Paul's wider thought. For example, Paul refers to the Corinthians as a bride, or "virgin (παρθένος)," explaining "For I am jealous for you with a godly jealousy, for I betrothed (ἡρμοσάμην) you to one husband (ἑνὶ ἀνδρὶ), to present you to Christ (τῷ Χριστῷ) as a pure virgin (παρθένον ἁγνὴν)" (2 Cor 11:2).³⁴ While Rom 7:1–6 lacks this explicit betrothal language, it still likens the Romans to a wife and Christ to a husband. Such a marital metaphor emanates from OT descriptions of Yhwh's marriage to Israel, though it is not without Pauline reconfiguration which I will discuss below. Within the *history of interpretation*, some interpreters have recognized Paul's use of this marital metaphor, though they assess its impact on the text in different ways.³⁵ Jewett specifically notes the OT "precedents" for "speaking of the relationship between God and Israel in marital terms."³⁶ Paul's reconfiguration of the OT motif has both rhetorical and christological implications. With respect to the latter, just as Paul sometimes replaces the divine referent of an OT citation with Jesus, he does something similar here by replacing Yahweh the husband with Christ the husband (ἀνήρ).³⁷

---

31. Best does not hesitate to see a marital metaphor based on the phrase εἰς τὸ γενέσθαι ὑμᾶς ἑτέρῳ and the wider context. See Best, *The Letter of Paul to the Romans*, 77–78.

32. See also Hos 1:2.

33. Cf. Isa 54:5 MT. See also Ezek 16:8.

34. See also Eph 5:25–33.

35. After analyzing the presence of the metaphor in Rom 7:1–6, Campbell concludes "Thus, it is appropriate to suggest that this passage evokes something akin to the bond of marriage with respect to the relationship between Christ and believers. Participation with Christ is explicit and believers belong to Christ in a manner that characterizes the pledge of marriage." Campbell, *Paul and Union with Christ*, 301. See also Batey, *New Testament Nuptial Imagery*, 19; Gieniusz, "Rom 7,1–6: Lack of Imagination?" 389–98; Earnshaw, "Reconsidering Paul's Marriage Analogy," 68–88.

36. Jewett, *Romans*, 434. See also Dunn, *Romans*, 1:362

37. See, e.g., Rom 10:13. For a full discussion on the way Paul sometimes replaces divine referents in OT citations with Jesus, see Capes, *Old Testament Yahweh Texts*.

Romans 7:4–5 and Echoes of Fruit Bearing

In Rom 7:4–5, Paul's references to "bearing fruit (καρποφορέω)" echo the OT motif of fruit bearing from a missional and eschatological perspective.[38] Paul contrasts bearing fruit either to death or to God:

> Therefore, my brothers, also you died to the law through the body of Christ, that you might belong to another, to the one who has been raised from the dead, in order that we might bear fruit to God (καρποφορήσωμεν τῷ θεῷ). For when we were in the flesh, the sinful desires, which were through the law, were at work in our members, to bear fruit to death (εἰς τὸ καρποφορῆσαι τῷ θανάτῳ); but now we have been released from the law having died to that by which we were being bound, so that we serve in the newness of the Spirit and not in the oldness of the letter.

Paul does not pull the metaphor of "fruit bearing (καρποφορέω)" out of thin air nor is it an abstraction untethered to his historical milieu, a milieu largely defined by his reading of a sacred text.[39] Instead, he draws from Israel's Scriptures. As I noted in the analysis of Rom 1:13, "fruit (καρπός)" has missional and eschatological connotations in the OT.[40] God promised that Israel's return from exile would result in world-wide fruitfulness:

> Those who are coming, the children of Jacob, will bloom and Israel will flourish, and the world will be filled with its fruit (ἡ οἰκουμένη τοῦ καρποῦ αὐτοῦ) (Isa 27:6).[41]

> But I will show peace; the vine will give its fruit (καρπόν), and the earth will yield its produce, and heaven will give its dew, and I will give as an inheritance all these things to the remnant of this people (Zech 8:12).

> And I will return to captivity of my people Israel, and they will build the cities which have been destroyed and they will dwell and they will plant vineyards

---

38. Some interpreters suggest that bearing fruit (καρποφορέω) in Rom 7:4–5 is a metaphor for the progeny produced through the union between Christ and believers. As Matthew Black puts it, "The believer is free to contract a new union with his Risen Lord, and obtain new progeny through this fresh 'marriage.'" Black, *Romans*. Similarly, Barrett notes "In vi. 21 f. Paul used the image of 'fruit-bearing' in quite general terms, but when he employs it in the present context it can hardly be doubted that he has in mind the birth of children. We are joined to Christ (for he not only died but was raised from the dead), but the children are born 'to God.'" Barrett, *The Epistle to the Romans*, 137. Cranfield is opposed to the notion of "progeny" being produced between the union of Christ and the believer. He notes, "The image of our bearing offspring to God is altogether grotesque." Cranfield, *Romans*, 1:337.

39. In the LXX, the verb καρποφορέω only occurs in Hab 3:17. See also Wis 10:7. For NT uses, see Matt 13:23; Mark 4:20, 28; Luke 8:15; Col 1:6, 10.

40. See volume 1.

41. Cf. Isa 37:30.

and they will drink their wine and they will plant gardens and they will eat their fruit (τὸν καρπὸν αὐτῶν) (Amos 9:14).[42]

It is against this scriptural backdrop that one should understand Paul's reference to the Romans who bear fruit to God based on their marriage to the risen Christ (Rom 7:4).

In Paul's thought and use of the scriptural metaphor, the referent of fruit is not limited to earthly blessings for ethnic Israel in ancient Palestine nor righteous conduct detached from its eschatological implications. Even Paul's famed "fruit of the Spirit (ὁ καρπὸς τοῦ πνεύματος)" in Gal 5:22–23 is tethered to the eschatological inheritance of the kingdom.[43] Similarly, in Rom 7:1–6, the Romans' marriage to the risen Christ produces the kind of fruit, or obedience, which Israel's Scriptures promised beyond exile and judgment but were left unrealized apart from Christ.[44] Apart from their marriage to Christ, both Jew and Gentile only producded fruit "to death (τῷ θανάτῳ)" (Rom 7:5). Paul describes their condition prior to union with Christ as living "in the flesh (ἤμεν τῇ σαρκί)." The phrase τῇ σαρκί refers to a sinful state that adversely affected the individual and the age/world in which they lived.[45] In such a state, sinful passions (τὰ παθήματα τῶν ἁμαρτιῶν) were being produced in the members (ἐν τοῖς μέλεσιν) of the Romans through sin's use of the law so that they were bearing fruit "to death (τῷ θανάτῳ)." In other words, given their condition "in the flesh," everything the Romans produced prior to their union with Christ resulted in death.

Romans 7:6 and Echoes of the Mosaic Law

This brings us to the sixth intertextual consideration in Rom 7:1–6. It stems from Paul's contrastive phrases "in newness of the Spirit" and "in oldness of the letter." As Paul puts it in v. 6, "But now we have been released from the law having died to that by which we were being bound, so that we serve in the newness of the Spirit (ἐν καινότητι πνεύματος) and not in the oldness of the letter (παλαιότητι γράμματος)." As he did in Rom 2:27–29, Paul contrasts Spirit and letter.[46] As Seifrid suggests, the contrast represents "two different ways in which God addresses the human being."[47] Understanding the contrast in this way does not entirely preclude other explanations such as

---

42. See also Joel 2:22; Mal 3:11; Jer 36:28 (29:28 MT); 38:12 (31:12 MT); Ezek 36:30; 47:17.

43. This is clear from Paul's closing remark about the "deeds of the flesh (τὰ ἔργα τῆς σαρκός)" which is that "those who do such things will not inherit the kingdom of God" (Gal 5:21).

44. Hultgren notes that bearing fruit to God in both the OT and NT "signifies doing good." Hultgren, *Romans*, 271. Indeed, the metaphor significes "doing good." However, it is "doing good" in an eschatological sense in accordance with Israel's Scriptures.

45. BDAG 915. As Moo describes the phrase, "Existence in the domain of the flesh is determined by the three others 'powers' of the old age: sin, the law, and death." Moo, *Romans*, 419.

46. He does not develop the contrast here as he keeps his focus on sin's use of the law in Rom 7:7–25. Paul's most concentrated teaching on πνεῦμα in this letter occurs in Rom 8. For intertextual analysis of Rom 2:27–29, see volume 1.

47. Seifrid, *Christ Our Righteousness*, 98.

a contrast between two covenants or two ages.⁴⁸ It simply stresses what Paul stresses which is that in these contrasting covenants/ages the divine address is either "in the letter" or "in the Spirit." These two different ways of divine address are anticipated in Israel's Scriptures.

The intertextual referent of "in the oldness of the letter/script (παλαιότητι γράμματος)" is not located in specific pre-texts but rather in what Paul labels as the "old" mode of communication in which God addressed his people through what was inscribed in the written code of the Mosaic Law.⁴⁹ Nevertheless, as I have noted several times throughout this work already, Paul's use of OT motifs and or large swaths of the scriptural narrative are ultimately informed by specific pre-texts. Therefore, it is necessary to consider specific passages. We should be particularly interested in OT pre-texts that stress the "written" nature of the Mosaic Law. We find such an emphasis in Pentateuchal accounts of Moses' reception of the tablets written by God on Mt. Sinai:

> And the Lord said to Moses, "Go up to me in the mountain and be there; and I will give to you the stone tablets, the law and the commandments, which I wrote (ἔγραψα) to instruct them (Exod 24:12).

> And he gave to Moses, when he finished speaking to him in the mountain of Sinai, the two tablets of testimony, stone tablets written with the finger of God (γεγραμμένας τῷ δακτύλῳ τοῦ θεοῦ) (Exod 31:18).⁵⁰

> And he proclaimed to you his covenant, which he commanded you to do, the ten words, and he wrote (ἔγραψεν) them on two stone tablets (Deut 4:13).⁵¹

God (θεός) functions as the subject of γράφω in each of these examples. He conveyed to his covenant people how he wanted them to live/serve by writing it down on stone tablets. Moses penned the larger book of the law at the direction of Israel's God.⁵² Moses inscribed in that book curses and blessings incurred for breaking and keeping the commands. Divine communication via writing continued beyond the ministry

---

48. With respect to the contrast of two covenants, Schreiner suggests "The contrast between 'newness' and 'oldness' here also signifies the disjunction between two covenants." Schreiner, *Romans*, 353. Regarding the contrasts between two ages, Moo explains "The antithesis is not between the misunderstanding or misuse of the law and the Spirit, nor even, at least basically, between the outer demand and in the inner disposition to obey, but between the Old Covenant and the New, the old age and the new." Moo, *Romans*, 421. Regarding the contrast of two ages, Käsemann notes "It clearly characterizes the standing of the Christian after the change of aeons, which is still at issue in 2:29." Käsemann, *Romans*, 190.

49. In discussing Paul's use of γράμμα in 2 Cor 3:6–7, Hays suggests that the noun should be translated as "script" rather than "letter." See Hays, *Echoes of Scripture in the Letters of Paul*, 130–31. We should not ignore Paul's specific choice of γράμμα rather than νόμος. The former noun accentuates the written mode through which God addressed his people.

50. See also Exod 32:15, 32; 34:1, 27, 28.

51. See also Deut 5:22; 9:10; 10:2, 4.

52. See, e.g., Deut 31:24.

of Moses. Joshua was encouraged to constantly meditate on what God wrote in the Mosaic Law (Josh 1:8). He then gives the same admonition to all of Israel towards the end of his life (Josh 23:6). David instructed Solomon to live by what had been written in the Law of Moses (1Kgs 2:3). The exilic and post-exilic periods stressed adherence to the commands written in the Law of Moses (Dan 9:11; Ezr 3:2).[53] While God had communicated to Israel through other means such as prophets and visions, he mainly addressed them through what was written in the Law.[54]

Paul describes this written form of divine address as "oldness of the letter" (παλαιότητι γράμματος) which implies that another and better form of address has arrived. To be sure, as Paul will make clear in his subsequent argument, the law is holy (ἅγιος) (Rom 7:12). Nevertheless, the expression of God's will through written commands does not perform what the Spirit does, namely circumcision of the heart.[55] Paul does not explicitly mention circumcision of the heart as he does in Rom 2:29. Instead, he refers to this circumcision and its effect as "newness of the Spirit (ἐν καινότητι πνεύματος)." In this way, he evokes an OT motif of promised newness, especially the promise of a new heart and spirit.

Romans 7:6 and the Echo of Ezekiel 36

Ezekiel 36:16–38 contains the most explicit link in Israel's Scriptures between newness and spirit/Spirit.[56] The prophet relays God's promise to renew Israel after its exile which includes the gift of a new heart and spirit/Spirit, "And I will give to you a new heart (καρδίαν καινὴν) and I will give a new spirit (πνεῦμα καινὸν) in you and I will take away the heart made of stone from your flesh and I will give to you a heart of flesh. And I will give my Spirit (τὸ πνεῦμά μου) in you and I will make it that you should go in my righteous requirements and you should keep and do my judgments" (Ezek 36:26–27). The *volume* of this echo in Rom 7:6 is moderate to substantial based on the semantic overlap of καινόν/καινότης and πνεῦμα.

We also find significant *contextual consistency*. The larger contexts of both the pre-text and text refer to God delivering/freeing captives which results in fruitfulness. As the prophet puts it, "And I will save you (σώσω ὑμᾶς) from all your uncleannesses (ἐκ πασῶν τῶν ἀκαθαρσιῶν) and I will call for the grain and I will multiply it and I will not place famine upon you; and I will multiply the fruit of the tree (τὸν καρπὸν τοῦ ξύλου) and the produce of the field, in order that you might not receive the disgrace of

---

53. See also Dan 9:13.

54. Even prophecies and visions were tethered to what was written in the Law of Moses.

55. As Seifrid puts it, "Unlike the 'written code,' the Spirit performs a 'circumcision of the heart.'" Seifrid, *Christ Our Righteousness*, 99.

56. The noun καινότης which Paul uses in Rom 7:6 only occurs twice in the LXX. See 1 Kgs 8:53 and Ezek 47:12. The adjective καινός, which obviously shares the same root as καινότης, occurs frequently. See LEH 298.

famine among the nations" (Ezek 36:29–30). Similarly, within Paul's marriage metaphor, the death of the husband results in the wife's freedom "but if the husband should die, she is free (ἐλευθέρα) from the law." As a result, the believer bears fruit to God (ἵνα καρποφορήσωμεν τῷ θεῷ) (Rom 7:4).

This proposed echo also passes the tests of *recurrence* and representation within the *history of interpretation*. With respect to the former, as I discussed in the previous chapter, Rom 6:19–23 echoes Ezek 36:16–38. Among interpreters who have noted the echo of this pre-text in Rom 7:6, pointing to both Jer 31:31–34 and Ezek 36:26–27, Schreiner observes "The newness of the Spirit fulfills the old covenant promise that the new covenant would give people ability to keep the statutes and commandments of the law."[57]

Interpretive Impact of Pre-Texts in Romans 7:1–6

The interplay between various pre-texts and Rom 7:1–6 produce multiple unstated points of resonance that shed light both on Paul's immediate argument and wider thought in the letter. Five salient points emerge.

First, Paul reconfigures the danger of adultery expressed in Israel's Scriptures (Prov 6:29; Deut 24:1–4) around the Romans' "marriage" to the Mosaic Law and Christ. The only acceptable and effectual separation from the law, like the only acceptable and effectual separation of a Jewish wife from her husband, requires death. Paul locates that acceptable and effectual death in the death of Christ and the believer's participation in it. As Paul puts it, "You died (ἐθανατώθητε) to the law (τῷ νόμῳ) through the body of Christ (διὰ τοῦ σώματος τοῦ Χριστοῦ)" (Rom 7:4a).[58] The reference to death in Christ's body (σῶμα) is a reference to the crucifixion which Paul portrays here as a kind of death of the "first husband."[59] Unlike Deut 24:1–4, the wife (believer) can marry the deceased husband who has been raised from the dead (τῷ ἐκ νεκρῶν ἐγερθέντι) (Rom 7:4). However, the crucified and risen husband is not the "first husband," which is the law, but "another" husband (εἰς τὸ γενέσθαι ὑμᾶς ἑτέρῳ).

Second, if the Romans allowed the law to rule over (ὁ νόμος κυριεύει) them after their death to the law in the crucified and risen Christ, it would be akin to the abominable act (βδέλυγμα, Deut 24:4) described in Deut 24:1–4 wherein the wife returned to her first husband after the death of her last husband. This unstated point is consistent with Rom 6:1–23 where Paul combats the false inference that those who

---

57. Schreiner, *Romans*, 353.

58. Cf. Gal 2:19.

59. See ὁ ἀνὴρ ὁ πρότερος in Deut 24:4. Regarding σῶμα as a metonymy for Christ's crucifixion, Murray notes "'The body of Christ' refers to the crucifixion of our Lord in the body and places in relief the concreteness of that event by which we have been discharged from the law." Murray, *Romans*, 243.

have died to sin can continue to live in it. Similarly, one cannot "remarry" the law after Christ died to free the Romans from it.⁶⁰

Third, the Romans' marriage to Christ echoes ancient Israel's marriage to Yahweh which places Christ within the divine identity of Israel's God.⁶¹ As noted above, multiple OT pre-texts describe Israel's union with its God as a marriage.⁶² Israel's Scriptures restrict such a marriage to God alone. Paul adapts this metaphor to describe Christ's union with his followers. In this way, Paul portrays Christ as fulfilling a role that in Israel's Scriptures only Yahweh could fulfill.

Fourth, bearing missional and eschatological fruit promised in Israel's Scriptures is the purpose behind death to the law, freedom from the law, and marriage to Christ. Multiple OT passages include fruitfulness as a post-exilic and cosmological outcome of God's deliverance.⁶³ As Isaiah puts it, "Those who are coming, the children of Jacob, will bloom and Israel will flourish, and the world will be filled with its fruit (τοῦ καρποῦ αὐτοῦ)" (Isa 27:6). Paul finds such fruit bearing in the believer's death to the law with the crucified Christ and their marriage to the risen Christ. The purpose of the experience is "in order (ἵνα) that we might bear fruit (καρποφορήσωμεν) to God" (Rom 7:4). The concrete referent of the fruit metaphor is obedience by Jews and Gentiles to God rather than the disobedience to death. Bearing fruit to death was the outcome of an existence "in the flesh (ἐν τῇ σαρκί)" where sinful passions were being produced in the "members" (ἐν τοῖς μέλεσιν ἡμῶν) of the Romans through the law. Christ delivered the Romans from this existence to bear fruit to God just as the prophets promised.

Finally, the Romans were released from the law (κατηργήθημεν ἀπὸ τοῦ νόμου) through their death (ἀποθανόντες) with Christ, and the result is a new kind of service to God (δουλεύειν) promised in the prophets where God addresses the Romans in their hearts by the Spirit rather than in stone by the script of the Mosaic Law. The latter form of address is abbreviated in the phrase "in the oldness of the letter (παλαιότητι γράμματος)" (Rom 7:6). As I noted above, Paul evokes the OT's description of the law as God's written address to his people from Sinai to the post-exilic era.⁶⁴ Paul personifies the law in Romans as something that speaks to people, but this old form of divine address does not result in the kind of service that God demands.⁶⁵ The "new" divine

---

60. Cf. Gal 3:23–29; 4:8–11; 5:2–6.

61. Bauckham argues that early Christian writers portray Christ as participating in actions that are restricted to Yhwh in Israel's Scriptures. His argument can be extended to include divine metaphors. Early Christian writers used metaphors to describe Christ's relationship to his followers which in Israel's Scriptures described Yhwh's relationship to ancient Israel. See Bauckham, *Jesus and the God of Israel*.

62. See Isa 62:5; Hos 2:16.

63. E.g., Isa 27:6; Zech 8:12; Amos 9:14.

64. See, e.g., Exod 24:12; Deut 4:13; Josh 23:6; 1 Kgs 2:3; Dan 9:11; Ezra 3:2.

65. E.g., in the very next verse of Paul's argument we find "for I was not knowing coveting except the law was saying (ὁ νόμος ἔλεγεν), 'You shall not covet'" (Rom 7:6). See also Rom 3:19.

address is by the Spirit which both Jeremiah and Ezekiel promised (Jer 31:31–34; Ezek 36:16–38). Seifrid nicely summarizes Paul's scripturally informed contrast in Rom 7:6:

> 'Letter' and 'Spirit' represent two different ways in which God addresses the human being. The written code encounters the human being from without, requiring obedience as a condition of life. In contrast, the Spirit writes the will of God upon the heart through the proclamation of what God has done for us in Christ. Unlike the 'written code,' the Spirit performs a 'circumcision of the heart.' Those who believe in Christ render service to God in 'the newness of the Spirit.' They share in the new creation which has been inaugurated in Christ. Their obedience does not derive from 'the oldness of the letter' by which God addresses the fallen human being.[66]

---

66. Seifrid, *Christ Our Righteousness*, 98–99.

6

Romans 7:7–25

WE COME NOW TO one of the most debated passages in the entire Pauline corpus. It is unlikely that a single ἐγώ from ancient Greek literature has ever sparked as much conversation as the one employed by Paul in these verses.[1] The two main exegetical questions that swirl around the identity of this enigmatic ἐγώ are: (1) Is the "I" autobiographical? (2) Is this an instance of speech-in-character?[2] One must also consider how this text fits with Paul's ongoing rhetorical argument.

The intertextual subtext of this passage has the potential to shed a great deal of interpretive light on these exegetical questions. Although this text only contains one fragmented citation, the citation of Exod 20:17 (Deut 5:21) in Rom 7:7, its intertextual force should not be underestimated. Nothing shapes Paul's "I" here like Israel's Scriptures.[3] Even if Paul employs a speech-in-character (προσωποποιΐα) in the vein of his rhetorical contemporaries, as Stowers and others have argued, the speech itself is an OT lament as I will explain in what follows.[4] While echoes of lament dominate the intertextual subtext here, other pre-texts are in play as well. Collectively, Paul describes an individual's hellish experience with sin and the Mosaic Law which can only be articulated with such vivid detail from the retrospective viewpoint of someone who is in Christ (ἐν Χριστῷ).

---

1. Paul uses an emphatic ἐγω in Rom 7:9, 10, 14, 17, 20, 24, and 25.

2. Gaventa, "The Shape of the 'I,'" 79.

3. For intertextual studies of Rom 7:7–25, or studies that lean heavily on intertextual analysis, see Bornkamm, "Sin, Law, and Death," 87–104; Bruckner, "The Creational Context of Law," 91–110; Busch, "The Figure of Eve," 1–36; Campbell, *Pauline Dogmatics*, 113–18; Dochorn, "Röm 7,7," 59–77; Elder, "Wretch I Am!," 743–64; "Gaventa, "The Shape of the 'I,'" 77–91; Goodrich, "Sold Under Sin," 476–95; Jervis, "The Commandment," 193–216; Karlberg, "Israel's History Personified," 65–74; Meyer, "The Worm at the Core," 62–97; Moo, "Israel and Paul," 122–35; Packer, "The 'Wretched Man,'" 70–81; Seifrid, "The Voice of the Law," 1–51; Timmins, *Romans 7 and Christian Identity*; Ziesler, "The Role of the Tenth Commandment," 41–56.

4. See Stowers, "Romans 7.7–25 as a Speech in Character," 180–202; Tobin, *Paul's Rhetoric in Its Contexts*, 227–45. f

Romans 7:7–13

(7:7–13) What then shall we say? Is the law sin? May it never be; but I would not have known sin except through the law; for I was not knowing coveting except the law was saying, "You shall not covet." But sin having seized an opportunity through the commandment produced in me all coveting; for apart from the law sin is dead. And I was living formerly apart from the law, but after the commandment came sin sprang to life, and I died and the commandment which was for life this was found in me for death; for sin having seized an opportunity through the commandment deceived me and through it killed me. Therefore, the law is holy and the commandment is holy and righteous and good. Therefore, did that which was good become death for me? May it never be; but sin, in order that it might be shown to be sin, producing death in me through the good, in order that through the commandment sin might become utterly sinful.

Paul once again anticpates and responds to a false inference which one might draw from his statements about the law in Rom 7:1–6. One might falsely conclude that the Mosaic Law is sinful, "What then shall we say? Is the law sin?" (Rom 7:7). Paul quickly responds to this inference with his familiar "may it never be (μὴ γένοιτο)." He follows his interjection by identifying the problem as sin's use of the law rather than the law itself. Paul's discussion of how sin uses, or abuses, the law contains several well-known exegetical difficulties.[5] I will address these difficulties as we encounter them in our intertextual analysis.[6] Our primary focus remains the interplay between OT pre-texts and Paul's argument. The pre-texts here mainly emanate from Gen 2–3 and Exod 20:17 (Deut 5:21).

Suggested Pre-Texts in Romans 7:7–13

Hübner lists the following pre-texts: Exod 20:17 (Rom 7:7); Gen 2:16–17 (Rom 7:7–9); Gen 3:5–7, 13, 22; Lev 11:45; 18:5; Deut 6:24; 30:15, 16–18; Prov 6:23 (Rom 7:10–12).[7]

Nestle-Aland 28th ed. lists the following pre-texts in its margins: Exod 20:17; Deut 5:21 (Rom 7:7); Lev 18:5 (Rom 7:10); Gen 2:17; 3:13 (Rom 7:11).[8] Hays does not discuss any pre-texts in these verses.

---

5. For an overview of the difficulties associated with Rom 7:7–25, see Cranfield, *Romans*, 1:342–47; Hultgren, *Romans*, 681–91.

6. For the interpretive history of Rom 7:7–25, see Lichtenberger, *Das Ich Adams und das Ich der Menschheit*, 13–105.

7. Hübner, *Vetus Testamentum in Novo*, 2:102–108. See also 4 Macc 18:8; Sir 45:5; Pss Sol 14:2; Bar 3:9; 4:1.

8. See also 4 Macc 2:5; Pss Sol 14:2.

Seifrid includes the following pre-texts in his analysis: Gen 3:6, 13; Exod 20:17; and Deut 4:5–8; 5:16, 21, 29; 6:3, 18, 24; 7:10–12; 10:13; 12:25, 28; 22:7; 30:15–20. He suggests that Paul combines the deception of Eve and the citation of the Mosaic Law noting, "Paul sees in the human encounter with the commandment the recapitulation of Adam's transgression."[9]

Intertextual Analysis of Romans 7:7–13

The bulk of the intertextual subtext here emanates from the citation of Exod 20:17 (Deut 5:21) and the echo proper of Gen 3. Additionally, as well shall see, Paul's argument also contains an echo proper of Lev 18:5 and Deut 30:15.

Romans 7:7 and the Citation of Exodus 20:17 (Deut 5:21)

Paul begins his response to the false inference that the law is sin by explaining that the law gave him a knowledge of sin, and he cites the Decalogue to illustrate his point.[10] He points to the example of coveting, "For I was not knowing coveting except the law was saying, "You shall not covet (οὐκ ἐπιθυμήσεις)" (Rom 7:7). The phrase οὐκ ἐπιθυμήσεις (לא תחמד) is an exact citation from Exod 20:17 or Deut 5:21.[11] In their full forms, the prohibition reads "You shall not covet (οὐκ ἐπιθυμήσεις) the wife of your neighbor. You shall not covet (οὐκ ἐπιθυμήσεις) the house of your neighbor nor his field nor his servant nor his female servant nor his ox nor his donkey nor any of his cattle nor as much as belongs to your neighbor."[12]

Paul removes the specific objects of coveting which are listed in Exod 20:17 (Deut 5:21). The result is that the prohibition becomes broader so that the object of coveting could be almost anything. Moreover, the precise object of coveting is likely not Paul's main concern as much as it is a person's base desire to possess what does not belong to them regardless of what God says and regardless of how that desire impacts one's

---

9. Seifrid, *Romans*, 632.

10. Cf. Rom 3:19–20.

11. It is not possible to determine if Paul is citing Exod 20:17, Deut 5:21. For other uses of the phrase οὐκ ἐπιθυμήσεις, see Deut 7:25; 4 Macc 2:5. Kujanpää argues, "Since Paul's quotation of the commandments in Rom. 13:9 follows the order of Deuteronomy 5 rather than Exodus 20, I have presented Deut. 5:21 as Paul's source text, although the words οὐκ ἐπιθυμήσεις are identical in Exod. 20:17. Yet it is questionable whether it makes sense to select between two source texts for such a central piece of tradition and teaching." Kujanpää, *The Rhetorical Functions*, 316n74.

12. Exod 20:17 and Deut 5:21 are in exact match in the LXX. However, the MT contains a few differences between the two. Exod 20:17 MT reads, "You shall not covet (תחמד) your neighbor's house; you shall not covet (תחמד) your neighbor's wife, or his male servant, or his female servant, or his ox, or his donkey, or anything that belongs to your neighbor." Deut 5:21 reads, "And you shall not covet (תחמד) your neighbor's wife; and you shall not desire (תתאוה) your neighbor's house, his field, or his male servant or his female servant, his ox, or his donkey, or anything that belongs to your neighbor."

neighbor.¹³ As Kujanpää observes, "The omission of all objects and the resulting more abstract command not to covet is not Paul's own innovation; several Jewish writings by his contemporaries present ἐπιθυμία ('desire') as the origin of sin and its prohibition as a central commandment of the law. Paul continues this tradition of interpretation when he picks up exactly the command not to covet as if it were representative of the law's commandment as a whole."¹⁴ Whether or not Paul sees the prohibition as "representative of the law's commandment as a whole," coveting certainly plays a key role in the narratives of Adam and Israel which, as we shall see, are important parts of the intertextual subtext here. Of all the commands in the Decalogue, the prohibition against coveting provides Paul with a powerful example of how the law is powerless against the power of sin.¹⁵

Romans 7:7–13 and the Echo of the Serpent

This brings us to the second intertextual consideration in our text, namely the echo proper of Gen 3 where coveting plays a key role in the interaction between God, Adam/Eve, and the serpent. Rom 7:7–12 echoes the interaction in a few different ways.

First, Paul's description of how sin deceived the "I" (ἐγώ) evokes Eve's complaint to God against the serpent:

> For sin having seized an opportunity through the commandment deceived me (ἐξηπάτησέν με) and through it killed me (Rom 7:11).

> And the Lord God said to the woman, "Why did you do this?" And the woman said, "The serpent deceived me (ἠπάτησέν με), and I ate" (Gen 3:13).

The *volume* of the echo is strong based on the semantic and grammatical consistency between ἐξηπάτησέν με and ἠπάτησέν με.¹⁶ Paul's use of the verb ἐξηπάτησέν rather than ἠπάτησέν does not mitigate the volume. Paul uses the same verb in 2 Cor where he explicitly mentions the serpent's deception of Eve, "But I fear lest somehow, as the serpent deceived Eve (ὄφις ἐξηπάτησεν Εὔαν) by his trickery, your minds might be lead astray from the sincere devotion and simplicity in Chirst" (2 Cor 11:3).

---

13. See Dunn, *Romans*, 1:380; Ziesler, "The Role," 41–56.

14. Cf. 4 Macc 2:6; Philo Decal. 142, 150, 173; Spec. 4.84, 85. Kujanpää, *The Rhetorical Functions*, 316.

15. Kujanpää observes, "It is noteworthy that Paul's argument would not have worked with most other commandments of the law. Since his purpose is to demonstrate the powerlessness of the law that is being 'hijacked' by sin (7:11), he needs a commandment that is, first, difficult to keep and that thus indirectly proves the powerlessness of the law, and second, that concerns the internal processes of the mind: one's intentions and desires." Kujanpää, *The Rhetorical Functions*, 317.

16. For other uses of ἐξαπατάω in the Pauline corpus see Rom 16:18; 1 Cor 3:18; 2 Cor 11:3; 2 Thess 2:3; and 1 Tim 2:14. In the LXX, ἐξαπατάω only occurs in Exod 8:25. The only occurrence of the phrase ἠπάτησέν με in the LXX is in Gen 3:13.

The *contextual consistency* between Gen 3 and Rom 7:7–12 is also substantial based on several parallels. For example, just as the serpent used a prohibition against coveting to deceive and kill Adam/Eve, sin does some the same thing to Paul's "I." The serpent evokes God's prior command in his deception of Eve:

> Now the serpent was craftier than all the animals which are upon the earth, which the Lord God made; and the serpent said to the woman, "Did God really say, 'You certainly shall not eat from every tree which is in the garden?'" And the woman said to the serpent, "From the fruit of the tree of the garden we will eat, but from the fruit of the tree, which is in the midst of the garden, God said, 'You shall not eat from it nor shall you touch it, in order that you might not die.' And the serpent said to the woman, "You certainly shall not die; for God was knowing that in whatever day you should eat from it, your eyes will be opened, and you will be like gods knowing good and evil." And the woman saw that the tree was good for eating and that it was pleasing to the eyes to look at and that it was beautiful to consider, having taken its fruit she ate; and she gave also to her husband, and they ate (Gen 3:1–6).[17]

The prior command in question is Gen 2:16–17, "And the Lord God commanded Adam saying, 'From every tree which is in the garden you shall certainly eat, but from the tree to know good and evil, you shall not eat from it; but in whatever day you should eat from it, you will surely die.'" Obviously, this prohibition does not contain the phrase οὐκ ἐπιθυμήσεις (Exod 20:17; Deut 5:21); however, it is implied in God's command that Adam and Eve not eat from the tree of knowing good and evil. It is also implied in Eve's covetous response to the serpent's temptation, "And the woman saw that the tree was good for eating and that it was pleasing to the eyes to look at and that it was beautiful to consider, having taken its fruit she ate; and she gave also to her husband, and they ate" (Gen 3:6).[18] The narrator underscores that Eve looked at the fruit in a covetous way. She deemed the fruit so desirous that she tossed aside the divine prohibition and warning against eating it.

This narration of the serpent's deceptive work against Eve is refracted in Paul's description of sin's deceptive work against the "I."[19] Sin, like the serpent, used the divine command as an opportunity to produce within the "I" the coveting that God prohibited in the law, "But sin having taken an opportunity (ἀφορμήν) through the commandment (διὰ τῆς ἐντολῆς) produced in me (κατεῖργάσατο ἐν ἐμοί) all coveting (πᾶσαν ἐπιθυμίαν); for without the law sin is dead" (Rom 7:8).[20] In Gen 3, the referent

---

17. There are no significant differences between Gen 3:1–6 in the LXX and MT.

18. Gen 3:6 and Deut 5:21 in the MT contain catchwords (תאוה/אוה) that may indicate a link between Eve's transgression and the prohibition not to covet. On this point, see Dochorn, "Röm 7,7 und das zehnte Gebot," 63–64.

19. In this way, just as we saw in our intertextual analysis of Rom 5:12–19, the power of sin and the scriptural description of the serpent overlap with another at several points.

20. Cf. Gen 3:1, 4–5.

of "opportunity" (ἀφορμή) is Eve's encounter with the serpent.[21] It is more difficult to pinpoint the precise referent of ἀφορμή in Rom 7:7–12, because the referent is tied to the identity of the "I" which, as I discsucced above, poses the largest exegetical difficulty in our text. We will return to this discussion below. Here I would simply note that Gen 3 informs Paul's perception of the opportunity. Simply put, sin's opportunity to deceive and kill is the divine command. Just as the serpent used God's command in Gen 2–3 to deceive and kill Adam and Eve, sin uses the same opportunity. Sin produced (κατεῖργάσατο) all kinds of coveting (πᾶσαν ἐπιθυμίαν) in the "I" through God's command in the law, "You shall not covet."[22]

In Rom 7:8–13, Paul expands on this Adamic shaped experience which is recapitulated in ancient Israel, in Paul, and, as I will discuss below, any embodied person in whom sin dwells. Verse 8 ends with the explanatory comment χωρὶς γὰρ νόμου ἁμαρτία νεκρά. The present ἔστιν, or perhaps even the imperfect ἦν, should be supplied here.[23] However, Paul's statement does not suggest the general principle that "if the law were not present, people would not be troubled by sin."[24] Instead, the statement underscores the inactivity of sin apart from the law. Apart from the law, sin is, as Fitzmyer puts it, "a corpselike being, powerless to make the evildoing of humanity a flagrant revolt against God's will."[25] The pre-text, likewise, draws a close link between the activity of the serpent and the divine command.

Romans 7:8–13 and Echoes of the Adamic Experience

Paul continues his description of this Adamic shaped experience in vv. 9–10 noting, "And I was living once apart from the law, but after the commandment came, sin sprang to life, and I died and the commandment which was to result in life proved to result in death for me." Here the interpreter is even more hard pressed to consider the identity of the "I." As Longenecker puts it, the question arises "Who is this 'I' that is spoken of in this passage, and to what time is the passage referring?"[26] Additionally, one must consider the relationship between the "I" in vv. 7–12 and the "I" in vv. 13–25.

---

21. Of course, the term ἀφορμή does not occur in Gen 3. Nevertheless, it is an apt description of what transpires in the garden.

22. Cf. the use of κατεργάζομαι in Rom 1:27; 2:9; 4:15; 5:3; 7:8, 13, 15, 17, 18, 20; 15:18.

23. Murray suggests, "There is no verb in the Greek. The translators in this case have inserted 'is' and have construed Paul as enunciating a general principle. The propriety of this interpretation is disputable. It would seem that the verb to be inserted should be 'was.' Paul is describing his experience. His experience is indeed representative and in that respect the clause in question states what is the common feature of the experience which the apostle here describes and analyzes. It must not be assumed, however, that what the apostle is dealing with here is the principle stated elsewhere that 'where no law is, there is no transgression.'" Murray, *Epistle to the Romans*, 250.

24. Longenecker, *Romans*, 641.

25. Fitzmyer, *Romans*, 467.

26. Longenecker, *Romans*, 642.

At this point, I would note that in vv. 7–12 Paul likely recounts his own experience with sin's deceptive and deadly use of the law. The vivid language employed throughout vv. 7–25 makes it unlikely that the account is entirely unreflective of Paul's own experience. However, it does not follow that the identity of the "I" is purely autobiographical in force. Paul describes his own experience in relation to Gen 3 with the result that the "I" recapitulates Adam's experience.[27] It follows then that if Paul recapitulates Adam's experience others do as well. This would include Israel and anyone else in whom sins dwells which defines all human beings for Paul.

With respect to the time that Paul has in view in vv. 9–13, interpreters often want to pinpoint a specific moment in the apostle's life. Such an urge stems from Paul's statement, "I was living formerly apart from the law (ἔζων χωρὶς νόμου ποτέ)" (Rom 7:9a).[28] The verb ἔζων with its temporal dexis marker ποτέ indicates a past ongoing action. Some have inferred from this construction, coupled with the genitive absolute ἐλθούσης τῆς ἐντολῆς ("after the commandment came"), that Paul refers to a teenage experience perhaps around time of his bar mitzvah "when the commandment shifted from a written text to an obligation."[29] At that moment in Paul's youth, "sin sprang to life (ἀνέζησεν)." When the arrival of the command not to covet woke sin from its dormancy in Paul, he died (ἐγὼ ἀπέθανον). The command which he thought would result in life resulted in death instead (Rom 7:10). This proposed autobiographical referent is quite possible, but it is not something that the interpreter can be certain about.

We can be certain that Paul recounts this experience retrospectively from the standpoint of faith in Christ. Moreover, based on strong intertextual echoes, the experience of the "I" bears a strong resemblance to what transpired in Gen 3. Adam lived for an indeterminate amount of time without the command announced in Gen 2:16–17.[30] From a narrative standpoint, and presumably in Paul's reading of Gen 2–3, the serpent remained dormant until Adam received the divine prohibition and his helper Eve. It was then that serpent sprang into deceptive and deadly action. As Eve

---

27. Seifrid notes, "Paul sees in the human encounter with the commandment the recapitulation of Adam's transgression." Seifrid, *Romans*, 632.

28. Jewett notes that Rom 7:9 contains the NT's only occurrence of the form ἔζων and that it parallels reminiscences of death and or suicides in Greco-Roman literature. See, e.g., Eur Alc 295; Plut Amat 768 D. See Jewett, *Romans*, 451. Additionally, in his comparison of Sir 15 and Rom 7:7–25, Jason Maston observes that these two texts share "verbal and thematic points of contact." However, Maston ultimately concludes that the two texts "have quite distinctive perspectives on the relationship between the human, the law, and sin." Maston, "Sirach and Romans 7:1–25, 97.

29. Maston, "Sirach and Romans 7:1–25, 97.

30. Stuhlmacher suggests that Adam is the only biblical figure who lived without a command. Therefore, he identifies Adam as the "I" in Rom 7:7–12. Moreover, he argues that Paul's description here resembles Jewish tradition of his day. He explains, "First of all, the Law, identified with the wisdom at work in creation, is considered in this tradition to have been created long ago before the creation of the world. Then, very definite periods of time are again seen to existe between the creation of Adam, his transfer into the garden of paradise, and the decree of the commandment in Gen. 2:16f. Finally, the one commandment given to Adam and Eve is understood to be the embodiment of the entire Law." See, e.g., Sir 24; Bar 4:1; m. Abot 3:14. See Stuhlmacher, *Romans*, 106.

explains in the aftermath and shame of transgressing the command, "The serpent deceived me (ὁ ὄφις ἠπάτησέν με), and I ate" (Gen 3:13). Something similar occurred with Paul and those like him. Sin seized the arrival of the command "you shall not covet" as an opportunity for decpeiton and death.[31] As Paul puts it in v. 11, "For sin having seized the opportunity through the commandment deceived me and through it killed me."

Within the *history of interpretation*, not all interpreters are enthusiastic about the prospect of Adamic echoes in Rom 7:7–12. For example, L. Ann Jervis refers to the proposed echo of Gen 2–3 in Rom 7:7–12 as a "phantom appearance of the Genesis fall narrative."[32] This is simply misguided. As the preceding analysis has demonstrated, the Gen 2–3 pre-text and Paul's text have substantial intertextual *volume*, *contextual consistency*, and *recurrence*. As Dodd plainly puts it, "The importance of that passage for Paul's thought is obvious; he has many allusions to it."[33]

Romans 7:7–13 and the Echo of Leviticus 18:5

While the Adamic narrative dominates the intertextual subtext of Rom 7:7–13, two other OT pre-texts are woven into Paul's argument at this point. They both involve Paul's juxtaposition of life and death. First, v. 10 echoes Lev 18:5:

> And I was living formerly apart from the law, but after the commandment came sin sprang to life, and I died and the commandment which was for life (ἡ ἐντολὴ ἡ εἰς ζωήν) this was found in me for death (αὕτη εἰς θάνατον) (Rom 7:10).

> And you shall keep all my commands (τὰ προστάγματά μου) and all my judgments (πάντα τὰ κρίματά μου) and you shall do them, the things which if a man should do them he will live by them (ζήσεται ἐν αὐτοῖς); for I am the Lord your God (Lev 18:5).[34]

The *volume* of the echo is low to moderate. Some semantic overlap occurs with the phrases ἡ ἐντολὴ ἡ εἰς ζωήν and ζήσεται ἐν αὐτοῖς. What the echo lacks in volume it makes up for in the way it passes other tests.

For example, the *contextual consistency* is strong. In the wider context of Lev 18:1–5, Moses instructs the Israelites to adopt neither the practices of Egypt where they once lived nor those of Canaan which they are slated to enter. If they abstain from such practices, God promises life. Lev 18:6–30 focuses on specific sexual practices,

---

31. Again, it is not possible to pinpoint the precise moment of this "arrival."
32. Jervis, "'The Commandment which is for Life,'" 214.
33. Dodd, *Romans*, 123.
34. Cf. Deut 6:24, "And the Lord commanded us to do all these righteous requirements to fear the Lord our God, in order that it might go well with us all of our days, in order that we might live (ἵνα ζῶμεν) just also today."

but the instructions in vv. 1–5 applies to all the commands contained in the Mosaic Law. The referent of life in the Leviticus pre-text is a long life in Canaan with the warning that curses and death await those who fail to carry out the commandments.[35] This is the instruction by which Paul's "I" was formerly living. From the perspective of the "I" in Rom 7:10, the referent of life (ζωή) is ultimately resurrection life which I will discuss further below.[36] Paul extends the referent of "life" in Lev 18:5 to include life in this fullest sense, but it remained contingent upon obedience to the Law.

One question that arises at this point is how Paul weaves together Gen 2–3, Exod 20:17 (Deut 5:21), and Lev 18:5 to describe the experience of the "I." To put it another way, how did sin use the prohibition against coveting (Exod 20:17) and instruction about living (Lev 18:5) to deceive (Gen 3:13) and kill the "I"? If Gen 2–3 is the backdrop for Rom 7:7–12, as I have suggested thus far, it follows that sin acted as the serpent did, though not without reconfiguration by Paul to fit the circumstances of the "I."[37] Therefore, at some point in the life of the "I," sin that lie dormant within the "I" sprang to life through the command "you shall not covet." Sin brought the command to the attention of the "I" just as the serpent brought the command from Gen 2:16–17 to the attention of Eve in Gen 3:2. At that point, the "conversation" between sin and the "I," like that between the serpent and Eve, most likely involved a denial that coveting would lead to death. Sin "produced (κατειργάσατο, Rom 7:8)" in the "I" all kinds of coveting through the command "you shall not covet" which resulted in death rather than life. In this way, sin's use of the law turned the promised result of Lev 18:5, "if a man will do them he will live by them," into its converse.

Before proceeding, we need to consider the precise referent of "life" (ζωή/ζάω) and "death" (θάνατος/ἀποθνῄσκω) in Rom 7:7–13. Two considerations are helpful for identifying these referents.

First, life and death described in Gen 1–3 inform life and death in Paul's argument here. Gen 1–2 indicates that life for Adam and Eve consisted of God being the gracious source of their existence, their provision, their instruction, and their authority to rule over creation. In the immediate aftermath of succumbing to the serpent's temptation in Gen 3, death became a divine sentence against them which stripped away everything God gave them and culminated in the termination of their physical existence. Prior to that termination point, Adam and Eve still experienced their sentence of death in a variety of ways such as the pain of childbirth, emnity with the serpent, difficulty in obtaining necessities of life, and even the murder of a son. Their

---

35. See Lev 18:26–30.

36. In his comparison of how 4 Ezra and Paul engage texts such as Lev 18:5 and Deut 30:19, Watson notes "In both cases, law observance is the way to life; in both cases, the 'life' in question is resurrection life, on the far side of the universal judgment; and in both cases, his clear scriptural teaching constitutes a problem." Watson, *Paul and the Hermeneutics of Faith*, 505.

37. E.g., Seifrid notes, "Unlike the situation of the fall, sin is already present within the human being who hears the law: the commandment provides only the opportunity for sin to effect 'all coveting.'" Seifrid, *Romans*, 632.

exile from the garden and separation from God put the sentence of death in motion. For Paul's "I," death consisted of similar experiences under the same sentence of death.[38] Life would be the opposite of these experiences and culminate in resurrection from the dead.

Second, we must also consider Paul's tendency to personify death as we identify the referent of death in Rom 7:7–12. For example, when he first evokes the Adamic narrative in Rom 5, Paul portrays death as "entering (εἰσῆλθεν)" the world through sin, "spreading (διῆλθεν)" to all people, and "reigning (ἐβασίλευσεν)" from Adam until Moses (Rom 5:12–14). Union with Christ ends the reign of death in the life of the believer (Rom 6:9).[39] And in Rom 7:24 the lamenting "I" cries out for deliverance from the "body of this death (ἐκ τοῦ σώματος τοῦ θανάτου τούτου)." Death is obviously a power in Paul's estimation whose reign of terror begins with Adam. Therefore, the experience of death for the "I" in Rom 7:7–12 includes an experience of death's tyrannical power.

Romans 7:7–13 and the Echo of Deuteronomy 30:15

A second echo related to Paul's juxtaposition of life and death in Rom 7:7–13 emanates from Deut 30:15, "Behold, I have set before you today life and death (τὴν ζωὴν καὶ τὸν θάνατον), good and evil (τὸ ἀγαθὸν καὶ τὸ κακόν)." The *volume* of this echo is high based on the combination of the terms ζωή, θάνατος, and ἀγαθόν in both the pre-text and text. Paul juxtaposes life (εἰς ζωήν) and death (εἰς θάνατον) in Rom 7:10, and he refers to the law and its commandments as "good (τὸ ἀγαθόν)" in 7:13.

Contextual consistency occurs at the point of juxtaposing the results of obedience and disobedience to the Mosaic Law. The wider context of the pre-text elaborates on this juxtaposition:

> Behold, I have set before you today life and death (τὴν ζωὴν καὶ τὸν θάνατον), good and evil (τὸ ἀγαθὸν καὶ τὸ κακόν). If you should listen to the commandments of the Lord your God, which I am commanding you today, to love the Lord your God, to go in all of his ways, to keep his righteous requirements and his judgments, you will live (ζήσεσθε) and multiply, and the Lord your God will bless you in all the earth, into which you are entering there to inherit it. And if your heart should change and you should not listen and having been deceived you should worship other gods and serve them, I am proclaiming to you today that you will certainly be destroyed and you certainly shall not live long upon the land, which the Lord God is giving to you, into which you are going through the Jordan to inherit it. I call both heaven and earth this day

---

38. As Cranfield notes in his comments on ἐγὼ δὲ ἀπέθανον in Rom 7:10, "Though he continues to live, he is dead—being under God's sentence of death. Physical death, when it comes, is but the fulfillment of the sentence already passed." Cranfield, *Romans*, 1:352.

39. See also Rom 6:16, 21, 23; 8:38.

to testify against you, I have set life and death (τὴν ζωὴν καὶ τὸν θάνατον) before you, blessing and curse; choose life (ἔκλεξαι τὴν ζωήν), in order that you might live (ἵνα ζῆς) and your seed, to love the Lord your God, to obey his voice and cleave to him; for this is your life (τοῦτο ἡ ζωή σου) and the length of your days, for you to dwell in the land, which the Lord swore to your fathers Abraham and Isaac and Jacob to give them (Deut 30:15–20).

As the nation stood poised to enter the promised land, the choice (ἔκλεξαι τὴν ζωήν, Deut 30:19) between obedience or disobedience to the Mosaic Law was clearly a choice between death and life. Paul depicts the "I" as an individual faced with the same choice and accompanying results but not withtout significanct reconfiguration. The pre-text juxtaposes life and death as a choice left to the Israelites, but the text in Romans underscores sin's deceptive and deadly use of the Mosaic Law. One hardly gets the sense in reading Rom 7:7–13 that the "I" had the ability to choose obedience and thereby experience life. That is not to suggest that the "I" understood this inability at the time. As Matson rightly notes in his comparison of Sirach 15 and Rom 7:7–25, "Although in the narrative as told by Paul the speaker's pessimism dominates Rom 7, one must not miss that he views himself, like Ben Sira, as morally capable of keeping the Torah."[40] However, Paul inserts into the experience of the "I" something which the Deuteronomic pre-text does not explicitly mention, the agency of sin. Paul retrospectively recognizes that sin used the Mosaic Law to deceive the "I" in two interrelated ways. As I noted above, sin raised doubts about the deadly consequences of coveting in the mind of the "I." At the same time, sin deceived the "I" into thinking that he could acquire life before God through obedience to the Mosaic Law, even using the promise of Lev 18:5 to accomplish this deceitful and deadly outcome.[41]

Romans 7:7–13 and Additional Echoes

We come now to Paul's conclusion in v. 12. After describing sin's deceitful and deadly use of the Mosaic Law agasint the "I," Paul concludes "Therefore (ὥστε), the law is holy (ὁ νόμος ἅγιος) and the commandment is holy (ἡ ἐντολὴ ἁγία) and righteous (δικαία) and good (ἀγαθή)" (Rom 7:12). Paul concludes that sin's use of the law does not tarnish the law's inherent purity and perfection nor the upright and worthy nature

---

40. Matson goes on, "When the narrative begins, he is ignorant of sin and disobedience (7:7c) and claims to posess life prior to the arrival of the law (7:9a). Moreover, while, 7:15–20 describes the failings of the speaker, the twice-repeated pattern of desiring and attempting good and yet performing evil (7:15–17, 18–20) reveals the speaker's initial, mistaken optimism: he thinks he can be obedient, if only he keeps trying." Matson, "Sirach and Romans 7:1–25," 97.

41. Deut 30:15 also passes the tests of *recurrence* and *history of interpretation*. With respect to the former, as I will discuss in a later chapter, Paul cites Deut 30:12 in Rom 10:6. With respect to the latter, in examining the "four co-ordinates" of life and death as well as good and evil in Rom 7:7–25, Watson notes "In their abstract form, however, the four co-ordinates appear to derive from Deuteronomy 30:15." Watson, *Paul and the Hermeneutics of Faith*, 506–7.

of its commands.⁴² This description of the Mosaic Law echoes descriptions in Israel's Scriptures:

> And what kind of nation is so great, for whom there are righteous requirements (δικαιώματα) and righteous judgments (κρίματα δίκαια) according to all this law (κατὰ πάντα τὸν νόμον τοῦτον), which I am placing (δίδωμι) before you today (Deut 4:8)?

> For I am giving (δωροῦμαι) a good gift (δῶρον ἀγαθὸν) to you, you shall not abandon my law (τὸν ἐμὸν νόμον) (Prov 4:2).

Both pre-texts emphasize that the Mosaic Law is a gift (δίδωμι/δῶρον) from God. It is a unique gift that set ancient Israel apart from its religious contemporaries and held the promise of life for those who obeyed it in the promised land.⁴³ Similarly, the speaker in Ps 19 (18 LXX) gushes over the instruction found in the Mosaic Law "The law of the Lord (ὁ νόμος τοῦ κυρίου) is blameless, restoring the soul; the testimony of the Lord is faithful, instructing the simple; the righteous requirements of the Lord are upright, rejoicing the heart; the commandment of the Lord (ἡ ἐντολὴ κυρίου) is bright, enlightening the eyes" (Ps 118:8–9 LXX).⁴⁴ Although Paul's statement about the Mosaic Law does not necessarily evoke any of these pre-texts specfically, these are the kinds of pre-texts that undoubtedly shaped his perception of the law. As Hultgren observes, "Here Paul stands within the mainstream of Jewish tradition, joining the voice of others who speak of the law in glowing terms, praising it for its perfection and goodness."⁴⁵

Romans 7:13 is often taken as a transitional verse that bridges vv. 7–12 to 14–25.⁴⁶ Based on his discussion of sin's use of the law in vv. 7–11, as well as his full-throated endorsement of the law in v. 12, Paul anticipates a false inference. "Therefore, did that which was good become death for me? May it never be; but sin, in order that it might be shown to be sin, producing death in me through the good, in order that through

---

42. See BDAG 3–4, 10–11, and 246–47.

43. "And now, Israel, hear the righteous requirements and the judgments, as much as I am teaching you to do today, in order that you might live (ἵνα ζῆτε) and become numerous and having entered you might inherit the land, which the Lord of your fathers is giving to you" (Deut 4:1).

44. As Westerholm notes, "That God gave the law to Israel must be reckoned among the greatest proofs of his love. Sympathetic readers of Psalm 119 will grasp something of the treasured place occupied by torah for those who horizons included the holy and the good and who saw torah's law as their embodiment. Paul was certainly among them. Before his adoption of the Christian cause, he excelled his contemporaries in his devotion to the law. Nor did his coming to Christian faith do anything to alter his convictions about the sacredness of torah's demands." Westerholm, *Understanding Paul*, 112–13.

45. Hultgren, *Romans*, 280. See also Wolter, *Der Brief an die Römer*, 1:439. With respect to Second Temple texts that speak highly of the Mosaic Law as Paul does in Rom 7:12, see, e.g., 2 Macc 6:23, 28; Josephus, *Ant.* 4:295; Philo, *Mos* 2.3.14; 3 En. 11.

46. Consequently, some interpreters treat Rom 7:13 in their discussions of vv. 7–12 while others treat it in their discussions of 14–25.

the commandment sin might become utterly sinful" (Rom 7:13). "That which is good (τὸ ἀγαθόν)," or the law, did not cause the death of the "I."[47] Rather, the death of the "I" stemmed from sin's use of the good law (διὰ τοῦ ἀγαθοῦ). Paul explains that sin was producing death (κατεργαζομένη θάνατον) in the "I" through the good law.[48] He has already laid out how sin accomplished this in vv. 7–11. Here Paul notes the dual purposes behind sin's deadly use of the law: (1) in order that (ἵνα) sin might be shown to be sin; and (2) in order that (ἵνα) sin would become "utterly sinful (γένηται καθ' ὑπερβολὴν ἁμαρτωλὸς ἡ ἁμαρτία)" through the commandment.[49] In short, the purpose behind God allowing, or perhaps orchestrating, this scenario was to make apparent (ἵνα φανῇ) how utterly sinful, even demonic and evil, sin was.[50] Therefore, in this way, as Thiselton puts it, "The law, Paul asserts, *serves God's deepest purposes.*"[51]

Interpretive Impact of Pre-Texts in Romans 7:7–13

The interplay between OT pre-texts and Rom 7:7–13 is made complex by questions about the identity of the "I." To reiterate, we are treating the "I" as a polyvalent figure within an Adamic framework. In keeping with Adam's primeval experience, Israel, Paul, and all other embodied figures find themselves entangled in the same scenario described here. Paul lays out a scenario that is both autobiographical and gnomic in its character. In retrospect, Paul recognizes sin's deceitful and deadly use of the Mosaic Law. However, it does not follow that Paul restricts the experience to the past. There is a gnomic quality to his description which, as we shall see below, is even more apparent in vv. 14–25. As Westerholm frames it, "Paul dramatizes the encounter between God's law and the flesh in Rom 7:7–13, then explains its outcome in 7:14–25. Though he speaks in the first person of what 'I' have experienced, the account is intended to be generic, not strictly autobiographical."[52] With that said, there is an autobiographical

---

47. The referent of the neuter τὸ ἀγαθὸν in Rom 7:13 is the νόμος described in Rom 7:12.

48. Rom 7 contains six uses of κατεργάζομαι. See Rom 7:8, 13, 15, 17, 18, 20. The concentrated usage of this verb indicates an emphasis on the results that emerge from the work of sin and the "I." See BDAG 531.

49. Cf. use of καθ' ὑπερβολὴν in 1 Cor 12:31; 2 Cor 1:8; 4:17; Gal 1:13.

50. We can infer from the ἵνα clauses in Rom 7:13, as well as Paul's wider theology, that sin's deceitful and deadly actions are somehow tied to God's larger purposes and oversight. Schreiner frames this divine oversight as a question, "What was God's purpose in allowing this state of affairs to occur?" Schreiner, *Romans*, 371. With respect to the description of sin here, in reflecting on Paul's use of Gen 3 in Rom 7:7–13, Stuhlmacher notes "While in the early Jewish interpretation of Genesis 3 the nature and activity of the tempter in the form of the snake are, in part, intensively reflected upon and reported, Paul, in contrast, speaks in concise theological abstraction only of the demonic appearance of 'the sin' which uses the divine commandment in order to tempt the person to transgress the will of God." Stuhlmacher, *Romans*, 107.

51. Thiselton, *Discovering Romans*, 159.

52. Westerholm, *Understanding Paul*, 115.

and gnomic quality to the points of resonance generated here by the interplay between OT pre-texts and text.

To begin, the prohibition against coveting and the transgression of this prohibition has decisively plagued Adam and Eve, Israel, Paul, and any other embodied figure. As noted above, God essentially gave Adam and Eve a command not to covet when he prohibited them from partaking of the tree of the knowledge of good and evil (Gen 2:16-17). Israel of course received an explicit prohibition against covering in the Decalogue (Exod 20:17; Deut 5:21) which Paul cites in Rom 7:7. Their subsequent history bears out a failure to abide by this prohibition. Paul points to this prohibition as an example of how he came to a knowledge of sin through the law (διὰ νόμου, Rom 7:7).[53] Nevertheless, as vv. 8-13 indicate, he failed to keep this command just as Adam and Israel failed. The wider Pauline corpus underscores the impossibility to overcome coveting.[54]

Next, sin operates in a serpentine, or even demonic, fashion.[55] The echoes of Gen 3 in Rom 7:8-11 signal a clear Adamic framework which should not be limited to the identification of the "I." Instead, just as the identity of the "I" bears an Adamic stamp, sin (ἁμαρτία) does as well. Some ancient interpreters went as far as to seen sin as a synonym for Satan in these verses. As Ambrosiaster put it long ago in reflecting on the reference to coveting in v. 8 (πᾶσαν ἐπιθυμίαν), "By all kinds of covetousness, Paul means the whole range of sins. Earlier, he specified that covetousness which the law forbids; now he includes all the other vices in saying that all kinds of covetousness were activated in humanity at the instigation of the devil—whom Paul signifies by the term sin."[56] Although I have not suggested in my analysis that sin and Satan are interchangeable in this text, the overlap between the two is clear. Like the serpent in Gen 3, sin uses the command against coveting to produce coveting in the "I" and thereby death.

Romans 7:14-25

(7:14-25) For we know that the law is spiritual, but I am fleshly having been sold under sin. For that which I do I do not understand; for that which I want I do not do this, but that which I hate this I do. But if that which I do not want this I do, I agree with the law that it is good. But now I am no longer doing it but sin which dwells in me. For I know that there does not dwell in me, that is in my flesh, good; for the willing is present in me, but doing the good is not;

---

53. Cf. Rom 3:20.

54. E.g., in Colossians coveting (ἐπιθυμία) is described as idolatry "Therefore, put to death the parts which are on the earth, fornication, impurity, passion, evil desire, and covetousness (ἐπιθυμίαν) which is idolatry (εἰδωλολατρία)" (Col 3:5).

55. Once again, see Stuhlmacher, *Romans*, 107

56. Burns, *Romans*, 164.

for the good which I want this I do not do, but the evil which I do not want this I do. But if that which I do not want this I do, it is not longer I doing it but sin which dwells in me. So I find the law, in me the one who wants to do good, that evil is present in me; for I agree with the law of God in the inner man, but I see another law in my members warring against the law of my mind and taking me captive in the law of sin which is in my members. O wretchted man that I am; who will deliver me for the body of this death? But thanks be to God through Jesus Christ our Lord. So then I myself in my mind I serve the law of God but in my flesh the law of sin.

Grammatical signals indicate a shift between Rom 7:7-13 and 14-25. For example, the aorist and imperfect tense verbs in vv. 7-13 are replaced with present tense verbs in vv. 14-25. Rhetorically, as Witherington suggests, "This signals that Paul is talking about something that is now true of someone or some group of persons, but nonetheless a group of persons that has some integral relationship with Adam."[57] Or, as Westerholm explains it, "Paul dramatizes the encounter between God's law and the flesh in Rom 7:7-13, then explains its outcome in 7:14-25."[58] The "outcome," as we shall see, is that the "I" (ἐγώ) suffers a hellish experience akin to lamenters from Israel's Scriptures.

Suggested Pre-texts for Romans 7:14-25

Hübner lists the following pre-texts: Isa 50:1, 7 (Rom 7:14); Ps LXX 13:3-4; 77:10; Isa 5:24; Jer 5:4 (Rom 7:15-16); Ps LXX 30:13; 34:25; 57:3; Prov 12:20; Ezek 36:26 (Rom 7:17-20); Ps LXX 1:2; 118:16 (Rom 7:22); 1 Kgs 19:9 (Rom 7:23).[59]

Nestle-Aland 28th ed. lists one pre-text in its margin, Rom 7:14 (Ps 51:7). Hays does not discuss any pre-texts in Rom 7:14-25.

Although in his commentary on the use of the OT in Romans Seifrid does not discuss any OT pre-texts related to Rom 7:14-25, a later essay explores echoes of OT lament in Paul's depiction of the ἐγώ.[60]

Intertextual Analysis of Romans 7:14-25

Paul portrays the ἐγώ here as a lamenter from Israel's Scriptures. As we shall see, these verses echo both lament pre-texts and the pattern of lament prevalent in Israel's Scriptures. We shall begin with a brief overview of the pattern of lament, because it is the intertextual framework reflected in Rom 7:14-25.

---

57. Witherington, *Romans*, 193.
58. Westerholm, *Understanding Paul*, 115.
59. Hübner, *Vetus Testamentum in Novo*, 2:108-11.
60. Seifrid, "Romans 7: The Voice of the Law," 1-51.

Seminal works by Hermann Gunkel and Claus Westermann in the twentieth century brought much needed attention to the prayer form of lament.[61] While Gunkel focused primarily on form critical concerns, Westermann also gave attention to the theological implications of this prayer form. He defined lament as a traumatic "event" involving the lamenter, God, and enemies.[62] In short, the lamenter cries out to God for deliverance from enemies. Within this recurring event, Westermann detected a recurring pattern. He explains, "The events making up the deliverance form a sequence which is always encountered (though it is not always the same) where a deliverance is related: distress, a cry of distress, a hearkening (promise of deliverance), deliverance, response of those saved (praise of God)."[63] As I have written about elsewhere, I have slightly modified Westermann's suggested pattern.[64] Lament in Isarel's Scriptures and in the NT consists of a five-fold pattern: (1) prior promise; (2) suffering; (3) cry of distress; (4) deliverance; and (5) praise. In short, lamenters experience a tension between God's *prior promise* and their *suffering*. The tension elicits a *cry of distress*, an element most often associated with the prayer form.[65] God then answers that cry with the *deliverance* of the lamenter, though the form of the deliverance varies.[66] The divine answer elicits the lamenter's praise. However, the shift to praise is never permanent, because tensions between prior promise and suffering persist. Additionally, in OT lament, this pattern is flexible so that some of these elements may be assumed rather than explicitly stated, or they may occur out of order.[67]

Psalm 13 (12 LXX), a classic individual lament, provides us an example of this pattern. The psalm begins with a *cry of distress*, "How long, O Lord, will you forget me forever? How long will you hide/turn (תסתיר/ἀποστρέψεις) your face from me? How long will I take counsel in my soul, having sorrow in my heart all day long? How long will my enemy be exalted over me?" (Ps 13:2–3; 12:2–3 LXX). This cry assumes the tension between a *prior promise* of deliverance and *suffering* at the hands of enemies, a tension that elicits the opening *cry of distress*. This *cry of distress* continues in v. 4, but, as is common in lament, the cry shifts from complaint to petition "Look and answer me, O Lord my God; lighten my eyes, lest I sleep in death." Immediately after this request, the cry shifts back to an explanatory complaint "Lest my enemy say, 'I

---

61. Gunkel, *Introduction to the Psalms*; Westermann, *Praise and Lament in the Psalms*. For a brief overviev of the contributions to lament studies by Gunkel and Westermann, see Crisler, *Reading Romans as Lament*, 17–21.

62. Westermann, *Praise and Lament in the Psalms*, 213.

63. Westermann, *Praise and Lament in the Psalms*, 259–60.

64. See Crisler, *Reading Romans as Lament*, 3; Crisler, "The 'I' Who Laments," 64–83; Crisler, *Echoes of Lament and the Christology of Luke*, 1–2.

65. Two classic cries of distress in the Psalms of Lament are questions: (1) Why? and (2) How Long? See, e.g., Pss 13:2–3 (12:2–3 LXX); and 22:1 (21:2 LXX).

66. Deliverance can consist of a reiteration of the prior promise to save, an oracle of salvation, or actual deliverance.

67. See Mandolfo, *God in the Dock*.

have overcome him.' Lest my enemies rejoice when I am shaken" (Ps 13:5; 12:5 LXX). Within this pattern, *deliverance* comes in the form of a reiterated promise to save. The psalm then ends with a shift to *praise* where the lamenter asserts confidence in divine deliverance, "I have trusted in your mercy; I will rejoice in your salvation (בישותך/ἐπὶ τῷ σωτηρίῳ σου). I will sing to the Lord, because he has dealt bountifully with me" (Ps 13:6; 12:6 LXX).

It is also worth noting that the seminal moment in Israel's history, the Exodus, follows this pattern of lament in Exod 1–15.[68] Exod 2:23–25 expresses the tension between God's *prior promise* to Abraham's descendants and Israel's *suffering* as slaves in Egypt which elicits a *cry of distress*, "And after those many days the king of Egypt died. And the sons of Israel groaned (κατεστέναξαν) because of their works, and they cried out (ἀνεβόησαν), and their cry (ἡ βοὴ αὐτῶν) went up to God because of their works. And God heard their groaning (τὸν στεναγμὸν αὐτῶν), and God remembered his covenant (ἐμνήσθη ὁ θεὸς τῆς διαθήκης αὐτοῦ) which was with Abraham and Isaac and Jacob." In Exod 3–14, God gives the *deliverance* Israel requested by sending Moses who serves as the agent of divine plagues and signs which culminate in the Passover and in the drowning of the Egyptians at the Red Sea. Exod 15 shifts the nation's *cry of distress* to *praise* in the form of a song which celebrates God's defeat of Israel's enemies, "Let us sing to the Lord, for he has been greatly glorified; he has thrown the horse and its rider into the sea" (Exod 15:1).

In Israel's Scriptures, on both an individual and communal level, this pattern of lament provides a framework for articulating recurring bouts of affliction.[69] The lamenter, God, and enemies, the three participants of lament, are repeatedly locked in an event which is excruciatingly painful for the lamenter. In this way, lament is more than a prayer form in the OT. It is the quintessential language of suffering which Paul takes up in Rom 7:7–25 to describe the hellish event involving a lamenter (ἐγώ), God (θεός), and the enemy of sin (ἁμαρτία). As we shall see, Rom 7:7–25 not only contains a pattern of OT lament. This text also employs the register of lament to describe the participants of lament. The five-fold pattern of OT lament can be clearly identified in Rom 7:7–25. It will help frame the following intertextual analysis.

Romans 7:7–25, the Lamenter's Promise and Internal Struggle

The *prior promise* is God's promise of life embedded in his commands. This promise is evoked through the echoes of Gen 2:16–17, Lev 18:5, and Deut 30:15–20 which I discsucced above in the analysis of Rom 7:7–13. Adam and Israel had a promise of life that Paul ties to the command "you shall not covet." Their respective experiences with the command result in death rather than life. They suffer from sin, death, and

---

68. On this point, see Westermann, "The Role of Lament," 20–38.

69. OT lament can be broadly divided into two main categories, individual and communal laments. On this distinction, see Ferris, *The Genre of Communal Lament in the Bible*.

divine wrath rather than enjoying the life God promised beforehand. Here we find the tension between the prior promise of God and the suffering of the ἐγώ.

The prior promise of life is in tension with the *suffering* that the "I" experiences. This part of the lament pattern dominates Rom 7:7–25. Paul provides a protracted description of what the "I" suffers, and the description echoes the register of lament. He takes up lament language to describe each participant.

Paul depicts the suffering of the "I" (ἐγώ) as an internal struggle that takes a colossal toll on the "body" (σῶμα) of the "I." The whole depiction echoes the description of lamenters in the OT in a multitude of ways. For example, Paul uses the personal pronoun ἐγώ emphatically just as we find in the Psalms of Lament. Paul couples the pronoun with δέ just as the speaker often does in these psalms.[70] In Rom 7, we find the following:

> And I (ἐγὼ δέ) was living apart from the law formerly, but after the commandment sin sprang to life, and I (ἐγὼ δέ) died and this commandent, which was to result in life, proved to result in death for me (Rom 7:9–10).

> For we know that the law is spiritual, but I (ἐγὼ δέ) am fleshly having been sold under sin (Rom 7:14).

Paul uses this expression to set the "I" apart from the enemy of sin. Similarly, the Psalms of Lament in the LXX most often use ἐγὼ δέ to set themselves apart from their enemies.[71] We find for example the following:

> For I heard the censure of many who dwelled around me; when they were gathered together against me they plotted to take my life. But I (ἐγὼ δέ) hoped in you, O Lord (Ps 30:14–15 LXX).

> May those who accuse my soul falsely be ashamed and fail, may those who seek my harm be clothed with shame and dishonor. But I (ἐγὼ δέ) will hope continually, and I will continue my praise more and more (Ps 70:13–14 LXX).

In these examples and many others, the ἐγὼ δε signals a shift from the lamenter's complaint about an enemy to a statement of trust in God's ability to save.[72] However, Paul reconfigures this shift to underscore the tortous experience unfolding within the "I."

---

70. As Gaventa notes, "And twenty-three times the emphatic ἐγώ is coupled with *de*: 'but I,' i.e., setting the speaker apart from what (or more often *who*) has preceded (as also in Romans 7:9, 10, 14)." Gaventa, "The Shape of the 'I,'" 82.

71. Cf. ואני in MT. See, e.g., Ps 38:14 MT.

72. See also this use of ἐγὼ δε in Pss LXX 5:7–8; 12:5–6; 25:10–11; 30:7; 34:12–13; 37:13–15; 51:9–10; 54:16–17, 24; 55:3–4; 58:16–17; 68:13–14; 108:3–4; 118:69–70, 78, 87.

Romans 7:7–25 and the Lamenter's Enemy

Paul describes the suffering of the "I" by using the OT, especially OT lament, in at least four ways. First, Paul describes sin as an enemy in the mold of enemies from OT lament who afflict the "I" through deceit that leads to death. Sin is deceitful and opportunistic as Paul has already made clear in Rom 7:7–12, "But sin having seized an opportunity (ἀφορμὴν λαβοῦσα) thorugh the commandment deceived me (ἐξηπάτησεν με) and through it killed me (Rom 7:11)."[73] As I noted above, Paul evokes the Gen 3 narrative including the serpent's deception of Eve. The same opportunitistic tactic of the serpent is reflected in the deceitful and opporunitistic enemies described in the Psalms of Lament which Paul has already cited in his catena (Rom 3:10–18). For example, the lamenter in Ps 5 complains "There is no truth in their mouth, their heart is empty; their throat is an open grave, with their tongues they deceive (ἐδολιοῦσαν)" (Ps 5:10).[74] Contextually, the deceit can take the form of either false accusations or flattery.[75] Other depictions of enemies using deceptive speech against lamenters include:

> The words of his mouth are lawlessness and deceit (δόλος), he has ceased to be wise and good. He plans iniquity on his bed; he stations himself on a road that is not good, he does not despise evil (Ps 35:4–5 LXX).

> They were divided from the anger of his face, and his heart came near; his words were softer than oil and they are darts (Ps 54:22 LXX).

> And they deceived (ἠπάτησαν) him with their mouth and with their tongue they lied (ἐψεύσαντο) to him (Ps 77:36 LXX).

These enemies use their deceptive speech to hide their deadly intentions just as the serpent does in Gen 3. In Rom 7:7–12, sin, like the serpent in the garden and like enemies in the Psalms of Lament, use the divine command as an opportunity to flatter the "I" into thinking that transgressing the prohibition against coveting would lead to life rather than death.

Second, Paul employs the description of enemies in the OT to depict sin as an enemy to whom God sells the "I." The "I" cries out, "For we know that the law is spiritual, but I am fleshly having been sold under sin (πεπραμένος ὑπὸ τὴν ἁμαρτίαν) (Rom 7:14)."[76] The phrase "having been seen sold under sin" (πεπραμένος ὑπὸ τὴν ἁμαρτίαν) is unique in Greek literature.[77] However, it echoes familiar OT depictions of

---

73. See also Rom 7:8.

74. See Rom 3:13.

75. See Terrien, *The Psalms*, 107.

76. Rom 7:14 contains the only use of πιπράσκω in the Pauline corpus. While the verb occurs in a handful of NT texts outside the Pauline corpus, it is never used with God as the subject or the implied divine agent. See Matt 13:46; 18:25; 26:9; Mark 14:5; John 12:5; Acts 2:45; 4:34; 5:4.

77. Jewett notes, "An extensive TLG search indicates that the expression 'sold under sin'

God "selling (πιπράσκω)" his people to their enemies as an expression of his judgment against them:

> For I and my people have been sold (ἐπράθημεν) into destruction and plundering and slavery, we and our children for servants and female servants (Esth 7:4 LXX).[78]

> Thus says the Lord, "What kind of bill of divorce is your mothers, which I sent her? Or to which debtor have I sold (πέπρακα) you? Behold, you were sold (ἐπράθητε) because of your sins (ταῖς ἁμαρτάις ὑμῶν), and for your transgressions (ταῖς ἀνομίαις) I sent out your mother" (Isa 50:1).

> For thus says the Lord, "You were sold (ἐπράθητε), and you will not be ransomed with silver" (Isa 52:3).

The uses of πιπράσκω in these OT pre-texts cleary have a divine agent which is subsequently reflected in Second Temple literature.[79] This agency is also reflected in Paul's description of sin as an enemy who afflicts the "I."[80] While sin afflicts the "I" through deception and overwhelming force, it is God who "sold" the "I" to sin.

Within the *history of interpretation*, some interpreters have noted parallels between these OT pre-texts and Paul's statement in v. 14, though they come to different conclusions regarding the exegetical significance of the parallels.[81] Many interpreters do not elaborate on God's involvement here. However, Seifrid interprets the phrase in relation to Paul's previous statements about God "handing over" idolaters in Rom 1:24, 26, 28 and the phrase "under sin" in 3:9. 8. Seifrid explains, "He later describes the divine action upon the fallen human being in more direct manner as being 'sold under sin.' 'Being under sin' therefore signifies both guilt and condemnation, both human

---

(πεπραμένος) appears here for the first time in Greek literature, and thereafter is entirely restricted to patristic writers dependent on this verb." Jewett, *Romans*, 461.

78. Esth 7:4 MT contains the phrase נמכרנו.

79. See, e.g., the use of πιπράσκω with a divine agent in Jdt 7:25, "And now there is no help for us, but God has sold us (πέπρακεν ἡμᾶς ὁ θεός) into their hands to be slayed before them with thirst and great destruction." See also Bar 4:6. See also 4Q504 1–2 ii 15; 11QPs 19:9–10.

80. The use of the passive voice with the participle πεπραμένος excludes other OT pre-texts where the subjects sell themselves to their enemies. See, e.g., Deut 28:68; 1 Kgs 21:20; 2 Kgs 17:17. Murray rightly dismisses interpreters of Rom 7:14 who seek to downplay the divine agency implied in Rom 7:14 by appealing to OT pre-texts where the subject is actively involved in selling himself to an enemy. Murray notes, "It is one thing to sell oneself to do iniquity; it is another to be sold under the power of sin. In the former case the person is the active agent, in the latter he is subjected to a power that is alien to his own will. It is the latter that appears here." Murray, *Romans*, 261.

81. E.g., Jewett mentions Isa 50:1 in his analysis of Rom 7:14. However, he does not see it as especially important to understanding Paul's phrase, because in Isa 50 there is "no suggestion that sin itself is the slaveholder." Jewett, *Romans*, 461. However, Paul often reconfigures the descriptions of political enemies in the OT to personify entities immaterial such as sin and death. Cf. the more optimistic treatment of Isa 50:1 in Rom 7:14 by Philonenko, "Sur l' expression," 41–52.

rebellion and God's sovereign judgment upon the human being in rebellion."[82] We will return to the implications of this divine agency within the flow of Paul's argument.

A third OT echo related to how Paul describes the enemy of the "I" stems from the way he depicts sin as a power that overpowers and captures the "I." As Paul cries out in v. 23, "For I see another law warring (ἀντιστρατευόμενον) in my members in the law of my mind and taking me captive (αἰχμαλωτίζοντά με) in the law of sin which is in my members." This description of sin echoes the way lamenters cry out to God in the face of national and individual enemies in ancient Israel. With respect to the former, at critical points in their history, Israel lamented that kingdoms such as Egypt and Babylon had overpowered them:

> And now behold the cry (κραυγή) of the sons of Israel has come to me, and I have seen their affliction, with which the Egyptians afflicted them (Exod 3:9).[83]

> From the days of our fathers we are in great error until this day and on account of iniquities we have been handed over, and our kings, and our sons in the hand of the kings of the nations in sword, and in captivity, and in plunder and in our open shame, as it is this day (Ezra 9:7).

Egypt's strength and brutality, juxtaposed alongside God's prior promise, elicited a cry of distress. Following the Exodus narrative, Egyptian bondage becomes the benchmark for Israel's overpowering enemies whom God must overcome on behalf of his people and in accordance with his promise. Subsequent overpowering enemies elicit the same kind of prayers from lamenters. This is evident in the prayers offered during the conquest and period of the Judges.[84] Moreover, both pre- and post-exilic prayers vocalize complaints about the overpowering nature of Israel's enemies.[85] Many times the affliction suffered at the hands of foreign kingdoms is self-inflicted on Israel's part. This is reflected in the prayer of Ezra cited above (Ezra 9:7). Ezra cries out on behalf of the post-exilic community whose affliction at the hands of overpowering enemies is in step with all those who preceded them. Israel's liturgy reflects poetically on the recurring theme of overpowering enemies in the nation's history. For example, the psalmist observes:

> And the Lord was exceedingly angry with his people and he abhorred his inheritance; and he handed them over (παρέδωκεν) into the hands of the nations (εἰς χεῖρας ἐθνῶν), and those who hated them lorded over them (ἐκυρίευσαν αὐτῶν); and their enemies (οἱ ἐχθροὶ αὐτῶν) afflicted them, and they were lowered under their hands (ὑπὸ τὰς χεῖρας αὐτῶν). Many times

---

82. Seifrid, *Christ Our Righteousness*, 60.
83. See also Exod 2:23–25.
84. See, e.g., Josh 7:6–9; Judg 3:7–11.
85. See, e.g., Neh 9:6–38.

he delivered them (ἐρρύσατο αὐτούς), and they rebelled against him in their counsel and they were lowered in their lawlessness (ἐταπεινώθησαν ἐν ταῖς ἀνομίαις αὐτῶν). And he saw when they were being afflicted when he heard their supplication (τῆς δεήσεως αὐτῶν); and he remembered his covenant and regretted according to the multitude of his mercy (Ps 105:40–45 LXX).

The psalmist lays out a recurring pattern from Israel's history. The nation sins against God; therefore, in his anger, God hands the nation over to its enemies. The people then cry out for deliverance, and God hears their cry. He delivers them based on his mercy and in faithfulness to his promise. Nevertheless, even with the deliverance, the nation sins again. Consequently, the pattern repeats itself. What we find then is that Israel suffered under an overpowering enemy as part of the divine judgment against them. We will return to this inference momentarily.

The "I" in Rom 7 also echoes individual lamenters who decry overpowering enemies in Israel's Scriptures. Both in their complaints and statements of trust, lamenters liken their enemies to overpowering armies, hunters, and wild animals.[86] For example, the psalmist cries out "They seize me (ὑπέλαβόν) like a lion (ὡσεὶ λέων) ready for prey and like a cub dwelling in hiding places" (Ps 16:12 LXX). Enemies in OT lament overpower their victims through a combination of deceit and overwhelming force.[87] Paul ascribes the same characteristics to describe sin's actions against the "I" in Rom 7:7–12 (ἐξηπάτησέν με) and in 7:23 (ἀντιστρατευόμενον, αἰχμαλωτίζοντά με). They also overpower their prey through relentless pursuit which is a characteristic reflected in the lamenter's complaint that enemies pursue them "all day long." As the psalmist puts it, "My enemies (οἱ ἐχθροί μου) trampled me all day long (ὅλην τὴν ἡμέραν), many are those who battle against me from on high" (Ps 55:3 LXX).[88] Similarly, Paul's "I" complains about the unrelenting presence and activity of sin crying out in exasperation "So I find the law, in me the one wants to do good, that evil is present (τὸ κακὸν παράκειται) in me" (Rom 7:21). Sin is always present when the "I" wants to do good which is Paul's version of the lamenters' complaint that enemies pursue them "all day long."

The fourth OT echo reflected in Paul's description of the enemies and the suffering of the "I" involves internal bodily & psychological trauma. Paul underscores the internal location of the suffering:

---

86. Hans-Joachim Kraus notes that the Psalms of lament often use three images to describe enemies: (1) an attaching army; (2) a hunter; and (3) a wild animal. See Kraus, *Psalms 1–59*, 95–99. For broader discussions of enemies in the Psalms of Lament, see, e.g., Dhanaraj, *Theological Significance of the Motif of Enemies*; Westernamm, *Praise and Lament*, 180–81, 188–95. See also my discussion in Crisler, *Reading Romans as Lament*, 38–40; Crisler, *Echoes of Lament and the Christology of Luke*, 55–59.

87. See, e.g., Pss LXX 7:3; 55:6–7; 58:3–4.

88. See also Pss LXX 31:3; 37:7; 73:22; 87:18; 101:9; 139:3.

But now I am no longer doing it but sin which dwells in me (ἡ οἰκοῦσα ἐν ἐμοὶ ἁμαρτία). For I know that there does not dwell in me (οὐκ οἰκεῖ ἐν ἐμοί), that is in my flesh (ἐν τῇ σαρκί μου), good; for the willing is present in me (τὸ θέλειν παράκειταί μοι), but doing the good is not; for the good which I want this I do not do, but the evil which I do not want this I do. But if that which I do not want this I do, it is not longer I doing it but sin which dwells in me (ἡ οἰκοῦσα ἐν ἐμοὶ ἁμαρτία). So I find the law, in me the one wants to do good, that evil is present in me (ἐμοὶ τὸ κακὸν παράκειται); for I agree with the law of God in the inner man (τὸν ἔσω ἄνθρωπον), but I see another law in my members (ἐν τοῖς μέλεσίν μου) warring against the law of my mind (τοῦ νοός μου) and taking me captive in the law of sin which is in my members (ἐν τοῖς μέλεσίν μου) (Rom 7:17–23).

Paul repeatedly employs phrases that stress the inner turmoil of the "I" including the following: (1) ἡ οἰκοῦσα ἐν ἐμοὶ ἁμαρτία; (2) οὐκ οἰκεῖ ἐν ἐμοί; (3) ἐν τῇ σαρκί μου; (4) τὸ θέλειν παράκειταί μοι; (5) ἐμοὶ τὸ κακὸν παράκειται; (6) τὸν ἔσω ἄνθρωπον; (7) τοῦ νοός μου; and (8) ἐν τοῖς μέλεσίν μου.[89] Some interpreters suggest that Greco-Roman, or even Second Temple, influences are reflected here in Paul's depiction of what can be summarized as the affliction of the "inner man (τὸν ἔσω ἄνθρωπον, Rom 7:22)".[90] While such influences, or parallels, may be reflected here, there are drastic differences from a Platonic inner person and the person whom Paul describes.[91] Moreover, Greco-Roman influences do not preclude the influence of the psalmist whose description of inner turmoil is echoed here.

Romans 7:7–25 and Echoes of Psalm 37 LXX

Psalms of Lament sometimes describe the condition of lamenters by considering the impact of the suffering on their bodies and minds. Ps 37 LXX is especially exemplary

---

89. The dative case especially stands out Rom 7:17–23.

90. E.g., Käsemann refers to this emphasis on the inner man (τὸν ἔσω ἄνθρωπον) of the "I" as a "pneumatic" experience. He explains, "The pneumatic, determined by a heavenly nature and belonging to the new world, is true human being, and he is this in participation in Christ as his prototype, in whom the divine image has manifested itself again at the end of the times. He has in the pneuma the νοῦς Χριστοῦ." Käsemann suggests that Paul's portrayl of the "pneumatic" man here "derives from the tradition of the man within man as our true existence which participates in the divine reason and which in its rationality is constitutively open to the divine will." With respect to historical parallels, he points to what he sees as Plato's influence on Philo. Käsemann, *Romans*, 206. See also Heckel, *Der Innere Mensch*; Markschies, "Innerer Mensch," 266–312.

91. Keeneer notes, "The sort of struggle depicted in 7:14–25 would resonate with many people in antiquity. Some philosophers depicted the struggle between reason and the body's passions, an image relevant here (especially 7:22–23). Judaism spoke of an evil impulse (*yetzer*), and later teachers argued that learning Torah would strengthen one's good impulse to defeat the evil impulse. Some Diaspora Jews also argued that the law enabled one to rule one's passions." Keener, *Romans*, 93–94. On drastic differences between the inner man of Greco-Roman philosophy and Paul's conception, see Dunn, *Romans*, 1:393–94.

here, and it functions as an echo proper in Rom 7. In this individual lament, the speaker mentions internal distresss multiple times:

> There is no healing in my flesh (ἐν τῇ σαρκί μου) because of your anger (ἀπὸ προσώπου τῆς ὀργῆς σου), there is no peace in my bones (τοῖς ὀστέιοις μου) because of my sins (ἀπο προσώπου τῆς ἁμαρτιῶν μου) (Ps 37:4 LXX).

> For my loins (ψύαι) have been filled with scorn, and there is no healing in my flesh (ἐν τῇ σαρκί μου) (Ps 37:8 LXX).

> My heart (καρδία) was disturbed, my strength (ἰσχύς) failed me, and the light of my eyes also was not with me (Ps 37:11 LXX).

The terms flesh (σάρξ), bone (ὀστέον), loins (ψύα), heart (καρδία), and strength (ἰσχύς) collectively underscore the lamenter's bodily and psychological suffering. With respect to the echo of Ps 37 LXX in Rom 7:14–25, the *volume* is high based on semantic and syntactical points of congruence. The phrase ἐν τῇ σαρκί μου in Ps 37:4 and 37:8 LXX occurs in the same same form in Rom 7:18, "For I know that there does not dwell in me, that is in my flesh (ἐν τῇ σαρκί μου), good; for the willing is present in me, but doing the good is not."[92]

Psalm 37 LXX and Rom 7:7–25 also share *contextual consistency*. In the former, the lamenter suffers from a "trilogy of affliction."[93] Sickness, sin, and enemies afflict the lamenters' body and mind.[94] A concern with divine wrath accompanies this trilogy of affliction as indicated by the lamenter's request, "Lord, do not convict me in your anger (τῷ θυμῷ σου) nor discipline me in your wrath (τῇ ὀργῇ σου). For your arrows were stuck to me and you rested your hand upon me; there is no healing in my flesh because of your wrath (ἀπὸ προσώπου τῆς ὀργῆς σου), there is no peace in my bones because of my sins" (Ps 37:2–4 LXX). The description of the internal harm caused by the combined weight of these afflictions is quite vivid at various points in the psalm, "My bruises smelled and decayed because of my foolishness" (Ps 37:6 LXX). The lamenter describes this entire ordeal as misery, "I was in misery (ἐταλαιπώρησα) and I was bent down completely, all day long I was going looking sulluen" (Ps 37:7 LXX). Therefore, the lamenter seeks both mercy and deliverance.[95] The closing request encapsulates the pain and cry for help by the psalmist, "Do not abandon me, O Lord; my

---

92. The only occurrences of the phrase ἐν τῇ σαρκί μου in the LXX are found here in Ps 37:4 and 37:8. In Ps 38:4 and 38:8, we find בבשׂרי. These are the only two occurrences of the phrase in the MT. The limitation of the phrase to this psalm increases the probability that Paul has it in view. One should also note the semantic overlap between ἐταλαιπώρησα in Ps 37:7 LXX and ταλαίπωρος in Rom 7:24. I will discuss the significance of this overlap below. Additionally, the phrase ἐν τῇ σαρκί μου only occurs two other times in the Pauline corpus. See Gal 4:14; Col 1:24.

93. Terrien, *The Psalms*, 326.

94. See this "trilogy of affliction" in Ps 37:2–4, 20 LXX.

95. See Ps 37:2, 19–20 LXX.

God, do not be far from me; pay attention for my help, O Lord of my salvation" (Ps 37:22–23 LXX).

The "I" in Rom 7:14–25 faces a similar "trilogy of affliction" within his flesh and mind, and, it is compounded by a concern with divine wrath. Sin is the enemy of the "I" who experiences affliction in the flesh and in the mind as the lamenter does in Ps 37 LXX. Moreover, although the "I" does not overtly express concern with divine wrath as the psalmist does, it is implied throughout the text and ultimately given expression in Rom 8:1 with the reference to divine condemnation (κατάκριμα). Given this predicament, like the lamenter in Ps 37 LXX, the "I" cries out about his miserable condition "Wretched (ταλαίπωρος) man that I am" (Rom 7:24a).[96] However, Paul reconfigures certain features of Ps 37 LXX. For example, he replaces the political enemies of the psalmist with the immaterial power of sin. Additionally, while the lamenter in the psalm expresses confidence that God will deliver him, Paul's lamenter is in such dire straits that he does not know who can deliver him "Who (τίς) will deliver me (με ῥύσεται) from the body of this death?" (Rom 7:24b). I will return to these reconfigurations below.[97]

Romans 7:24 and the Lamenter's Cry of Distress

To this point, in analyzing Rom 7:7–25 from the perspective of the five-fold pattern of OT lament, we have seen the *prior promise* in 7:7–13 and the *suffering* of the "I" in 7:14–24. The tension between the prior promise of life, which has been co-opted through sin's use of the law, and the suffering of the "I," which takes it toll on body and mind, produces the *cry of distress* in v. 24, "O wretchted (ταλαίπωρος) man that I am; who will deliver me for the body of this death?"[98] This third piece of the lament pattern, the *cry of distress*, echoes Israel's Scriptures in two ways.

First, Paul evokes the miserable state of lamenters as it is sometimes described in the OT. The adjective ταλαίπωρος in v. 24, along with its surrounding context, echoes the miserable state of individuals described in the Psalms of Lament:

> I was in misery/wretchedness (ἐταλαιπώρησα) and I was bent down completely, all day long I was going looking sulluen (Ps 37:7 LXX).[99]

---

96. Cf. ἐταλαιπώρησα in Ps 37:7 LXX.

97. The lamenter in the psalm confidently asserts, "For I have hoped in you, O Lord; you will hear, O Lord my God" (Ps 37:16 LXX).

98. The adjective ταλαίπωρος does not occur very often in the LXX. See Judg 5:27; Ps LXX 136:8; Isa 33:1. See also the use of ταλαίπωρος in Tob 13:12; 2 Macc 4:47; 5:22; 3 Macc 5:47; 4 Macc 16:7; Wis 3:11; 13:10; Rev 3:17.

99. Cf. the use of ταλαιπωρέω in Mic 2:4; Joel 1:10; Zech 11:2, 3; Isa 33:1; Jer 4:13, 20; 9:18; 10:20; 12:12. See also the use of ταλαιπωρέω in Jas 4:9.

And he brought me up from the pit of misery (λάκκου ταλαιπωρίας) and from the mud of the mire and set my feet upon the rock and directed my steps (Ps 39:3 LXX).[100]

As I noted above, the lamenter's misery and wretched state stems from suffering caused by disease, sin, guilt, political enemies, and divine wrath. This motif of misery informs the cry of distress in v. 24 in multiple ways.

For instance, a few psalms personify sin (ἁμαρτία) and or wickedness (κακόν) as the cause of the lamenter's misery, and it resembles the personification of sin as a hostile power in Rom 7. Once again, Ps 37 LXX is informative at this point. The lamenter cries out, "My lawless deeds (αἱ ἀνομίαι μου) rose over my head, like a heavy load they were made heavy on me" (Ps 37:5 LXX). Similarly, in Ps 39 LXX, the lamenter complains "Because wickedness (κακά) surrounded me, of which there is no number, my lawless deeds (ἀνομίαι μου) seized me (κατέλαβον με), and I was not able to see; they multiplied more than the hairs of my head, and my heart failed" (Ps 39:13 LXX). As I have discussed at several points already, Paul personifies sin as a power in Rom 7 and elsewhere in the letter. The personification of sin already extant in OT lament may shape Paul's personification in the letter. Specifically, as Pss 37 and 39 LXX demonstrate, sin afflicts the "I" like an enemy who drowns, surrounds, deceives, and kills.

Descriptions of the lamenter's misery also employ a few different images that may be evoked in Rom 7:24. For example, the lamenter in Ps 16 LXX links his misery to being surrounded by enemies; therefore, he cries out "Keep me as the apple of your eye; in the protection of your wings shelter me before the ungodly who made me miserable (ταλαιπωρησάντων). My enemies encompassed (περιέσχον) my soul" (Ps 16:8–9 LXX). We also find a link between misery language and the image of a pit (בור/λάκκος). As noted above, the psalmist praises God for delivery from misery exclaiming "And he brought me up from the pit of misery (λάκκου ταλαιπωρίας) and from the mud of the mire and set my feet upon the rock and he directed my steps" (Ps 39:3 LXX).[101] Multiple figures in the OT are literally thrown into a pit (λάκκος) by their enemies.[102] Given the link between misery and the image of a pit in the OT, the miserable/wretched "I" in Rom 7:24 may see "the body of this death" as a kind of pit from which he cannot escape. We will return to this echo below.

We must also note the way that lamenters sometimes link their misery to divine wrath. For example, the psalmist cries out "For day and night your hand was heavy on me, I was turned to misery (εἰς ταλαιπωρίαν) when the thorny bush had been fixed" (Ps 31:4 LXX). As the wider context of Ps 31 LXX indicates, God made

---

100. Cf. the use of ταλαιπωρία in Pss LXX 11:6; 13:3; 68:21; 87:19; 139:11; Job 30:3; Amos 3:10; 5:9; Joel 1:15; Hab 1:3; 2:17; Isa 47:11; 59:7; 60:18; Jer 4:20; 6:7, 26; 15:8; 20:8. See also the use of ταλαιπωρία in Rom 3:16; Jas 5:1.

101. The literal sense of the noun λάκκος is a reservoir, dungeon, or pit. LEH 364. The metaphorical use of the term is sometimes associated with Sheol/Hades. See, e.g., Pss LXX 27:1; 39:3.

102. See, e.g., Joseph (Gen 37:24); Jeremiah (Jer 45:6 LXX; 38:6 MT); and Daniel (Dan 6:18).

the lamenter miserable because of the lamenter's sin. The image of God's heavy hand coming down upon the lamenter signals his guilt. Similarly, faced with the prospect of Israel's impending judgment, the prophet Joel laments "Woe is me, because the day of the Lord is near and misery will go out from misery (ταλαιπωρία ἐκ ταλαιπωρίας)" (Joel 1:15). The day of the Lord will move the nation from peace to utter misery as the idiom ταλαιπωρία ἐκ ταλαιπωρίας indicates.[103] Jeremiah likewise links the day of the Lord to misery crying out, "Their widows will be multiplied more than the sand of the sea; I brought misery (ταλαιπωρίαν) in midday upon the mother of the young man, I suddenly threw upon them trembling and anxiety" (Jer 15:8). In short, misery in OT lament can be a theological abbreviation for the pain caused by God's judgment against the guilty. This abbreviation is echoed by the "I" in Rom 7:24. The misery, or wretchedness, of Paul's "I" emanates in part from divine judgment against the guilt of the "I." The wider context of the cry in Rom 7:24 confirms that divine judgment is a concern of the "I." We see this in the inference that Paul draws from Rom 7:7–25 where Paul explicitly employs forensic language, "Therefore, there is no condemnation (κατάκριμα) for those who are in Christ Jesus" (Rom 8:1). We will return to the connection between the misery of the "I" and divine wrath below.

The second OT echo in Rom 7:24 is related to the lamenter' question, "Who will deliver me (με ῥύσεται) from the body of this death?" The combination of ῥύομαι + με + ἐκ (ἀπό) occurs frequently in OT lament as part of a request for deliverance:

> My times are in your hands; deliver me from the hand of my enemies (ῥῦσαι με ἐκ χειρὸς ἐχθρῶν μου) and from those who persecute me (Ps 30:16 LXX).

> Deliver me from all my lawlessness (ἀπὸ πασῶν τῶν ἀνομιῶν ῥῦσαί με), you have given me as a reproach to the fool (Ps 38:9 LXX).

> He himself will deliver me from the trap of the hunters (ῥύσεται με ἐκ παγίδος θηρευτῶν) and from a terrifying word (Ps 90:3 LXX).

As these examples indicate, lamenters request deliverance from political enemies and their own sin.[104] The same combination of ῥύομαι + με + ἐκ (ἀπό) occurs in statements of trust such as, "Behold the eyes of the Lord are upon those who fear him, those who hope in his mercy to deliver their souls from death (ῥύσασθαι ἐκ θανάτου) and to feed them in famine" (Ps 32:18–19 LXX).[105] The phrase ῥύσασθαι ἐκ θανάτου in Ps 32:19 LXX bears a strong resemblance to ῥύσεται ἐκ τοῦ σώματος τοῦ θανάτου τούτου in Rom 7:24. In both the pre-text and text, the speaker seeks deliverance "from death"

---

103. For a discussion on lament in Joel, see Dillard, *Joel*, 243; Hayes, "When None Repents, Earth Laments," 119–43; Ogden, "Joel 4 and Prophetic Responses," 97–106.

104. See also Pss LXX 7:2; 9:14; 21:22; 58:2–3; 70:4; 141:7; 142:9; 143:11.

105. See also Pss LXX 17:18, 20; 33:20; 36:40; 88:49; 90:3; 96:10.

(ἐκ θανάτου).¹⁰⁶ However, Paul supplements the ablative expression ἐκ θανάτου with τοῦ σώματος—"from the body of this death."¹⁰⁷ Paul wants to be delivered from the body where he experiences "this death" that he has just described which is caused by the indwelling power of sin.

One stark difference between the OT lamenter's request for deliverance and Paul's lamenter who seeks deliverance is that the former has a confident awareness of God's ability to save while the latter does not. The "I" in Rom 7:24 asks "who" (τίς) will deliver him. Although the register of OT lament can be marked by questions directed to God, "who" is never one of them.¹⁰⁸ Lamenters in the Psalms of Lament cry out with piercing questions such as "How long (ἕως πότε) will you turn your face from me (Ps 12:2b LXX)?", or "Why (ἵνα τί) are you turning your face? (Ps 43:25 LXX)."¹⁰⁹ Such questions indicate the intensity of the lamenter's suffering and the bewilderment over God's absence or actions in that moment. Nevertheless, OT lamenters always know to direct their cries of distress to God. Contrastively, Paul's "I" asks "who" will deliver him. This question indicates both the intensity and the theo-logic of the lamenter. The internal struggle against sin is so great and deadly that the lamenter has concluded God is against him; therefore, he cannot cry out to God for deliverance. This elicits the question of "who?". In this way, Paul replaces the lamenter's typical vocative address such as κύριε or θεός with τίς. We will return below to the implications of this reconfiguration of OT lament.

Romans 7:25 and the Lamenter's Praise

The shift to *praise* often marks the fifth and final piece of the OT lament pattern, and it also marks the end of Paul's lament. In keeping with sudden shifts in OT lament from cries of distress to praise, the "I" shifts from a cry of distress in Rom 7:24 to praise in v. 25a "But thanks be to God (χάρις τῷ θεῷ) through Jesus Christ our Lord."¹¹⁰ This

---

106. See also the statements of trust that God will deliver the lamenter ἐκ θανάτου in Pss LXX 55:14; 114:8.

107. The demonstrative pronoun τούτου in Rom 7:24 either modifies τοῦ σώματος at the beginning of the prepositional phrase or τοῦ θανάτου at the end of the phrase. Regarding these two options, Longenecker notes "The expression ἐκ τοῦ σώματος τοῦ θανάτου τούτου has been often understood somewhat differently by NT commentators." Longenecker, *Romans*, 668. My translation reflects the choice to make τούτου the modifier of τοῦ θανάτου rather than τοῦ σώματος.

108. One possible exception is the question in Ps 13:7 LXX, "Who (τίς) will give the salvation of Israel from Zion? When the Lord returns the captivity of his people, let Jacob be glad and let Israel rejoice." However, the wider context of the entire psalm characterizes the lamenter as someone who is confidently aware that God can and will save his people. The question "who" in this instance is rhetorical in nature.

109. See also ἕως πότε in Pss LXX 73:10; 78:5; 79:5; 88:47; 89:13; 93:3. See also ἵνα τί in Pss LXX 9:22; 41:10, 12; 42:2, 5; 43:24–25; 73:1, 11; 87:15.

110. The expression χάρις τῷ θεῷ as a doxological statement does not occur in the LXX. Cf. χάρις τῷ θεῷ in Rom 6:17; 1 Cor 15:57; 2 Cor 2:14; 9:16; 9:15.

kind of sudden shift from cry to praise occurs frequently in the Psalms of Lament. For example, in Ps 12 LXX, a classic individual lament, the speaker spends the entirety of the psalm complaining about God's absence and requesting his deliverance. Yet, the psalm suddenly ends with praise "But I have hoped in your mercy, my heart will exult in your salvation; I will sing to the Lord who showed kindness to me, and I will sing psalms to the name of the Lord most high" (Ps 12:6 LXX).[111] Similarly, Paul's "I" makes a sudden shift to praise, but the explanation of the deliverance is delayed until Rom 8:1–4 which I will discuss below and in the next chapter.

What immediately follows the praise in Rom 7:25a is shorthand for the experience of the "I" as it is laid out in Rom 7:7–24, "So then, I myself in my mind I serve the law of God but in my flesh the law of sin."[112] Paul describes the ongoing experience within the "I" as a struggle between serving (δουλεύω) two opposing laws in two opposing ways. On the one hand (μέν), the "I" serves the "law of God (νόμῳ θεοῦ)" with his "mind (τῷ νοΐ)." On the other hand (δέ), the "I" serves the "law of sin (νόμῳ ἁμαρτίας)" with his "flesh (τῇ σαρκί)." Once again, it is a challenge to pinpoint the precise referent of "law" (νόμος). To be sure, the law of God (νόμῳ θεοῦ) largely refers to the Mosaic Law based on the wider context of the lament.[113] Paul in fact begins the lament by citing Exod 20:17 (Deut 5:21), "You shall not covet" (Rom 7:7). He praises the Mosaic Law as holy and spiritual (Rom 7:12, 14). However, given the fact that Paul juxtaposes the "law of God" with the "law of sin," the referent of νόμος is not limited to the Mosaic Law. Instaed, Paul juxtaposes two theological abbreviations that encapsulate the struggle of the "I." With his mind (τῷ νοΐ), that is with that part where thoughts and plans are initiated, the "I" wants to serve God by obeying the commands articulated in the Law of Moses.[114] However, with the flesh of the "I," that is with an instrument dominated by sin, the desire in the mind of the "I" is always challenged by sin's deceptive and deadly use of the Mosaic Law.[115] The situation of the "I" is clearly bleak, but the praise in Rom 7:25a indicates that Paul sees deliverance beyond this predicament. He lays out the details of that deliverance in Rom 8:1–4 which I will discuss in the next chapter. When it is understood that Rom 7:25b summarizes the experience of the lamenting ἐγώ, its placement after the praise in 7:25a is

---

111. See also, e.g., Pss LXX 5:12–13; 6:11; 7:18; 10:7; 16:15.

112. Interpreters have often struggled to make sense of the placement of Rom 7:25b. As Longenecker notes, "It has been frequently asked: Why, after giving thanks to God for deliverance in 7:25a (which seems to present a positive conclusion to all that has been expressed in 7:14–24), should Paul revert back in this final lament of 7:25b to speaking about the inability and futility of human action to do good apart from divine intervention (which continues the negative laments of 7:14–24)?" Longenecker, *Romans*, 670.

113. This includes Rom 7:7–25 as well as 7:1–6 where the referent of νόμος is the Mosaic Law.

114. BDAG 680. For other uses of νοῦς in the Pauline corpus, see Rom 1:28; 7:23; 11:34; 12:2; 14:5; 1 Cor 1:10; 2:16; 14:14, 15, 19; Eph 4:17, 23; Phl 4:7; Col 2:18; 2 Thess 2:2; 1 Tim 6:5; 2 Tim 3:8; Titus 1:15.

115. BDAG 915.

less inconceivable.[116] Moreover, one does not have to resort to solutions that have no representation within the textul tradition.[117]

Within the *history of interpretation*, the role of lament in Rom 7:7–25 that I have laid out has generally received cursory treatment. Some have noted that the description of the "I" resembles the kinds of laments sometimes heard in Greco-Roman literature.[118] Others have identified OT lament as a parallel or source of Paul's reflection; however, they do not necessarily engage in robust intertextual engagement.[119] A few exceptions to this trend include my own work, which is reflected in the preceding analysis, as well as works by Beverly Gaventa and Will Timmins.[120] Gaventa argues that the ἐγώ of Rom 7 is "shaped" by the Psalms of Lament.[121] She explains, "As Paul brings to a culmination his long argument about Sin, he does so neither by telling nor by showing but by drawing his audience into the experience of the collision between the psalmist's voice and the workings of Sin as those workings have been revealed in the gospel."[122] She gives focused attention to Pss 17, 69, and 119.[123] Timmins focuses almost exclusively on the impact of Ps 119 on the "I" in Rom 7 concluding, "The suffering and affliction in the body that the 'I' of Ps 119 experienced, on account of

---

116. As Dodd puts it, "It is scarcely conceivable that, after giving thanks to God for deliverance, Paul should describe himself as being in exactly the same position as before." Dodd, *Romans*, 114–15. However, when Rom 7:7–25 is reading from the perspective of OT lament, the sudden shift is less confusing.

117. As Longenecker notes, "Although there is no external evidence in the textual tradition that would support their views, a number of NT interpreters have resorted to one or another of the following expedients: (1) to reverse the positions of the material in 7:25a (the seeming conclusion) and the material in 7:25b (the final lament of the passage), (2) to declare that 7:25b is 'very likely a gloss, which, in addition, has landed in the text at the wrong place; it belongs to vs. 23,' (3) to suggest that 7:25b can safely be eliminated, since it appears to be an interpolation or an error that has crept into the text in the process of dictation, or (4) to argue that not only is 7:25b rightly placed when it precedes 7:24–25a, but that 8:2 must also be transposed to follow immediately after 7:25a." Longenecker, *Romans*, 670.

118. E.g., Keener points to "tragic laments" such as Aeschylus, *Ag.* 1260; Ovid, *Metam.* 9.474; Apulieus, *Metam.* 3.25. Keener notes that some of these tragic laments described the bodily state as "wretched." See, e.g., Epictetus, *Disc.* 1.3.5–6; 1.9.12. Keener, *Romans*, 95n29. See also Longenecker, *Romans*, 656–68.

119. E.g., Stuhlmacher explains the shift from lament in Rom 7:24 to praise in 7:25a based on the shift that often occurs in the Psalms of Lament. He points to the shifts between Ps 22:22 to 22:23 and Ps 69:30 to 69:31. He explains, "For on the occasion of a religious celebration of thanksgiving, the lament is publicly presented by the one has been saved as a remembrance of the need which has been overcome with God's help. In Romans, the change from the lament in 7:7–24 to gratitude in 7:25a (8:2ff) is to be explained in a quite similar way, especially in view of the public reading of the letter in the gatherings of the churches and the teaching style of the apostle." Stuhlmacher, *Paul's Letter to the Romans*, 113.

120. Crisler, *Reading Romans as Lament*, 94–118; Crisler, "The 'I' Who Laments," 64–83.

121. Gaventa, "The Shape of the 'I,'" 90.

122. Gaventa, "The Shape of the 'I,'" 90.

123. Gaventa, "The Shape of the 'I,'" 81–86.

personal sin and a lawless enemy, remains the lot of the believer in Christ, for as long as he or she inhabits the pre-resurrection body of death."[124]

Interpretive Impact of Pre-Texts in Romans 7:14–25

As we have seen, the Psalms of Lament are the dominate intertextual influence in Rom 7:14–25. The interplay between the lament pre-text, namely the pattern of lament and Ps 37 LXX, produces several points of resonance that shed interpretive light on the text and the identity of the "I."

To begin, the pattern of OT lament evoked in Rom 7:7–25 shapes the structure of Paul's argument. All five parts are clearly distinguishable: (1) God's prior promise of life (Rom 7:10); (2) suffering caused by sin's deceptive and deadly use of the law (Rom 7:7–23); (3) the cry of distress (Rom 7:24); (4) deliverance in the crucified and risen Christ (Rom 8:1–4); and (5) praise (Rom 7:25). Obviously, the five elements do not occur in order; however, as I noted already, the pattern of lament is often flexible so that elements can occur "out of order."

Next, just as the identity of the lamenter in the Psalms of Lament is ambiguous enough for hearers to see themselves in the lamenter's distress, the identity of the "I" has a similar ambiguity. As noted above, the "I" represents Adam, Israel, Paul, and anyone in whom sin dwells, deceives, and kills. It follows that preoccupations with dichotomous readings such as pre-Christian/Christian, or autobiographical/rhetorical, may miss Paul's point.[125] The experience of the "I" resonates with anyone in whom sin dwells, deceives, and kills. The one caveat here is perspective. Only from the perspective of faith in Christ, with the help of the Psalms of Lament, can Paul recognize and articulate the tortous experience with sin in the body.[126] Without that faith-informed perspective, sin's deceptive and deadly ways are not as clearly seen or as loudly lamented.

---

124. Timmins, "Romans 7 and the Resurrection of Lament in Christ," 407.

125. As Timmins puts it, "The lament character of Rom 7 leads us, therefore, to reject the common binary distinction between a 'pre-Christian' 'I' and a 'Christian' 'I.' On the one hand, it would be a mistake to conclude from the exilic nature of his experience that he is an unbeliever, out of Christ. Lament presupposes a posture of hopeful faith. On the other hand, in Rom 7:7–25 the 'I' does not bear witness to the empowering of the Spirit. He does not bear witness to the arrival of the new (except in v. 24), but to the continuance of the old. We witness a Christ-believer confessing to a fleshly condition that has not yet caught up with the life that he has been given in Christ. Such a jarring juxtaposition has its origin in the language of psalmic lament. As such, the χάρις δὲ τῷ θεῷ of Rom 7:25a does not swallow up the wretchedness experienced by the 'I.' Rather, now refracted through the lens of eschatological fulfillment in Christ, it boths sharpens it to a point of greater intensity, and suffuses it with the new-found assurance of hope. That is the resurrection of lament in Christ." Timmins, "Romans 7 and the Resurrection of Lament in Christ," 407–8.

126. In this way, we see that Paul's Christian epistemology is grounded in the interplay between his suffering, prayer (especially lament), faith in Christ, and reading of Israel's Scriptures. For extended analysis on this interplay as a way of understanding Pauline theology, see Crisler, *Pauline Theology as Agonizing Struggle*.

Third, the interplay between Ps 37 LXX and Rom 7:14–25 indicate the "thickness" of the misery (ταλαίπωρς) experienced by the "I." Paul's description of sin bears a strong resemblance to enemies in the Psalms of Lament. Like the latter, sin is always present, overpowering in its war against the "I," deceptive, and deadly. However, the misery of the "I" also stems from divine wrath. The lamenter in Ps 37 LXX not only requests deliverance from enemies but also mercy in the face of God's wrath.[127] The "I" in Rom 7 is likewise troubled with the prospect of divine wrath. Without the echo of this underlying concern, Paul's conclusion in 8:1, "So then, there is no condemnation (κατάκριμα) for those who are in Christ," becomes non-sensical. The underlying concern with divine wrath is exacerbated by the fact that the "I" is entirely powerless against sin which uses the law to deceive and kill. In this way, there is a "thickness" to the misery which even lamenters in the Psalms of Lament have not experienced. Therefore, Paul escalates the cry of misery from typical lament questions such as "how long," or "why," to the stunning question of "who." The intensity of the cry must capture the intensity of the suffering.

Finally, if Rom 7:7–25 is Paul's attempt at *prosopopoeia*, as many schoalrs have suggested, the "I" is ultimately impersonating an OT lamenter.[128] In this way, we find another instance in which Paul combines a Greco-Roman literary device with Israel's Scriptures to explain an aspect of his gospel.[129] Interpreters do not have to drive a wedge between Paul's use of Greco-Roman rhetorical devices and his use of Israel's Scriptures. Paul blends these elements together as he constructs his epistolary arguments.

---

127. The request for mercy is in fact the initial request by the lamenter. See Ps 37:2–4 LXX.

128. Witherington defines the rhetorical technique noting, "Impersonation, or prosopopeia, is a rhetorical technique which falls under the heading of figures of speech and is often used to illustrate or make vivid a piece of deliberative rhetoric. This rhetorical technique involves the assumption of a role, and sometimes the role is marked off from the surrounding discourse by a change in tone, inflection, or accent, by form of delivery, or by an introductory formula signaling a change in voice." Witherington, *Paul's Letter to the Romans*, 179. See also the description of speech-in-chater in Parsons and Martin, *Ancient Rhetoric*, 141–73. For proponents of this kind of reading of Rom 7:7–25, see Elder, "Wretch I am!", 743–63. Stowers, *A Rereading of Romans*, 260–64.

129. Cf. the use of *syncrisis* in Rom 5:12–19.

7

Romans 8:1–11

ALTHOUGH ROM 8 CONTAINS only one citation (Rom 8:36; Ps 43:23 LXX), it has one of the richest intertextual subtexts of the entire letter.[1] The subtext consists of multiple narrative strands which are shaped by Paul's reading of Israel's Scriptures.[2] These strands include God's subjection of creation to futility, the role of the Mosaic Law, the testing of Abraham described in Gen 22, the promise of a new creation, and Ezekiel's vision of dry bones. Paul also continues his use of OT lament to describe the experience of Roman believers. In keeping with the ethos of Abraham, Habakkuk, and others, justifying faith is a painful experience. Of course, Paul reconfigures these intertextual features in relation to God's work in the crucified and risen Christ. The interplay between these various pre-texts and texts generate unstated points of resonance that shed interpretive light on some of the most important chapters in the entire Pauline corpus.

Romans 8:1–4

(8:1–4) There is therefore now no condemnation for those who are in Christ Jesus. For the law of the Spirit of life in Christ Jesus freed you from the law of sin and death. For what the law was unable to do in that it was weakened through the flesh, God, by having sent his own Son in the likeness of sinful flesh and for sin, also condemned sin in the flesh, in order that the righteous requirement of the law might be fulfilled in us who do not walk according to the flesh but according to the Spirit.

---

1. For intertextual studies of Rom 8:1–11, or studies that lean heavily on Paul's use of the OT in this pericope, see, e.g., Keck, "The Law and the Law of Sin and Death," McFadden, "The Fulfillment of the Law's," 483–97.

2. See Dodd, *Romans*, 133–61; Hays, *Echoes of Scripture in the Letters of Paul*, 57–63.

The particle ἄρα in Rom 8:1 signals that Paul draws a conclusion, "Therefore (ἄρα), there is now no condemnation for those who are in Christ Jesus" (Rom 8:1). Interpreters sometimes struggle to explain the logical flow of Paul's argument at this point.[3] What is the logical relationship between Rom 7:7–25 and 8:1? Clearly, as Schreiner notes, the relationship cannot be construed as "Because I am enslaved to sin, therefore I am no longer under condemnation."[4] Some interpreters suggest that Rom 8:1 reaches back to statements that precede Rom 7:7–25. For example, Cranfield argues that 8:1 reaches back to 7:1–6 where Paul "elucidated" the assertion "you are not under the law" in 6:14. In this way, Paul's statement in 8:1 confirms what he laid out in 7:1–6.[5] Longenecker suggests that the pronouncement of "no condemnation" (οὐδὲν κατάκριμα) in 8:1 reaches back to 5:12–21, particularly 5:16 and 18 which contain the only other uses of the noun κατάκριμα. He explains, "Here in 8:1 that awful heritage of Adam's sin, humanity's inherited depravity and people's own resultant sins, which together have brought about the universal sentence of 'judgment unto condemnation' (κρίμα εἰς κατάκριμα), is countered by God's wondrous grace through the work of Jesus of Nazareth and the proclamation of 'no condemnation for those who are in Christ Jesus' (οὐδὲν κατάκριμα τοῖς ἐν Χριστῷ Ἰησοῦ)."[6] While I agree that 8:1 reaches back to pieces of Paul's argument that precede Rom 7:7–25, 8:1–4 logically flows from the lament of the "I." Specifically, as we shall see, it is the answer to the cry of distress in 7:24.

Not surprisingly, Rom 8:1–4 echoes Israel's Scriptures in several ways. These echoes inform both the lament from 7:7–25 and what follows in 8:5–11.

Suggested Pre-Texts in Romans 8:1–4

Hübner lists one pre-text here, Lev 5:6; 16:3 (Rom 8:3). Nestle-Aland 28th ed. lists one pre-text, Lev 16 (Rom 8:4).

Hays does not discuss any OT echoes in Rom 8:1–4 in *Echoes of Scripture in the Letters of Paul*.[7] However, elsewhere he acknowledges that these four verses contain "pivotal scriptural allusions" related to the "sin offering" in Rom 8:3 and τὸ δικαίωμα τοῦ νόμου in Rom 8:4.[8] Seifrid's analysis in his Romans commentary focuses almost exclusively on Paul's use of the OT in Rom 8:31–39.

---

3. As Hultgren puts it, "It is not immediately obvious how chapter 8 follows from what has gone before it in the previous chapter. Yet a link does exist." Hultgren, *Romans*, 295.

4. Schreiner, *Romans*, 398.

5. Cranfield, *Romans*, 1:373.

6. Longenecker, *Romans*, 684.

7. Therefore, he continues a large interetextual lacunae that began with 5:1 and continues until 8:18. See Hays, *Echoes of Scripture in the Letters of Paul*, 158.

8. Hays, *The Conversion of Imagination*, 182. He points the reader to Wright's argument that περὶ ἁμαρτίας in Rom 8:3 is a "metaphorical reference to the Torah's offering for unwilling sin." See Wright, *Climax of the Covenant*, 220–25.

Intertextual Analysis of Pre-Texts in Romans 8:1-4

The answer to the cry of distress by the "I" in Rom 7:24 is summarized in Rom 8:1-4. Those who are plagued by the deceitful and deadly work of sin find deliverance through God's work in the crucified and risen Christ. Paul specifically underscores that those in Christ are delivered from God's condemnation which, as I noted in the previous chapter, functions as the underling source of suffering for the "I" in Rom 7. Divine condemnation for sin has caused affliction since Adam (Rom 5:16, 18), and it has the potential to cause great affliction on the last day. From a scriptural perspective, divine condemnation is often marked by suffering at the hands of enemies. Paul must reassure the Christians in Rome that their sufferings are not indications of divine condemnation, something he began to do in Rom 5:1–5 and continues through 8:31–39.[9] That reassurance continues here in 8:1–4 with a compact explanation of where God has directed his condemnation. These verses evoke multiple OT pre-texts.

Romans 8:1-2 and Echoes of Divine Condemnation

The reference to "condemnation" (κατάκριμα) in 8:1 echoes once again Gen 3. We are alerted to this echo by Paul's previous use of κατάκριμα in Rom 5:16 and 18:

> And not as through the one who sinned is the gift; for the judgment from one resulted in condemnation (εἰς κατάκριμα), but the gift from the many transgressions resulted in justification (Rom 5:16).

> So then as through the one transgression there resulted condemnation (εἰς κατάκριμα) for all men, in this way also through one transgression there resulted the justification of life for all men (Rom 5:18).

In Rom 5, Paul describes God's judgment against Adam and Eve as "condemnation" (κατάκριμα) for their transgression of the command. The divine κατάκριμα doled out in Gen 3 consisted of both the pronouncement of death and the execution of that sentence by removing Adam and Even from the life-giving presence of God. They were essentially handed over to sin and death. Moreover, all subsequent human beings experience the same condemnation. It is an experience especially discerned from the perspective of faith as the lamenting "I" in Rom 7 indicates. The "wretched" (ταλαίπωρος) condition of the "I" stems from God condemning, or selling (πεπραμένος, Rom 7:14), the "I" to sin, who like an enemy, deceives and kills. However, the answer to the cry of the wretched "I" is that "now" (νῦν), in Christ, God no longer condemns Adam's descendants in this way. It does not follow that those in Christ will never again experience the hellish experience of the "I." To the contrary,

---

9. As I noted previously, in Rom 5:1–10, Paul assures the Romans that they will be saved from eschatological wrath based on what God has already done for them in Christ and in the gift of his Spirit.

they are all too aware of it. What does follow is that they "now" always have an answer to their cry when sin inevitably attempts to deceive, overpower, and kill.[10]

In 8:2, Paul explains his assertion from 8:1 noting "For the law of the Spirit of life in Christ Jesus freed you from the law of sin and death." As we shall see, these two "laws" echo OT pre-texts.[11] The phrase ὁ νόμος τοῦ πνεύματος τῆς ζωῆς ἐν Χριστῷ Ἰησοῦ is a theological abbreviation informed by Israel's Scriptures. As I have noted already, Paul's use of the term νόμος is polyvalent in the sense that a single usage can have interrelated ties to both the Mosaic Law and a principle/norm.[12] To put it another way, Paul uses wordplay to combine both meanings in a single phrase.[13] As Seifrid reminds us, "Words not only 'refer' to things but 'signify' concepts."[14] In this instance, νόμος, from the phrase "the law (νόμος) of the Spirit of life in Christ Jesus," refers to the Mosaic Law while also signaling a concept that Paul has been working out since Rom 7. The phrase evokes the Mosaic Law, particularly the promise of life embedded in it which Paul has already evoked in the letter.[15] Here Lev 18:5 stands out once again, "And you shall keep all my commandments and my judgements and you shall do them, the things which if a man does them he will live (ζήσεται) by them; I am the Lord your God." Obedience to the law would result in life; however, as Paul has made it abundantly clear in Rom 7, sin's use of the law results in death rather than life.

Romans 8:2 and Echoes of Life through the Spirit

This bring us to a second cluster of pre-texts that inform the phrase "the law of the Spirit of life in Christ Jesus." Paul tethers νόμος to the Spirit and life in Rom 8:2 (ὁ νόμος τοῦ πνεύματος τῆς ζωῆς) which evokes the OT promise that God would give

---

10. This is not to mitigate Paul's strong statements about the death to sin in Rom 6. To the contrary, Rom 7:7–8:11 qualifies that death to sin. As I will discuss further below, Paul makes it clear in Romans 8 that sin is an ongoing problem for those in Christ for the duration of their existence in unredeemed bodies. See, e.g., Rom 8:10, 23–25.

11. As Dodd notes in his analysis of Rom 8:1–4, "His real background is, first, the Old Testament; and, secondly, the experience of primitive Christianity." Dodd, *Romans*, 134.

12. See, e.g., the use of νόμος in Rom 3:27. See BDAG 677–78.

13. As Hultgren notes, interpreters are divided in four ways regarding the referent/meaning of νόμος in Rom 8:2. See Hultgren, *Romans*, 297n257. First, some interpret it as a reference to the Mosaic Law. See, e.g., Dunn, *Romans*, 1:416–17; Jewett, *Romans*, 480–81; Lohse, *Römer*, 229; Wilckens, *Römer*, 2:122. Second, other interpreters treat νόμος here as a figure of speech. See, e.g., Cranfield, *Romans*, 375–76; Fitzmyer, *Romans*, 482–83; Keck, "The Law and 'the Law of Sin and Death' (Rom 8:1–4)," 41–57; Moo, *Romans*, 473–77; Räisänen, *Paul and the Law*, 52; Winger, *By What Law?* 195. Third, some interpreters treat it as Paul's use of wordplay. See, e.g., Sanders, *Paul, the Law, and the Jewish People*, 26, 98. Fourth, some interpreters treat as a reference to a principle or rule. See, e.g., Bertone, "The Law of the Spirit," 178–79.

14. Seifrid, *Christ Our Righteousness*, 96.

15. E.g., the echo of Lev 18:5 in Rom 7:10.

new life through the gift of his Spirit.[16] The Spirit gives life in Christ in accordance with pre-texts from Israel's Scriptures such as:

> And I will give to you a new heart and I will give a new spirit (πνεῦμα καινόν) in you and I will take away the heart of stone from your flesh and I will give to you a heart of flesh. And I will give my Spirit (τὸ πνεῦμά μου) in you and I will make it that you might go in my righteous requirements (ἐν τοῖς δικαιώμασίν μου) and you might keep my judgments and you might do them. And you will dwell on the earth, which I gave to your fathers, and you will be my people and I will be your God. And I will save (σώσω) you from all your impurities and I will call for the grain and I will multiply it and I will not give a famine upon you (Ezek 36:26–29).
>
> And I will give my Spirit (τὸ πνεῦμά μου) in you, and you will live (ζήσεσθε), and I will place you in your land, and you will know that I the Lord have spoken and I will do it, says the Lord (Ezek 37:14).[17]

The *volume* of the pre-text is moderate to high based on the semantic overlap between πνεῦμα, ζάω/ζωή, and δικαίωμα. The latter term appears in Ezek 36:27 (ἐν τοῖς δικαιώμασίν μου) and Rom 8:4 (τὸ δικαίωμα τοῦ νόμου).

The *contextual consistency* is substantial as well, because both the pre-texts and text combine Spirit, life, deliverance, walking in God's ways, and resurrection. In Ezek 36–37, the gift of the Spirit is accompanied by God's deliverance of his people from impurities— "And I will save (σώσω) you from all your impurities (ἐκ πασῶν τῶν ἀκαθαρσιῶν ὑμῶν)" (Ezek 36:29a). Similarly, in Ezek 37:1–14, God promises to deliver the bones of his people from death by giving his Spirit to them and thereby giving life to them— "And I will give my spirit (τὸ πνεῦμά μου) in you, and you will live (ζήσεσθε)" (Ezek 37:14a). God's deliverance from sin and death in conjunction with the gift of the Spirit results in the people walking in his ways— "And I will give my Spirit (τὸ πνεῦμά μου) in you and I will make it that you might go in my righteous requirements (ἐν τοῖς δικαιώμασίν μου) and you might keep my judgments and you might do them" (Ezek 36:27).

Paul takes up these same divine promises from Ezek 36–37 and reconfigures them around Christ. Ezekiel's promise of deliverance from sin and death is now realized in Christ as Paul indicates in Rom 8:2, "For the law of the Spirit of life in Christ Jesus freed you (ἠλευθέρωσέν σε) from the law of sin and death (ἀπὸ τοῦ νόμου

---

16. If Rom 5:1 marked a "turn to Christ" in the letter, 8:2 marks a turn to the Spirit in Christ. The noun πνεῦμα appears 21 times in Rom 8:1–39. Once again, for a discussion of the "turn to Christ," see Seifrid, "Paul's Turn to Christ in Romans," 15–24.

17. See also, "For I will give water to those who come in thirst in a waterless place, I will place my spirit (τὸ πνεῦμα μου) upon you and my blessing upon your children, and they will spring up like grass between the water and like willows upon the water flowing by (Isa 44:3–4)."

τῆς ἁμαρτίας καὶ τοῦ θανάτου)." Additionally, in keeping with pre-text from Ezek 36–37, Paul explains that the purpose of God freeing the Romans from sin and death through the crucified Christ was to fulfil the "righteous requirement of the law" (τὸ δικαίωμα τοῦ νόμου) (Rom 8:4; Ezek 36:27). God's work in Christ frees them to "walk" (περιπατοῦσιν) according to the Spirit (Rom 8:4; Ezek 36:27). Even more, for Paul, the promise of resurrection by the Spirit in Ezek 37:1–14 is realized in the Spirit of Christ (πνεῦμα Χριστοῦ, Rom 8:9) as he indicates in his wider argument, "But if the Spirit of the one who raised Jesus from the dead dwells in you, the one who raised Christ from the dead will also make alive your mortal bodies through the same Spirit who dwells in you" (Rom 8:11).

Within the history of *interpretation*, some interpreters identify Ezek 36–37 as pre-texts that inform Rom 8:2. For example, Stuhlmacher recognizes the exegetical importance of Ezek 36, in conjunction with other OT pre-texts, noting "It is natural to interpret Rom. 8:2–7 against the background of Jer. 31:31ff; Ezek. 36:27; and the early Jewish expectation that the end-times people of God, in fulfillment of the promise of a son from 2 Sam. 7:12–14, will be led into the perfect obedience of the 'sons of God.'"[18]

Romans 8:3 and Echoes of περὶ ἁμαρτίας

In Rom 8:3, the phrase "for sin" (περὶ ἁμαρτίας) echoes OT sacrificial language related to sin offerings. Paul explains how the "law of the Spirit of life in Christ Jesus" freed the Romans from "the law of sin and death" noting, "For what the law was unable to do in that it was weakened through the flesh, God, by having sent his own Son in the likeness of sinful flesh and for sin (περὶ ἁμαρτίας), also condemned sin in the flesh." The phrase περὶ ἁμαρτίας occurs several times in the LXX, especially in Leviticus and Numbers.[19] Given Paul's echo of Lev 16 in Rom 3:25 and his use of Isa 53 elsewhere in the letter, we should consider the use of περὶ ἁμαρτίας in these pre-texts.[20]

The instructions for the day of atonement in Lev 16 include seven uses of the prepositional phrase περὶ ἁμαρτίας.[21] The phrase is associated with two sacrifices. First, Aaron is instructed to bring a young bull as a sin offering to atone for his sins and those of his household. For example, "And Aaron will bring forward a bull for a sin

---

18. Stuhlmacher, *Romans*, 118. See also Dunn, *Romans*, 1:417–18; Keener, *Romans*, 99.

19. See the use of περὶ ἁμαρτίας in Lev 5:6, 7, 11; 7:37; 9:2, 3; 12:6, 8; 14:13, 31; 15:15, 30; 16:3, 5, 9; 23:19; Num 6:11, 16; 7:16, 22, 28, 34, 40, 46, 52, 58, 64, 70, 82, 87; 8:8, 12; 15:24, 27; 28:15, 22, 30; 29:5, 11, 16, 19, 22, 25, 28, 31, 34, 38; 2 Kgs 12:17; 2 Chr 29:21, 23, 24; Ezra 6:17; 8:35; Neh 10:34; Ps 39:7; Job 1:5; Isa 53:10; Ezek 42:13, 19, 21. See also 2 Macc 12:43; Bar 1:10. In the NT, see John 8:46; 16:8, 9; Heb 10:6, 8, 18; 13:11. See also περὶ τῆς ἁμαρτίας in Exod 32:30; Lev 4:3, 14, 28, 35; 5:6, 7, 8, 9, 10, 13; 6:18, 23; 7:7; 8:2, 14, 9:7, 8, 10, 15, 22; 10:16, 17, 19; 14:19; 16:6, 11, 15, 27; 19:22; Num 15:25; 29:11; Lam 3:39. See also 2 Macc 2:11. In the NT, see John 15:22.

20. Lev 5 is also a helpful pre-text where instructions for sin offerings in general are laid out.

21. We find both the anarthrous περὶ ἁμαρτίας and the articular περὶ τῆς ἁμαρτίας in Lev 16. See Lev 16:3, 5, 6, 9, 11, 15, 27.

offering (περὶ τῆς ἁμαρτίας) which is for himself and his household only and he will make atonement (ἐξιλάσεται) for himself and his household and he will slaughter the bull for his sin offering (περὶ τῆς ἁμαρτίας)" (Lev 16:11).[22] Second, Aaron is instructed to offer a goat as a sin offering to atone for the sins of the entire nation. For example, "And he will slaughter the goat which is for the sin offering (περὶ τῆς ἁμαρτίας) which is for the people before the Lord and he will bring from his blood inside of the veil and he will do with its blood in which manner he did with the blood of the bull, and he will sprinkle its blood upon the mercy seat before the mercy seat" (Lev 16:15).[23]

The *contextual consistency* between Lev 16 and Rom 8:3 revolves around the function of these respective sin offerings. The sin offerings in Lev 16 atone (ἐξιλάσκομαι) for Israel's sins by removing the stain of sin and thereby propitiating God's wrath against the nation. Similarly, in the larger context of Romans, Paul infuses Jesus' death with the same atoning function. God puts the crucified Jesus forward as the mercy seat (ἱλαστήριον) (Rom 3:25).[24] Christ died on behalf of and in place of the ungodly (Rom 5:8). His sacrificial death is the means of the Romans' justification and the certainty that he will save them from future wrath, "Therefore, how much more having been justified now by his blood (ἐν τῷ αἵματι αὐτοῦ) we will be saved through him from the wrath (ἀπὸ τῆς ὀργῆς)" (Rom 5:9). Additionally, in Rom 8, Paul underscores the sacrificial nature of Christ's death. For example, he describes God as the one "Who did not spare (οὐκ ἐφείσατο) his own son but handed him over (παρέδωκεν) for us all (ὑπὲρ ἡμῶν πάντων)" (Rom 8:32a). As I will discuss below, this description echoes multiple OT pre-texts including Gen 22 and Abraham who, in the attempted sacrifice of Isaac, did not "spare" (φείδομαι) his son.[25]

As I have already noted, outside of Lev 16, the LXX contains several uses of περὶ ἁμαρτίας as a reference to sin offerings in general. These other uses likely shape Paul's use of the phrase as well. Lev 4–5 are especially instructive, because these chapters describe the sin offering in detail. According to Hartley, a sin offering, or purification offering, can be organized into four categories: (1) offering for sins commited inadvertently or a sin that has become hidden (Lev 4:1–35; 5:1–7); (2) a "rite of aggregation" for someone who has touched something that makes one unclean; (3) a ritual for the consecration of people or objects; and (4) offering prescribed for "certain high days" or festivals.[26] The overall function of these sin offerings, as they are described in Lev 4–5, include separating the guilty party from responsibility and impurity, purifying

---

22. See also Lev 16:6, 9.

23. See also Lev 16:3, 5, 15, 27.

24. As I noted previously in my analysis of Rom 3:21–26, in keeping with the context of Lev 16, Jesus becomes the appointed time, place, and means of atonement for both Jew and Gentile. For intertextual analysis of Rom 3:21–26, see volume 1.

25. See the use of φείδομαι in Gen 22:12, 16.

26. Hartley, *Leviticus*, 55–56.

something or someone for service, and forgiveness.[27] Moreover, while it is unpopular in many corners of biblical scholarship to maintain a link between atonement and divine wrath, a concern with divine wrath underlies all of the functions of the sin offering in both Leviticus and thereby in Paul's thought.[28] We will return to the way that Paul reconfigures the various functions of the sin offering and its relationship to divine wrath.

Within the *history of interpretation*, Stuhlmacher complains that many translations of the expression περὶ ἁμαρτίας eclipse the intertextual link to OT sin offerings.[29] He observes, "In the Greek translation of Lev. 4:3, 14, 21; 5:6, 7, 8, and so on (which was also used among the Christians in Rome), the phrase 'the sin offering to be presented for the sake of sin' is simply given in shortened form as (the sin offering presented) 'for the sake of sin.' The phrase 'for the sake of sin' is thus a technical expression from the language of sacrifice, and is to be understood in this way as well in Rom. 8:3."[30] Other interpreters note that, even with the echo of a sin offering in Leviticus, this pre-text does not exhaust Paul's use of the expression to describe the death of Christ.[31] This brings us to another echo related to περὶ ἁμαρτίας in Rom 8:3.

We must also consider the echo of Isa 53 with the use of περὶ ἁμαρτίας in Rom 8:3. Part of the description of Isaiah's suffering servant includes, "And the Lord wants to cleanse him from his blow; if you might give an offering for sin (περὶ ἁμαρτίας), your soul will see a long-lived seed" (Isa 53:10 LXX). One difficulty that arises here is that the LXX differs significantly from the MT. The latter reads, "But the Lord was pleased to crush him, putting him to grief; when his soul makes an offering for sin (אשם), he will see his offspring, he will prolong his days, and the pleasure of the Lord will propser in his hand" (Isa 53:10 MT). One of the main differences here is that in the MT the servant offers the sin offering, but, in the LXX, the second-person plural δῶτε indicates that a group puts forward the sin offering. In any case, the connection between the servant and sin offering stands in Isa 53. Part of the divine will for the servant is for him to make, or be, such an offering.

The *contextual consistency* between Isa 53 and Rom 8:3 involves not only the use of περὶ ἁμαρτίας but also the role of a divine agent. The παῖς in Isa 52:13–53:12

---

27. Hartley, *Leviticus*, 56–57.

28. E.g., Hultgren plainly states, "One cannot derive from Paul any theory of atonement that implies that the Son has to appease the wrath of God (the Father)." Hultgren, *Romans*, 299.

29. Some commentators do not take περὶ ἁμαρτίας as an intertextual reference to "sin offering." E.g., Fitzmyer suggests that the phrase simply refers to "the mission on which the Son was sent." Fitzmyer, *Romans*, 486.

30. Stuhlmacher, *Romans*, 120. See also Witherington, *Romans*, 213–14; Wright, *Climax of the Covenant*.

31. E.g., Sanday and Headlam note, "Still we need not suppose the phrase περὶ ἁμαρτ. here specially limited to the sense of 'sin-offering.' It includes every sense in which the Incarnation and Death of Christ had relation to, and had it for the object to remove, human sin." Sanday and Headlam, *Romans*, 193.

carries out the divine will by suffering divine wrath for the sins of the people as their sin offering. As noted at the close of the description, "For this reason he will inherit many and he will divide the spoils of the mighty, because his soul was handed over to death, and he was reckoned with the lawless; and he himself bore many sins and he was handed over because of their sins" (Isa 53:12). Paul likewise depicts Jesus as the divine agent whom God sent (ὁ θεὸς τὸν ἑαυτοῦ υἱὸν πέμψας) as a sin offering to carry out his will by suffering for the Romans. Of course, Paul reconfigures the divine agency expressed in Isa 53. For example, he makes sin the direct object of the divine condemnation "he condemned sin (κατέκρινεν τὴν ἁμαρτίαν) in the flesh." Paul does not here deny that God condemned Jesus in his crucifixion. However, he qualifies his description of what God accomplished by sending his Son as a "sin offering" (περὶ ἁμαρτίας). He pronounced a sentence of death on sin and executed that sentence in the death of his Son.

To put it in a way that continues the description of sin as enemy in the vein of OT lament which we saw in Rom 7:7–25, God righteously judged and defeated sin in response to the cry for deliverance in 7:24. Therefore, the function of this "sin offering" is not only to expiate sin and propitiate wrath. Jesus, as the divinely sent sin offering, also frees (ἠλευθέρωσεν, Rom 8:2) the believer from sin and death. The law did not have this ability (τὸ ἀδύνατον τοῦ νόμου), because it was weakened through the flesh (ἠσθένει διὰ τῆς σαρκός). The Adamic state of the world and humanity debilitated the Mosaic Law's ability to accomplish what only the Son could accomplish in his death.

Romans 8:4 and Various Echoes

We now come to Rom 8:4 and its intertextual subtext. Paul expresses the purpose behind God condemning sin in the flesh of his Son. It was "in order that the righteous requirement of the law (τὸ δικαίωμα τοῦ νόμου) might be fulfilled in his us who do not walk (τοῖς περιπατοῦσιν) according to the flesh but according to the Spirit (κατὰ πνεῦμα)." This purpose statement contains three OT echoes.

First, the phrase τὸ δικαίωμα τοῦ νόμου obviously evokes a requirement from the Mosaic Law. However, it is not immediately clear which requirement Paul has in view.[32] The noun δικαίωμα occurs five times in the letter, and three of the uses are related to requirements laid out in the Mosaic Law.[33] In Rom 2:26, Paul uses τὰ δικαιώματα τοῦ νόμου in describing the possibility of an uncircumcised Gentile keeping (φυλάσσω) the righteous requirements of the law. In Rom 1:32, Paul uses τὸ δικαίωμα τοῦ θεοῦ. He specifies that God requires "death" for those who do the things described in the vice list of 1:29–31. As I noted in my previous discussion of Rom 1:32, τὸ δικαίωμα τοῦ θεοῦ does not evoke a specific OT pretext. Instead it evokes a

---

32. Longenecker lists the referent of τὸ δικαίωμα τοῦ νόμου as one of the main interpretive problems in Rom 8:3–4. See Longenecker, *Romans*, 694–96.

33. See the use of δικαίωμα in Rom 1:32; 2:26; 5:16, 18; 8:4.

larger motif from the Mosaic Law in which God requires that death of a transgressor. This is part of what Paul refers to with his use of τὸ δικαίωμα τοῦ νόμου in 8:4. The crucified Jesus, "in the likeness of sinful flesh," fulfilled (πληρωθῇ) the requirement in the Mosaic Law, namely that transgressors must die.

However, the inverse of this OT motif is also evoked with the use of δικαίωμα in 8:4. Not only does Christ fulfill the righteous requirement of death for the transgressor, he also fulfills the requirement that results in life for those who obey.[34] Among OT pre-texts that inform this motif, the juxtaposition of life and death in Deuteronomy stands out:

> Behold, I have set before you today life and death (τὴν ζωὴν καὶ τὸν θάνατον), good and evil (τὸ ἀγαθὸν καὶ τὸ κακόν). If you should listen to the commandments of the Lord your God, which I am commanding you today, to love the Lord your God, to go in all of his ways, to keep his righteous requirements (τὰ δικαιώματα αὐτοῦ) and his judgments, you will live (ζήσεσθε) and multiply, and the Lord your God will bless you in all the earth, into which you are entering there tok inherit it. And if your heart should change and you should not listen and having been deceived you should worship other gods and serve them, I am proclaiming to you today that you will certainly be destroyed and you certainly shall not live long upon the land, which the Lord God is giving to you, into which you are going through the Jordan to inherit it. I call both heaven and earth this today to testify against you, I have set life and death (τὴν ζωὴν καὶ τὸν θάνατον) before you, blessing and curse; choose life (ἔκλεξαι τὴν ζωήν), in order that you might live (ἵνα ζῇς) and your seed, to love the Lord your God, to obey his voice and cleave to him; for this is your life (τοῦτο ἡ ζωή σου) and the length of your days, for you to dwell in the land, which the Lord swore to your fathers Abraham and Isaac and Jacob, to give them (Deut 30:15–20).

This pre-text passes multiple intertextual tests including *contextual consistency*.[35] While ancient Isarelites were guaranteed life in the promised land if they kept the righteous requirements (τὰ δικαιώματα, Deut 30:16) of the law, that requirement is eschatologically fulfilled (πληρωθῇ) in the Roman believers through the crucified and risen Christ.[36] Christ's obedience in the crucifixion becomes the obedience of the Romans which results in life just as the law promised. In this way, through his death,

---

34. As Seifrid puts it, "For a number of reasons, it is best to understand this 'righteous ordinance' as the 'life' which the law offered on the condition of obedience." Seifrid, *Christ Our Righteousness*, 119.

35. It passes the test of *recurrence*, because Paul cites Deut 30:12 in Rom 10:6.

36. We should not overlook Paul's use of the passive voice with the verb πληρωθῇ. As Moo notes, "The passive verb 'might be fulfilled' points not to something that we are to do but to something that is done in and for us." Moo, *Romans*, 483. However, Wolter insists that πληρωθῇ "ist kein *passivum divinum*." Wolter, *Der Brief an die Römer*, 1:480.

Christ fulfills both the requirement that lawbreakers die and that lawkeepers live. We will return to this dynamic below.

A second echo in Rom 8:4 stems from Paul's use of the "walking" (הלך/περιπατέω) metaphor so common in Israel's Scriptures. As I noted previously in the analysis of Rom 6:4, Israel's Scriptures employ the walking metaphor to describe prominent figures from the nation's history and to describe what God requires in the Mosaic Law. The latter is most consistent with Rom 8:4. If Israel walks in God's commands, the result will be blessing and life. As indicated in Leviticus, "You shall do my judgments and you shall keep my statutes to walk (ללכת) in them, I am the Lord your God." If they do not walk in the commands, the result will be curse and death. Therefore, you shall keep my statutes and my judgments which, if a man will do them, then he will live (וחי) by them, I am the Lord" (Lev 18:4–5).[37] Contrastively, if Israel does not "walk" in the divine commands, the result will be curse and death. As indicated in Leviticus, "Then if you walk (תלכו) in hostility with me, and you are not willing to obey me, then I will increase the plague on you seven times according to your sins" (Lev 26:21).[38] In short, "walking" or "not walking" in God's commands is the difference between life and death. As the psalmist puts it, "Blessed is everyone who fears the Lord, the one who walks (ההלך) in his ways" (Ps 128:1).[39] Paul reconfigures this juxtaposition of life and death in the Mosaic Law, based on how one "walks" in it, around God's work in Christ and the gift of the Spirit. God has fulfilled the righteous requirement of the law, that is condemnation for lawbreaking and life for lawkeeping, in the crucified and risen Christ with the aim that the Romans would "walk," or live, in accordance with the Spirit rather than the flesh.

This brings us to the third intertextual echo in Rom 8:4, namely the eschatological promise of the Spirit. Paul contrasts walking "according to the flesh" (κατὰ σάρκα) with walking "according to the Spirit (κατὰ πνεῦμα).[40] As noted at various points already, the prepositional phrase κατὰ σάρκα refers to life in an Adamic state and in a world where the "I" is helplessly deceived, defeated, and killed by the powers of sin and death. Contrastively, κατὰ πνεῦμα refers to life in Christ where the "I" has his or her cry for deliverance answered. The crucified and risen Christ defeats the powers of sin and death which at the same time frees one from divine condemnation. The Spirit's role in this experience with Christ, based on the larger context of Rom 8:5–27, is to direct the thinking of the believer, enable death to sin, bear witness to the believer's filial status with God, elicit the cry "Abba Father," intercede in their prayers, and ultimately

---

37. See Paul's citation of Lev 18:5 in Rom 10:5 and Gal 3:12. For other statements linking "walking" in the commands to life, see, e.g., Deut 5:33; 8:6–7; 10:12–13; 26:17–19; 30:16.

38. See also Lev 26:22–46.

39. See also the metaphor of walking linked to life and the penalty of not walking in Pss 1:1; 15:2; 26:1, 11; 78:10; 81:13; 82:5; 84:11; 85:14; 86:11; 89:31; 101:2, 6; 116:9; 119:1, 3.

40. Cf. the use of κατὰ σάρκα in Rom 8:5, 12, 13; 9:3, 5; 1 Cor 1:26; 10:18; 2 Cor 1:17; 5:16; 10:2, 3; 11:18; Gal 4:23, 29; Eph 6:5; Col 3:22. Cf. the use of κατὰ πνεῦμα in Rom 8:5; Gal 4:29.

raise believers from the dead just as he raised Christ. All of this constitutes walking "according to the Spirit," and it is in accordance with Israel's Scriptures.

On this point, the most formative pre-texts for Paul likely emanate from Ezekiel's prophecy where we find the combination of "walking" (הלך/πορεύω/περιπατέω) and the Spirit:

> And I will give to them a new heart and I will give a new Spirit (πνεῦμα καινόν) in them and I will remove the heart of stone from their flesh and I will give to them a heart of flesh, in order that they might walk (ילכו/πορεύωνται) in my commandments and they might keep my righteous requirements (τὰ δικαιώματα μου) and do them; and they will be my people, and I will be their God (Ezek 11:19–20).

> And I will give to you a new heart and I will give a new Spirit (πνεῦμα καινόν) in you and I will remove the heart of stone from your flesh and I will give to you a heart of flesh. And I will give my Spirit (τὸ πνεῦμά μου) in you and I will make it that you might walk (תלכו/πορεύησθε) in my righteous requirements (ἐν τοῖς δικαιώμασίν μου) and you shall keep my judgments and do them (Ezek 36:26–27).[41]

The *volume* of these pre-texts is moderate to high based on the semantic overlap of הלך/πορεύω/περιπατέω, πνεῦμα, and δικαίωμα.[42] The *contextual consistency* is also substantial, because, in both the pre-text and text, walking in the righteous requirements of God requires the gift of his Spirit. Even more, when we consider Ezekiel's vision of resurrection in Ezek 37:1–14, which also requires the gift of the Spirit, it is apparent that Paul draws from Ezekiel's thought given his statement in Rom 8:11 which we will discuss below. Paul reconfigures these pre-texts from Ezekiel around what God has "fulfilled" in Christ Jesus. The Mosaic requirement of death for the transgressor and life for the lawkeeper is fulfilled in the obedience of Christ. The gift of the Spirit enables the believers to share in Christ's obedience and live out that experience in his suffering and glory.

Interpretive Impact of Romans 8:1–4

The interplay between these four verses and various OT pre-texts produce several points of resonance that shed interpretive light on Paul's argument at this point.

First, when Paul concludes (ἄρα) in Rom 8:1 "Therefore, there is now no condemnation (κατάκριμα) for those who are in Christ Jesus," he announces an end to the judgment first doled out in Gen 3 which had a perpetually deleterious impact on

---

41. See also Isa 44:3; 48:16–17; 63:14.

42. As I noted in the discussion of the walking metaphor in Rom 6:4, Paul's use of περιπατέω reflects the Hebraic use of הלך more than the LXX's use of πορεύω. In any case, the latter term can bear the sense of "walk." See LEH 508.

Adam's progeny. They had been sentenced and subjected to the enemy of sin (serpent) and death since the Adamic transgression.[43] The "I" relays the experience of that condemnation in Rom 7:7–25 from the perspective of faith in Christ. It is an experience still lived out by all those in whom sin dwells, but it can only be articulated by those who are in Christ. Moreover, only those in Christ receive a response to the cry of distress, and it is that response that Paul lays out in Rom 8:1–4. While there is an end to the Adamic condemnation in Christ, it does not follow that those who are in Christ are insulated from the ongoing and internal experience of that condemnation. In keeping with the pattern of OT lament, the shift to deliverance and praise is never permanent. Just as enemies persist in their affliction of the lamenter, sin persists in the body of believers. As Paul puts it in Rom 8:10, "But if Christ is in you, the body is dead because of sin, but the Spirit is life because of righteousness.[44] Therefore, we should not conclude from Paul's statement in Rom 8:1 that those who are in Christ are no longer impacted by the Adamic condemnation. Sin continues to afflict, and death remains largely inescapable. As we shall see, this lingering reality, or norm (νόμος), is the catalyst for many of the points that Paul underscores in Rom 8.[45]

Second, the manner of the "I's" *deliverance* from Adamic condemnation described in Rom 8:2–4 fulfills the promise of life in the Mosaic Law and the promise of the life-giving Spirit in the prophets, promises which Paul weds through the theological abbreviation "For the law of the Spirit of life in Christ Jesus freed you from the law of sin and death." The Mosaic Law, particularly pre-texts such as Lev 18:5 and Deut 30:15–20, promises life for those who obey. Yet, as the lament of the "I" in Rom 7 demonstrates, sin uses the Mosaic Law to produce coveting and death rather than life. This is in fact a recurring experience, or norm (νόμος), within the "I." Paul abbreviates this experience with the phrase "the law of sin and death." It is also the experience from which those in Christ are freed (ἠλευθέρωσεν) through "the law of the Spirit of life in Christ Jesus." The intertextual subtext of this abbreviation stems from pre-texts such as Ezek 36:26–29 and 37:14 where the prophet envisions a time when God's people would be cleansed from sin and endued with the very Spirit of God. For Paul, the Spirit gives the believer life with God in all the ways undone in Eden and in all the ways laid out in the law and the prophets. Paul explains this life throughout Rom 8, but he prefaces all of it with the "in Christ Jesus" (ἐν Χριστῷ Ἰησοῦ) in v. 2, "The law of the Spirit of life *in Christ Jesus*."

Third, as Paul explains how God has freed those in Christ from a life condemned to the powers of sin and death, he describes Jesus as the sin offering (περὶ ἁμαρτίας)

---

43. As I noted in the previous chapter, Paul's description of sin and the description of the serpent in Gen 3 overlap at several points. However, the Pauline corpus never explains in detail how the power of sin and Satan are related to one another. See also the overlap between sin and the serpent in Rom 5:12–19.

44. See also Rom 7:25b and the discussion in the previous chapter.

45. Part of what informs Paul's use of νόμος in Rom 7:25b and 8:2 is the norm or principle that sin and death are every present enemies even for those who are in Christ.

par excellence which is anticipated in the Levitical sacrificial system and promised in the messianic figure of Isaiah's suffering servant. The phrase περὶ ἁμαρτίας, often obscured in translations as "for sin," evokes the sin offering discussed at length in Leviticus. Once again, in Leviticus and throughout Israel's Scriptures, sin offerings separate guilty parties from responsibility for their transgressions, secure their forgiveness, purify them for service, and thereby propitiate divine wrath. For Paul, the crucified Christ is the sin offering who finally accomplishes all of this on an eschatological scale. By sending his Son as a sin offering, God did in Christ what the law, weakened as it was by the Adamic state of affairs (ἠσθένει διὰ τῆς σαρκός), did not have the ability to do, namely "condemn" sin in a way that it freed a person from the deceptive and deadly clutches of sin. God condemned (κατέκρινεν) sin, that is he announced a judgment against the power of sin and carried that judgment out, in the flesh (κατέκρινεν τὴν ἁμαρτίαν ἐν τῇ σαρκί) of his crucified Son. Such liberating condemnation required a sin offering. In other words, God could not condemn sin and thereby free believers from sin without a sacrifice that he himself required by law and that he himself promised in the prophets. We will return to the former requirement in just a moment. Here I want to highlight the promise of a sin offering in the prophets, specifically in the suffering servant described in Isa 52:13–53:12.

In Isa 53:10, differences between the MT and the LXX notwithstanding, life, or justification (Isa 53:11), before God requires a sin offering (περὶ ἁμαρτίας).[46] The suffering servant provides that sin offering as God hands him over to death for the sins of the people (Isa 53:6). Paul identifies Jesus as the Isaianic servant/sin offering.

A fourth point of resonance generated here is that God sent his Son to be a sin offering (περὶ ἁμαρτίας) in his crucifixion to fulfill the dual requirement of the Mosaic Law (τὸ δικαίωμα τοῦ νόμου). The law requires death for the transgressor and guarantees life for the one who obeys. Paul assures the Romans that God himself fulfills this requirement "in us" by condemning in the flesh of his Son the enemy who deceives and kills the Romans through its use of the Mosaic Law, namely the enemy of sin. Rom 8:3–4 indicate that Paul sees a close connection between the need for forgiveness and freedom. The "I" needs both forgiveness of sin and freedom from it. God meets both needs through Jesus as the sin offering in whose death God cleanses the "I" from sin and condemns sin with the aim of freeing the "I" from sin. This is in keeping with Paul's wider soteriology in Romans and elsewhere.[47] Not coincidentally, it is also in

46. Once again, the difference between Isa 53:10 MT and 53:10 LXX is that in the former the servant offers the sin offering while in the latter the people make the offering, though it is in conjunction with the servant.

47. In this way, Rom 8:3–4 resembles Paul's explanation of God's righteousness in Rom 3:21–26. By putting Jesus forward as the "mercy seat," God simultaneously acts to forgive, deliver, and condemn. He cleanses the ungodly from sin while also righteously judging the sinner in the death of Jesus. In this way, he is both "righteous and the one who justifies the one from the faith of Jesus" (Rom 3:26). It is not a coincidence that in both Rom 3:21–26 and 8:3–4 Paul evokes Lev 16, an OT pre-text which typifies God's soteriological work in Christ. Additionally, in Gal 1:4, Paul links Jesus as a sin offering to freedom from the present evil age describing Jesus as "the one who gave himself for our sins (ὑπὲρ

keeping with the OT soteriology that shapes Paul's thought where, on both a communal and individual level, the need for forgiveness and deliverance from oppressive forces go hand in hand.

Finally, by fulfilling the dual requirement of the Mosaic Law in the crucified Christ, those who are in Christ become people who live, or "walk," in accordance with the Spirit of God just as God promised through Ezekiel. Rom 8:1–4 echoes the prior promise of the Spirit from Ezek 11:19:20, 36:26–27, and 37:14. In this way, the Ezekiel pre-texts become a key part of the intertextual subtext for Rom 8:5–17 which I will discuss below. As we shall see, walking in accordance with the Spirit that God promised in Ezekiel culminates in resurrection from the dead just as the prophet promised.[48]

Romans 8:5–11

(8:5–11)For those who are according to the flesh set their minds on the things of the flesh, but those who are accorindg to the Spirit the things of the Spirit. For the way of thinking of the flesh is death, but the way of thinking of the Spirit is life and peace; because the way of thinking of the flesh is hostile towards God, for it is not subject to the law of God, for it is not even able to. But you are not in the flesh but in the Spirit, if indeed the Spirit of God dwells in you. But if anyone does not have the Spirit of Christ, he is not of him. But if Christ is in you, the body is dead because of sin, but the Spirit is life because of righteousness. But if the Spirit of the one who raised Christ from the dead dwells in you, the one who raised Christ from the dead will also make alive your mortal bodies through his same Spirit who dwells in you.

Paul's juxtaposition of the Spirit (τὸ πνεῦμα) and flesh (σάρξ) dominates these verses. His juxtaposition expands upon the initial contrast stated in v. 4, "to those who do not walk according to the flesh (κατὰ σάρκα) but according to the Spirit (κατὰ πνεῦμα)." He focuses especially on the way of thinking (φρόνημα) that distinguishes these two groups and the ultimate outcome of the Spirit's presence in the beliver, namely resurrection from the dead. Paul's reflection on the Spirit here also expands upon his initial statement in Rom 5:3–5 regarding hope which will not become an eschatological disappointment.[49] Although these seven verses contain no OT citations, they have a richer intertextual subtext than is sometimes appreciated.

τῶν ἁμαρτιῶν), in order that he might deliver (ἐξέληται) us from the present evil age."

48. See Ezek 37:1–14.

49. As noted already, Rom 5–8 coalesces around hope from affliction and the gift of Spirit.

Suggested Pre-Texts in Romans 8:5–11

Hübner lists the following pre-texts: Num 23:27; 1 Kgs 3:10; Ps 68:32; Mal 3:4 (Rom 8:8).[50] These pre-texts focus upon the use of ἀρέσκω which Paul uses in Rom 8:8, "But those who are in the flesh are not able to please (ἀρέσαι) God."

Nestle-Aland 28th ed. lists no pre-texts in its margins. Once again, Hays does not reengage Paul's use of the OT until Rom 8:18.[51] Additionally, Seifrid's analysis, as noted above, focuses primarily on the use of the OT in Rom 8:31–39.[52]

Intertextual Analysis of Pre-Texts in Romans 8:5–11

The pre-texts here are consistent with many of those that comprise the intertextual subtext of Rom 7:7–8:4. Specifically, the Adamic narrative, the Mosaic Law, and Ezekiel's promise of the Spirit continue to influence Paul's thought at this point. However, as well shall see, a handful of other pre-texts are echoed here as well.

In Rom 8:5–8, Paul explains the difference between those who walk before God according to flesh and those who walk according to the Spirit (Rom 8:4). It is a difference in what they set their minds upon, or what they are intent on doing. The noun φρόνημα occurs three times in Rom 8:6–7, and the verb φρονέω occurs once in Rom 8:5.[53] In this way, Paul clearly draws attention to the distinctive ways that these two groups think and to their cognitive intent. Their contrastive ways of thinking contain three OT echoes.

Romans 8:5–8 and Echoes of the Inner Life

First, the multiple references to "flesh" (σάρξ) should once again be understood in relation to the Adamic narrative which underlies multiple sections of Rom 5–8.[54] To live and think "according to the flesh" (κατὰ σάρκα), is to live and think in a way that conforms to the fallen Adamic condition and world.[55] Paul has already described that condition as one in which sin and death reign (βασιλεύω) through a deceptive use of

---

50. Hübner, *Vetus Testamentum in Novo*, 2:112–15.

51. Hays, *Echoes of Scripture in the Letters of Paul*, 57–63, 158.

52. Seifrid, *Romans*, 633–38.

53. See BDAG 1063–64.

54. E.g., the allusion to Gen 3 in Rom 5:12–21 and the echoes proper of Gen 3 in Rom 7:7–25.

55. Paul makes it clear in Rom 5:12–14 and 8:19–22 that Adamic rebellion not only impacted human beings but also the material world. As he puts in Rom 5:12, "just as through one man sin entered the world (εἰς τὸν κόσμον)." From a broader perspective, σάρξ in the Pauline corpus can have a broad range of meaning. Hultgren notes, "The concept of life in the flesh can express the normal manner of earthly existence (Gal 2:20; 2 Cor 10:3; Phil 1:22, 24; Phlm 16); typical human standards of thought and action (1 Cor 1:26; 2 Cor 1:17; 5:16; Gal 3:3); or the arena in which sinful inclinations reside." Hultgren, *Romans*, 301. In Rom 8:5–11, σάρξ fits into the third category. I would only add that the "arena" of sinful inclinations has ties to the Adamic narrative.

the divine command, whether it is the command in Gen 2:16–17 or commands in the Mosaic Law, through persistently overpowering its victims, and ultimately by killing them.[56] Such a condition had persisted from Adam until Moses and continued up to Paul's day. Therefore, to live and think "according to the flesh" is to continue in this Adamic state and epoch which is to continue in sin and death. As Paul puts it in Rom 8:6, "The mind-set/way of thinking of the flesh (τὸ φρόνημα τῆς σαρκὸς) is death (θάνατος)." In other words, thinking that is always intent on sin, that is "the mind-set of the flesh," is itself a form of death where one is separated presently and eschatologically from God.[57]

In v. 7, Paul further qualifies the "the way of thinking of flesh" by identifying it as "enmity towards God (ἔχθρα εἰς θεόν)." Enmity towards God exists, because the flesh's way of thinking is not able to be subject to the law of God (Rom 8:7). Although the phrase ἔχθρα εἰς θεόν does not evoke a specific OT pre-text, it does reflect an OT motif which portrays unlawful people as God's enemies. For example, Isa 63:7–10 recounts how God became Israel's enemy "But they were disobedient and they provoked his holy spirit; and he turned to be an enemy (εἰς ἔχθραν), and he fought against them" (Isa 63:10). Similarly, in the poetic description of Jerusalem's destruction, God is likened to an enemy:

> He stretched out his bow like an enemy (ἐχθρός), he strengthened his right hand like an opponent (ὑπεναντός), and he killed all the desireable things of my eyes in the tent of the daughter of Zion, he poured out his wrath on me. The Lord became like an enemy (ἐγενήθη κύριος ὡς ἐχθρός), he drowned Israel, he drowned all of its palace, he ruined its strongholds, and he multiplied to the daughter of Judah the afflicted and humbled (Lam 2:4–5).

In both Isa 63:10 and Lam 2:4–5, God becomes an enemy (ἐχθρός) to Israel because of their disobedience to the Mosaic Law.

Other pre-texts describe enmity with God from the perspective of ungodly enemies. Paul has already appealed to some of these pre-texts in his catena of citations in Rom 3:10–18.[58] For example, the psalmist vocalizes the enemy's disposition noting "The lawless one (ὁ παράνομος) says in himself, in order that he might sin, that 'There is no fear of God before his eyes'" (Ps 35:2 LXX).[59] Overall, the OT link between divine enmity and human lawlessness shapes the way Paul links the "mind-set on the flesh" which results in "enmity towards God." The enmity stemming from an inability to

---

56. See the use of βασιλεύω in Rom 5:14, 17, 21; 6:12. See also the use of κυριεύω Rom 6:9, 14 with θάνατος and ἁμαρτία as the subjects of the verb respectively.

57. The subject-predicative nominative construction in Rom 8:6, τὸ γὰρ φρόνημα τῆς σαρκὸς θάνατος, indicates a fatal state of being stemming from the the mind-set of the flesh.

58. For a discussion of the catena, see volume 1.

59. See also Pss LXX 13:1.

obey God began with Adam's transgression, continued until Moses, and persists unless one is in Christ.[60]

Second, in v. 6, when Paul compares the flesh's way of thinking to that of the Spirit (τὸ φρόνημα τοῦ πνεύματος), the latter echoes the OT in a few different ways. As Paul puts it, "the way of the thinking of the Spirit is life and peace (ζωὴ καὶ εἰρήνη)" (Rom 8:6b). The inverse of the "the way of the thinking of the flesh" that results in death presently and eschatologically is "the way of the thinking of the Spirit" which results in life and peace both presently and eschatologically.[61] Interpreters do not always give attention to the combination of ζωὴ καὶ εἰρήνη.[62] Paul likely pairs the terms under the influence of Israel's Scriptures.[63] Yet, one looks in vain for the overt combination of life + peace + Spirit (ζωή + εἰρήνη + πνεῦμα) in an OT pre-text. The terms life and peace only appear together twice in the OT, and neither occurrence is especially consistent with Paul's text.[64]

However, it does not follow that Paul's combination of ζωή + εἰρήνη + πνεῦμα is entirely uninformed by Israel's Scriptures. As I have noted already at various points in this work, these terms resound with OT echoes in the letter.[65] For example, in the letter's *propositio*, Paul's reference to life originates from Hab 2:4 "But the righteous will live (ζήσεται) by faith" (Rom 1:17b). To reiterate, based on the original context of Habakkuk, this is a promise of life *in* and *beyond* divine judgment based on whether one believes God's promise of deliverance.[66] Similarly, Paul has demonstrated that peace with God is a present and eschatological reality in Christ which is informed by Israel's Scriptures. When Paul concludes "Therefore, having been justified by faith we have peace (εἰρήνην) with God through our Lord Jesus Christ" in Rom 5:1, this "peace" is intertextually informed. For example, as I noted previously, Paul reconfigures OT pre-texts such as Isa 32, Psalms LXX 71, and 84 around the crucified and risen Christ who secures "peace" for believers according to the messianic promises

---

60. As noted in previous chapters, Paul uses OT descriptions of divine enemies to describe those who are outside of Christ. See, e.g., the use of the Psalms of Lament in Rom 3:10–18. See also the use of ἐχροί in Rom 5:10.

61. It is hard to imagine that Paul could employ "life and peace" together in a way that is entirely devoid of eschatological consideration. Dunn argues that the terms are "primarily future eschatological blessings." Dunn, *Romans*, 1:426.

62. On this point, see Jewett, *Romans*, 487.

63. As I noted in the introduction to this work, we must also allow for other influences such as Greco-Roman thought, early Christian tradition, and Paul's own unique perspective. Nevertheless, none of these additional influences are entirely detached from Israel's Scriptures.

64. See Prov 3:2; Mal 2:5. As noted by Wolter, *Der Brief an die Römer*, 484n55.

65. See the use of ζάω/ζωή in Rom 1:17; 2:7; 5:10, 17, 18, 21; 6:2, 4, 10, 11, 13, 22, 23; 7:1, 2, 3, 9, 10; 8:2, 12, 13, 38; 9:26; 10:5; 11:15; 12:1; 14:7, 8, 9, 11. See the use of εἰρηνεύω/εἰρήνη in Rom 1:7; 2:10; 3:17; 5:1; 12:18; 14:17, 19; 15:13, 33; 16:20. See the use of πνεῦμα in Rom 1:4, 9; 2:29; 5:5; 7:6; 8:2, 4, 5, 6, 9, 10, 11, 13, 14, 15, 16, 23, 26, 27; 9:1; 11:8; 12:11; 14:17; 15:13, 16, 19, 30.

66. See also Rom 5:10 where Paul has in view salvation from eschatological wrath "by his (i.e., Christ's) life (ἐν τῇ ζωῇ αὐτοῦ)."

of Israel's Scriptures. The peace that the Christ ultimately brings is a peace with God himself. Finally, as we have seen repeatedly, Paul's references to the Spirit are intertextually charged as well. Pre-texts such as Ezek 11 and 36–37 are especially informative.

It follows then that the expression "the way of thinking of the Spirit is life and peace" in Rom 8:6 should be understood against this intertextual backdrop. Israel's Scriptures promise life beyond judgment and peace with God in conjunction with the gift of the Spirit. Paul's point here in v. 6 is that the Spirit's way of thinking, in contrast to the deadly results of the flesh's way of thinking, directs the thinking and actions of those who are in Christ to a hope-filled experience of these promises.

A third intertextual element in Rom 8:5–8 involves Paul's statement about "pleasing" (ἀρέσκω) God, "But those who are in the flesh are not able to please (ἀρέσαι) God" (Rom 8:8). The verb ἀρέσκω, along with the adjective ἀρεστός-ή-όν, often appear in the LXX in contexts where God is the object of this "pleasing" action.[67] Sometimes the pleasing action takes the form of a command such as, "And you shall do what is pleasing (τὸ ἀρεστόν) and good before the Lord your God, in order that it might be well with you and you might enter and inherit the good land, which the Lord swore to your fathers" (Deut 6:18).[68] In other instances, focus is placed on individual figures who do, or do not do, what is pleasing to God. The most well-known example is probably Enoch as he is described in Gen 5. As the narrator puts it, "And Enoch pleased God (εὐηρέστησεν) and he was not being found, because God transferred him" (Gen 5:24).[69] Other OT figures fit this same profile.[70] For example, in praying to be delivered from his fatal illness, Hezekiah appeals to the fact that he had done what was pleasing before God during his lifetime. He cries out, "Remember, Lord, as I went before you with truth in a true heart and I did the things that were pleasing (τὰ ἀρεστά) before you" (Isa 38:3).[71] The psalmist reflects on the internal disposition of those who strive to please God by obeying his commands, "I will praise the name of God with a song, I will magnify him with praise, and it will be more pleasing (ἀρέσει) to God than a new bull having horns and hoofs" (Ps 68:32 LXX).[72] In short, what pleases God is heartfelt obedience to the commands laid out in the Mosaic Law.

This OT motif of pleasing God through heartfelt obedience to the law is *contextually consistent* with Paul's statement in Rom 8:8. In the immediate context, Paul links the inability (οὐ δύνανται) of those "who are in the flesh (οἱ ἐν σαρκὶ ὄντες)" to please God (θεῷ ἀρέσαι) with their inability (οὐδὲ γὰρ δύνανται) to be subject to the law

---

67. See LEH 81.

68. See also Exod 15:26; Deut 12:8, 25, 28; 13:19; 21:9; Ezra 7:18; 10:11; Prov 21:3. See also Jdt 12:14; Tob 4:21; Wis 4:14; 9:9, 18; Sir 48:22.

69. See also Gen 5:22. In Gen 5:22 and 5:24 MT, we find the verb הלך. The LXX translator renders it with εὐαρεστέω which obviously contains the ἀρεστ root. See LEH, 247. See also the use of εὐαρεστέω in Heb 11:5–6 which the author employs to describe Enoch.

70. See also Noah in Gen 6:9 and the patriarchs in Gen 48:15.

71. See also Num 22:34; 23:27; 1 Kgs 3:10.

72. See also Prov 24:18; Isa 59:15; Mal 3:4.

of God (τῷ νόμῳ τοῦ θεοῦ) (Rom 8:7–8). He recontextualizes the motif by broadly incorporating a broad swath of people into the Adamic condition, or "in the flesh."[73] From Paul's perspective, only those who are in Christ and walking according to the Spirirt can please God.[74] He grounds their ability to please God in what God has done in the crucified and risen Christ and what he has given in the Spirit. Within the *history of interpretation*, Jewett notes a link between the OT motif of pleasing God and Rom 8:8. He summarizes the OT motif noting, "The idea is that if one please God, good fortune will follow, but the one not pleasing God will face misfortune and wrath."[75]

Romans 8:9–11 and Echoes of the Spirit

We now turn our attention to Rom 8:9–11 where Paul assures the Romans that they are "in the Spirit" (ἐν πνεύματι) rather than "in the flesh" (ἐν σαρκὶ).[76] He briefly describes life in the Spirit now and resurrected life by the Spirit later. Paul's explanation evokes the OT in a few different ways.

In Rom 8:9, by using the phrases "Spirit of God" (πνεῦμα θεοῦ) and "Spirit of Christ" (πνεῦμα Χριστοῦ) interchangeably, Paul applies an OT description of Israel's God to its messiah. He writes, "But you are not in the flesh but in the Spirit, if indeed the Spirit of God (πνεῦμα θεοῦ) dwells in you. But if anyone does not have (ἔχει) the Spirit of Christ (πνεῦμα Χριστοῦ), he is not of him."[77] The phrase πνεῦμα θεοῦ occurs thirteen times in the LXX, and πνεῦμα κυρίου occurs twenty-three times.[78] The creation account includes a reference to the "Spirit of God" (πνεῦμα θεοῦ) upon the primordial waters (Gen 1:2). Subsequent occurrences describe the Spirit of God as being either "in" or "upon" individuals. For example, in his description of Joseph, Pharaoh

---

73. As Murray puts it, "It is implied, of course, that 'the law of God' enunciates what is well-pleasing to God. But what is pleasing to God comprehends more than is included in the term 'law.' Hence by saying that 'they that are in the flesh *cannot please God*' the extent of the impossibility is expanded to cover the whole range of what is pleasing ot God." Murray, *Romans*, 287.

74. Cf. Paul's use of ἀρέσκω in Rom 15:1, 3; 1 Cor 7:32–34, Gal 1:10; 1 Thess 2:4, 15; 4:1; 2 Tim 2:4. See also 1 John 3:22. In reflecting on the prominence of this motif in the wider Paulien corpus, Wright notes "Despite its prominence in various Pauline passages, the idea that one can actually please God, or the Lord, is foreign to much thinking and writing on the apostle, perhaps because it suggests to some the thin end of a wedge that will end in works-righteousness." Wright, *Romans*, 583.

75. Jewett, *Romans*, 489.

76. The dative nouns πνεύματι and σαρκὶ are best understood as indicating the "sphere" in which the Romans live before God.

77. The only other use of πνεῦμα Χριστοῦ is found in 1 Pet 1:11. We do find τὸ πνεῦμα Ἰησοῦ in Acts 16:7 and Phil 1:19.

78. The phrase πνεῦμα θεοῦ is the translation of רוח אלהים. See Gen 1:2; 41:38; Exod 31:3; 35:21; Num 24:2; 1 Sam 10:10; 11:6; 19:20, 23; 2 Chr 15:1; 24:20; Job 27:3; 33:4; Ezek 11:24. For other uses of πνεῦμα θεοῦ in the Pauline corpus, see Rom 8:14; 15:19; 1 Cor 2:11, 14; 7:40; 12:3; Eph 4:30; Phil 3:3. See πνεῦμα κυρίου in Judg 3:10; 6:34; 11:29; 13:25; 14:6, 19; 15:14; 1 Sam 10:6; 16:13, 14; 2 Sam 23:2; 1 Kgs 18:12; 22:24; 2 Kgs 2:16; 2 Chr 18:23; 20:14; Isa 11:2; 40:13; 61:1; 63:14; Ezek 11:5; 37:1; Mic 3:8. See also Luke 4:18; Acts 5:9; 8:39; 2 Cor 3:17.

asks "Will we find such a man, who has (ἔχει) the Spirit of God in him (πνεῦμα θεοῦ ἐν αὐτῷ)?" (Gen 41:38).[79] Additionally, God "fills" (ἐμπίμπλημι) those who are involved in the design and construction of the tabernacle with a divine spirit, "I filled him with a divine spirit (πνεῦμα θεῖον) of wisdom and understanding and skill in every work" (Exod 31:3).[80] The Spirit of God comes upon, or is in, those who prophesy as in the case of Balaam, "And Balaam having lifted up his eyes looked down at Israel encamped according to their tribes, and the Spirit of God was in him (πνεῦμα θεοῦ ἐν αὐτῷ)" (Num 24:2).[81] God's Spirit also empowers individuals in battle as we often see in Judges, "And the Spirit of God/Lord (πνεῦμα θεοῦ/πνεῦμα κυρίου) strengthened Gideon " (Judg 6:34).[82] In the midst of his pain, Job acknowledges "the spirit of God (πνεῦμα θεῖον) remains in my nostrils" (Job 27:3) which is obviously an echo of Gen 3:7, "And God formed man out of the dust from the earth and breathed into his face the breath of life (πνοὴν ζωῆς), and man became a living soul."[83]

Similarly, Ezekiel's vision of the dry bones underscores the role of God's Spirit in giving life to the dead "And you will know that I am the Lord when I open your tombs in order that I might bring my people out from the tombs. And I will put my Spirit (τὸ πνεῦμα μου) in you, and you will will live (ζήσεσθε), and I will place you in your land, and you will know that I the Lord have spoken and I will do it, says the Lord (Ezek 37:13–14)."[84] Other uses of τὸ πνεῦμα μου in Ezekiel include the promise that God would place his Spirit within his people in order that they might obey him, "And I will place my Spirit (τὸ πνεῦμα μου) in you and I will make it that you might go in my righteous requirements and you might keep and do my judgments" (Ezek 36:27).[85]

Finally, in Isaiah, God's Spirit anoints his messiah "The Spirit of the Lord (πνεῦμα κυρίου) is upon me, because he has anointed me (ἔχρισέν με); he has sent me to proclaim good news to the poor, to heal those crushed in heart, to preach release to the captives and the recovery of sight to the blind" (Isa 61:1).[86]

To summarize up to this point, the divine title τὸ πνεῦμα θεοῦ, along with its variations such as τὸ πνεῦμα κυρίου and τὸ πνεῦμα μου, occurs in contexts where writers emphasize the following divine actions: (1) creative and life-sustaining work (Gen 1:2; Job 27:3); (2) supplying wisdom to human agents tasked with doing his work

---

79. It is worth noting that the *volume* of this pre-text in Rom 8:9 is high based on the semantic and grammatical involving ἔχει and πνεῦμα θεοῦ.

80. The phrase πνεῦμα θεῖον is the rendering of רוח אלהים. See also Exod 35:31.

81. See also the link between πνεῦμα θεοῦ and prophecy in 1 Sam 10:10; 19:20, 23; 2 Chr 5:1; 24:20. The πνεῦμα θεοῦ gives Ezekiel a vision. See Ezek 11:24.

82. Judg 6:34 A contains πνεῦμα θεοῦ. See also the references to πνεῦμα in Judg 3:10; 11:29; 13:25; 14:6, 19; 15:14.

83. See also Job 33:4.

84. The phrase τὸ πνεῦμα μου occurs elsewhere in the LXX as a refrence to God's Spirit. See Gen 6:3; Isa 30:1; 42:1; 44:3; 59:21; Ezek 36:27; 37:14; 39:29; Joel 3:1–2; Hag 2:5; Zech 4:6; 6:8.

85. Cf. Joel 3:1–2.

86. See also Isa 11:2; Mic 3:8.

(Exod 31:3); (3) empowering leaders in battle (Judg 6:34); (4) enabling obedience to his commands (Ezek 37:26); (5) anointing his messiah (Isa 61:1); and (6) raising the dead (Ezek 37:13–14). Some of these divine actions associated with τὸ πνεῦμα θεοῦ inform Rom 8:9–11. Obedience, life with God, and resurrection by means of God's Spirit especially stand out here.

The wider context of Paul's argument indicates a concern with obedience for those who are "in the Spirit" rather than "in the flesh." However, it is not obedience detached from the person and work of Christ. As I noted above, God sent his Son to fulfill the righteous requirement of the Mosaic Law wherein the transgressor must die but the obedient figure must live (Rom 8:4). Therefore, being "in the Spirit" means sharing in the experience and benefits of Christ's obedience. This is part of what having (ἔχει) the Spirit of God, or the Spirit of Christ, entails (Rom 8:9). The title πνεῦμα Χριστοῦ drives home the point that the those who are "in the Spirit" share in the experience and benefit of Christ's obedience. The experience involves suffering with Christ, and the benefit includes sharing in his resurrection.[87]

In Rom 8:10, Paul plainly summarizes the current state of those who have the Spirit of Christ in Rome "But if Christ is in you, the body is dead because of sin but the Spirit is life and righteousness." What does Paul mean by describing the body (σῶμα) as "dead" (νεκρόν) because of sin?[88] The answer lies in Paul's vivid description of sin and death throughout Rom 5:12–7:25.[89] Sin and death are closely related powers that entered the world and human bodies through Adam's transgression. Not even those who are in Christ, or in the Spirit, escape the fatal effects of these powers which have been active since the garden. While those baptized into Christ's death should not remain in sin, and though they should consider themselveas as dead to sin, it does not follow that they are entirely insulated from the present deleterious effects of sin and death. As the lamenting "I" of Rom 7 reminds the Romans, an internal war rages on, and sin still kills the body.[90] The apodosis of "If Christ is in you (εἰ δὲ Χριστὸς ἐν ὑμῖν)," is not "then sin will have no ill-effects on you." It is that "the body is dead because of sin." As Seifrid puts it, "In the present world, our graves will testify to our continuing godlessness–indeed, there we shall be properly God-less–'the body is dead on account of sin' (Rom 8:10a)."[91]

---

87. This formulation becomes explicit in Rom 8:17 with συμπάσχομεν and συνδοξασθῶμεν which I will discuss below.

88. As Jewett notes, "A bewildering variety of interpretive suggestions has been proposed." Jewett, *Romans*, 491.

89. E.g., Murray notes, "'Because of sin' points back to 5:12 and 6:23 and reasserts the truth so often emphasized that the reason why death has invaded the physical aspect of our being is the fact of sin. Bodily death is the wages of sin." Murray, *Romans*, 289.

90. Paul's statement that the "body is dead because of sin" primarily focuses upon physical death but not to the exclusion of the internal struggle of the "I" caused by sin which Paul describes in Rom 7:7–25.

91. Seifrid, *Christ Our Righteousness*, 184–85.

However, Paul's apodosis also includes "but the Spirit is life because of righteousness." In this way, Paul juxtaposes the following: (1) body and Spirit (σῶμα/πνεῦμα); (2) dead and life (νεκρόν/ζωή); and (3) sin and righteousness (ἁμαρτία/δικαιοσύνη). The power of sin kills the body; however, the Spirit's presence provides internal life and the hope of a resurrected life. This life through the presence of the Spirit is "because of righteousness (διὰ δικαιοσύνην)," namely the righteousness of Christ.

The referent of δικαιοσύνη in Rom 8:10 should be understood in relationship to both the life of righteousness described in Rom 6:12–23 and God's righteous verdict which is reckoned on the basis of faith in the gospel. I am not speaking here of a "meta-concept" of justification which combines the gift of a righteous verdict and the power to live righteously so that one becomes new.[92] Instead, the righteous verdict brings with it the gift of the Spirit who Paul says is "life" (ζωή) (Rom 8:10). The Spirit is "life" not only in juxtaposition to a body that is dead because of sin. As the wider context will bear out, the Spirit is life in the sense that the believer lives with Christ in his suffering and ultimately in his resurrection from the dead.[93]

Romans 8:9–11 and the Echo of Ezekeil 37

Paul underscores the latter aspect of life in v. 11, and it echoes Ezek 37:1–14. He explains, "But if the Spirit of the one who raised Jesus from the dead dwells in you, the one who raised Christ from the dead will also make alive your mortal bodies through the same Spirit who dwells in you."[94] As I noted above, one of the divine actions associated with the πνεῦμα τοῦ θεοῦ in the LXX is resurrection from the dead as it is described in Ezekiel's vision. The larger context of the vision provides a vivid backdrop for Paul's assertion that the Spirit will raise the Romans from the dead.

The vision begins with God posing a question to Ezekiel, "Will these bones live?" (Ezek 37:3). God then instructs Ezekiel to prophesy over the bones with these words, "Behold, I will bring upon you the breath of life (πνεῦμα ζωῆς), and I will place upon you sinews (νεῦρα) and I will bring flesh (σάρκας) upon you and I will stretch out skin (δέρμα) upon you and I will place my Spirit (πνεῦμα μου) in you, and you will live (ζήσεσθε); and you will know that I am the Lord" (Ezek 37:5–6). Once Ezekiel prophesies, he witnesses the bones coming together complete with sinews, flesh, and skin (Ezek 37:7–8). However, Ezekiel observes "there was no breath (πνεῦμα) in them (ἐν αὐτοῖς)" (Ezek 37:8). God then commands Ezekiel to "prophesy to the breath (ἐπὶ τὸ

---

92. On this point, see Seifrid, *Christ Our Righteousness*, 172.

93. As Seifrid notes, "Paul does know of a distinction between 'declaratory' and 'effective' (or 'transofrmatory') righteousness." He agrees that God's justifying work "brings with it the entrance of the new creation into the fallen world, in the form of the gift of 'justification by the Spirit.'" However, the gift of the Spirit "proceeds from the justifying verdict which God has rendered in Christ." *Christ Our Righteousness*, 172.

94. Cf. the use of οἰκέω with πνεῦμα as the subject in Rom 8:9 and 1 Cor 3:16. The verb οἰκέω in these contexts bears the sense of "residing" in the body of the Christians in Rome. BDAG 694.

πνεῦμα)" (Ezek 37:9). He is instructed to prophesy, "Come from the four winds and breathe in these dead (εἰς τοὺς νεκροὺς τούτους) and let them live (ζησάστωσαν)" (Ezek 37:9). After Ezekiel prophesied these words, "The breath (πνεῦμα) entered them, and they lived and they stood on their feet, an exceedingly great gathering (Ezek 37:10).[95] The Lord then informs Ezekiel that the bones are "the house of Israel" who had lost hope complaining, "Our bones dried up, our hope has perished, we are lost" (Ezek 37:11). Due to their lost hope, Ezekiel is to prophesy one last time:

> For this reason, prophesy and say, thus says the Lord, "Behold, I am opening to you the tombs and I will bring you up from the tombs and I will bring you into the land of Israel, and you will know that I am the Lord when I open your tombs in order that I might bring my people from the tombs. And I will give my Spirit in you (τὸ πνεῦμα μου εἰς ὑμᾶς), and you will live (ζήσεσθε), and I place you in your land, and you will know that I the Lord have spoken and I will do it," says the Lord (Ezek 37:12–14).

This pre-text passes several intertextual tests in relation to Rom 8:9–11. The *volume* is moderate based on the semantic overlap between πνεῦμα μου/πνεῦμα θεοῦ, ζάω/ζωή, and νεκρός.

We also find *contextual consistency* as both the pre-text and text envision bodily, that is material, resurrection through God's gift of the Spirit. The pre-text refers to bones, sinews, skin, and flesh which the text summarizes as the Romans' "mortal bodies" (τὰ θνητὰ σώματα ὑμων). Of course, as I will discuss further below, Paul reconfigures the Ezekiel pre-text which envisioned a post-exilic life of Israel in terms of resurrection and new creation.[96] For Paul, the Spirit already dwells in the Romans prior to their bodily resurrection, the Spirit already raised Christ from the dead, and the resurrection of the "house of Israel" will include both Jews and Gentiles.

Within the *history of interpretation*, Wolter notes that Paul's description of resurrection in v. 11 stands "in jener jüdischen Tradition" first tangible in Ezek 37:1–14 and then reflected in later Second Temple writings.[97] Hultgren notes that Rom 8:11 is "somewhat comparable to the conceptuality to the vision in Ezek 37:1–14, in which the Spirit (or breath) of the Lord breathes life into the dry bones, bringing them to life."[98]

It is also worth noting that when Paul asserts that the Spirit "will make alive (ζωοποιήσει) your mortal bodies" it echoes a similar expression from Ps 70 LXX.

---

95. The noun πνεῦμα (רוח) in Ezek 37:1–14 LXX is a paronomasia. The writer/translator plays on the polyvalence of the term, because it can refer to wind, breath, and or spirit/Spirit which are all under divine control. LEH 500.

96. See Kirk, *Unlocking Romans*, 20n24.

97. Wolter points specifically to Test Abr 18:11. See Wolter, *Der Brief in die Römer*, 1:490. See also Keener, *Romans*, 101.

98. However, Hultgren stresses the link between Rom 8:11 and the "early creedal formula of Romans 1:3." Hultgren, *Romans*, 306.

After the psalmist requests protection and deliverance from enemies (Ps 70:13 LXX), there is a shift towards statements of trust and praise (Ps 70:14–24 LXX). As part of the latter, the psalmist confidently asserts "What many afflictions and calamities you showed to me, and having turned you made me alive (ἐζωοποίησάς με), and you brought me up again from the abysses of the earth (ἐκ τῶν ἀβύσσων τῆς γῆς)" (Ps 70:20 LXX). The use of ζωοποιέω and the phrase ἐκ τῶν ἀβύσσων τῆς γῆς correspond to Paul's use of the verb in Rom 8:11 and ἐκ νεκρῶν.[99]

Interpretive Impact of Pre-Texts in Romans 8:5–11

The interplay between various OT pre-texts and Rom 8:5–11 produce unstated points of resonance that shed interpretive light on Paul's argument at his point. They are points that are consistent with explicit statements within the letter. Five points stand out.

First, Paul describes those who are "in the flesh" in the vein of OT figures who are at enmity (ἔχθρα εἰς θεόν) with God based on their violation of the Mosaic Law. In the OT, Israel is sometimes described as an unlawful figure who becomes God's enemy due to its disobedience. This dynamic is exemplified in Israel's Babylonian captivity, "But they were disobedient and they provoked his holy spirit; and he turned to be an enemy (εἰς ἔχθραν), and he fought against them" (Isa 63:10).[100] Paul expands this OT description to include both Jews and Gentiles. We saw this intertextual expansion on full display in Rom 3:10–18 where Paul employs the description of enemies in the Psalms of Lament to describe both Jews and Gentiles who are "under sin" (Rom 3:9). Here Paul describes these enemies as those who are "in the flesh," and he stresses their "way of thinking" (φρόνημα). Their mind-set conflicts with God, because the mind-set of the flesh "is not subject to the law of God." That is because the "way of thinking of the flesh" is not able to be subjected to God's law (Rom 8:7). This inability stems from the Adamic state of the flesh wherein the powers of sin and death rule and reign as Paul has made clear in Rom 5–7. In this way, those who are in the flesh simply cannot "please" God.

This brings us to the second point of resonance, namely that those are in the flesh cannot please God based on their unacceptable inward disposition as described in Israel's Scriptures. When Paul asserts "But those who are in the flesh are not able to please (ἀρέσαι) God (Rom 8:8)," it evokes an OT motif that stresses an inward and heartfelt obedience to divine commands. To be sure, the Mosaic Law demands that Israel do what is pleasing to God "And you shall do what is pleasing (τὸ ἀρεστόν) and good before the Lord your God, in order that it might be well with you and you might enter and inherit the good land, which the Lord swore to your fathers" (Deut 6:18). However, Israel's Scriptures also note that Israel often lacked the proper inward

---

99. See Jewett, *Romans*, 492–93.
100. See also Lam 2:4–5; Ps 35:2 LXX.

disoposition in their obedience to the Mosaic Law. The psalmist describes the acceptable disposition noting, "I will praise the name of God with a song, I will magnify him with praise, and it will be more pleasing (ἀρέσει) to God than a new bull having horns and hoofs" (Ps 68:32 LXX). Similarly, in Hosea we find, "For I want mercy and not sacrifice and a knowledge of God rather than whole burnt offerings" (Hos 6:6).[101] Israel's Scriptures highlight figures whose inward disposition pleased God such as Enoch, Noah, Hezekiah, and others. Paul reconfigures this scriptural motif to describe those who are in the flesh whose inward disposition is unpleasing to God. Up to this point in the letter, Paul has already stressed the importance of one's inward disposition through multiple references to the "heart" (καρδία).[102] Later in the letter, Paul locates faith in the heart, and he disqualifies all works as unacceptable unless faith, presumably from the heart, is their catalyst.[103] In short, those who are in the flesh are not able to "please" God, because their Adamic condition leaves their inward disposition enslaved to sin and to death which makes their way of thinking unacceptable before him.

Third, Paul's combination of life + peace + Spirit in Rom 8:6 and 8:10 pulls together multiple promises in Israel's Scriptures. The promise of life (ζάω/ζωή) beyond judgment characterizes much of the prophetic literature in the OT. Paul has already signaled this through his citation of Hab 2:4 in Rom 1:17, "But the righteous will live (ζήσεται) by faith," that his gospel is consistent with this kind of promise. Similarly, Israel's Scriptures promised a time when the presence of God's Spirit (πνεῦμα) would result in peace (εἰρήνη) for his people:

> Until the Spirit (πνεῦμα) should come upon you from on high, and Chermel will be desert, and Chremel will be counted for a forest. And justice will rest in the wilderness, and righteousness will dwell in Carmel; and the works of righteousness will be peace (εἰρήνη), and righteousness will take hold of rest, and they wil be confident forever; and his people will dwell the city of peace (εἰρήνης), they will dwell in confidence, and they will rest with wealth (Isa 32:15–18).

The peace envisioned here is characterized by cessation of God's judgment, a defeat of foreign enemies, and dwelling in the promised land when the Spirit comes upon the people. Paul reconfigures this characterization of peace so that there is a cessation of enmity with God, a defeat of sin and death, and resurrection from the dead in Christ when the same Spirit who raised him raises the Christians in Rome.

This brings us to the fourth point of resonance which emerges from the interplay between Ezek 37:1–14 and Rom 8:9–11. For Paul, Ezekiel's vision of resurrection, ultimately carried out when the Spirit breathes life into the dead, is a promise already

---

101. Cf. Matt 9:13; 12:7.
102. See, e.g., Rom 2:5, 15, 29; 5:5; 6:17.
103. See Rom 10:8; 14:23.

realized but not yet experienced by all.[104] The Spirit already raised Christ from the dead, and that same Spirit dwells in the Romans where he is poised to "make alive" (ζῳποιήσει) their mortal bodies in accordance with the Scriptures.[105] The "already but not yet" aspect of resurrection results in the tension which Paul describes in Rom 8:10, "But if Christ is in you, the body is dead because of sin, but the Spirit is life because of righteousness." This tension underlies much of Paul's discussion in Rom 8, and it is crystallized in v. 17 with the juxtaposition of suffering with Christ and being glorified with him.[106]

Finally, Paul includes Jesus Messiah in the divine identity of Israel's God who, according to Israel's Scriptures, alone gives life, even life from the dead. As noted above, the divine title πνεῦμα τοῦ θεοῦ, along with its variations, occurs in contexts where God gives life to human beings such as at creation or in Ezekiel's vision of dry bones. However, Paul uses πνεῦμα τοῦ θεοῦ and πνεῦμα Χριστοῦ interchangeably. This does not suggest that Paul collapses Father, Son, and Spirit into one. It does indicate that Paul includes Israel's Messiah in the life-giving work normally reserved for Israel's God.[107] Based on Paul's reading of Israel's Scriptures, in conjunction with early Christian tradition and his own experience with the risen Christ, the promised Messiah participates in what only God can do, namely give life from the dead. As Stuhlmacher puts it, "On the basis of Ezek. 37:5f., God's Spirit is the power of God which creates life from the dead. The messiah Jesus, indwelt by God's Spirit, crucified and resurrected, is for the apostle (and other early Christian witnesses) the real representative of the Spirit. By the power of the Spirit, he determines the life of those who are his."[108]

---

104. Although G.E. Ladd's formulation of "already but not yet" is not without its problems, it is helpful for understanding the dynamics of resurrection in Rom 8:9-11. See Ladd, *A Theology of the New Testament*. I also think the formulation could be expressed locatively. The kingdom is "here but there." The kingdom is "here," on earth, because the Spirit of Christ is here. At the same time, the kingdom is "there," in heaven, because Christ is seated at the right hand of God.

105. See once again the use of ζῳοποιέω in Ps 70:20 LXX.

106. It also underlines Rom 5-8 as indicated by the inclusio of suffering in Rom 5:1-5 and 8:31-39 along with the affliction and hope highlighted between these two poles.

107. "Life" is one of the dominate motifs in Rom 8:1-11. As Wright puts it in his analaysis of Rom 8:1-11, "'Life' is the golden thread that runs through 8:1-11." Wright, *Romans*, 574.

108. Stuhlmacher, *Romans*, 122.

8

Romans 8:12–17

SINCE THE "SPIRIT OF Christ" dwells in the Romans, resulting in life both now and ultimately in resurrection from the dead, Paul draws the inference (Ἄρα οὖν, Rom 8:12) that his recipients are not "obligated" (ὀφειλέται) to the flesh which means they do not have to live in conformity with the flesh. He grounds this inference in two first-class conditional statements: (1) if you live according to the flesh, you are about to die; and (2) if by the Spirit you put to death the deeds of the body, you will live (Rom 8:13). The Romans obviously fit into the latter category which Paul goes on to describe as those who are "led by the Spirit of God" which means they are "sons of God" (Rom 8:14). The latter description dominates vv. 15–17. The Romans are no longer enslaved to fear. Rather, they have received the "Spirit of adoption" by whom, as children, they cry to God as "Abba Father." This Spirit of adoption testifies to the spirits of the Romans assuring them they are God's children. These divine children are at the same time heirs of God and co-heirs with Christ. However, the latter status hinges upon their suffering with Christ, a focus that Paul has had since Rom 5:1 and will continue to have throughout the letter.

As we shall see, this argument presents a unique intertextual challenge.[1] As we shall see, Paul combines three strands of thought: (1) Israel's Scriptures; (2) Greco-Roman imagery; and (3) early Christian tradition. While our primary focus is on the engagement with Israel's Scriptures, it is necessary to consider how this engagement is impacted by the other strands of thought from which Paul draws.

---

1. For analyses of Rom 8:12–17 that emphasize its intertextual features, see, e.g., Byrne, *Sons of God*; Keesmaat, "Exodus and the Intertextual Transformation," 29–56.

Romans 8:12-17

(8:12-17) So then, brothers, we are not debtors to the flesh, that is to live according to the flesh, for if you are living according to the flesh, you are about to die; but if by the Spirit you are putting to death the deeds of the body, you will live. For as many as are led by the Spirit of God, they are sons of God. For you did not receive a spirit of slavery again resulting in fear but you received a Spirit of adoption by whom we cry out "Abba Father." The same Spirit testifies with our spirit that we are children of God. But if children, also heirs; heirs of God, and fellow heirs with Christ, if indeed we suffer with him in order that we might also be glorified with him.

This is one of the more emotionally charged portions of the letter. As part of a larger description of how the Roman Christians are to understand their suffering in the present age (Rom 5-8), the cry "Abba" captures the tension between the intensity of the affliction and the certainty of the hope. Although this text contains no citations or explicit citations, several echoes support the intertextual subtext.

Suggested Pre-Texts in Romans 8:12-17

Hübner lists the following pre-texts: Deut 30:15-18 (Rom 8:13); 8:14-15; Exod 4:22; Deut 14:1; 1 Kgs 16:14; Isa 11:2, 4; Jer 3:19; Hos 1:10-11 (Rom 8:17); Deut 4:20; 9:26, 29; 32:9; 1 Kgs 8:51, 53; 2 Kgs 21:14 Ps 32:12 LXX.[2]

Nestle-Aland 28th ed. does not list any OT pre-texts. Similarly, once again, Hays does not resume his intertextual analysis until Rom 8:18.[3] Additionally, as I have noted multiple times already, most of Seifrid's analysis focuses upon Paul's use of the OT in Rom 8:31-39.[4]

Intertextual Analysis of Romans 8:12-17

The main intertextual feature in these six verses are the narrative strands reflected in Paul's argumentation. He specifically draws on the narratives of Adam and Israel in an overlapping manner just as we saw in Rom 7:7-25. In addition to these narrative strands, Paul also draws from a handful of pre-texts and scriptural motifs.

---

2. Hübner, *Vetus Testamentum in Novo*, 2:116-20.
3. Hays, *Echoes of Scripture in the Letters of Paul*, 158.
4. Seifrid, *Romans*, 633-37.

Romans 8:12–17 and Echoes of the Slavery Motif

To begin, as often as Paul contrasts "flesh" and "Spirit," he evokes the narratives of both Adam and Israel. We noted this in the analysis of Rom 7:7–25—8:11, and it bears repeating here based on references to the flesh (σάρξ) and "deeds of the body" (τὰς πράξεις τοῦ σώματος) in vv. 12–13. Specifically, Paul notes "we are not debtors (ὀφελέται) to the flesh" which he qualifies as living in conformity with the flesh (κατὰ σάρκα). He warns that such living results in death, "For if you are living according to the flesh, you are about to die (μέλλετε ἀποθνήσκειν)" (Rom 8:13a). With his use of ὀφελέται, Paul evokes well-known "social obligations" of the Greco-Roman world.[5] Jewett explains:

> Roman ethicists taught that such obligations are owed to everyone in one's social sphere, to parents, friends, and patrons; a "gradation of duties" (*gradus officiorum*) placed obligations to the gods first, to country second, to parents third, etc. Although commentators consistently overlook this social background in interpreting v. 12, to be obligated τῇ σαρκί ("to flesh") would entail the entire range of social and religious obligations in the Roman environment.[6]

For Paul, the "regulative principle" in carrying out these obligations is either the flesh or the Spirit with their divergent outcomes, namely death or life.[7] However, Paul combines his metaphorical use of social obligations from the Greco-Roman world with the narratives of Adam and Israel.[8] Since the time of Adam, apart from Christ, all are obligated to live in the realm of the flesh where the powers of sin and death hold sway.

Furthermore, in v. 15a, Paul's explanation, "For you did not receive a spirit of slavery (πνεῦμα δουλείας) again (πάλιν) resulting in fear (εἰς φόβον)," hearkens the outcome of Adam's transgression which is recapitulated in all of Adam's descendants. The phrase πνεῦμα δουλείας, along with the adverb πάλιν, which implies a prior experience of slavery, evokes the judgment that all have received since Adam, namely slavery.[9] Although the Adamic narrative does not contain overt references to slavery (δουλεία), conceptually, the divine judgment doled out in Gen 3:13–19 resembles a kind of enslavement to fear. God enslaves, or subjects, men and women to the following: (1) emnity with the serpent; (2) contention between one another; (3) pain in childbirth; (4) a cursed earth; and (5) separation from God's life-giving presence. Paul evokes part of this Adamic subjection to slavery (δουλεία) in Rom 8:21 where he describes creation's longing to be freed "from its slavery to corruption (ἀπὸ τῆς δουλείας τῆς φθορᾶς)."[10] We will return to this below. Here I would note that Paul paints with

---

5. Jewett, *Romans*, 493.
6. Jewett, *Romans*, 493.
7. See Jewett, *Romans*, 493.
8. Once again, Paul combines features of his Greco-Roman culture with Israel's Scriptures.
9. Cf. the use of πάλιν in Gal 4:9.
10. Cf. the use of δουλεία in Gal 4:24; 5:1.

broad strokes in describing the condition of Jewish and Gentile Christians in Rome prior to their adoption as God's children through faith in Christ. In short, like Adam, they lived in fearful slavery to the power of sin and death under God's judgment and separated from his life-giving presence.

Paul's reference to living in the flesh, along with the phrases πνεῦμα δουλείας and πάλιν, evoke another intertextual layer in conjunction with Geneis 3, namely Israel's slavery in Egypt and Babylon. The term δουλεία (עבדה) occurs frequently in the LXX to describe Israel's experience in Egypt. Prior to the plagues and the parting of the Red Sea, God promises "I am the Lord, and I will bring you out from the domination of the Egyptians and I will deliver you from slavery (ἐκ τῆς δουλείας), and I will ransom you with an uplifted arm and with great judgment" (Exod 6:6).[11] Subesquently, God's identity is consistently tethered to this deliverance from Egyptian slavery, "I am the Lord your God who brought you out from the land of Egypt from the house of slavery (ἐξ οἴκου δουλείας)" (Deut 5:6).[12] Similarly, in Ezra's post-exilic prayer, he describes Israel's ordeal in Babylon as slavery "For we are slaves (δοῦλοί), and our Lord God did not leave us in our slavery (ἐν τῇ δουλείᾳ ἡμῶν), and he has turned mercy on us before the king of Persia to give to us a quickening so that they should restore its deserted things and to give to us a wall in Judea and in Jerusalem" (Ezra 9:9).[13]

In this way, Paul does not use δουλεία in Rom 8:15 abstractly but intertextually. He evokes and reconfigures the defining experiences of slavery from Israel's past to describe God the Father's adoption of believers in Rome. Just as God delivered his children from slavery to the Egyptians and Babylonians, he has delivered his adopted children from the flesh where they languished under the power of sin which used the law to bring death. Paul abbreviates this scripturally-informed experience as receiving a "spirit of slavery" (πνεῦμα δουλείας). The syntax of the phrase πνεῦμα δουλείας can be understood in a variety of ways, but it most likely functions to clarify the character of the Holy Spirit.[14] The Spirit, by whom the Romans are to put to death the deeds of

---

11. Cf. the use of δουλεία in Exod 13:13, 14; 20:2.
12. Cf. the use of δουλεία in Deut 6:12; 7:8; 8:14; 13:6, 11; 1 Kgs 9:9; Mic 6:4; Jer 41:13 (34:13).
13. Cf. the use of δουλεία in Ezra 9:8; Neh 9:17.
14. The genitive δουλείας in the phrase πνεῦμα δουλείας could be rendered in the following ways: (1) attributive genitive—"enslaving spirit;" or (2) attributed genitive—"spiritual slavery." One of the exegetical questions that arises here in Rom 8:15 is whether πνεῦμα in πνεῦμα δουλείας and πνεῦμα in πνεῦμα υἱοθεσίας have the same referent. Cranfield observes, "The contrast between πνεῦμα δουλείας and πνεῦμα υἱοθεσίας has been variously explained. Some have argued that πνεῦμα δουλείας is most naturally understood as denoting a human disposition, and that πνεῦμα υἱοθεσίας, since it is contrasted with it (the same verb, ἐλάβετε, being used in both cases), can scarcely be the Holy Spirit but must also be here a human disposition (albeit one inspired by the Holy Spirit), a filial sentiment; others, assuming that πνεῦμα υἱοθεσίας must refer to the Holy Spirit, have felt obliged to understand πνεῦμα δουλείας also of the Holy Spirit (seeing a reference to life under the Old Dispensation). In either case the tendency has been to see a connexion between πνεῦμα δουλείας and the law. Another way has been to disallow the argument that πνεῦμα must have the same sort of meaning in both parts of the sentence and to understand the first πνεῦμα to denote a disposition and the second the Holy Spirit. Yet another explanation which has been given—and this seems the most probable—is that the sentence

the body, and by whom they are to be lead, does not enslave them to the flesh, a state which results in fear of God's condemnation and wrath. Instead, the Spirit assures the Christians in Rome that they are God's children with all the promises and pain which such a status entails.

Romans 8:12–17 and Echoes of Sonship

This brings us to another cluster of OT echoes in Rom 8:12–17 involving Paul's description of his recipients as "sons of God" (υἱοὶ θεοῦ), or "children of God" (τέκνα θεοῦ), whom God the Father has adopted (υἱοθεσία) and who are "led" (ἄγνονται) by the Spirit.[15] We will begin by identifying the background for understanding Paul's use of υἱοθεσία.[16]

Some have suggested that Paul's reference to adoption can only be understood in relation to Roman law in a way that excludes Jewish thought/Israel's Scriptures. For example, Witherington argues "This language of adoption would be especially appropriate in Rome, where legal adoption was a means to a brighter future. This practice was very common, even in the imperial family. The language would, however, be surprising if Paul were speaking in a Jewish manner to a largely Jewish audience, because Jews basically did not practice adoption."[17] Regarding the "language" of adoption within a Greco-Roman context, Jewett notes "Francis Lyall tried to show that υἱοθεσία ('sonship, adoption') in the legal sense was available only in Romans laws concering the *adoptio* or *adrogatio* of someone to become the child of a new *paterfamilias*. However, G.H.R. Horsley has shown that this term appers in Greek sources before and after the development of the Latin terminology, referring for example to a petition from Isidora, 'the adopted child of Dionysios (τεκνοθεσίαν Διονυσίο[υ]).'"[18] Nevertheless, while the use of υἱοθεσία in Rom 8:15 undoubtedly evokes legal concepts from the Greco-Roman world, such usage does not entirely exclude the OT from shaping Paul's thought on adoption.[19]

---

does not imply the actual existence of a πνεῦμα δουλείας but means only that the Holy Spirit whom they have received is not a spirit of bondage but the Spirit of adoption." Cranfield, *Romans*, 1:396.

15. Jewett reminds us that some interpreters prefer the rendering of "sonship" for υἱοθεσία rather than "adoption." See Jewett, *Romans*, 498.

16. Cf. other uses of υἱοθεσία in Rom 8:23; 9:4; Gal 4:5; Eph 1:5. For lengthy studies on Paul's use of the adoption metaphor, see Burke, *Adopted into God's Family*; Scott, *Adoption as Sons of God*; Stevenson-Moessner, *The Spirit of Adoption*.

17. Witherington, *Romans*, 217.

18. Jewett, *Romans*, 498. See also Lyall, "Roman Law," 66.

19. Longenecker summarizes the features of Greco-Roman adoption that "would have come to the fore in the consciousness of Paul's hearers in his mission to pagan Gentiles." According to Longenecker, this include the following: (1) An adopted son was taken out of his previous situation and placed in an entirely new relationship to his new adopting father, who became his new *paterfamilias*. (2) An adopted son started a new life as part of his new family, with all his old debts canceled. An adopted son was considered no less important than any other biologically born son in his adopted

It is true that υἱοθεσία does not appear in Jewish sources. Nevertheless, some OT texts characterize Yahweh's father-son relationship with Israel in an adoptive sense.[20] There is no question that the OT likens the relationship between Israel and its God to a relationship between father and son. For example, God instructs Moses to identify the Israelites as his "son" (υἱός) when addressing Pharaoh, "Then you shall say to Pharaoh, 'Thus says the Lord, Israel is my first-born son (υἱὸς πρωτότοκός μου)" (Exod 4:22). God disciplined Israel as a son, "And you shall know in your heart that as a man might discipline his son (υἱὸν), in this way the Lord your God will discipline you" (Deut 8:5). Israel's sonship separated them from the idolatrous nations around them and provided them with the guidance they needed, "You are sons of the Lord your God (υἱοὶ κυρίου τοῦ θεοῦ ὑμῶν); you shall not seek oracular ecstasy, you shall not place baldness between your eyes for the dead" (Deut 14:1). Hosea likens Israel's deliverance from Egypt to that of a loving father calling his son out of captivity, "Since Israel was a child (νήπιος), and I loved him and out of Egypt I have called his children (τὰ τέκνα αὐτοῦ)" (Hos 11:1).[21]

However, Israel often proved to be disobedient children as the divine complaint through Isaiah indicates, "Hear, O heaven, and give ear, O earth, because the Lord has spoken; I brought forth (ἐγέννησα) sons (υἱούς), and I exalted them, but they rejected me" (Isa 1:2).[22] Similarly, even as Jeremiah envisions a time of restoration beyond Babylonian judgment, he likens Israel's past disobedience to that of a son disappointing his father's expectations. The divine voice in Jer 3:19 speaks from the perspective of divine expectations for Israel upon their initial entrance into the promised land, "And I said, 'May it be, Lord;' for I will appoint you for children (εἰς τέκνα), and I will give to you choice land as an inheritance of God almighty of the nations; and I said 'You will call me father (Πατέρα), and you shall not turn away from me.'" As the subsequent husband and wife metaphor demonstrates, these expectations were dashed.[23] Therefore, the divine father calls his disobedient sons to repentance "Turn, sons who turn away (υἱοὶ ἐπιστρέφοντες), and I will heal your wounds. Behold we will be your servants, because you O Lord are our God" (Jer 3:22).

Nevertheless, such disobedience notwithstanding, promises of blessing and protection remain for God's children. As the psalmist notes, "Just as a father (πατήρ) has compassion on sons (υἱούς), the Lord has compassion on those who fear him" (Ps

---

father's family. 4. An adopted son experienced a changed status, with his old name set aside and a new name given him by his adopting father." Longenecker, *Romans*, 704.

20. As Jewett notes, "Despite the lack of comparable legal terminology in Jewish sources, there are some links here with the ethos of ancient Israel, in which Yahweh was thought to have adopted the people of Israel as his kinsfolk." Jewett, *Romans*, 498. See also Keesmat, *Paul and His Story*, 60–75. The entry for υἱοθεσία in BDAG acknowledges the absence of the term in the LXX while also affirming the LXX as a shaping influence noting. See BDAG 1024.

21. Hos 11:1 MT contains "my son" (לבני). Cf. the citation of Hos 11:1 in Matt 2:15.

22. See also Deut 32:5.

23. See Jer 3:21.

102:13 LXX).²⁴ Even more, Jeremiah envisions a time beyond Babylonian judgment when God will have mercy upon his sons/children "Ephraim is my beloved son (υἱὸς ἀγαπητός), a pleasing child (παιδίον), because my words are in him, I will certainly remember him; for this reason I will hasten to him, I wil certainly have mercy on him, says the Lord" (Jer 38:20; 31:20 MT).²⁵

This summary of the father-son/child metaphor in Israel's Scriptures indicates the following: (1) God disciplines and delivers Israel as a father would do for his son/child; (2) Israel proved to be both a pleasing and disobedient child of God; and (3) no real emphasis is placed upon whether Israel is a "natural" or "adopted" son/child.²⁶ The third inference is significant at this point, because it demonstrates that Paul's reference to "adopted" sons does not exclude the OT metaphor of Israel as God's child/son. Finally, as the use of υἱοθεσία in Rom 9:4 indicates, Paul had no reservations about describing Israel's elect filial status as adoptive in nature. As Wolter plainly notes, "In Röm 9,4 nennt Paulus auch Israels Erwählung υἱοθεσία.²⁷

Paul reconfigures this OT father-child metaphor around the gift of the Spirit and the person of Jesus Christ. In short, the Spirit leads the sons of God, testifies to the filial status of the Christians in Rome, and enables their lament "Abba Father." (Rom 8:14–17). This reconfiguration of the OT's father-child metaphor contains other intertextual echoes to which we now turn our attention.

To begin, when Paul describes the Spirit as "leading" (ἄγω) the sons of God, the description evokes the way Israel's Scriptures describe God as leading his Israelite children in the wilderness. Paul explains in v. 14, "For as many as are being lead (ἄγονται) by the Spirit of God, these are sons of God." This statement evokes the description of God leading the Israelites out of Egyptian slavery and through the wilderness. Israelites were encouraged not to forget this divine leading, "And you shall remember all the way, which the Lord your God lead you (/ἤγαγέν σου) in the wilderness, in order that he might afflict you and he might test you and the things in your heart might be perceived, if you shall keep his commandments or not" (Deut 8:2). Additionally, later in Deut 8 God is described as "the one who lead you (ἀγαγόντος) through that great and fearful wilderness, where there is the biting serpent and the scorpion and thirst, where there is no water, the one who brought out to you a fountain of water from a sharp-edged rock" (Deut 8:15). Additionally, God reminds the Israelites that his leading involved provision in the wilderness, "And he led you (ἤγαγεν) forty years in the wilderness; your garments did not become old, and your sandals were not worn out from your feet" (Deut 29:4). We see from these Deuteronomic pre-texts that God's

---

24. See also Ps 104:6 LXX.

25. See also Isa 63:8.

26. Isa 1:2 and the use of γεννάω is one of the few OT texts that portray God as "bringing forth" Israel as a child in the "natural sense. LEH 118. However, even here, emphasis is not placed upon the means how Israel became God's child.

27. Wolter, *Der Brief an die Römer*, 1:496.

"leading" involved the following: (1) guidance to the promised land; (2) protection until Israel arrived there; and (3) provision until Israel arrived there. A few lines from Moses' song in Deut 32 captures the nature of this divine leading in the wilderness:

> He supplied them with their needs in the wilderness, in burning thirst in a waterless place; he surrounded him and disciplined him and kept him as the pupil of his eye, as an eagle would watch over its brood and yearn for its young, having spread out his wings he receives them and takes them up on his back. The Lord alone lead (ἦγεν) them, and there was not a strange god with them (Deut 32:10-12).[28]

This poetic reflection on Israel being "lead" in the wilderness underscores God's protection and provision on the way to the promised land. Before testing and evaluating how Rom 8:14 evokes the pre-text of God leading Israel through the wilderness, it is necessary to consider how subsequent OT writers evoked this moment in the nation's history.

Among these subsequent evocations, Isa 63 is most pertinent to Rom 8:14. Contextually, Isaiah seeks vindication from Israel's enemies (Isa 63:1-6) and offers a prayer of penitence (Isa 63:15-19. The prayer form resembles lament, and, in typical lament fashion, Isaiah grounds his request in the way God had acted towards Israel in the past (Isa 63:7-14).[29] Isaiah specifically remembers (ἐμνήσθη, Isa 63:7) the mercy God displayed towards his "children" (τέκνα, Isa 63:8) in the Exodus and wilderness wanderings. However, although he saved them and exalted them, they rebelled against him (Isa 63:9). As Isaiah describes it, "They were disobedient, and they provoked his Holy Spirit (τὸ πνεῦμα τὸ ἅγιον αὐτοῦ); and he turned for enmity, and he battled against them" (Isa 63:10).[30] Isa 63:11-14 hearkens God's mercy in the wilderness:

> Then he remembered the ancient days, saying, "Where is He who brought (ὁ ἀναβιβάσας) the flock of sheep up from the land; where is the one who set the Holy Spirit (τὸ πνεῦμα τὸ ἅγιον) among them? The one who led (ὁ ἀγαγών) them by the hand of Moses, the arm of his glory? He overpowered the water from before him to make a name for himself. He led (ἤγαγεν) them through the abyss like a horse through the wilderness, and they did not grow weary. And like animals through a plain, the Spirit (πνεῦμα) came down from the Lord and guided (ὡδήγησεν) them; in this way you led (ἤγαγες) your people to make a glorious name for yourself.[31]

---

28. Cf. Exod 15:13; Num 24:8; Josh 24:3.
29. See Miller, *They Cried to the Lord*.
30. Cf. the echo of Isa 63:10 in Acts 7:51; Eph 4:30.
31. The verbs ἄγω and ὁδηγέω are used interchangeably in Isa 63:11-14. The latter verb occurs several times in the LXX with a divine subject. See, e.g., Exod 13:17; 15:13; 32:34; Deut 1:33; Josh 24:3; 2 Sam 7:23; 1 Chr 17:21; Neh 9:12, 19; Pss LXX 5:9; 22:3; 24:5, 9; 26:11; 30:4; 42:3; 44:5; 59:11; 60:4; 66:5; 72:24; 76:21; 77:14, 53, 72; 79:2; 85:11; 89:16; 105:9; 106:7, 30; 107:11; 118:35; 138:10, 24; 142:10. See also Wis 9:11; 10:10, 17. In the NT, see Rev 7:17.

This Isaianic pre-text echoes the Deuteronomic pre-texts described above. Therefore, we can test both divine "leading" pre-texts together.

The *volume* of the pre-text is moderate. The Deuteronomy pre-texts and Isa 63 overlap with Rom 8:14 based on the use of ἄγω and the description of Israel as God's son (υἱός)/children (τέκνα). The *volume* of the Isa 63 pre-text is even stronger than the Deuteronomic pre-texts based on the occurrence of τὸ πνεῦμα τὸ ἅγιον/πνεῦμα.

Contextual consistency occurs in multiple ways. For example, the divine "leading" in both Deuteronomy and Isa 63 occurs in contexts of tremendous affliction just as it does in Rom 8:14. God led Israel out of bondage, through the wilderness, and into the promised land. Such leading required the defeat of enemies too powerful for Israel. It required providing manna from heaven, because transient people could obviously not produce their own food supply. It required protection from harmful, even fatal, elements, internal threats to the people such as rebellion against leadership, and external threats such as nation states that stood between Israel and the promised land and nation states which occupied the promised land. Moreover, the tension between God's mercy and judgment charged this affliction. Therefore, the Spirit's presence and guidance was needed as Isa 63:11–14 indicates.

Based on the wider context of Rom 8:14, the Christians in Rome face similar, though obviously not identical, circumstances. The enemies of sin and death are too powerful for them. They must suffer with Christ before they can be glorified with him (Rom 8:17). The Romans, along with creation and the Spirit himself, lament the hope of the resurrection. Moreover, the entire experience is charged by the tension between judgment and mercy. Therefore, the Romans need the Spirit to lead them in much the same way that Israel needed divine guidance in the wilderness. Based on the intertextual subtext of OT pre-texts outlined above, it follows that Paul envisions the Spirit "leading" the Romans via deliverance, protection, and provision. Of course, Paul recontextualizes the Spirit's leading in relation to what God has done in Christ and in relation to the circumstances of the Romans. God condemned sin in the flesh of his crucified son, and, as the risen Lord, Jesus overcomes death. However, the Romans' ongoing existence in bodies where sin dwells results in ongoing affliction. The Spirit's presence "leads" the Romans through this experience by putting to death the sinful deeds of the body, testifying to their filial status with Christ in the face of affliction that raised serious questions about that status, and interceding for them with inexpressible lamenting as they await the hope of resurrection.[32] We will return to Paul's recontextualization of this OT motif below.

Within the *history of interpretation*, some interpreters have identified God's guidance to the wilderness generation as part of the intertextual subtext in Rom 8:12–17.[33]

---

32. Cf. Gal 5:18 where Paul's reference to the leading of the Spirit (πνεύματι ἄγεσθε) occurs in a context involving affliction.

33. E.g., Keesmaat provides extensive analaysis of the link between sonship, being led by God, and the exodus tradition suggesting that it informs Paul's thought in Rom 8:12–17. See Kessmaat, *Paul*

Wright is one of the most prominent interpreters to suggest this connection noting that in Rom 8:14, "The image here is taken from the wilderness wanderings of Israel, led by the pillar of cloud and fire."[34] While I am not adopting Wright's intertextual suggestions at every point, it is the case that Paul reconfigures the external leading of God in the wilderness to the indwelling Spirit who leads those who are in Christ.

It is also worth noting that Ps 142 LXX, a psalm echoed in Rom 3:20, combines divine guidance with God's Spirit. Towards the end of this individual lament, the psalmist requests "Teach me to do your will, because you are my God; your good Spirit (τὸ πνεῦμα σου τὸ ἀγαθόν) will guide (ὁδηγήσει) me in the level ground" (Ps 142:10 LXX). The wider context of the Psalm describes the affliction of the lamenter. The affliction stems from concern with the lamenter's status before God and enemies who pursue him. (Ps 142:2–3LXX). This affliction produces internal exhaustion, "My spirit is exhausted in me, and my heart has been disturbed in me" (Ps 142:4 LXX). Therefore, the lamenter requests deliverance which includes a request that God's "good Spirit" guide him in doing God's will (Ps 142:10 LXX). The entire scenario maps onto Paul's argument quite nicely. The larger context of Romasn 8:14 shows a concern with divine judgment as well as the personified enemies of sin and death. Such affliction elicits the cry "Abba Father" which I will consider next.

Romans 8:12–17 and Echoes of Lament

The cry "Abba Father" evokes another OT pre-text in Rom 8:12–17, though, as we shall see, the cry is also linked to Jesus tradition reflected in Mark 14:36. Paul explains the relationship between being led by the Spirit and the Romans' filial status noting, "For you did not receive a spirit of slavery again resulting in fear, but you received a Spirit of adoption by whom we cry out (κράζομεν), 'Abba, Father' (αββα ὁ πατήρ)" (Rom 8:15). While the transliterated Aramaic vocative αββα (אבא) has received its fair share of attention over the years, my concern is with the intertextual pre-texts evoked through the combination of κράζομεν and αββα ὁ πατήρ.[35] In short, Paul's expres-

---

and His Story, 60–74.

34. Wright continues, "Those symbols of God's powerful presence are here replaced, as we might have guessed from the 'indwelling' theme in 8:9–11, by the Spirit, who now does for God's people that which the tabernacling presence of God did in the wilderness, assuring them of divine adoption and leading them forward to their inheritance. The idea of Christians as God's sons and daughters is rooted in the same exodus narrative, again reapplied in the prophets." Wright lists the following pre-texts: Exod 13:21–22; 14:19, 24; 40:38; Num 9:15–23; 10:34; 14:14; Deut 1:33; Neh 9:12, 19; Pss 78:14; 105:39; Wright, *Romans*, 593.

35. E.g., Joachim Jeremias popularized the notion that in the first century "Abba" functioned as a childish address for the male parent equivalent to "Daddy." Jeremias, *Abba*, 15–67. However, those such as James Barr largely debunked this argument by showing that "Abba" was an address employed by both adults and children. See Barr, "*Abba* Isn't Daddy," 35–40. See also the discussion in Jewett, *Romans*, 499. Additionally, Longenecker summarizes the various ways that interpreters have understood the link between κράζομεν and αββα ὁ πατήρ. He notes, "Some have suggested that this

sion "by whom we cry out Abba, Father" echoes both OT lament and Jesus tradition reflected in Mark 14:36 which itself is shaped by OT lament. The expression does not evoke a single OT pre-text. Rather, it evokes the OT prayer form and ethos of lament.[36]

The Psalms of Lament in the LXX frequently employ the verb κράζω in contexts where lamenters face affliction from a variety of sources including guilt for sin, political opponents, disease, death, and divine wrath.[37] The verb is often paired with a divine vocative such as "O God" (θεός) or "O Lord" (κύριε/κύριος).[38] For example, when afflicted on a variety of fronts, a psalmist recalls, "O Lord my God (κύριε ὁ θεός μου), I cried (ἐκέκραξα) to you, and you healed me" (Ps 29:3 LXX). These addresses and cries to God are personal in tone. They are usually followed by complaints and requests, which, though expressed in variety of ways, are pleas for deliverance. Therefore, though Paul does not specify the request that accompanies the divine address "Abba, Father," the lament-like address implies a request which we will consider below. Here I would simply note that, in keeping with these addresses from OT lament, it is ultimately a request related to deliverance.

Before considering how Rom 8:15 recontextualizes OT lament, we must also consider the relationship of Paul's text to the Jesus tradition reflected in Mark 14:36. The latter text is one of the three NT uses of the phrase αββα ὁ πατήρ.[39] Mark's passion narrative includes Jesus' prayer in the Garden of Gethsemane the night of his arrest where he repeats the same prayer three times.[40] Mark 14:36 provides the specific content of the thrice repeated prayer, "And he was saying, 'Abba, Father (αββα ὁ πατήρ), all things are possible for you; remove this cup from me; but not what I will but what you will.'" With this request, Jesus seeks deliverance from the divine judgment he is about to endure through the hands of his Roman executioners. Nevertheless, he is resolved to do his Father's will, though not without the internal affliction which characterizes OT lamenters. The surrounding context of Jesus' prayer adopts the language of OT

'crying out to God as Father' should be understood in the context of the early Christians praying the 'Lord's Prayer,' which begins with the familial affirmation 'Our Father.' Others, however, have postulated that Paul had in mind (1) some portion of an early Christian confession, (2) some early Christian baptismal formula, (3) some other early Christain liturgical formulation of his day, or (4) some prominent ecstatic utterance that had been expressed in early Christian worship." Longenecker, *Romans*, 705.

36. For a discussion of "ethos of lament," see Eklund, *Jesus Wept*.

37. See the use of κράζω in Pss LXX 3:5; 4:4; 16:6; 17:7, 42; 21:3, 6, 25; 26:7; 27:1; 29:3, 9; 30:23; 31:3; 33:7, 18; 54:17; 56:3; 60:3; 64:14; 65:17; 68:4; 76:2; 85:3, 7; 87:2, 10, 14; 106:6, 13, 19, 28; 118:145, 146, 147; 119:1; 129:1; 140:1; 141:2, 6.

38. The LXX Psalms do not contain the actual vocative case θεέ, only the use of the nominative θεός for the vocative.

39. See also Gal 4:6 which combines κράζω and αββα ὁ πατήρ. We will return to this occurrence below.

40. See Mark 14:36, 39, 41. Cf. Matt 26:36–46; Luke 22:40–46. Neither of these parallel accounts contain the divine vocative αββα ὁ πατήρ.

lament.⁴¹ For example, just prior to praying, Jesus tells his disciples "My soul is grieved (περίλυπός ἐστιν ἡ ψυχή μου) unto death" (Mark 14:34). The phrase περίλυπός ἐστιν ἡ ψυχή μου evokes Ps 41 LXX, an individual lament, where the lamenter cries out "Why are you grieved (περίλυπος), O my soul (ψυχή), and why are disturbed within me?" (Ps 41:6a LXX).⁴² I note the lament-laden language of Jesus' prayer, because, if Rom 8:15 relies upon this tradition, the tradition itself is shaped by lament language. Therefore, the intertextual subtext in Paul's argument would still include OT lament.

With respect to the direct influence of the Jesus tradition on Paul's expression, along with the hermneutical implications of such an influence, interpreters display varying degrees of enthusiasm. Many interpreters note the parallel between Mark 14:36 and Rom 8:15, but it does not greatly impact their exegesis.⁴³ Others directly incorporate the influence of Jesus tradition into their interpretation of Rom 8;15. For example, Stuhlmacher suggests that believers in Rome participated in Jesus' sonship through the Spirit to the point that they "address God with Jesus' own words" reflected in Mark 14:36.⁴⁴ I share Stulhmacher's enthusiasm for the impact of the Jesus tradition on Rom 8:15.

Witht that said, Paul recontextualizes OT lament and Jesus' lament to explain the nature of the Romans' adoption and how the Spirit leads them as God's sons. Their cries to God are not as slaves to sin and death. Rather, the Spirit leads them to utter laments as children whom God has delivered from sin and death through his son Jesus. The Romans can in fact address God as the son did, namely as "Abba, Father." Given the contexts of such divine vocatives in OT lament and the Jesus tradition, it follows that the circumstances of the Romans is one of great affliction. Moreover, their cry to God as "Abba, Father" implies a request for deliverance from this affliction in the vein of OT lamenters who requested deliverance and in the vein of Jesus who requested deliverance from the cup of God's wrath, though he remained resolute in carrying out the divine will. We will explore the nature of the Romans' affliction in our analysis of Rom 8:18–39 where Paul specifies what afflicts his recipients. Here I would note that the overlap between Jesus' lament in Mark 14:36 and the lament in Rom 8:15 implies an underlying concern with divine wrath. While the father's answer to Jesus' cry resulted in having to endure the cup of wrath through enemies, the father's answer to the Romans is wrapped up in that response in a way that avoids the divine wrath but not the enemies. The Romans must suffer with Christ, even addressing God as he did prior to his crucifixion. However, it does not follow that their suffering is the direct

---

41. For fuller discussions of OT lament in the passion narratives of the Gospels, see, e.g., Ahearne-Kroll, *The Psalms of Lament in Mark's Passion*; Campbell, *Of Heroes and Villains*; Crisler, *Echoes of Lament and the Christology of Luke*, 226–73; Eklund, *Jesus Wept*.

42. See also Pss LXX 41:12; 42:5.

43. See, e.g., Fitzmyer, *Romans*, 498–501; Käsemann, *Romans*, 228; Longenecker, *Romans*, 702–703; Wolter, *Der Brief an die Römer*, 497.

44. Stuhlmacher, *Romans*, 130.

experience of divine wrath. Nevertheless, their cry "Abba, Father" implies a request for deliverance.

Romans 8:16 indicates how the divine father responds to his children's cry for deliverance, "The same Spirit testifies (συμμαρτυρεῖ) with our spirit that we are children of God."[45] In typical OT lament fashion, God responds to the cry of deliverance by reassuring lamenters of his prior promise to deliver. Such reassurance could come in the form of an oracle or a prophetic messenger.[46] Paul escalates God's reassurance by noting that it is the very Spirit of God who testifies with the human spirit regarding the status of the Romans, namely that they are "children of God" (τέκνα θεοῦ). That status comes with the promise of deliverance in Christ and thereby an inheritance in Christ.

Romnas 8:12–17 and Echoes of an Inheritance

This brings us to still another intertextual feature of Rom 8:12–17, the inheritance of God's children. Paul qualifies "children of God" in v. 16 by explaining, "But if children, also heirs (κληρονόμοι); heirs of God (κληρονόμοι θεοῦ), and fellow heirs with Christ (συγκληρονόμοι Χριστοῦ), if indeed we suffer with him in order that we might also be glorified with him" (Rom 8:17). "Inheritance" is a robust leitmotif in Israel's Scriptures which undoubtedly shapes Paul's use of the language here and elsewhere.[47] Four kinds of pre-texts need consideration.

To begin, we need to consider the intertextual echoes from Paul's previous use of inheritance language in Rom 4:13–14. As I noted in my analysis of these verses, Paul escalates the original promise of land to Abraham and his descendants to an inheritance of the entire world (τὸ κληρονόμον αὐτὸν εἶναι κόσμου, Rom 4:13).[48] The same escalated promise to Abraham likely informs the inheritance language in Rom 8:17 which Paul reconfigures around the Romans' union with Christ. The logical progress is straightforward. If the Romans are God's children, as the Spirit testifies, it follows that they are God's heirs. In other words, they inherit what God promises to his children. That includes the promise that Abraham's children would inherit the world.[49] The Romans share in this cosmic inheritance with Christ as "joint heirs" (συγκληρονόμοι Χριστοῦ) with him. The wider context of Rom 8 confirms that at least part of the inheritance in view here is the escalated promise that Abraham's descendants would inherit the world. Paul's rhetorical question in Rom 8:32 bears this

---

45. For the only other uses of συμμαρτυρέω, see Rom 2:15; 9:1.
46. See, e.g., the answer to Hezekiah's lament in Isa 38.
47. Cf. 1 Cor 6:9; 15:50; Gal 3:18, 29; 4:1, 7, 30; 5:21; Eph 1:14; 5:5; Col 3:24.
48. See volume 1.
49. See Gen 12:1–13; Rom 4:13–14.

out, "He who did not spare his own son but handed him for us all, how will he not also with him graciously give us all things (τὰ πάντα)."⁵⁰

Second, inheritance language in Rom 8:17 also evokes OT pre-texts in which God promises a cosmic reign and inheritance to his Davidic messiah. A primary pre-text in this regard is 2 Sam 7:1–17.⁵¹ God promises David, "And it will be that whenever your days should be filled up and you will lie with your fathers, I will raise your seed (ἀναστήσω τὸ σπέρμα σου) after you, who will be from your lineage, and I will prepare his kingdom; he will build for me a house for my name, and I will establish his throne forever" (2 Sam 7:12–13). Along these lines, Ps 2 also stands out. As the nations resist God and his anointed (משיח/χριστός), God appoints him as king in Zion (Ps 2:1–6). Those who seek shelter in God's begotten and anointed son will be protected from his impending wrath (Ps 2:7–12). The verbal exchange between God and his anointed son embedded in the Psalm includes the command, "Ask from me, and I will give the nations to you as your inheritance (ἔθνη τὴν κληρονομίαν σου), and the ends of the earth as your possession (τὴν κατάσχεσίν σου τὰ πέρατα τῆς γῆς)" (Ps 2:8). Similarly, the suffering servant in Isa 53 is slated to receive an inheritance, "For this reason he will inherit (κληρονομήσει) many and he will divide the spoils of the mighty, because his soul was handed over to death, and he was reckoned with the lawless; and he bore the sins of many and he was handed over because of their sins" (Isa 53:12). Finally, God promises an inheritance to the son of man in Daniel's apocalyptic vision:

> I saw in the vision of the night and behold upon the clouds of heaven one like a son of man was coming, and he came near to the ancient of days, and those who had stood by brought him near. And all authority was given to him, and the all the nations of the earth (πάντα τὰ ἔθνη τῆς γῆς) according to kinds and all the glory serving him; and his authority is an eternal authority, which certainly shall not be taken away, and his kingdom, which certainly shall not be ruined (Dan 7:13–14).⁵²

The gift to the son of man is clearly cosmic in scope.

Paul recontextualizes these pre-texts in Rom 8:17 in two ways. First, he includes the Romans in the cosmic inheritance originally promised to God's messiah. They are co-heirs of "all the nations of earth" with the crucified and risen Christ. Second, before enjoying that inheritance with Christ, they suffer with him (συμπάσχομεν). While pre-texts such as Ps 2 and Isa 53 indicate that God's messiah would suffer, they do not clearly spell out that his followers would share in that experience. Yet, sharing in Christ's glory hinges upon suffering with him and like him, an experience which Paul elaborates on in Rom 8:31–39.

---

50. Cf. 1 Cor 3:21–23.
51. Cf. echoes of 2 Sam 7:1–17 in Rom 1:2–4. For analysis of this echo, see volume 1.
52. Cf. differences in Dan 7:13–14 θ.

Another pre-text that informs Rom 8:17 is Isa 52:13, "Behold, my servant will understand, and he will be exalted, and he will be glorifed (δοξασθήσεται)." Contextually, this promise prefaces the description of a servant who was rejected by people and afflicted by God on behalf of the very ones who rejected him (Isa 52:14–53:11). Because of his service, he will be glorified and inherit many (Isa 52:13; 53:12). God reverses the servant's lowliness and disdain in the eyes of others by placing him in a position of authority. Paul evokes Isaiah's juxtaposition of the servant's glory and suffering in the conditional clause of Rom 8:17, "If ineed we suffer with him (συμπάσχομεν) in order that we might also be glorified with him (συνδοξασθῶμεν)." Paul reconfigures the Isaianic pre-text in a few different ways. For example, while the Isaianic pre-text does not specify how God will glorify the servant, Paul grounds God's glorification of Jesus Christ in his resurrection and in the resurrection of those who believe. We can infer this grounding based on the way that Paul sometimes uses glory language (δόξα) in references to the resurrection:

> Therefore, we have been buried with him through baptism into death, in order that just as Christ was raised from the dead (ἐκ νεκρῶν) through the glory of the father (διὰ τῆς δόξης τοῦ πατρός), in this way we might also walk in newness of life (Rom 6:4).

> For also creation itself will be freed from slavery to ruin in the freedom of the glory of the children of God (τῆς δόξης τῶν τέκνων τοῦ θεοῦ) (Rom 8:21).

> It is sown dishonor, it is raised in glory (ἐγείρεται ἐν δόξῃ); it is sown in weakness, it is raised in power (1 Cor 15:43).[53]

Additionally, Paul's argument in Rom 8:18–25 signals a clear link between glory and resurrection. The noun δόξα functions as one of the hook words between Rom 8:17 and 18 where the phrase "glory which is to come" (τὴν μέλλουσαν δόξαν) refers to resurrection from the dead. Therefore, for Paul, the glorification of the Isaianic servant is the resurrection of Jesus Christ which results in the inheritance that God promised to the servant.

Within the *history of interpretation*, some interpreters have noted the various Abrahamic and messianic echoes of a promised inheritance in Rom 8:17. Stuhlmacher notes that in Rom 4:13 Paul had in view the inheritance promised to Abraham. However, in Rom 8:17, Stuhlmacher suggests "But in our context, the apostle now has in view the promise from 2 Sam. 7:12–14 that one will be brought into the relationship of a child in regard to God. This promise is now made available anew to those who believe through Jesus' sending, death, and resurrection. The crucified and resurrected Christ is its decisive guarantee."[54] In his analysis of Rom 8:17, Jewett casts a wider

---

53. See also 1 Cor 15:40, 41; Phil 3:21; Col 3:4; 2 Thess 2:14.
54. Stuhlmacher, *Romans*, 131.

intertextual net for understanding the reference to inheritance noting, "So in the case of the children of God in Paul's discourse, every promise and possession once granted to Israel are now granted in a new and symbolic sense to each and every believer and to each believing community."[55] In the analysis above, I framed all the prior promises to Israel around the figures of Abraham and a Davidic messiah. Whatever God promised Israel is now inherited by his children who suffer with Christ. At the heart of all that God promised Israel there is a promise of his presence, of himself. What the Romans ultimately inherit is Christ, and Christ is God himself in accordance with his prior promises.

This brings us to the final intertextual consideration related to Rom 8:17. While συγκληρονόμοι Χριστοῦ is a unique expression, its uniqueness should not overshadow the significance of the phrase which precedes and informs it, κληρονόμοι θεοῦ.[56] The genitive in the latter phrase functions as a plenary genitive.[57] In other words, Paul simultaneously describes God as the Romans' inheritance and the Romans as God's inheritance. To put it another way, the Romans inherit God and God inherits the Romans. This syntactical decision is based largely on the phrase's OT echoes which evokes the thick description of inheritance from Israel's Scriptures.

Most inheritance (κληρονομία/κληρονομέω) language in the LXX is related to Israel's possession of the land that God first promised to Abraham and his descendants, "I will give this land (τὴν γῆν ταύτην) to your seed" (Gen 12:7).[58] God later identifies himself to Abraham in relation to the promised land, "I am the God who brought you out from the land of the Chaldeans to give to you this land (τὴν γῆν) to inherit it (κληρονομῆσαι)" (Gen 15:7).[59] However, not all of Abraham's descendants inherited a portion of the land, namely the tribe of Levi. As God informed Aaron, "In their land you will not inherit (οὐ κληρονομήσεις), and there will not be a portion (μερίς) for you among them, because I am your portion and your inheritance (ἐγὼ μερίς σου καὶ κληρονομία σου) in the midst of the sons of Israel" (Num 18:20).[60] Subsequent descriptions of this promise elaborate on the nature of Levi's inheritance, "For there is no portion (μερίς) to the sons of Levi among you, for the priesthood of the Lord is his portion (ἱερατεία κυρίου μερὶς αὐτοῦ)" (Josh 18:7). Therefore, the Levites "inherited God" in the sense that they were given the cultic responsibilities and privileges within the nation.

---

55. Jewett, *Romans*, 501.

56. For the only other occurrences of συγκληρονόμος in the NT, see Eph 3:6; Heb 11:9; 1 Pet 3:7.

57. For an objective genitive reading of κληρονόμοι θεοῦ, see Schreiner, *Romans*, 427.

58. For a discussion of how NT writers viewed the promised land, see, e.g., Burge, *Jesus and the Land*; Davies, *Christian Engagements with Judaism*, 112.

59. See also γῆ + κληρονομία/κληρονομέω in Gen 17:8; 22:18; 26:3-4; 28:4, 13, 14; 35:12; 50:24; Josh 1:15; Pss LXX 24:13; 36:9, 11, 22; 43:4; 68:36; 104:11; Isa 14:21; 49:8.

60. See also Num 18:23; Josh 13:14

OT poetic expressions employ inheritance language to describe the relationship between all of Israel and its God. For example, Moses' song describes Israel as God's portion "And the portion of the Lord (μερὶς κυρίου) is his people Jacob, and the allotment of his inheritance (σχοίνισμα κληρονομίας) is Israel" (Deut 32:9).[61] The psalmist describes God as Israel's portion/inheritance and vice versa:

> The Lord is the portion of my inheritance (ἡ μερὶς τῆς κληρονομίας) and of my cup; you are the one who restores my inheritance (τὴν κληρονομίαν) to me (Ps 15:5 LXX).[62]

> For the Lord will not reject his people, and he will not abandon his inheritance (τὴν κληρονομάιν αὐτοῦ) (Ps 93:14 LXX).[63]

Prophetic literature likewise describes Israel as God's inheritance whom he both judges and delivers.[64] Both divine actions are present in God's exchange with Jeremiah. God responds to Jeremiah's lament by explaining, "I have abanonded my house, I have left my inheritance (τὴν κληρονομίαν μου), I have given the beloved of my soul into the hands of its enemies" (Jer 12:7). Beyond the judgment against his inheritance, he promises its deliverance "And it will be after I have thrown them out I will turn and I will have mercy upon them and I will cause each of them to dwell in his inheritance (τὴν κληρονομίαν αὐτοῦ) and each one in his land" (Jer 12:15).

Overall, the OT motif of "inheritance" describes the land promised to Abraham's descendants, the tribe of Levi, and the relationship between Israel and its God. One overarching characteristic in this motif is that God "chooses" (ἐκλέγομαι). He chose the land, the inheritance of Levi, and Israel as his people. As the psalmist puts its, "Blessed is the nation, whose God is the Lord, the people, whom he chose (ἐξελέξατο) for his own inheritance (εἰς κληρονμίαν ἑαυτῷ)" (Ps 32:12 LXX).

When we consider Paul's reference to κληρονόμοι θεοῦ against this intertextual backdrop, it becomes clear that the phrase is teeming with meaning. God is the inheritance of the Romans, and the Romans are the inheritance of God. In keeping with the OT motif, God chose the Romans as his inheritance which he will explain in Rom 8:28–30. Of course, Paul recontextualizes the OT motif of inheritance around the Romans being coheirs with Christ (συγκληρονόμοι Χριστοῦ). Simply put, in Christ, God obtains the Romans and the Romans obtain God in accordance with Israel's Scriptures. I will return to this interplay below.

---

61. For Israel as God's κληρονομία, see also 1 Kgs 8:51, 53.

62. Most Psalms describe Israel as God's κληρονομία.

63. For Israel as God's κληρονομία in the LXX Psalms, see Pss LXX 32:12; 46:5; 68:9; 73:2; 77:62, 71; 93:5; 105:40.

64. See Israel as God's κληρονομία in Isa 19:25; 47:6; 63:17; Jer 10:16; 12:8, 9; 16:18; 28:19 (51:19 MT); Ezek 44:28.

Interpretive Impact of Pre-Texts in Romans 8:12–17

Romans 8:12–17 contains a rich intertextual subtext consisting of at least five elements: (1) the recapituatlion of Adam's slavery in Israel; (2) divine leading; (3) the vocative of divine address; (4) divine reassurance; and (5) the children's inheritance. The interplay between these intertextual elements and Paul's text generate several unstated points of resonance.

To begin, the two modes of living described in Rom 8:12–17, living according to the flesh and putting to death the deeds of the body, are a juxtaposition of recapitulating Adam's slavery and sharing in Christ's inheritance. To be sure, Paul does not explicitly refer to Adam or the Genesis narrative as he did in Rom 5:12–19. Instead, he abbreviates his wider reflection on the Adamic narrative and its effect using phrases such as τῇ σαρκί, κατὰ σάρκα, and πνεῦμα δουλείας. The latter phrase evokes Israel's recapitulation of Adam's sin which resulted in captivity and death. Paul describes this experience as a "spirit that enslaves" (πνεῦμα δουλείας).[65] It enslaves and kills not only Adam and Israel but all who live as they did, "according to flesh." He contrasts that experience with the "Spirit of adoption." Those who receive this Spirit have an experience consisting of the following: (1) they put the deeds of the body to death; (2) they lament to "Abba, Father;" (3) they receive a response to their lament; (4) they inherit God; (5) God inherits them; and (6) they inherit with Christ. These interrelated experiences are intertextually informed.

The cry "Abba, Father" (αββα ὁ πατήρ) is reminiscent of divine vocatives found in the Psalms of Lament, and it is an imitation of Jesus' lament in the Garden of Gethsemane. The diverse interplay here implies that the Spirit of adoption prompts the Romans to cry out in the vein of OT lamenters, particularly Christ himself who was portrayed in early Christian tradition as a righteous lamenter in the vein of OT lamenters.[66] This means the cry "Abba, Father" assumes a request by the Romans to be delivered from both divine wrath and their enemies. This inference is drawn from intertextual echoes in Rom 8:12–17, and it is confirmed by the wider contents of the letter along with the more immediate context. As I have noted at several points, Paul shows an extensive, though it is sometimes underemphasized by interpreters, concern with divine wrath throughout the letter.[67] The same concern underpins much of the argument from Rom 7:7—8:39. Otherwise, declarations such as "There is no condemnation (κατάκριμα) for those who are in Christ Jesus" are difficult to explain. Paul has also portrayed sin and death as enemies from whom the Romans have been rescued through Christ. However, despite deliverance from both divine condemnation and

---

65. For a "spirit that enslaves," see Matera, *Romans*, 197.

66. For a discussion of Jesus' depiction as a righteous lamenter, see, e.g., Crisler, *Echoes of Lament and the Christology of Luke*; Ahearne-Kroll, *The Psalms of Lament in Mark's Passion*.

67. See Rom 1:18–32; 2:1–16; 3:1–8; 3:19–20, 26; 4:15; 5:9, 15–21; 6:23; 8:1.

enemies such as sin and death, the Romans continue to suffer which elicits their request to Abba that he might yet deliver them.

God answers the cry "Abba, Father" by reassuring the Romans, through the testimony of the Holy Spirit with the spirit of the Romans, that they are God's children which affords them a remarkable inheritance promised in Israel's Scriptures. God promised an inheritance to his messiah and to his children. When we collate the promises made to David (2 Sam 7:11–14), Isaiah's suffering servant (Isa 53:1–12), God's son (Ps 2), and Daniel's son of man (Dan 7:13–14), God promised that his messiah would inherit a people and an eternal reign over the world. With respect to God's children, they were slated to inherit the promised land and beyond, the gates of their enemies, and even God himself. Paul merges these promissory strands in Messiah Jesus. The crucified and risen Christ has been glorified through his resurrection; therefore, he has inherited a people and an eternal reign over the world. As Paul put it in his letter opening, Jesus is "from the seed of David according to the flesh who has been declared the son of God in power according to the Spirit of holiness from the resurrection of the dead." Paul describes the people whom Christ has inherited, both Jews and Gentiles, as coheirs with him. It is in sharing the inheritance of Christ that the children ultimately inherit God and God them.

Finally, integral to all of Paul's argument in Rom 8:12–17 is the intertextually informed description of the Spirit who "leads" (πνεύματι θεοῦ ἄγονται, Rom 8:14) believers. Pre-texts such as Ps 142 LXX and Isa 63 associate the Spirit's presence and leading with the affliction of God's people. Specifically, the Spirit leads God's children out of exile and death into the promised inheritance and life. Paul reconfigures these OT pre-texts so that the Spirit's presence "leads" the Romans by putting to death the sinful deeds of the body, testifying to their filial status with Christ in the face of affliction, affliction which raised serious questions about that status, and interceding for them with inexpressible lamenting as they await the hope of resurrection. The latter hope, which Paul refers to as being glorified with Christ, does not become a realization without suffering with Christ. It is the Spirit who will "lead" the Romans through suffering with Christ and being raised with Christ just as he raised Christ from the dead.

9

Romans 8:18–27

THE RHETORICAL LINK BETWEEN between vv. 17 and 18 is the juxtaposition between suffering and glory. Although Paul reasurres the Romans that the glory to come far outweighs their present suffering, he focuses throughout this section of the letter on hope in suffering. He accentuates the eager expectation for resurrection on the part of creation and the children of God. Both creation and the children utter laments requesting resurrection from the dead. The Spirit of God even joins in this lament. As we shall see, Paul's line of argument in these verses contains an intertextual subtext that coalesces around a tripartite lament by creation, the sons of God, and the Spirit of God.[1]

The στενα-root is the semantic thread that binds these ten verses together.[2] Groans can be heard from creation (πᾶσα ἡ κτίσις συστενάζει), the children of God (στενάζομεν), and the Spirit of God (τὸ πνεῦμα ὑπερεντυγχάνει στεναγμοῖς ἀλαλήτοις). They are groans for resurrection from the dead. That is because the resurrection of God's children liberates creation from its divinely prescribed subjection to futility, fulfills the very hope with which the Romans were saved, and answers the Spirit's intercession. As we shall see, these "groans" are in fact laments based on a whole matrix of intertextual allusions and echoes that Paul's language evokes.

---

1. For studies that engage the intertextual subtext of Rom 8:18–27, see, e.g., Allen, "The Old Testament Background," 104–8; Braaten, "All Creatio Groans," 131–59; Christofferson, *The Earnest Expectation of the Creature*; Cranfield, "The Creation's Promised Liberation," 224–30; Hahne, *The Corruption and Redemption of Creation*; Keesmaat, "Exodus and Intertextual Transformation," 29–56; Moo, "Romans 8.19–22," 74–89; Tsmura, "An OT Background," 620–21.

2. For a full discussion of the στενα-root in Rom 8:18–27, see Crisler, *Reading Romans as Lament*, 120–34.

Romans 8:18–22

(8:18–22) For I consider that the present sufferings are not worthy to be compared to the glory which is about to be revealed to us. For the eager expectation of creation eagerly awaits the revelation of the sons of God. For creation was subjected to futility, not willingly but because of the one who subjected it, in hope that also creation itself will be freed from slavery to corruption in the freedom of the glory of the children of God. For we know that all creation is lamenting and suffering the pains of childbirth until now.

Although v. 18 strikes a note of eschatological hope, it is situated in a larger context of the present realities that the Christians in Rome must face. They are part of a trio of lamenters whose cries collectively protest present affliction and request the realization of the gospel's eschatological promise. In vv. 19–22, Paul highlights creation's participation in these trio of lamenters. Not surprisingly, Paul leans heavily on Israel's Scriptures which contain a rich tradition of creation lamenting the suffering of God's people.

Suggested Pre-Texts in Romans 8:18–22

Hübner identifies the following pre-texts: Gen 3:17–19; Ps 61:10 LXX; Eccl 1:2 (Rom 8:19–20).[3] Nestle-Aland 28th ed. lists the following pre-texts in its margins: Gen 3:14–19; Eccl 1:2 (Rom 8:20).[4]

Hays's intertextual analysis remains thin at this point. He acknowledges that Rom 8:20–21 contains scriptural allusions to "the fallen creation subjected to decay," but he does not discuss which pre-texts shape Paul's thought.[5] Once again, Seifrid reserves his comments for Rom 8:31–39.[6]

Intertextual Analysis of Romans 8:18–22

In Rom 8:19–22, Paul describes creation's (κτίσις) eager expectation (ἀποκαραδοκία) and lament (συστενάζω) which is wrapped up with the revelation of God's son/children at their resurrection from the dead. Interpreters are divided on what Paul means by κτίσις.[7] Based on the surrounding context of κτίσις and the intertextual subtext

---

3. Hübner, *Vetus Testamentum in Novo*, 2:124–29.
4. See also 2 Bar. 15:8 (Rom 8:18); 4 Ezra 10:9; 23:26 (Rom 8:22).
5. Hays, *The Conversion of the Imagination*, 182.
6. Seifrid, *Romans*, 633–37.
7. BDAG 573. Longenecker summarizes eight positions from the time of the church fathers until today. The eight interpretations of κτίσις in Rom 8:19–22 are as follows: (1) an all-encompassing reference to human, subhuman (animate/inanimate), and angelic creation; (2) a reference to "nonrational creation," or "nature;" (3) a reference to "all of humanity" but not subhuman creation; (4) a reference

of Rom 8:19–22, the term most likely "refers to created subhuman earthly life, both animate and inanimate–that is, to 'the nonrational creation' or what people today call 'nature.'"[8] Paul's reflection on creation, or "nature," needs to be read in relation to five intertextual considerations.

Romans 8:19–22 and Echoes of Creation's Futility

To begin, when Paul describes creation's condition as being "subjected to futility" (τῇ ματαιότητι ἡ κτίσις ὑπετάγη) and in need of being freed "from slavery to ruin" (ἀπὸ τῆς δουλείας τῆς φθορᾶς), it evokes God's curse against creation/nature in the aftermath of Adam's transgression. God announces this judgment to Adam:

> And he said to Adam, "Because you listened to the voice of your wife and you ate from the tree, of which I commanded you from this one only not to eat, cursed is the ground (ἐπικατάρατος ἡ γῆ) in your labors; in pains you will eat from it all the days of your life; thorns and thistles it will bring forth to you, and you will eat the herb of the field. By the sweat of your face you will eat your bread until you return to the ground from which you were taken; for you are earth and you will return to the earth (Gen 3:17–19).

God curses creation as part of his judgment against Adam. The curse has two deleterious effects on nature: (1) the ground struggles to be fruitful for human beings as signaled by the thorns and thistles that it bears; and (2) the ground becomes a tomb to which human beings return rather than the domain they rule over. The effects of the curse are felt by nature, and they have fatal consequences for humanity.

When we test the intertextual echoes of Gen 3:17–19 in Rom 8:19–22, the *volume* is admittedly low. The Genesis pre-text does not employ Paul's terminology such as "subjected" (ὑποτάσσω) or "slavery" (δουλεία) to describe the way God cursed nature.[9] Likewise, the Romans text does not contain descriptors found in the Genesis pre-text such as "accursed" (ἐπικατάρατος).

Nevertheless, the pre-text and text share *contextual consistency*. When God curses the ground with its deleterious effects on humanity, it is tantamount to a divine subjection or enslavement to futility. Paul description of creation's condition aptly describes what began in the garden and continued up to his own day (ἄχρι τοῦ νῦν, Rom 8:22). God subjected creation to a meaningless existence which surely elicited its lament which I will discuss below. This suggested echo also passes the test of *recurrence*. As

---

to believers in Jesus; (5) a reference to the "created body of a believer in Jesus;" (6) a reference to unbelievers; (7) a reference to "subhuman creation and unbelieving humanity;" and (8) a reference to angels. See Longenecker, *Romans*, 719–20.

8. Longenecker, *Romans*, 719.

9. Gen 3:17–19 does not even contain the noun κτίσις, or it verbal cognate κτίζω. However, Paul's use of κτίσις obviously evokes the Genesis narrative even if it does not reflect the semantic choices of the Genesis pre-text.

I have noted at several points already, the Adamic narrative is one of the main pillars of Paul's intertextual subtext in Rom 5–8. Finally, within the *history of interpretation*, many interpreters have noted Paul's use of Gen 3:17–19. As Dunn puts it, "The reason why the created order awaits so longingly man's redemption is because creation itself is caught up in man's fallen state. Paul assumes that his readers would recognize the allusion, once again, to the narrative of Adam's creation and fall."[10]

Second, when Paul explains creation's eager expectation for the resurrection of God's children, his observation that "creation was subjected to futility" (τῇ ματαιότητι ἡ κτίσις ὑπετάγη) evokes the description of creation in Eccl 1. Qohelet's wisdom commences with a thesis-like statement which he subsequently unpacks, "'Vanity of vanities (ματαιότης ματαιοτήτων)' says the preacher, 'Vanity of vanities (ματαιότης ματαιοτήτων), all is vanity (τὰ πάντα ματαιότης)'" (Eccl 1:2). What then follows is a description of creation's futility:

> What benefit is there to man in all his toil, for which he toils under the sun? A generation comes and a generation goes, and the earth has stood forever. And the sun rises and the sun sets and it drags toward its place; arising it goes there to the south and goes around to the north; it goes around and around, the wind goes, and the wind returns on its circuits. All the rivers go into the sea, and the sea will not be filled up; to the place, where the rivers go, there they retrun to go (Eccl 1:3–7).

Qohelet describes nature as something that churns on in a meaningless way. The larger context of Ecclesiastes locates this meaningless estate in the fact that nature continues but human beings do not.[11] The *volume* of Ecclesiastes in Rom 8:20 is moderate based on the use of ματαιότης, and the implication, in both the pre-text and text, is that God subjected nature to its meaningless estate.[12]

The pre-text and text are *contextually consistent* with one another. Ecclesiastes and Paul both link nature's futility to the mortality of human beings. With this consistency in view, Paul recontextualizes the futility motif from Ecclesiastes in a few ways. For example, he links it with other OT pre-texts such as the Gen 3:17–19 and OT lament which I will discuss below. Paul also links the suffering of nature with the suffering of the Romans who live in a world subjected to meaninglessness by the God whom they call "Abba, Father." Therefore, both creation and the children of God cry out for deliverance. Some interpreters note the influence of Ecclesiastes on Paul's thought at this point. As Hultgren observes, "The term for 'futility' (ματαιότης) refers

---

10. Dunn, *Romans*, 1:487. Hultgren notes that the allusion/echo of Gen 3:17–19 is "almost universally the view of major interpreters." Hultgren, *Romans*, 322 fn. 331.

11. See, e.g., Eccl 9:9.

12. BDAG 621; LEH 386. The noun ματαιότης (הבל) occurs several times in the LXX of Ecclesiastes. See Eccl 1:2, 14; 2:1, 11, 15, 17, 19, 21, 23, 26; 3:19; 4:4, 7, 8, 16; 5:6, 9; 6:2, 4, 9, 11, 12; 7:6, 15; 8:10, 14; 9:2, 9; 11:8, 10; 12:8.

at least to the transitory nature of the creation, but undoubtedly also its seeming lack of purpose, reflecting the language and thought of Ecclesiastes."[13]

Romans 8:19–22 and Echoes of Creation's Lament

This brings us to the third OT pre-text in Rom 8:19–22. It stems from Paul's description of creation's lament in v. 22, "For we know that all creation laments (συστενάζει) and suffers the pains of childbirth together (συνωδίνει) until now." Paul's personification of creation as groaning/lamenting evokes similar OT personifications of creation. Two prophetic pre-texts directly reflect this personification:

> The earth mourns (ἐπένθησεν), the world has been ruined, the heights of the earth mourn (ἐπένθησεν). And the earth has been corrupted because of those who dwell in it, because they have transgressed the law and changed the law, the eternal covenant. Because of this a curse will consume the earth, because those who dwell in it sinned; because of this those who dwell in the earth will be poor and few people will be left (Isa 24:4–6).

> Let the earth mourn (πενθείτω), and let the sky above be darkened, because I have spoken and I will not relent, I have sworn and I will not turn from it (Jer 4:28).

The *volume* of these echoes is low, though the verbs συστενάζω, συνωδίνω, and πενθέω are in the same semantic domain.

With respect to *contextual consistency*, creation laments for similar reasons in both the pre-text and text. Isa 24 is an apocalyptic vision in which God desolates the entire earth due to humanity's sinfulness. Consequently, the earth cries out to mourn God's judgment. Jer 4 is not a prophecy of cosmic judgment. Rather, the prophet envisions judgment against Jerusalem and its inhabitants for its sinfulness.[14] Nevertheless, like Isa 24, the desolation of the land elicits a cry from the earth as it mourns the judgment. Paul recontextualizes this personification with the result that creation and the children of God lament. Much like the wider contexts of Isa 24 and Jer 4, hope remains that God will answer the lament.[15] Though God subjected creation to futility and slavery, he did so "in hope" (ἐφ᾽ἐλπίδι) (Rom 8:20). Paul identifies that hope as resurrection from death to life for children who are in Christ.[16]

Paul's description of creation groaning/lamenting (συστενάζω) echoes a similar description of the earth by Job. In Job's final defense of his innocence before God,

---

13. Hultgren, *Romans*, 322–23.
14. See Jer 4:17–22, 27.
15. See Isa 25:1–12; Jer 4:27.
16. With respect to the *history of interpretation*, some interpreters note the echo of pre-texts such as Isa 24:4–6 and Jer 4:28. See, e.g., Jewett, *Romans*, 516.

he insists that the land would testify against him if he were guilty of the accusations levelled against him by his "friends." He asserts, "If the land groaned against me (ἡ γῆ ἐστέναξεν), and if its furrows have cried out together (οἱ αὔλακες αὐτῆς ἔκλαυσαν ὁμοθυμαδόν), and if I ate its strength alone without price, and if I also grieved the heart of the owner of the land, then may the nettle come up in place of wheat, and bramble in place of barley" (Job 31:38–40). The *volume* here is moderate based on the land groaning in the pre-text (ἡ γῆ ἐστέναξεν) and creation groaning in the text (ἡ κτίσις συστενάζει).

Contextual consistency lies in the shared interest of how nature participates in the pain and hope of the righteous. In the pre-text, the land could groan against an unrighteous Job through its fruitlessness; however, it does not.[17] The personified land acts as a witness to the innocence or guilt of Job. Similarly, in Paul's text, creation does not cry out against the children of God but rather with them. Paul recontextualizes the pre-text with the result that creation shares in the children's lament for resurrection from the dead.

Romans 8:19–22 and Echoes of the Pangs of Childbirth

The fifth cluster of OT pre-texts stems from Paul's personification of creation as a pregnant woman, "And it (creation) suffers birth pangs together (συνωδίνει) until now" (Rom 8:22b). OT writers sometimes employ a woman's pain in childbirth as a metaphor that symbolizes the tension between Israel's hope and pain. Several pre-texts likely inform Paul's use of the metaphor in Rom 8:22.[18]

To begin, the metaphor occurs in Isa 26 which is part of a larger apocalyptic section (Isa 24–27) wherein Judah sings a song of salvation, "In that day they will sing this song in the land of Judah" (Isa 26:1). The song divides the world's inhabitants into the ungodly and the humble who hope in Israel's God. The latter hope and request that God would usher in their salvation by judging the ungodly.[19] Waiting for this salvific moment is likened to a woman on the cusp of giving birth, and the outcome of the birth is nothing less than resurrection from the dead:

> And like one who suffers the pains of child birth (ἡ ὠδίνουσα) comes near to give birth and she cries out in her pain (ἐπὶ τῇ ὠδῖνι αὐτῆς ἐκέκραξεν), in this way we have been to your beloved because of fear of you, O Lord. We conceived and we suffered the pains of child birth (ὠδινήσαμεν) and we gave birth; we made the spirit of salvation upon the earth. The dead will

---

17. Hartley links Job 31:38–40 to portions of the Mosaic Law such as Lev 19:19 and Exod 23:10–11. He suggests, "When the people are disobedient, the land whithers and mourns beneath the weight of their sins. Conversely, when the people obeyed God's laws, he blessed the land so that it yielded abundantly." Hartley, *Job*, 422.

18. See Braaten, "All Creation Groans," 131–59.

19. See, e.g., Isa 26:11–12.

rise (ἀναστήσονται οἱ νεκροί), and those who dwell in tombs will be raised (ἐγερθήσονται οἱ ἐν τοῖς μνημείοις), and those who are in the earth (οἱ ἐν τῇ γῇ) will rejoice; for the dew from you is healing to the them, but the land of the ungodly will perish (Isa 26:17–19).

The *volume* of the echo is moderate based on the semantic overlap involving ὠδίνω and συνωδίνω.[20]

Contextual consistency revolves around the divine response to suffering which is likened to that experienced by a woman in labor. In the pre-text, this metaphor captures the tension between the pain of the humble caused by their ungodly enemies and their hope that God would deliver them, ultimately in resurrection from the dead. Paul recontextualizes Isaiah's metaphor by expanding the participants of the lament to include both creation and God's children.[21]

Next, Paul's use of the child bearing metaphor may evoke and repurpose its use in Jer 4:19–31 which describes Israel's impending judgment at the hands of the Babylonians. God vows to destroy the promised land because of his people's foolish rebellion against him, "Thus says the Lord, 'All the land will be desolate, but I certainly shall not make a full end'" (Jer 4:27). The conclusion of this divine announcement employs the child bearing metaphor, "For I heard the sound like that of one suffering the pains of child birth (ὠδινούσης), your groaning (τοῦ στεναγμοῦ σου) like that of one giving birth to her first child (πρωτοτοκούσης); she will weaken her hands, saying, 'Woe is me, for my soul faints because of the slain'"(Jer 4:31). The *volume* of the echo is moderate based on the shared use of ὠδίνω/συνωδίνω and στεναγμός/συστενάζω.

There is also *contextual consistency* based on the wider context of the pre-text. As I noted above, Jer 4:28 personifies the land (ἡ γῆ) as mourning the nation's impending judgment. However, the gloominess of the prophecy notwithstanding, there is still a modicum of hope based on the Lord's promise that his judgment would not "bring a full end" (συντέλεια) to his people (Jer 4:27b). These features are reflected in Rom 8:19–22. Creation laments the way God subjected it to futility, but, like a mother about to give birth, the hope of a new beginning is hidden in the pain. Paul escalates the personification of the pregnant daughter of Zion in Jeremiah by applying the metaphor of an expectant mother to the whole of creation.[22] Like the land in Jeremiah, creation senses the tension between the divine judgment of futility and the hope that God will raise his children from the dead thereby bring the judgment of futility to an end.

---

20. The use of συνωδίνω in Rom 8:22 is a hapax legomenon in the NT. It never occurs in the LXX.

21. On Paul's use of Isa 24–27 in Rom 8:19–22, see Moo, "Romans 8.19–22," 74–89.

22. In Jer 4:30–31 LXX, the pain of childbirth emanates from the "daughter of Zion." However, Paul applies the metaphor to creation. See also the use of ὠδίνω in Jer 30:16 (49:22 MT); Mic 4:10; Hab 3:10.

Romans 8:23-25

> (8:23-25) But not only this, but also we ourselves having the firstfruits of the Spirit, we also groan in ourselves eagerly awaiting the adoption, the redemption of our body. For in hope we were saved; but hope being seen is not hope; for who hopes for that which he sees? But if we hope for that which we do not see, through endurance we eagerly await it.

In turning our attention to Rom 8:23-25, Paul observes that "it is not only" (οὐ μόνον δέ) creation who laments for the children's resurrection from the dead but also the Romans themselves. Paul's description of the Romans as lamenters evokes multiple OT pre-texts.

Suggested Pre-texts in Romans 8:23-25

Hübner lists the following pre-texts: Exod 22:29; 23:19; Lev 2:12; 23:10; Num 11:17; Deut 26:2; Ps 8:6; Isa 26:16-18; Jer 4:27-29; 12:4 (Rom 8:23-25).[23] Nestle-Aland 28th ed. lists no pre-texts.

Intertextual Analysis of Romans 8:23-25

The intertextual subtext of Rom 8:23-25 is supported by multiple pre-texts. As we shall see, the primary pre-texts here stem from three kinds of pre-texts: (1) the use of first fruits language; (2) OT lament language; and (3) the use of OT hope language.

Romans 8:23-25 and Echoes of ἀπαρχή

When Paul describes himself and the Romans as "having the first fruits of the Spirit" (τὴν ἀπαρχὴν τοῦ πνεύματος ἔχοντες), he merges the OT motif of first fruits with the eschatological gift of the Spirit. The term ἀπαρχή (בכורים) evokes the first offerings prescribed in the Mosaic Law, "And you shall take from the first of the fruits (ἀπαρχῆς τῶν καρπῶν) of your land, which the Lord your God gives to you, and you shall put them in a basket, and you shall go into the place, which the Lord your God might choose for his name to be called there" (Deut 26:2).[24] The wider context of Deut 26:2 indicates that God's saving actions were to be recited when the first fruits were offered:

---

23. Hübner, *Vetus Testamentum in Novo*, 2:124-29.

24. See also the use of ἀπαρχή in Exod 22:28; 23:19; Lev 2:12; 23:10; Num 15:20-21; 31:29; Deut 12:11; 18:4; 26:10; Neh 10:38; Mal 3:8; Ezek 44:30. Within the Mosaic Law, as Dunn notes, first fruits can be categorized as follows: (1) first-born son (Ps 104:36 LXX); (2) first offspring of sheep or cattle (Deut 12:6); (3) first offerings of goods (Exod 25:2-3); (4) first lump of dough (Num 15:21); and (5) the first fruits of a harvest, either from the winepress or threshing floor (Exod 22:29; 23:19). However, as Dunn rightly notes, in Rom 8:23, Paul has in view the first fruits of a harvest. See Dunn, *Romans*, 1:473.

And you shall answer and you shall say before the Lord your God, "My father left Syria, and he went down to Egypt and he dwelled there with a small number and he became there a might nation and a great multitude; and the Egyptians afflicted us and they placed on us harsh works; and we cried out (ἀνεβοήσαμεν) to the Lord God of our fathers, and the Lord heard our voice and he saw our low estate and our toil and our oppression; and the Lord himself brought us out of from Egypt by his great strength and by a mighty hand and by his high arm and with great vision and with signs and with wonders and he brought us into this place and he gave to us this land, a land flowing with milk and honey; and now behold I have brought the first of the produce (τὴν ἀπαρχὴν τῶν γενημάτων) of the land, which you gave to me, O Lord, a land flowing with milk and honey." And you shall leave it before the Lord your God and you shall worship there before the Lord your God (Deut 26:5–10).

By reciting God's saving actions, the one who offered the first fruits acknowledged that the produce was a blessing from God grounded in his prior saving work.[25]

Similarly, Paul identifies the Spirit as a kind of first fruits associated with the saving work of God in Christ. He recontextualizes ἀπαρχή so that it is God, rather than God's people, who gives the first fruits of an eschatological harvest. The Romans have (ἔχω) the same Spirit who raised Jesus from the dead, whom Paul describes elsewhere as the "first fruits (ἀπαρχή) of those who have fallen asleep" (1 Cor 15:20).[26] Jesus is the first fruits of the eschatological harvest raised by the Spirit whom God gave to the Romans. Such a gift, like the first fruits offered in the OT, signals that the Romans have and will receive an eschatological blessing.

Romans 8:23–25 and Echoes of Lament

The clause "we we also groan (στενάζομεν) in ourselves eagerly awaiting the adoption, the redemption of our body," like the use of the στενα-root in Rom 8:22 and 8:26, echoes OT lament. The στενα-root often signals an audible sigh or groan elicited by afflictions of various sorts.[27] As I have noted at various points in this work already, OT lament is a prayer form marked by a pattern, distinct idiom, set of participants, and theology.[28] Paul often employs prayer language apart from formal prayers/prayer reports, and that is certainly the case here.[29] Cries of distress, or "groaning," often arise

---

25. See Hartley, *Leviticus*, 31.

26. See also 1 Cor 15:23. We also find the first fruits reference in a description of the Thessalonians, "But we are obligated to give thanks to God always for you, brothers beloved by the Lord, because God chose you as the first fruits (ἀπαρχήν) for salvation by the sanctification of the Spirit and by faith in the truth" (2 Thess 2:13). See also the use of ἀπαρχή in Jas 1:18; Rev 14:4.

27. BDAG 942; LEH 567.

28. See especially the prior discussion of lament in Rom 1:16–17 and 7:7–25. For extensive analysis of lament in Rom 8:23–25, see Crisler, *Reading Romans as Lament*, 127–29.

29. For a discussion of Paul's use of prayer language beyond formal prayers and prayers reports in his letter, see Stendahl, "Paul at Prayer," 240–49.

because of the tension between God's prior promise of deliverance and the suffering of the lamenter. In Israel's Scriptures, these experiences unfold within the nation and in the lives of individuals. A classic example of the former is Israel's cry of distress just prior to their deliverance from Egypt, "And the sons of Israel groaned (κατεστέναξαν) because of their tasks and they cried out (ἀνεβόησαν), and their cry (ἡ βοή) because of their tasks went up to God. And God heard their groaning (τὸν στεναγμὸν αὐτῶν), and God remembered his covenant with Abraham and Isaac and Jacob" (Exod 2:23-24). In short, God promised Abraham's descendants deliverance from their enemies, but Israel was enslaved in Egypt. Therefore, they cried out for deliverance, and God "remembered" his prior promise which he then acted upon it as the larger Exodus narrative demonstrates.

From an individual perspective, various figures groan due to the tension they experience between their hope in God's prior promise of deliverance and their affliction. For example, Job complains "For before my food groaning (στεναγμοῖς) comes to near to me, and I cry while being gripped with fear (Job 3:24).[30] Similarly, the psalmist cries out "My life is left in pain and my years in groaning (στεναγμοῖς); my strength weakened in poverty, and my bones were disturbed" (Ps 30:11 LXX).[31] Such groaning is not a fait accompli by lamenters as if their affliction is irreversibly hopeless. To the contrary, the theology of OT assumes that God responds to such cries. The divine assurance to the lamenter is, "'Because of the misery of the poor and because of the groaning (στεναγμοῦ) of the needy now I will rise,' says the Lord, 'I will set him in salvation, I will deal openly with him'" (Ps 11:6 LXX).

This dynamic of OT lament, particularly the idiom of groaning (στεναγμός/στενάζω) from both an individual and communal perspective, shapes Paul's thought in Rom 8:23. The groaning by Paul and the Romans evokes the tension of a prior promise and current affliction. Paul identifies the tension as the defining aspect of "adoption" explaining, "We also groan in ourselves eagerly awaiting the adoption (υἱοθεσίαν), the redemption of our body (τὴν ἀπολύτρωσιν τοῦ σώματος ἡμῶν)." As I noted above, "adoption" (υἱοθεσία) is a filial metaphor informed by the father-child relationship between God and Israel in the OT.[32] This relationship guarantees the children an inheritance which Paul links to the inheritance of God's messiah. Like the risen Christ, the Romans groan as they eagerly await (ἀπεκδεχόμενοι) their own resurrection which Paul describes here as the "redemption of our body" (τὴν ἀπολύτρωσιν τοῦ σώματος ἡμῶν).[33] This is Paul's second use of ἀπολύτρωσις in the letter. Rom 3:24 contains the phrase "through the redemption (διὰ τῆς ἀπολυτρώσεως) which is in Christ Jesus" as Paul describes the means of God's gracious justification of the sinner. As I noted in the analysis of Rom 3:24, Israel's Scriptures contains a robust

---

30. See also Job 24:12; 30:25.
31. See also Pss LXX 6:7; 37:10; 78:11; 101:6, 21.
32. See the analysis of υἱοθεσία in Rom 8:15.
33. Cf. the use of ἀπεκδέχομαι in Rom 8:19; 1 Cor 1:7; Gal 5:5; Phil 3:20.

use of redemption language. The λυτ- word group is informed by the at least three interrelated descriptions of redemption in the OT: (1) redemption of Israel from Egypt; (2) redemption from individual plight; and (3) redemption patterned after deliverance from Egypt. As I concluded previously, all redemptive experiences from Israel's past, on both an individual and communal level, typify the climactic redemption through Jesus Christ. In Rom 8:23, Paul underscores the outcome of Christ's redemptive work, namely the "redemption of the body" which is "dead because of sin" (Rom 8:10). This is the hope, or promise, with which the Romans were saved, "For in hope we have been saved" (τῇ ἐλπίδι ἐσώθημεν) (Rom 8:24a). Being liberated from the "body of death" through resurrection in Christ is the hope that the Romans heard in the gospel and believed which resulted in their salvation. However, for as long as that hope is left unrealized, a tension is generated between what the Romans hope for and the suffering they experience in a world subjected to the futility of death and in bodies of death. Therefore, both creation and the children of God groan. They lament eagerly awaiting an end to the suffering they endure when the resurrection hope of the gospel is finally seen.

Romans 8:23-25 and Echoes of Hope

This brings us to a third and final intertextual consideration in Rom 8:23-25, the language of endurance and hope in Israel's Scriptures and its impact on Paul's thought here.[34] Paul explains why he and the Romans groan for the fullest experience of their adoption, which is redemption of their bodies, "For in hope (τῇ ἐλπίδι) we have been saved; but hope (ἐλπίς) being seen is not hope (ἐλπίς); for who hopes (ἐλπίζει) for that which he sees" (Rom 8:24-25). Hope is obviously the *leitwort* in these two verses, and it is language shaped by the OT. As Paul explains later in the letter, "For as much as was written beforehand (προεγράφη), it was written for our instruction, in order that through endurance (διὰ τῆς ὑπομονῆς) and through the encouragement of the scriptures (διὰ τῆς παρακλήσεως τῶν γραφῶν) we might have hope (τὴν ἐλπίδα ἔχωμεν) (Rom 15:4)."[35] For Paul, Israel's Scriptures are a primary source of hope for the Christians in Rome, both Jew and Gentile. Therefore, when Paul remarks in Rom 8:24-25 that the Romans "were saved in hope" (τῇ ἐλπίδι ἐσώθημεν), it follows that their soteriological hope has a scriptural underpinning.

These verses do not evoke specific pre-texts. Rather, they are reflective of a larger experience and narrative of hope in Israel's Scriptures which inform Paul's saving message. The LXX is flush with uses of ἐλπίς/ἐλπίζω, terms used by Greek translators

---

34. Paul's use of ἐλπίς in Rom 8:20 and 8:24 corresponds to the use of the same noun in Rom 5:2, 4, and 5. As noted previously, hope and suffering form an *inclusio* in Rom 5:1-5 and 8:18-39 which frames this entire section of the letter. On the *inclusio* in Rom 5-8, see Fowler, *The Structure of Romans*, 194.

35. Cf. Paul's statements about γραφή in Rom 1:2; 16:26.

to render a variety of Hebrew terms. The LXX Psalms and Isaiah contain several uses of this terminology. While these two books are not the only sources that likely shaped Paul's view of hope, the repeated use of them throughout Romans certainly indicate the magnitude of their hermeneutical impact on his thought.

In the Psalms and Isaiah, as well as in many other OT books, the common source of hope is the prior promises and prior saving actions of Israel's God. Individuals and the entire nation have an expectation of deliverance from their affliction based on what God promised and based on his deliverance of people in Israel's past.[36] Such promises and actions go hand in hand, and they are rooted in an overarching narrative propelled by key figures, events, and remembrances. Key figures include Abraham, Moses, and David. Key events include the birth of Isaac, the exodus from Egypt, the reception of the Mosaic Law, the wilderness wanderings, the conquest of the land, the golden age of Israel highlighted by David's rule and Solomon's construction of the temple, and eventual exile. Key remembrances include circumcision, festivals such as Passover, and prayers such as the Shema. This entire narrative, replete with its figures, events, and remembrances, is shot through with hope. Simply put, there is an overarching expectation embedded in the overarching narrative of Israel's Scriptures.

Hope language in LXX Psalms and Isaiah fits into the following taxonomy: (1) God as hope; (2) hope in God/the divine name; (3) hope in divine attributes; (4) misplaced hope; and (5) messianic hope.

The psalmist sometimes describes God himself as Israel's hope, "For you are my endurance, O Lord; the Lord is my hope (κύριος ἡ ἐλπίς μου) from my youth" (Ps 70:5 LXX).[37] However, the most prevalent use of hope language occurs in instances where hope is placed "in God."[38] For example, the psalmist exclaims "He put a new song into my mouth, a song to our God; many will see and they will fear and they will hope in the Lord (ἐλπιοῦσιν ἐπὶ κύριον)" (Ps 39:4 LXX).[39] Or, "For the way of the Lord is justice; we have hoped in your name (ἠλπίσαμεν ἐπὶ τῷ ὀνόματί σου) and in your memory" (Isa 26:8). Hope is also placed in divine attributes such as mercy, "Behold the eyes of the Lord are upon those who fear him, those who hope in his mercy (τοὺς ἐλπίζοντας ἐπὶ τὸ ἔλεος αὐτοῦ)" (Ps 32:18 LXX). Or, there is hope in divine protection "As you have multiplied your mercy, O God; and the sons of men will hope in the shelter of your wings (ἐν σκέπῃ τῶν πτερύγων σου ἐλπιοῦσιν)" (Ps 35:8 LXX). We

---

36. The afflictions of ancient Israel, as they are described in books such as Psalms and Isaiah, include guilt for sin, disease, hunger, death, captivity, the schemes and violence of various enemies, and the like. Such afflictions often have an underlying concern with God's disposition, either blessing or curse, towards the afflicted.

37. See also Pss LXX 13:6; 21:10; 39:5; 60:4; 64:6; 90:9; 141:6. Cf. Lam 3:18; 1 Tim 1:1; Titus 2:3.

38. In the LXX Psalms, the prepositional phrase is often ἐπὶ τὸν κύριον or ἐπὶ τὸν θεόν.

39. See also Pss LXX 4:6; 5:12; 7:2; 9:11; 15:1; 16:7; 17:3, 31; 20:8; 21:5, 6, 9; 24:20; 25:1; 27:7; 30:2, 7, 15, 20, 25; 31:10; 32:18, 21, 22; 33:9, 23; 36:3, 5, 40; 37:16; 39:4; 41:6, 12; 42:5; 54:24; 55:4, 5, 12; 61:9; 63:11; 68:4; 70:1, 14; 83:13; 85:2; 90:2, 14; 111:7; 113:17, 18, 19; 129:6; 130:3; 140:8; 142:8; 143:2; 144:15.

also find warnings about misplaced hope when hope is directed anywhere besides Israel's God, "For I will not hope in my bow (οὐ ἐπὶ τῷ τόξῳ μου ἐλπιῶ), and my sword will not save me" (Ps 43:7 LXX).[40] Finally, especially in Isaiah, hope is directed towards a messianic figure. For example, the description of the Davidic messiah in Isaiah includes a world-wide hope in him "And there will be a root of Jesse in that day, and he will rise to rule over the nations, the nations will hope in him (ἐπ᾽ αὐτῷ ἔθνη ἐλπιοῦσιν), and his rest will be glorious" (Isa 11:10).[41] As I will discuss later, Paul cites Isa 11:10 in Rom 15:12.

The entire taxonomy of hope in the Psalms and Isaiah is predicated on God's prior promise and work of salvation in ancient Israel. This becomes the catalyst for Israel's expectation of future deliverance by God. Several pre-texts in Isaiah and the Psalms explicitly wed salvation with hope just as Paul does in Rom 8:24–25. As the lamenter in Ps 21 LXX asserts, "Our fathers hoped in you (ἤλπισαν οἱ πατέρες ἡμῶν), they hoped (ἤλπισαν), and you delivered (ἐρρύσω) them; they cried to you and they were saved (ἐσώθησαν), they hoped in you (ἐπὶ σοὶ ἤλπισαν), and they were not disappointed (κατῃσχύνθησαν)" (Ps 21:5–6 LXX).[42] The parallelism between hope (ἐλπίζω) and disappoint (καταισχύνω) characterizes some of the hope language in the LXX, an intertextual feature reflected in the echo of Ps 21 LXX in Rom 5:5 which I discussed in earlier. While deliverance is the outcome of hope, disappointment is the outcome of hope denied if God fails in his promise to deliver. Additionally, hope in a prior promise and work of salvation in ancient Israel is not abstract. Rather, hopes are tethered to covenantal promises which have both a messianic and eschatological thrust, particularly the promises made to Abraham and David.

Hope in God's salvation characterizes righteous figures in the Psalms, "The righteous (δίκαιος) will rejoice in the Lord, and he will hope in him (ἐλπιεῖ ἐπ᾽ αὐτόν), and the upright in heart will be praised" (Ps 63:11 LXX).[43] The tension between the hope of deliverance and the experience of impending death elicits the cries of the righteous, "Keep my life, because I am holy; save (σῶσον) your servant, O my God, the one who hopes in you (τὸν ἐλπίζοντα ἐπὶ σέ)" (Ps 85:2 LXX). Of course, the hope of the righteous is not impervious to weariness and doubt. The psalmist complains, "I am weary (ἐκοπίασα) of crying, my throat has become sore, my eyes gave out from hoping in my God (ἐλπίζειν ἐπὶ τὸν θεόν μου)" (Ps 68:4 LXX).[44] They must endure (ὑπομένω/ὑπομονή) in their hope, "Because of your instruction I waited on you (ὑπέμεινά σε), O Lord, my soul waited (ὑπέμεινεν) for your word. My soul hoped in the Lord (ἤλπισεν

40. Objects of misplaced hope in Israel's Scriptures include the following: (1) hope in one's own strength; (2) hope in someone who betrays you; (3) hope in a foreign nation; and (4) hope in powerless idols. See, e.g., Pss LXX 40:10; 61:11; 117:9; Isa 26:8; 28:15, 17, 18; 29:8; 30:12, 32; 31:2; 47:10.

41. See also Isa 42:4.

42. For other examples of an explicit link between hope and salvation, see, e.g., Pss LXX 16:7; 24:20; 30:2; 36:40; 41:6, 12; 42:5; 85:2; 90:14; Isa 25:9; 51:5.

43. See also Pss LXX 83:13.

44. See also Pss LXX 140:8.

ἡ ψυχή μου ἐπὶ τὸν κύριον) from the watch in the early morning until night; from the watch in the early morning let Israel hope in the Lord (ἐλπισάτω Ισραηλ ἐπὶ τὸν κύριον)" (Ps 129:5–6).

When we bring this language of hope to bear on the interpretation of Rom 8:24–25, Paul's language comes into sharper focus. The surrounding context and larger rhetorical thrust of the letter places his language of hope within the OT taxonomy of hope outlined above. Just as God himself is the hope of ancient Israel in Isaiah and the Psalms, both God the Father and the Lord Jesus Christ are the object of the Romans' hope. They hope in God's promise and work through the crucified and risen Christ. God has revealed his righteousness in Christ; therefore, the Romans, like righteous figures in Isaiah and the Psalms who hope in divine attributes, hope in God's righteousness. Moreover, their hope in God and his revealed righteousness is not misplaced, because Christ, who is their righteousness, has been raised from the dead. Therefore, their hope of sharing in that resurrection, though unseen, is certain. Such certainty is essential given the affliction that the Romans face. This tension between hope and affliction echoes the same tension from the Psalms.[45]

However, as I will discuss further below, Paul reconfigures this tension around God's unique work in Christ and in the gospel. While in the Psalms and in Isaiah hope precedes salvation, Paul sees salvation as preceding hope. He confidently asserts, "we were saved in hope" (τῇ ἐλπίδι ἐσώθημεν) (Rom 8:24a).[46] Through the crucified and risen Christ, God has already delivered the Romans from sin, death, the forces marshalled against them, and even condemnation. Nevertheless, they do not yet experience the full effect of that deliverance, namely a redeemed body. The absence of that experience, coupled with the salvation they have already been promised in the gospel, elicits hope. It is a hope unseen, and one eagerly anticipated (ἀπεκδεχόμεθα) through endurance (δι' ὑπομονῆς) (Rom 8:25).[47] As noted above, hope in the OT is characterized by a need for endurance. One must wait for the deliverance God promised while experiencing so many afflictions that cast doubt upon the truthfulness of that

---

45. As Westerholm puts it, "Again, the psalmists who found such satisfaction in God's 'face' were fully aware of the darker aspects of life: is there anywhere a literature that more profoundly probes the lot of the despised, the slandered, the despondent, those ravaged by disease or war? God's ways are often disturbingly mysterious even for the psalmists. They feel that at times he has 'hidden' his 'face', and they cannot understand why. Nonetheless, what prevails in the ned is the unshakable in their bones, whatever the fate of their flesh, that underlying all is goodness, beyond human understanding but deserving of human trust: a goodness not only worth clinging to when all else fails, but more precious by far than anything else one might desire." Westerholm goes on to add that it is this framework from the Psalms, which I have described as a tension between hope and suffering, that Paul uses to interpret "the significance of Jesus" as it relates to righteousness in Romans. See Westerholm, *Understanding Paul*, 36.

46. To be sure, as I noted in the taxonomy of hope, ancient Israelites hoped in future salvation based on God's prior saving work. The Exodus functions as the nation's seminal soteriological moment. Even more, future generations of Israelites "participated" in that moment through Passover and other didactic means.

47. The LXX does not contain any uses of the verb ἀπεκδέχομαι.

promise. The Romans find themselves in a similar experience. Simply put, holding onto hope hurts; therefore, creation, the children of God, and even the Spirit lament.

Romans 8:26–27

(8:26–27) And likewise the Spirit helps in our weakness; for we do not know what to pray as is proper, but the same Spirit intercedes with inexpressible groanings; and the one who searches hearts knows what the way of the thinking of the Spirit is, because he intercedes for the saints according to God.

In Rom 8:26–27, we find that Paul includes the Holy Spirit in this tension between hope and lament.[48] Paul links these two verses to the laments uttered by creation (ἡ κτίσις συστενάζει) and the children (στενάζομεν) through one more use of the στενα–root, "the Spirit intercedes/pleads with inexpressible groanings (ὑπερεντυγχάνει στεναγμοῖς ἀλαλήτοις)" (Rom 8:26).[49] The Spirit participates in the laments by creation and the children of God to help in the weakness (τῇ ἀσθενίᾳ) of the latter.[50] The weakness in question is that the Romans do not know how to pray as they experience the tension between hope and suffering. The Spirit helps by interceding, or lamenting, for them in a way that corresponds with the divine will. These two verses have generated lively debates through the years, but my primary focus is the passage's intertextual subtext.[51] Two pretexts informs Paul's thought here.

Suggested Pre-texts in Romans 8:26–27

Hübner lists the following pre-texts: 1 Sam 16:7; 1 Kgs 8:39; Psalms LXX 16:3; 43:22; 138:1–5; Jer 12:3; 17:10 (Rom 8:27).[52] Nestle-Aland 28th ed. does not list any pre-texts for these two verses.

---

48. Fitzmyer describes these two verses as the "climax" of "Paul's discussion of the role of the Spirit in the Christian life." Fitzmyer, *Romans*, 517.

49. The verb ὑπερεντυγχάνω in this context bears the sense of interceding for someone by pleading for them. See BDAG 1033; Brill 706.

50. The adverb ὡσαύτως at the beginning of Rom 8:26 signals a similarity with what precedes. Specifically, just as creation and the children groan/lament in the tension between affliction and hope, the Spirit does as well. This is not to suggest that the Spirit is weak. Rather, the Spirit helps the children of God to pray/lament in accordance with God's will. For a lengthy discussion of ὡσαύτως in Rom 8:26, see Vollmer, *The Spirit Helps our Weakness*, 152–69.

51. For a helpful overview of how interpreters have addressed the exegetical difficulties related to Rom 8:26–27, see Vollmer, *The Spirit Helps our Weakness*, 9–40.

52. Hübner, *Vetus Testamentum in Novo*, 2:124–29.

Intertextual Analysis of Romans 8:26–27

The pre-texts evoked in these two verses stem from Israel's wilderness wanderings and God's ability to search the hearts of his people These are echoes often underappreciated by interpreters.

Romans 8:26–27 and Echoes of the Wilderness Generation

Paul's language echoes the OT motif of God's participation in the suffering of his people, particularly in the Exodus and wilderness wanderings. In the case of the former, God answers Israel's cries for deliverance by sending Moses. Through Moses, God delivers his people by judging their enemies. As I have noted at several points already, and as Westermann notes, lament frames the entire narrative of Exod 1–15.[53] God's actions in the narrative commence as a response to Israel's suffering and lament based on the "remembrance" of his prior promise, "And God heard their groaning (τὸν στεναγμὸν αὐτῶν), and God remembered his covenant with Abraham and Isaac and Jacob" (Exod 2:24).[54] Once God delivers Israel through the Red Sea by drowning the Egyptian army, the people praise God (Exod 15:1–21). In this way, the entire narrative of Exod 1–15 shifts from lament to praise. Between those two poles, God saves Israel by judging the Egyptians through Moses. Of course, immediately after the deliverance, there is a shift to grumbling and weakness as indicated in what transpires at Marah.[55] This episode portends subsequent moments in Israel's wilderness warnings.

One subsequent moment of interest for our purposes is Israel's faithless and ungrateful request for meat as it is described in Num 11. This request drives Moses to lament:

> Why have you mistreated your servant, and why have I not found favor before you so as to place the rage of this people upon me? I did not conceive all these people in the womb, or did I bear bear them, that you say to me "Take him into your bosom, like a nurse lifts up the one who nurses, into the land, which you swore to their fathers?" From where is there meat for me to give to this people? For they cry out against me saying, "Give meat to us, in order that we might eat." I alone will not be able to bear this, because this matter is too burdeonsome for me. But if you do in this way to me, indeed kill me if I have found mercy with you, in order that I might not see my affliction (Num 11:11–15).

Faced with answering an impossible request, Moses has no recourse except to lament. God answers Moses' lament by promising to help through the spirit, "And I will go down and I will speak there with you and I will take from the spirit (πνεύματος)

---

53. See Westermann, "The Role of Lament in the Theology of the Old Testament," 20–38.
54. See also the use of καταστενάζω/στεναγμός in Exod 2:23; 6:5.
55. See Exod 15:23–27.

which is upon you and I will place it upon them and they will help with you (συναντιλήμψονταί) the burden of the people, and you will not bear them alone" (Num 11:17).

Here we need to pause and test this echo in Rom 8:26–27. The *volume* of the echo from Num 11:17 is high based on the rarely used verb συναντιλαμβάνομαι.[56] The *contextual consistency* between the pre-text and text is also high. Even after deliverance, Moses is weak; therefore, he cries out for help. God helps by giving the spirit which rests upon Moses to others in Israel so that they can bear the burden of leadership together. Similarly, though not without recontextualization, the Romans are weakened by the tension between hope and suffering so that they do not know what to pray. God responds to their lament, as he responded to Moses, through the work of the Spirit. However, for Paul, the Spirit helps by sharing in the Romans' lament, though in knowledge and according to the divine will. As Paul describes it, "And he who searches hearts knows what the thinking of the Spirit is, because he intercedes for the saints according to the will of God" (Rom 8:27). Based on the interplay between the intertextual subtext and immediate argument, the content of the Spirit's intercession involves helping the Romans navigate life between hope and suffering until they receive what they ultimately hope for, redemption of the body. We will return to this interplay below. Here it is sufficient to note that the Spirit's lament indicates that the Spirit not only intercedes *for* the Romans but also *with* them. He is not a neutral agent who intercedes at a safe distance. Instead, the Spirit leads them from within and testifies to them that they are children of God from within which results in the cry "Abba, Father."[57] Simply put, a Spirit who laments for the Romans is a Spirit who suffers with them.[58]

In considering the wider Exodus and wilderness wandering motif echoed in Rom 8:26–27, the *contextual consistency* between pre-text and text indicates that Paul likens the Romans to sojourners who, though having been delivered through the crucified and risen Christ, are weak and in desperate need of help. Therefore, like the Israelites in Egypt and Moses in the wilderness, they cry out for help. That helps comes in the form of the Spirit who indwells the Romans and intercedes for them.

With respect to *recurrence* in Romans and the Pauline corpus, it is not uncommon for Paul to liken the experiences of believers to ancient Israel. We have already seen his use of Exodus motifs in Rom 6, and, in 1 Cor 10:1–13, Paul explicitly likens the Corinthians to the wilderness generation in his effort to warn them against idolatry and fornication. Additionally, the *history of interpretation* includes a few interpreters who have noted this echo. For example, Sylvia Keesmaat argues that Rom 8:18–27

---

56. In the LXX and GNT combined, there are five uses of συναντιλαμβάνομαι: Exod 18:22; Num 11:17; Ps LXX 88:22; Luke 10:40; Rom 8:26.

57. Cf. discussion on the Spirit in the analysis for Rom 8:12–17.

58. See Michel, *Brief an die Römer*, 273.

evokes the Exodus tradition wherein God suffers with his people.⁵⁹ She appeals to pre-texts such as Exod 2:23-25, Jer 3:19-20, 38:20 (31:20 MT), and Hos 11:8, 10-11. Her analysis of Rom 8:26-27 focues on Paul's contextual use of ἀσθένια which she translates as "suffering."⁶⁰ According to Keesmaat, through the Spirit, God shares in the suffering of the Romans in the same way that he shared in the "oppression of the Israelites in Egypt."⁶¹

Romans 8:26-27 and Echoes of the God Who Searches Hearts

Another echo stems from Paul's description of God as one "who searches the hearts" (ὁ ἐραυνῶν τὰς καρδίας) (Rom 8:26). Israel's Scriptures describe God in a similar way. One of the most-well known examples involves Samuel's inspection of Jesse's sons. As Samuel examines the sons in search of Israel's next king, he is struck by the outward appearance of Eliab thinking to himself, "Surely the Lord's anointed is before him" (1 Sam 16:6). However, God corrects Samuel's assessment "And the Lord said to Samuel, 'Do not look upon his appearance nor the outward appearance of his stature, because I have considered him of not account; because God does not see as man sees, because man looks at the outward appearance, but God looks at the heart (ὁ θεὸς ὄψεται εἰς καρδίαν)'" (1 Sam 16:7).⁶² Similarly, when the psalmist insists upon Israel's innocence before God, he grounds his claim in God's perception of the heart "Will God not seek these things? For he knows the secret things of the heart (αὐτὸς γινώσκει τὰ κρύφια τῆς καρδίας)" (Ps 43:22 LXX).⁶³ Overall, this OT description underscores God's ability to assess a person's inward intentions, motivations, needs, affections, and plans, an ability which human beings simply do not possess.⁶⁴

Paul recontextualizes this divine description to explain the relationship between the weakness of the Romans, God's ability to assess hearts, and the Spirit's intercession

---

59. See Keesmaat, *Paul and His Story*, 116-34.

60. For her reading of the Exodus tradition at this point, Keesmaat relies heavily on the work of Terrence Freitheim. Keesmaat, *Paul and His Story*, 117-18. He suggests that in the OT God suffers because of, with, and for the people. See Freitheim, *The Suffering of God*.

61. Keesmaat explains, "Paul clearly indicates that the Spirit who is leading the people of God through this wilderness of trial is a Spirit who participates with believers in this suffering walk. So we discover that underlying the various narratives of suffering, of groaning and bondage and liberation, lies the narrative of God, the God who felt the oppression of the Israelites in Egypt and liberated them, who grieved and mourned their disobedience and unfaithfulness throughout the prophetic literature, who continues to groan with her creation and people." Keesmaat, *Paul and His Story*, 27.

62. Cf. 1 Kgs 8:39.

63. Cf. Ps LXX 16:3; 138:1-5; Jer 12:3; 17:10.

64. With respect to the *volume* of this motif in Rom 8:27, it is moderate. Paul employs the verb ἐραυνάω which does not occur in the LXX. Cf. the use of ἐραυνάω in 1 Cor 2:10 where the πνεῦμα is the subject of the verb. Nevertheless, Paul's verbage is in the same semantic domain as the terms employed in OT passages which describe God as knowing/examining human hearts. See Fitzmyer, *Romans*, 519.

on behalf of the Romans. The Romans are weak in many ways including not knowing how to pray.[65] The Spirit brings the prayers of lament from the Romans before God in a way that both corresponds with the laments of these saints (ὑπὲρ ἁγίων) and with the divine will. Like the description of God searching hearts in the OT, God searches the hearts of the Roman saints and hears their eschatologically-laden requests in the laments of the Spirit. From an intertextual perspective, if God searches the hearts of the saints in Rome, as he did the Israelites in the OT, it follows that he assesses their inward intentions, motivataions, needs, affections, and plans. It is here that the Romans prove to be weak, because they lack understanding of what transpires in their hearts. Therefore, the Spirit must help. God, who searches the weak hearts of the Romans, knows the Spirit's mindset (οἶδεν τί τὸ φρόνημα τοῦ πνεύματος).[66] He "knows" (οἶδα) in the sense that he shares the Spirit's insight regarding the needs of the saints, because the Spirit's intercessory prayers (ἐντυγχάνω) for the saints corresponds to God's will (κατὰ θεόν).[67]

Interpretive Impact of Pre-Texts in Romans 8:18–27

Romans 8:18–27 explain Paul's statement in 8:17 that the Romans must suffer with Christ (συμπάσχομεν) if they are to be glorified with him (συνδοξασθῶμεν). The explanation focuses upon the tension that the Romans experience between their suffering with Christ and their hope of resurrection glory. Creation, the children of God, and the Holy Spirit experience this tension together. Paul binds their experiences through their shared prayers of lament via his use of the στενα-root in Rom 8:22, 23, and 27. In this chorus of lament, Paul's language is often shaped by a variety of OT pre-texts and motifs. The interplay betwewen these pre-texts and Paul's text generate several unstated points that shed light on Paul's explanation of the tension between suffering with Christ and the hope of sharing in his glorious resurrection.

First, creation cries out for deliverance from their slavery to futility, a judgment which God doled out in the aftermath of Adam's transgression and a judgment which continued in Paul's day. In Rom 8:19–22, Paul uses Qohelet's description of creation's futility (Eccl 1:2–7) to describe God's judgment against creation in Gen 3:17–19. God enslaved creation to futility in the sense that, though creation churned on, as Qohelet vividly describes, it did so in a meaningless way given the fact that creation far outlived Adam's descendants. Therefore, creation laments (ἡ κτίσις συστενάζει). The κτίσις cries out for deliverance in the vein of creation's laments in the prophets, particularly Isaiah and Jeremiah. These prophets personify creation as "groaning" which Paul then weaves into his description of creation. It also under the influence of these prophets that Paul personifies creation as a pregnant woman squezzed by the pain of

---

65. Based on Rom 7:7—8:17, there weaknesses also include indwelling sin and death in the body.
66. Cf. the use of φρόνημα in Rom 8:6, 7.
67. BDAG 693.

judgment and the hope which lies beyond it. For Paul, the answer to creation's lament lies in the way God answers the laments uttered by God's children and the Holy Spirit.

Second, the interplay between Rom 8:23–25 and its pre-texts produce thick points of resonance. When the expression "first fruits of the Spirit" (τὴν ἀπαρχὴν τοῦ πνεύματος) is read against the intertextual backdrop of pre-texts such as Deut 26:5–10, the expression indicates that the Romans hope for a greater eschatological harvest wherein the Spirit will redeem their bodies. Much like the "first fruits" in Deut 26, the first fruits of the Spirit are tied to the prior and future soteriological work of God. As Paul explains in v. 24, the Romans "were saved in hope" (τῇ ἐλπίδι ἐσώθημεν), but they also hope for what they do not yet see which is the redemption of their bodies. One unique feature in Paul's use of the phrase is that God gives the first fruits to the Romans whereas in Israel's Scriptures the people bring the first fruits to God. This reversal underscores the thoroughly gracious nature of the Romans' experience in Christ.

The tension between the hope of a redeemed body and suffering in an unredeemed body elicits a lament wherein the Romans eagerly await the full experience of their divine adoption. These laments resemble OT lamenters whose cries also stemmed from the clash between hope and suffering. However, the Romans' laments are unique, because they already possess what they hope for through the Spirit in the risen Christ. Nevertheless, like OT lamenters, the presence of Christ's Spirit within them notwithstanding, the Romans' hope relies upon a prior promise which they must cling to regardless of the affliction they are forced to endure.

This brings us to the way Paul's language of hope is informed by our OT taxonomy of hope as it is reflected in the Psalms and Isaiah.[68] While figures in the Psalms and Isaiah hope in God, the Romans hope in God and the Lord Jesus Christ. Moreover, just as their OT predecessors hoped in certain attributes of God, Paul and the Romans hope in God's righteousness as it is revealed in the gospel.[69] In this context, hope in righteousness highlights hope for a redeemed body. Despite the afflictions the Romans face, they do not have the kind of misplaced hope which the Psalms and Isaiah warn about. Hope for a redeemed body through the work of the Spirit in Christ will not disappoint.[70]

Finally, based on the intertextual features in Rom 8:26–27, the Holy Spirit suffers with the Christians in Rome as God suffered with the ancient Israelites in Egypt and in the wilderness. Paul escalates this motif in multiple ways. For example, the Spirit shares in the laments of the Romans rather than merely answering the laments as God did in Egypt and in the wilderness (Exod 2:23–25). Moreover, the Spirit does not merely rest on the leadership in Rome, as it did in the wilderness (Num 11:11–17),

---

68. Once again, the OT taxonomy is as follows: (1) God as hope; (2) hope in God/the divine name; (3) hope in divine attributes; (4) misplaced hope; and (5) messianic hope.

69. Rom 1:16–17; 3:21–22.

70. Rom 5:5; 9:33; 10:11.

but upon all the Romans. The Spirit's presence and work helps in the Romans' weakness, particularly their inability to know how they ought to pray. Paul briefly describes the dynamics of this divine help in accordance with Israel's Scriptures. God searches the hearts of the Romans which, based on intertextual echoes, means he knows their affections, needs, plans, and the like. However, Paul tethers this description of God to his knowledge of the Spirit's mindset. There is perfect symmetry between what God knows about the Romans, how the Spirit thinks, and how the Spirit laments with and for the Romans.

10

Romans 8:28–30

WHILE PAUL AND THE Romans do not know how to pray as they navigate the tension between hope and suffering, they do know (οἴδαμεν, Rom 8:28) that God is working for their good based on his robust work in Christ. In his foreknowledge, God predestined the Romans to be conformed to the image of his son, called them to salvation, justified them, sanctified them, and glorified them. Such divine work is the basis for hope and confidence in the face of great affliction which Paul proceeds to discuss in Rom 8:31–39. It is also work informed by Israel's Scriptures. The theological depth of these three verses and their treatment in Christian history sometimes overshadows their intertextual subtext. Therefore, the primary focus here is on this intertextual subtext.

Romans 8:28–30

(8:28–30) But we know that all things work together for good for those who love God, to those who are called according to his purpose. Because those whom he foreknew, he also predestined to be conformed to the image of his son, in order for him to be the firstborn among many brethren; and those whom he predestined, these he also called; and those whom he called, these he also justified; and those whom he justified, these he also glorified.

Contextually, these three verses contribute significantly to Paul's basis for hope in the face of suffering.[1] The interpreter must not lose sight of the tension between suffering and hope even though Paul crafts some of the most theologically robust statements

---

1. As Murray notes, "This is the ground of encouragement for the support of the children of God in the sufferings they are called upon to endure in this life." Murray, *Romans*, 313. Similarly, Jewett observes "Paul initiates the climactic celebration of the the thesis concerning the hopeful suffering of the children of God by reviewing what 'we know' as persons who 'love God.'" Jewett, *Romans*, 527.

in his letters.² Intertextually, it is historically implausible that Israel's Scriptures fail to shape such a theologically robust statement by Paul.

Suggested Pre-Texts in Romans 8:28–30

Hübner lists the following pre-texts: Exod 20:6; Deut 5:10; 6:5; 7:9 (Rom 8:28); Gen 1:26–27; Jer 1:5 (Rom 8:29); and Ps LXX 90:15–15 (Rom 8:30).³ Nestle-Aland 28th ed. does not list any pre-texts.

Hays briefly mentions an echo in Rom 8:29. He explains that the Christian's "trust," πίστις, is "prefigured in the Old Testament story of Abraham" and "becomes shaped by the patterns of Jesus' own faith-obedience. Hays suggests this is "part of what Paul means when he says that those whom God calls are to be 'conformed to the image of his Son'" in 8:29.⁴ Once again, Seifrid primarily focuses on the OT echoes in Rom 8:31–39.⁵

Intertextual Analysis of Romans 8:28–30

Paul's language in these three verses evokes a variety of OT pre-texts. Not surprisingly, given the substance of the argument at this point, many of the pre-texts describe God's soteriological work which Paul reconfigures around Christ.

Romans 8:28 and Echoes of Loving God

Romans 8:28 contains three intertextual echoes. Before analyzing these echoes, we must address one exegetical difficulty involving the case of πάντα. The substantival adjective is either accustative, resulting in the translation "God works all things (πάντα) for good," or nominative, resulting in the translation "all things (πάντα) work for good." While there are some important syntactical and text critical considerations here, I largely agree with Mounce's conclusion on the matter.⁶ He observes, "Since 'things' are incapable of independent action, the two translations actually come to the same conclusion. In both cases it would be God who is at work in the circumstances

---

2. As Calvin notes in his analysis of Rom 8:28, "But we must remember that Paul speaks here only of adversities, as though he had said, 'All things which happen to the saints are so overruled by God, that what the world regards as evil, the issue shows to be good.' For though what Augustine says is true, that even the sins of the saints are, through the guiding providence of God, so far from doing harm to them, that, on the contrary, they serve to advance their salvation; yet this belongs not to this passage, the subject of which is the cross." Calvin, *Romans*, 315.

3. Hübner, *Vetus Testamentum in Novo*, 2:130–36.

4. Hays, *The Conversion of the Imagination*, 195.

5. Seifrid, *Romans*, 633–37.

6. For a discussion of the syntax and textual variants related to Rom 8:28, see Jewett, *Romans*, 505–6, 526–28; Longenecker, *Romans*, 714, 736–39.

of life. God directs the affairs of life in such a way that, for those who love him, the outcome is always beneficial."[7]

Regarding intertextual echoes in 8:28, we begin with the phrase "to those who love God" (τοῖς ἀγαπῶσιν τὸν θεόν). A very similar expression occurs in the LXX.[8] A few examples stand out in the Pentateuch:

> You shall not worship them nor serve them; for I am the Lord your God, a jealous God repaying the sins of the fathers upon the children unto the third and fourth generations to those who hate me and doing mercy to thousands who love me (τοῖς ἀγαπῶσιν με) and keep my commandments (Exod 20:6).[9]

> And you will know that the Lord your God, he is God, a faithful God, who keeps the covenant and mercy to those who love him (τοῖς ἀγαπῶισν αὐτόν) and to those who keep his commandments unto a thousand generations (Deut 7:9).

In both instances, loving God is parallel to obeying his commands. God is merciful and faithful to those who love him and keeps his commands. The Israelite's inward affection for God, or love, was outwardly manifested in the way they obeyed the Mosaic Law. God promised to show mercy and faithfulness to those who loved and obeyed in this way.

We find a similar use of the expression τοῖς ἀγαπῶσιν με/αὐτον in a few other instances. Nehemiah's prayer contains the expression paralleled with obedience, "May it not be, O Lord God of heaven the mighty, great, and fearful one, keeping the covenant and mercy to those who love him (τοῖς ἀγαπῶσιν αὐτόν) and to those who keep his commandments" (Neh 1:5). The psalmist's prayer also includes the expression, "Request now the things for the peace of Jerusalem, and prosperity for those who love you (τοῖς ἀγαπῶσίν σε)" (Ps 121:6 LXX). In Proverbs, when personified wisdom speaks as a lady, she promises "I walk in the ways of righteousness, and I am conversant with the paths of judgment; in order that I might divide the substance to those who love me (τοῖς ἐμὲ ἀγαπῶσιν), and I might fill up their treasures with good things" (Prov 8:20–21).[10] Overall, each use of the expression shares two common traits: (1) loving God is parallel to obeying him; and (2) God promises mercy and faithfulness to those who love him in this way.

These common traits related to the expression τοῖς ἀγαπῶσίν με map on nicely to the larger theology of Israel's love for God in the OT. For example, the command to love lies at the heart of the Shema, "And you shall love the Lord your God (ἀγαπήσεις κύριον τὸν θεόν σου) with all your heart and with all your soul and with all your

---

7. Mounce, *Romans*, 187.

8. The participle τοῖς ἀγαπῶσιν is the translation of לאהבי in Exod 20:6; Deut 5:10. See also לאהביו in Deut 7:9; Neh 1:5.

9. Deut 5:10 contains the exact same wording including the phrase τοῖς ἀγαπῶσιν με.

10. Cf. Sir 1:10; Pss Sol 4:25; 6:6; 10:3 14:1.

power" (Deut 6:5).[11] Love of this nature results in divine blessing.[12] As the psalmist exhorts, "Love the Lord (ἀγαπήσατε τὸν κύριον), all his holy ones, because the Lord seeks truth and he pays back in excess those who do arrogance" (Ps 30:24 LXX). Israel's love for God was not predicated on a command alone. The nation loved God based on who he was and what he did for them. They loved his guidance, salvation, protection, and presence.[13] Their love for his person and his work is crystallized in their love for his name, "Look on me and have mercy on me according to the judgment of those who love your name (τῶν ἀγαπώντων τὸ ὄνομά σου)" (Ps 118:132 LXX).

Even more, Israel's love is predicated upon the fact that God loved them first. God's election of Israel signals the primacy of his love, "Behold the heaven and the heaven of heaven belongs to the Lord your God, the earth and everything, as much as is in it; yet, the Lord chose (προείλατο) your fathers to love them (ἀγαπᾶν αὐτούς) and he chose (ἐξελέξατο) their seed after them, you, beyond all nations according to this day" (Deut 12:14–15). This divine love and election prompted their deliverance from Egypt, "Because he loved your fathers (τὸ ἀγαπῆσαι αὐτὸν τοὺς πατέρας σου) and chose their seed (ἐξελέξατο τὸ σπέρμα αὐτῶν) after them, you, and brought you out of Egypt by his great strength" (Deut 4:37).

When we turn our attention back to the phrase "to those who love God" (τοῖς ἀγαπῶσιν τὸν θεόν) in Rom 8:28, these suggested pre-texts pass several intertextual tests. The *volume* of the OT expression "to to those who love me/him" (τοῖς ἀγαπῶσιν με/αὐτόν) is high based on semantic and syntactical overlap. The pre-texts and text also share *contextual consistency* at multiple points. Just as Israel's love for God was preceded by God's love for them in Israel's Scriptures, the same holds true for the Romans. Paul explicitly says as much earlier in the letter, "But God demonstrates his own love (τὴν ἑαυτοῦ ἀγάπην) for us, because while we we still sinners Christ died for us" (Rom 5:5).[14] Even more, as the immediate context indicates, God's election of the Romans signals the primacy of his love in the same manner as his election of Israel in the OT signaled the primacy of his love. Just as Israel loves God because of who he is and what he does, the same holds true for the Romans as indicated by the robust list of divine actions in Rom 8:29–30. Consistency can also be found in the way that obedience to God's commands runs parallel with the people's love for him. Of course, as always, Paul recontextualizes this OT theology of love for God around the person and work of Christ. Moreover, he recontextualizes love for God in relation to the gift and presence of the Spirit. We will return to this recontextualization below.

---

11. Cf. Deut 11:1.

12. See Deut 6:5–14; 7:12–14.

13. See, e.g., Pss LXX 5:12; 17:2–3; 39:17; 68:37; 69:5; 96:10; 118:47, 48, 97, 113, 119, 127, 140, 159, 165, 167; 144:20.

14. Cf. the use of ἀγάπη/ἀγαπάω in Rom 5:8; 8:35, 37, 39; 9:13, 25; 12:9; 13:8, 9, 10; 14:15; 15:30.

Some interpreters have recognized the intertextual qualities of τοῖς ἀγαπῶσιν τὸν θεόν in Rom 8:28. As Fitzmyer simply puts it, "To 'love God' is an OT idea."[15] In his analysis of τοῖς ἀγαπῶσιν τὸν θεόν, Cranfield notes "By being placed at the beginning of the clause these words have been given special emphasis. They have a rich OT and Jewish background. The love to God, which is commanded in Scripture, is nothing less than the response of a man in the totality of his being to the prior love of God. It thus includes the whole of true religion."[16]

Romans 8:28 and Echoes of God's Sovereign Work in Afflictions

A second echo in Rom 8:28 stems from the shared knowledge (οἴδαμεν) that God works all things together for good (πάντα συνεργεῖ εἰς ἀγαθόν).[17] This assertion bears a strong resemblance to what Joseph says to his brothers in the aftermath of Jacob's death, "You took counsel against me for evil, but God took counsel for me for good לטבה/εἰς ἀγαθά), in order that it might be as it is today, in order that a great people might be fed" (Gen 50:20). The *volume* is moderate based on the similarity between εἰς ἀγαθά and εἰς ἀγαθόν.[18] *Contextual consistency* is indicated in a few different ways. The larger Joseph narrative chronicles his afflictions which included being thrown into a pit, slavery, the false accusation of an attempted rape, and imprisonment. In retrospect, Joseph recognizes that his brothers intended evil (ἐβουλεύσασθε κατ᾽ἐμοῦ εἰς πονηρά) against him. However, at the same time, he also recognizes that God intended his afflictions for good (ὁ θεὸς ἐβουλεύσατο) (Gen 50:20). What God intended with Joseph's affliction resulted in good for Joseph and his brothers. The theological perspective reflected in Gen 50:20 underscores God's sovereign wisdom and power by which he accomplishes his purposes for Abraham's descendants.

Similarly, Paul's statement in Rom 8:28, given its larger context, underscores God's sovereign wisdom and power by which he works all things together (συνεργεῖ), especially afflictions, for the good of those who love him. The use of συνεργέω in Rom 8:28 indicates that God uses the Romans' various afflictions, which he will enumerate

---

15. Fitzmyer, *Romans*, 522.

16. Cranfield, *Romans*, 1:424–25. Similarly, Jewett notes "The language of this verse reflects Paul's adaptation of traditional Jewish teaching." Jewett, *Romans*, 526. See also Dunn, *Romans*, 1:480–81; Wolter, *Der Brief an die Römer*, 1:528–29.

17. Once again, regardless of how one renders πάντα συνεργεῖ εἰς ἀγαθόν, Paul knows God ultimately does the work.

18. Rom 8:28 contains the only use of the phrase εἰς ἀγαθόν in the GNT. In the LXX, εἰς ἀγαθόν occurs in 2 Chr 10:7; Ezr 8:22; Neh 2:18; 5:19; Pss LXX 85:17; 118:122; Jer 39:39 (32:39). See also Jdt 4:15; Sir 7:13. The phrase εἰς ἀγαθά never occurs in the GNT. In the LXX, besides Gen 50:20, it occurs in Deut 28:11; 30:9; 2 Chr 18:7; Amos 9:4; Mic 1:12; Jer 14:11; 15:11; 21:10; 24:5, 6; 46:16 (39:16). Fitzmyer notes that "for the good" is a "traditional Jewish expression." Fitzmyer, *Romans*, 522. See, e.g., Sir 39:25, 27. However, even as a "traditional Jewish expression," εἰς ἀγαθόν would be informed by Israel's Scriptures.

in 8:31–39, to assist them for good as he accomplishes his purpose.[19] For Paul, God's ultimate good and purpose for the Romans centers on being conformed to the image of his crucified and risen son. Within the *history of interpretation*, many interpreters do not note the similarities between Gen 50:20 in Rom 8:28. While some interpreters briefly note this OT parallel, it does not greatly impact their interpretation of the verse.[20]

Romans 8:28 and Echoes of the Divine Call

The final intertextual consideration in Rom 8:28 invovles the phrase "to those who are called according to his purpose" (τοῖς κατὰ πρόθεσιν κλητοῖς αὐτοῦ). Romans contains multiple uses of κλητός/καλέω which are informed by similar language from Israel's Scriptures.[21] In Paul's uses of this language, when God is the subject of the action, κλητός/καλέω refer to "God's effective summons by which people are brought into relationship with himself."[22] Israel's Scriptures describe God's call as effective in a few different senses.[23] For example, God "calls" to direct the cosmos "The God of gods, the Lord, has spoken and called (ἐκάλεσεν) the earth from the rising of the sun unto its going down" (Ps 49:1 LXX).[24] He can "call" disaster on earth as he did in the days of Joseph when he brought a famine upon the land, "And he called (ἐκάλεσεν) a famine upon the earth, all the support of bread was broken" (Ps 104:16 LXX).[25]

Of course, given Paul's use of κλητός as a reference to believers such as those in Rome, consideration needs to be given to instances where God effectively calls people. We find such instances in Isa 40–66:

> But you, Israel, my servant Jacob, whom I chose, the seed of Abraham, whom I loved, whom I helped from the ends of the earth and from its hilltops I called you (ἐκάλεσά σε) and I said to you, "You are my servant, I chose you and I did not abandon you" (Isa 41:8–9).

> I the Lord God have called you (ἐκάλεσά σε) in righteousness and I will seize your hand and I will strengthen youn and I have given you for the covenant of a people, for a light of the nations (Isa 42:6).

---

19. BDAG 969.
20. See, e.g., Cranfield, *Romans*, 1:429n1; Dunn, *Romans*, 1:481.
21. See the use of κλητός/καλέω in Rom 1:1, 6, 7; 4:17; 8:30; 9:7, 12, 24, 25, 26.
22. Moo, *Romans*, 530n126.
23. The adjective κλητός occurs eighteen times in the LXX. All uses bear the sense of either an appointed festival day or an invited guest. See, e.g., Lev 23:2–4; 2 Sam 15:11.
24. Cf. Isa 40:26.
25. Cf. Isa 22:12; 46:11; Ezek 36:29; 38:21; Amos 7:4.

As these examples indicate, the "call" language in Isa 40–66 is parallel with God's election and deliverance of Israel.[26] Such an effective call defines the nation from its inception, "Look at Abraham your father and Sarah who bore you; for he was one, and I called him (ἐκάλεσα αὐτόν) and I blessed him and I loved him and I multiplied him" (Isa 51:2). Isaiah described himself as someone God "called" to be a prophet before his birth, "He called my name (ἐκάλεσεν τὸ ὄνομά μου) from the womb of my mother" (Isa 49:1).

This use of "call" language in Israel's Scriptures informs Paul's description of the Romans as "those who are called according to his purpose." Like the description of God's call in the Psalms and Isaiah, God's effective call of the Romans parallels their election and deliverance which Paul describes in Rom 8:29–30, albeit in abbreviated fashion. God effectively calls them "according to his purpose." The referent of "purpose" (κατὰ πρόθεσιν) in 8:28 is the conforming of the Romans into the image of the crucified and risen Christ which makes him the "firstborn" among many brethren (Rom 8:29).

Romans 8:29–30 and Echoes of Divine Foreknowledge

In Romans 8:29–30, Paul explains the "foundational reason" for why all things work for the good of those who love God, and he briefly lays out the ultimate purpose for this work.[27] Each phrase is theologically robust and, at least for the sake of historical accuracy, needs to be understood more by Israel's Scriptures than later theological inferences.[28]

First, the clause "those whom he foreknew" (οὓς προέγνω), he also predestined (προώρισεν)" raises questions about Paul's understanding of divine foreknowledge and predestination, divine actions which are undoubtedly informed by the OT. As Jewett notes, "Paul assumes that the biblical themes of divine foreknowledge and election were familiar to the congregations in Rome."[29] The terms προγινώσκω/πρόγνωσις and προορίζω do not occur in the canonical LXX.[30] However, it does not follow that Israel's Scriptures are devoid of references to this divine activity. For example, when

---

26. See also Isa 43:1; 45:4; 48:12, 15; 49:1; 54:6. It should also be noted that in some instances Israel rejects God's call. See, e.g., Isa 65:12; 66:4.

27. Schreiner, *Romans*, 451. As Sanday and Headlam put it, Rom 8:29–30 is "the proof how 'God worketh all things for good to those who love Him.'" Sanday and Headlam, *Romans*, 216.

28. As Keener notes, "When modern readers encounter terms like 'choose' and 'predestine' (Rom 8:29–30) we tend to read them in light of later theological debates, such as the Greek fathers' defense of free will against fatalism, Augustine's defense of God's sovereign grace against Pelagius, or the debates of the Reformation era. Paul's own audience would think of Israel as the people God had chosen, and recognize that Paul's argument was designed to show that God was so sovereign that he was not bound to choose (with regard to salvation) based on Jewish ethnicity." Keener, *Romans*, 109–10.

29. Jewett, *Romans*, 528.

30. See the use of προγινώσκω in Wis 6:13; 8:8; 18:6 and the use of πρόγνωσις in Jdt 9:6; 11:19.

God reveals to Abraham his intent to destroy Sodom, he says of the patriarch and his descendants "For I know (ᾔδειν) that he will command his sons and his house after him, and they will keep the ways of the Lord to do righteousness and justice; in order that the Lord might bring upon Abraham all things, which he spoke to him" (Gen 18:19). Additionally, the psalmist observes:

> O Lord, you have examined me and you have known me (ἔγνως); you have known (ἔγνως) my sitting down and my rising, you have understood (συνῆκας) my thoughts from afar; you have traced out my path and my course and you have seen beforehand all (προεῖδες) all my ways. For there is not a word in my tongue, behold, O Lord, you have known all things (ἔγνως), the last things and the beginning things; you formed me and you placed your hand on me. Your knowledge (ἡ γνῶσις) is too wonderful for me; it is too strong, I am certainly not capable with respect to it (Ps 138:1–6 LXX).

The psalmist clearly portrays Israel's God as knowing, or seeing (προοράω, Ps 138:3 LXX), him beforehand.[31]

A pre-text that garners a great deal of attention in relation to Paul's understanding of divine foreknowledge and election in Rom 8:29 is Jer 1:4–5, "And the word of the Lord came to me saying, 'Before I formed you in the womb I knew you (ἐπίσταμαί σε) and before you came out from your mother's womb I sanctified you (ἡγίακά σε), I had set you (τέθεικά σε) as a prophet for the nations.'"[32] Although Jer 1:5 does not employ Paul's terminology (προγινώσκω/προορίζω), terminology never employed in the canonical LXX, it clearly links divine foreknowledge to divine election. God "knew" (ידע/ἐπίσταμαι) Jeremiah long before the prophet knew him, even prior to his conception and birth. The context does not stress that God knew beforehand whether Jeremiah would be obedient to his prophetic task or not, though such knowledge is axiomatic. Instead, the intent is to infuse Jeremiah with confidence given the suffering he will face as God's chosen prophet who is slated "to uproot and to tear down and to destroy and to rebuild and to plant" (Jer 1:10).[33] Jeremiah could find confidence in the fact that God knew him in an affectionate sense. With the knowledge of God's loving choice of him in hand, Jeremiah could face the afflictions which would define his prophetic ministry. One reduces God's knowledge of Jeremiah to mere divine cognition at the cost of the wider context.[34]

This is precisely where the Jeremiah pre-text is *contextually consistent* with Rom 8:29. Paul attempts to infuse the Romans with confidence given the suffering they are slated to experience given their status as God's children and given God's intent

---

31. Cf. Paul's use of προοράω in Gal 3:8.
32. See, e.g., Schreiner, *Romans*, 452.
33. See also Jer 1:11–19.
34. See Schreiner, *Romans*, 452.

to conform them to the image of his crucified and risen son. The Romans can be heartened that God will work for their good in all that they suffer, because he has affectionately known them and chosen them in the same way he knew and chose Jeremiah. Of course, Paul reconfigures the OT motifs of divine foreknowledge and election around God's work in Christ which I will discuss further below.

We should also consider Paul's use of προγινώσκω in Rom 11:2, because he ties the verb to an OT citation. While dispelling the false inference that God has rejected Israel, Paul asserts "God did not reject his people whom he foreknew (ὅν προέγνω)" (Rom 11:2a). The statement "God did not reject his people" is a slightly altered citation of 1 Sam 12:22/Ps 93:14 LXX.[35]

Romans 8:29–30 and Echoes of the Image of God

This brings us to a second OT pre-text which emanates from Paul's christological reference in Rom 8:29, "For those whom he foreknew, he also predestined to be conformed to (συμμόρφους) the image of his son (τῆς εἰκόνος τοῦ υἱοῦ αὐτοῦ), in order for him to be the firstborn (πρωτότκον) among many brethren." The phrase "image of his son" (τῆς εἰκόνος τοῦ υἱοῦ αὐτοῦ) echoes Gen 1:26–27, "And God said, 'Let us make man according to our image (κατ᾿ εἰκόνα ἡμετέραν) and likeness (καθ᾿ ὁμοίωσιν), and let them rule over the fish of the sea and over the birds of heaven and over all the livestock and over all the earth and over all the creeping things that creep upon the earth. And God made man, according to the image of God (κατ᾿ εἰκόνα θεοῦ) he made him, male and female he made them."[36] Contextually, given the parallelism with ὁμοίωσις (דמות), the noun εἰκών (צלם) refers to human creatures bearing a close resemblance to their creator.[37] The resemblance is not found in physical likeness but rather in the human being's ability to rationalize, relate, and communicate. The *volume* of this echo is moderate based on the use of εἰκών and its link to God in both the pre-text and text.

Contextual consistency rests upon God's creative work both in the creation of Adam and Eve and in the creation of the Romans. Semantically, given the use of ποιέω (ברא/עשה), God's creative work is more pronounced in the pretext than in the text of Romans. Nevertheless, σύμμορφος in Rom 8:29, used in conjunction with εἰκών, bears a creative and transformative sense.[38] The "same form" (σύμμορφος) is by divine

---

35. This citation will receive extended treatment in a later chapter. It is enough to note at this point that both 1 Sam 12:22 and Ps LXX 93:14 contain the phrase οὐκ ἀπώσεται κύριος τὸν λαὸν αὐτοῦ. Paul alters the verb and the divine subject.

36. See also the use of εἰκών in Gen 5:1, 3; 9:6; Deut 4:16. Cf. Wis 2:23; 7:26; Sir 17:3.

37. LEH 173, 437.

38. The term σύμμορφος does not occur in the LXX. For the only other GNT use, see Phil 3:21. See also the use of συμμορφόω in Phil 3:10. In his analysis of σύμμορφος in Rom 8:29, Jewett notes "It is especially the wording συμμόρφους τῆς εἰκόνος τοῦ υἱοῦ that points to a process of transformation that begins in baptism, in which an old self is buried and a new person arises out of the water to live henceforth in Christ, who was himself the image of God." Jewett, *Romans*, 528–29.

design.³⁹ Paul reconfigures Gen 1:26–27 with the result that God transforms the Romans into the image of his son. While in the pre-text God creates human beings to resemble himself, he conforms the Romans to resemble his crucified and risen son. This means that they bear a likeness not merely in terms of rationality, relationality, and the ability to communicate. They bear the likeness of Jesus' suffering, death, resurrection, and glorification. With respect to the test of *recurrence*, both Romans and the wider Pauline corpus contain multiple instances in which Paul juxtaposes God's work in Adam with his work in Christ.⁴⁰ The same juxtaposition occurs here, though in a subtle manner. Finally, among interpreters who have noted the echo of Gen 1:26–27 in Rom 8:29, Dunn notes "Almost certainly Paul has Adam in mind once again, man created in the image (εἰκών) of God (Gen 1:26–27)."⁴¹

Romans 8:29–30 and Echoes of the Firstborn

The second christological reference in Rom 8:29, "the firstborn among many brethren" (πρωτότοκον ἐν πολλοῖς ἀδελφοῖς), also evokes Israel's Scriptures. Specifically, the use of πρωτότοκος evokes the description of a Davidic king in Ps 88 LXX. Multiple references to "David" (Δαυίδ) signal the psalm's royal messianic emphasis.⁴² Part of the description includes, "He will call upon me saying, 'You are my father, my God and the helper of my salvation;' I will also set him as my firstborn (πρωτότοκον), higher than the kings of the earth" (Ps 87:27–28 LXX). The *volume* here is moderate based on the shared use of πρωτότοκος.⁴³

The *contextual consistency* is substantial for multiple reasons. The pre-text describes the relationship between God and the king in filial terms. God places the king in the position of a firstborn son with all the rights and privliges afforded by the position. In this instance, those rights and privileges include eternal rule and offspring "I made a covenant with my elect (τοῖς ἐκλεκτοῖς μου), I swore to David (Δαυιδ) my servant, I will establish your offspring (τὸ σπέρμα σου) forever and I will build your throne from generation to generation" (Ps 88:4–5 LXX).⁴⁴ God promises to defeat the enemies of his anointed firstborn king, and this promise functions as the backdrop to the lament in vv. 39–52. The suffering of God's people raises questions about his faithfulness to the Davidic covenant, "Where are your ancient mercies, O Lord, which you swore to David in your truth" (Ps 88:50 LXX). In short, what happens to God's

---

39. BDAG, 958.
40. See, e.g., Rom 5:12–19; 1 Cor 15:22, 45.
41. Dunn, *Romans*, 1:483. See also Stuhlmacher, *Romans*, 136.
42. See, e.g., Ps LXX 88:4, 21, 36, 50.
43. The OT contains a diverse motif of "firstborn" sons. See, e.g., Gen 27:19, 32; Exod 4:22–23; 11:5; Lev 27:26. However, Ps LXX 88:27 contains the only use of πρωτότοκος to describe a Davidic figure.
44. See also Ps LXX 88:20–21, 30, 36–37.

firstborn king happens to his offspring. In this scenario, the divine pledge of faithfulness to David and his offspring becomes even more important.⁴⁵

Similarly, Paul's description of Jesus as God's "firstborn" son occurs in a context where hope and suffering are held in tension with one another. Hope for the Romans, as in Ps 88 LXX, hinges upon God's faithfulness to his "firstborn" son. Of course, from Paul's perspective, God has "declared" (ὁρίζω) Jesus to be his son, his firstborn son, by raising him from the dead (Rom 1:4).⁴⁶ It follows that, as the risen and exalted firstborn son, the son's brethren will share in the same things. In this way, Jesus is the "firstborn" among many brethren who will also be raised and exalted, present afflictions notwithstanding. Moreover, as I will discuss further below, Rom 8:29 merges the figures of Adam and David. God conforms the Romans to the image of his firstborn son in both an Adamic and Davidic sense.

Although many interpreters do not detect the echo of Ps 87:27-28 LXX in Rom 8:29, Stuhlmacher makes this OT pre-text a key piece of his exegesis. He notes both the Gen 1:26-27 and Ps 87:27-28 LXX pre-texts evoked in Rom 8:29 noting:

> The apostle presupposes that this teaching is also known by the Christians in Rome. He therefore writes in our context that God has determined that those who love him will participate in the days to come in the same heavenly corporeality which Christ already possesses in the present. At the same time the messianic Son of God will be—in accordance with the promise of Ps. 89:28-30—the 'firstborn' among many brothers (who have been raised like him)."⁴⁷

Romans 8:29-30 and Echoes of Divine Actions

In Rom 8:30, Paul continues to explain the "foundational reason" for why all things work together for the good of those who love God.⁴⁸ Paul lays out in quick succession four divine actions, "And those whom he predestined (προώρισεν), these he also called (ἐκάλεσεν); and those who he called, these he also justified (ἐδικαίωσεν); and those whom he justified, these he also glorified (ἐδόξασεν)." Israel's Scriptures inform each of these divine actions, though, as we shall see, Paul reconfigures them.

As I noted in the analysis of Rom 8:29, God's work of predestination (προορίζω) is not without representation in the OT. The LXX does not employ the verb προορίζω.⁴⁹ Nevertheless, OT writers portray God as someone who decides, or plans, a matter

---

45. See Ps LXX 88:29-30.
46. See the intertextual analysis of Rom 1:2-4 in volume 1.
47. Stuhlmacher, *Romans*, 136-37; See also Hultgren, *Romans*, 329.
48. Schreiner, *Romans*, 451.
49. However, see the use of προορίζω in Test Sol 12:3.

beforehand and then carries it out. In other words, he "predestines/predetermines."⁵⁰ The theology proper of Israel's Scriptures take it as axiomatic that God's actions are not ad hoc in nature. Rather, all seminal moments in the nation's history are grounded in the decisions God made beforehand including (1) the Abrahamic covenant, (2) the births of Isaac and Jacob, (3) the rise of Joseph in Egypt, (4) Israel's bondage and exodus from Egypt, (5) the conquest of the promised land, and (6) exile and return.

He also predetermines the kingship of Israel as well as the life and death of every human being. As one psalmist puts it, "Your eyes saw my unformed substance; in your book all of them were written, the days that were formed for me, when there was not yet one of them" (Ps 139:16 LXX).⁵¹ Even the intercessory work of figures such as Moses is predetermined and built into divine actions.⁵² None of this implies a divine–human dynamic that is fatalistic in nature. God constantly holds Israel responsible for its actions, but the outcome of his work is thoroughly predetermined. OT writers provide no clear explanation of the relationship between divine sovereignty and human responsibility. What the work of predetermination provides in Israel's Scriptures is a confidence that God's purposes and promises will not be thwarted despite all appearances which would lead to the opposite conclusion, including their own failures. The rhetorical question in Isaiah captures this quite nicely, "For the things which the holy God has willed (βεβούλευται), who will scatter? And who will turn way his exalted hand?" (Isa 14:27).

In short, OT writers portray Israel's God as one who predetermines matters without fully explaining how that divine action is related to human responsibility. This portrayal functions to encourage ancient Israelites with the certainty of God's promises and plans regardless of the opposition they face.

This portrayal forms part of the backdrop for Paul's assertion in Rom 8:30 that God "predestined" (προώρισεν) him and his recipients.⁵³ Like OT writers, Paul highlights how God has predestined the Romans to give them certainty about their hope in God's purpose even as their suffering raised doubts about it. Paul identifies God's predetermined plan as conformity to the image of his crucified and risen son. Nothing and no one can thwart the conformity that God purposed. God's predestination of the Romans grounds their hope that God will work all things together for their good which is ultimately defined by their conformity to Christ in his suffering and

---

50. On the meaning of προορίζω, see BDAG 873; Brill 1780–81.

51. Cf. Ps 138:16 LXX.

52. This is reflected in the golden calf narrative and Moses' intercession on Israel's behalf. See, e.g., Exod 32:32. For a helpful discussion on the theological implications of Moses' intercessory work from an ancient Israelite perspective, see Widmer, *Moses, God, and the Dynamics of Intercessory Prayer*.

53. All the verbs in Rom 8:30 are in the aorist tense. With respect to the perfective verbal aspect encoded in the aorist tense form, the consistent choice of the aorist indicates that Paul presents these divine actions, as Campbell suggests, as "an undefined whole, from an external viewpoint." Campbell, *Paul and the Hope of Glory*, 260.

glorification. This becomes the crowning achievement of all the prior seminal moments from Israel's history which God had predestined.

God also called (ἐκάλεσεν) those whom he predestined. As I noted previously, this divine action evokes OT descriptions of God's effective call. God effectively calls creation and Israel into existence, and he does so by his word. As noted in the Psalms, "By the word of the Lord (τῷ λόγῳ τοῦ κυρίου) the heavens were established and by the breath of his mouth all their power" (Ps 32:6 LXX).[54] Similary, as Isaiah asserts, "For as the rain or snow come down from heaven and certainly do not return, until it should water the earth, and it should bring forth and bloom and give its seed to the one who sows and bread for eating, in this way my word (ῥῆμα μου) will be, whatever should come out from my mouth, it certainly shall not return, until it should complete as much as I willed and I will make your ways prosperous and my commandments" (Isa 55:10–11). I mention these pre-texts, because they are germane to the way Paul understands the means and effect of God's call to the Romans. Though Paul leaves it unstated in Rom 8:30, God called the Romans to salvation, which includes conformity to the image of his son, by means of the gospel. Like the divine word in Israel's Scriptures, the gospel by which God called the Romans is inevitably effective regardless of the resistance it faces.

Paul moves from God calling the Romans to justifying them which also has a rich intertextual subtext, "And those whom he called, these he also justified (ἐδικαίωσεν)." As I have discussed at length already, Israel's Scriptures definitively shape the way Paul understands God's justification of the ungodly through faith in Christ. We need only look at the intertextual subtext of Rom 1:17, 3:20, and 4:1–25 to identify the main pre-texts that inform the meaning of ἐδικαίωσεν in 8:30. Once again, the four main pre-texts include: Gen 15:6; Pss LXX 97:2; 142:2; and Hab 2:4. I will not rehash the analysis of these pre-texts here; however, I will offer two additional observations.

First, the wider contexts of these four pre-texts are *consistent* with the context in Rom 8:18–39. Like justification in Israel's Scriptures, the justification of the Romans unfolds amid suffering. God justified Abraham when he was distressed by the lack of an heir. Lamenters in the psalms seek justification when distressed by guilt, death, enemies, and the like. God responds to Habakkuk's suffering and lament by assuring the prophet that the "righteous one will live by faith" in and beyond the judgment to come. As with all of Paul's pastoral theology, the *Sitz im Leben* of justification is affliction.[55]

Second, Paul depicts final justification in a proleptic fashion to engender certainty within his recipients.[56] While in texts such as Rom 2:12–16 Paul depicts future

---

54. Cf. Gen 1:3.

55. For a discusson on suffering at the so-called center of Paul's theology, see Crisler, "Luther's Tentatio as the Center of Paul's Theology."

56. Within the Pauline corpus, this is the only occurence of δικαιόω as an aorist indicative. For other uses of the verb in the Pauline corpus, see Rom 2:13; 3:4, 20, 24, 26, 28, 30; 4:2, 5; 5:1, 9; 6:7; 8:33;

justification in an unsettled fashion, here he brings that future judgment into the present circumstances of the Romans. Stuhlmacher explains, "Verses 28–30, like v. 18, maintain the tone of prophetic certainty. From God's perspective and according to his will, that which can only be developed and completed in the future within salvation history is already accomplished. God has so acted in Christ, once for all, that all time is and remains determined by it."[57] Paul takes the certainty of justification expressed in the pre-texts mentioned above, and he configures them in a way that escalates that sense of certainty.

Lastly, we move to the final phrase in Rom 8:30 "And those whom he justified, these he also glorified (ἐδόξασεν)."[58] As noted previously, much of Paul's glorification language has resurrection as its referent.[59] This is especially evident in Rom 8. For example, when Paul speaks about the necessity of suffering with Christ if the Romans are to be glorified with him (συνδοξασθῶμεν), the latter phrase has resurrection from the dead as its referent (Rom 8:17). When he personifies creation as lamenting like an expectant mother, relief comes "in the freedom of the glory of the children of God (τῆς δόξης τῶν τέκνων τοῦ θεοῦ)" which, as Rom 8:23–25 makes clear, has resurrection from the dead as its referent.[60] However, what I want to consider here is how Israel's Scriptures may have influenced the way that Paul links the glorification of God's people to resurrection from the dead. To be sure, the OT most often makes God the recipient of glory (כבוד/δόξα). Creation and Israel are to "glorify" God in the sense that they display and praise his greatness.[61] As one psalmist famously put it, "The heavens declare the glory of God (δόξαν θεοῦ)" (Ps 18:1b LXX). However, some OT pre-texts make God's people the recipient of glory, and these texts are germane to the interpretation of ἐδόξασεν in Rom 8:30.

One pre-text that stands out in this regard is Ps 90:15 LXX, "He will call on me, and I will hear him, I am with him in tribulation and I will deliver and I will glorify him (δοξάσω αὐτόν)." This divine pledge comes towards the close of an individual

---

1 Cor 4:4; 6:11; Gal 2:16, 17; 3:8, 11, 24; 5:4; 1 Tim 3:16; Titus 3:7.

57. He goes on to add, "As far as the certainty of their salvation is concerned, those who believe therefore no longer need to express themselves within reservation, since God himself has laid the foundation for this certainty in the sending of Jesus." Stuhlmacher, *Romans*, 137.

58. Within the Pauline corpus, this is the only occurrence of δοξάζω in the aorist indicative. Jewett notes that interpreters have struggled to understand Paul's use of the verb here. See Jewett, *Romans*, 530.

59. Campbell has recently suggested, "It is difficult to explain what, exactly glory is for Paul. He never articulates its attributes, apart from its eternal and incomparable nature. But what is clear is that it pertains to God's nature as well as to his deeds. God is, in and of himself, glorioius. And his life-giving, resurrecting, and re-creating deeds are glorious in character." Campbell, *Paul and the Hope of Glory*, 285–86. I would lay stress on the link between glory and his "resurrecting" deed. It is in the resurrection that all of God's actions and character are put on full display in the resurrected Christ, and eventually, in those who are raised/glorified with him.

60. For others uses of δόξα/δοξάζω that have resurrection as their referent, see, e.g., Rom 5:2; 6:4; 1 Cor 15:40–43; Phil 3:21.

61. LEH 159–60.

lament in which the lamenter seeks deliverance from enemies and confidently asserts that God will protect and save him.⁶² God answers the lamenter with the assurance that his prayer will be answered and his hope of deliverance will be realized.⁶³ The deliverance includes God's glorification (δοξάσω αὐτόν) of the lamenter. Contextually, this means God will magnify the lamenter before his enemies by protecting and delivering him.

This pre-text passes multiple intertextual texts. The *volume* is moderate based on the use of δοξάζω with God as the subject of the verb and human beings as the direct object. These constructions occur infrequently in the LXX which raises the probability that Paul has this psalm in view.⁶⁴ *Contextual consistency* can be established based on the shared theme of deliverance from enemies with glorification of the afflicted parties as the ultimate outcome of the deliverance. As noted already, in the pre-text, God glorifies the lamenter in the sense that he is not only delivered from enemies but exalted above them. The text of Rom 8:18–39 likewise situates Paul's recipients in affliction where suffering with Christ apparently includes suffering at the hands of his enemies, a point that he makes clearer in vv. 31–39. Of course, Paul recontextualizes the divine answer to the lamenter in Ps 90:15 LXX by portraying God's glorification of the Romans proleptically so that it is as a settled matter.⁶⁵ Within the *history of interpretation*, while a few exegetes have noted the echo of this psalm in Rom 8:30, it largely goes unnoticed.⁶⁶

Interpretive Impact of Pre-Texts in Romans 8:28–30

The interplay between the pre-texts and text of Rom 8:28–30 impacts interpretation in a variety of ways. As we shall see, one of the primary effects is the reevaluation of how Paul wanted readers to respond to his robust theological flourish, particularly as it relates to his election and predestination language.⁶⁷

Romans 8:28 is bursting with intertextual echoes which sharpen the meaning of what might otherwise be taken as a somewhat abstract statement. These echoes collectively indicate that God is faithful to work all things, particularly the Romans'

---

62. See Ps LXX 90:1–13.
63. See Ps LXX 90:14–16.
64. See 1 Sam 2:30.
65. The shift is from δοξάσω αὐτον in Ps 90:15 LXX to τούτους καὶ ἐδόξασεν in Rom 8:30. As Fitzmyer notes, Paul speaks of it now in a proleptic sense: but it is the glorification 'that is going to be reavaled in us' (8:18).' Fitzmyer, *Romans*, 526.
66. See, e.g., Hübner, *Vetus Testamentum in Novo*, 2:136–37. I am surprised that in his recent and very fine analysis of Rom 8:28–30 Campbell does not attempt to interpret the text in relation to OT pre-texts. See Campbell, *Paul and the Hope of Glory*, 259–62.
67. As Matera notes in his analysis of Paul's election and predestination language in Rom 8:29–30, "Paul, then, is not so much developing a doctrine of double predestination as he is assuring the justified of their role in God's plan." Matera, *Romans*, 205.

afflictions, to the eschatological good of those who affectionately trust God and of those have been effectively called to his salvation and mission. The phrase "all things work together for good" (πάντα συνεργεῖ εἰς ἀγαθόν) evoke pre-texts such as the Joseph narrative which reaches its theological zenith in Gen 50:20, "You took counsel against me for evil, but God took counsel for me for good (לטבה/εἰς ἀγαθά), in order that it might be as it is today, in order that a great people might be fed." Paul and the Romans find themselves in a similar experience of affliction; however, under the direction of Israel's God, these afflictions actually assist in their eventual experience of the ultimate good which is conformity to the death and resurrection of Jesus.

Paul describes himself and his recipients as those who "love God" which, from the perspective of Israel's Scriptures, is a response that runs parallel with obedience.[68] For Paul, such love/obedience is defined by faith in the gospel and the gift of the Spirit. To put it another way, all things work together for the good of those who affectionately trust God and are led by his Spirit. Their love for God, like their scriptural predecessors, is predicated upon who he is and what he does. In Romans, Paul stresses that God has revealed his righteousness in Christ. Therefore, those who love God do so based on this revelation.

Paul qualifies his description of the Romans as those "who love God" with the additional descriptor "and those who are called according to his purpose." [69] Intertextually, God's "call" through his word is effective for accomplishing his purposes which fits with Paul's arugment and wider thought.[70] For Paul, God effectually called the Romans to salvation through the gospel. Elsewhere in the letter, he explicitly describes the gospel as effective with respect to salvation and faith.[71] Although divine purposes vary in Israel's Scriptures, as I noted above, they ultimately coalesce around God's faithfulness to his saving purposes crystallized in the kinds of promises made to Abraham and David. Paul refers to this scripturally charged purpose (πρόθεσις) as conformity to the image of his son.

As noted above, Rom 8:29–30 lays out the "foundational reason" that all things work together for good, and it evokes several OT pre-texts. The interplay between these pre-texts and Paul's "foundational reason" produce several unstated points. For example, based on pre-texs such as Ps 138:1–6 LXX and Jer 1:4–5, God's foreknowledge (οὓς προέγνω) is relational in nature and a source of comfort for the afflicted. Neither Israel's Scriptures nor Paul himself engage in philosophical speculation about the relationship between divine foreknowledge and human actions. Instead, stress is laid on God's prior and intimate knowledge of his people as a source of comfort in their pain.

---

68. See Exod 20:6; Deut 7:9.

69. As Schreiner rightly notes, "The believer's love for God is ultimately due to God's purpose in calling them to salvation." Schreiner, *Romans*, 450.

70. See, e.g., Ps LXX 32:6; Isa 55:9–10.

71. See Rom 1:16; 10:17. See also Gal 3:2, 5.

Similarly, Paul appeals to God's predestination (προώρισεν) of the Romans to both comfort them in their suffering and to explain it. The intertextual subtext at this point consists of the way God's plans and purposes, for both individuals and the whole nation in Israel's Scriptures, remain unthwarted regardless of the opposition they face. Israel's past contained endless examples of this truth. Paul escalates this truth by explaining to the Romans that God predestined them to be conformed to the image of the crucified and risen Jesus. On the one hand, this sheds light on the Romans' suffering. God predetermined that the Romans would be conformed to the image of his son by suffering with him. On the other hand, he predestined them to be conformed to the image of his son by being glorified with him. Sharing in his glory requires resurrection from the dead which is the ultimate hope of creation, God's children, and the Spirit himself.[72] As Paul puts it at the outset of this pericope, "But if children, also heirs; heirs of God, and coheirs with Christ, if indeed we suffer with him (συμπάσχομεν) in order that we might also be glorified with him (συνδοξασθῶμεν)" (Rom 8:17).

The christological descriptions embedded in the phrases the "image of his son" (τῆς εἰκόνος τοῦ υἱοῦ αὐτοῦ) and "firstborn among many brethren" (πρωτότοκον ἐν πολλοῖς ἀδελφοῖς) signal yet another intertextual layer involving the figures of Adam and David. As I noted above, these descriptions evoke Gen 1:26–27 and Ps 87:27–28 LXX. The interplay here produces the unstated point that the Romans are made in the divine image of the crucified and risen son who is at the same time the firstborn Davidic son. One implication of this interplay is that Paul places Israel's God and Jesus on the same divine plane.[73] While Adam was made in the image of God, the Romans are conformed to the image of the crucified and risen Jesus.[74] This is not to suggest that the two images are unrelated to one another. Rather, as Paul describes him to the Corinthians, Christ is the "image of God" (εἰκὼν τοῦ θεοῦ) (2 Cor 4:4).[75] A second implication of the interplay is that the Romans share in the experience of the firstborn Davidic son as he is described in Ps 87 LXX. It follows that these "brethren" will undergo both suffering and glory. Although their suffering is unavoidable, God

---

72. There is a soteriological component in being conformed to the image of the son. As Dodd puts it, "There is no end to the ideas (or fantasies) of salvation that the human mind can form—unending sensual bliss, absorption into the All, crowns and harps, Nirvana, or what not. Paul holds us to the essential thing: that, whatever else it may be, salvation means sharing the likeness of Christ, and Christ we know." Dodd, *Romans*, 156.

73. It follows that Paul's use of εἰκών in Rom 8:29 differs slighty from the use in 1 Cor 15:49. In the latter, Paul juxtaposes the images of Adam and Christ. Contrastively, in Rom 8:29, he juxtaposes the images of God and Christ.

74. Whether one sees the conformity (συμμόρφους τῆς εἰκόνος) in Rom 8:29 as "ethical" or something more, Paul places Jesus on the same divine plane. On an "ethical" image, see Campbell, *Paul and Union with Christ*, 232. See also Cranfield, *Romans*, 1:432.

75. As Sanday and Headlam put it, "As the Son is the image of the Father, so the Christian is to reflect the image of his Lord, passing through a gradual assimilation of mind and character to an ultimate assimilation of His δόξα, the absorption of the splendour of His presence." Sanday and Headlam, *Romans*, 218.

is ultimately faithful to the Romans through his faithfulness to the firstborn and risen son.[76]

In addition to divine foreknowledge and predestination, Paul finishes his flurry of divine actions in Rom 8:30 with "and those whom he predestined, these also called (ἐκάλεσεν); and those whom called these he also justified (ἐδικαίωσεν); and those whom he justified he is also glorified (ἐδόξασεν)." Each action has an analogue in Israel's Scriptures. The interplay between the pre-texts and text here supports Paul's pastoral effort to encourage the Romans in their suffering. For example, based on Israel's Scriptures, God's call through his word is inflexibly effective (Ps 32:6 LXX; Isa 55:10–11). The same holds true for the Romans whom God effectively called to salvation and comformity to Christ through the word of the gospel. Their sufferings do not thwart this call. Instead, since they are suffering with Christ, their suffering accomplishes God's saving purposes.[77]

Similarly, God's justification of the Romans through faith in Christ has as its intertextual backdrop justified and afflicted figures such as Abraham, lamenters in the Psalms, and Habakkuk. Suffering should not cast doubt on God's justification of the Romans. Rather, based on scriptural precedent, justification by faith always takes place in affliction. However, Paul escalates this scriptural precedent by bringing the Romans' final justification into the present and leveraging that assurance against their present affliction. He elaborates on this point in Rom 8:31–34 as we shall see.

Paul also escalates the promise of glorification in proleptic fashion. While in Ps 90:15 LXX God promises to glorify those who cry out to him (δοξάσω αὐτόν), Paul depicts the Romans' glorification as a present and accomplished fact in Christ (ἐδόξασεν).[78] The Romans are already glorified in Christ in the sense that they are already risen and exalted above their enemies, including death, because, as we shall see in the next chapter, the risen Christ has been exalted to the right hand of the father.

---

76. On this point, see Hultgren, *Romans*, 329.
77. Cf. 2 Cor 12:6–10; Phil 1:29; 2 Thess 1:4–5.
78. Cf. Eph 2:6.

Chapter 11

Romans 8:31–39

THESE NINE VERSES ARE a poetic and theological tour de force. Barrett observes that the paragraph is "in the rhetorical style of a diatribe" and "full of passionate eloquence."[1] It also rounds out Paul's discussion of the Romans' hope in the face of suffering which commenced in Rom 5:1–5. In the immediate context, these verses draw an inference from 8:28–30 where Paul assures his recipients that God works for their good in their suffering and proceeds to ground his assurance in the divine action of foreknowledge, predestination, effective calling, justification, and glorification. Paul concludes that nothing suffered by the Romans can separate them from God's love in Christ.

From an intertextual perspective, Rom 8:31–39 contains a rich intertextual subtext.[2] Paul's citation of Ps 43:23 LXX in Rom 8:36 is the main intertextual feature. However, as we shall see, several other intertextual echoes can be heard in these verses.

Romans 8:31–34

(8:31–34) What then shall we say to these things? If God is for us, who is against us? He who did not spare his own son but handed him over for us all, how will he not also with him graciously give to us all things? Who will bring a charge against God's elect? God is the one who justifies; who is the one who condemns? Christ Jesus is the one who died, rather who was raised, who also is at the right hand of God, who also intercedes for us.

The antecedent of ταῦτα in Rom 8:31, "What then shall we say to these things (ταῦτα)," is Paul's description of the divine actions which undergird his assertion that "all things

---

1. Barrett, *Romans*, 172.

2. With respect to the rhetorical structure of Rom 8:31–39, Thiselton notes "Verses 31b–39 constitute four rhetorical strophes consisting of verses 31b–32, 33–34, 35–37, and 38–39. All the major scholars, including Barrett, Käsemann, Fitzmyer, and Jewett, stress the diatribe form here." Thiselton, *Discovering Romans*, 183.

work together for the good of those who love God." Based on these actions, Paul infers that no one can afflict the Romans to the point that they are defeated, because God is on their side. He elaborates on this inference through a series of rhetorical questions and poetic assertions which are laden with intertextual references.

Suggested Pre-Texts in Romans 8:31–34

Hübner identifies the following pre-texts: Ps 55:12 LXX; 117:6–7 (Rom 8:31); Gen 22:12, 16; Exod 32:11–14, 30–32; Num 11:2, 13–19; Deut 9:25–26; Ps 22:4 LXX; 98:6 LXX; Isa 53:6, 12 (Rom 8:32); Exod 32:30–32; 1 Chr 16:13; Psalms LXX 88:4–5; 104:6; 105:23; 109:1; Job 42:8; Isa 42:1; 43:20; 45:4; 50:8–9; 65:9, 15, 23 (Rom 8:33–34).[3]

Nestle-Aland 28th ed. lists the following pre-texts: Ps 118:6 (Rom 8:31); Gen 22:16 (Rom 8:32); Ps 110:1; Isa 50:8 (Rom 8:34).[4]

Besides the citation of Ps 43:23 LXX, Seifrid identifies several other pre-texts: Gen 22:16; Isa 40:1–11; 43:1–17; 49:14–23; 52:13—53:7; 53:12; 54:1–17 (Rom 8:32); Psalms LXX 35:13; 109:4; Isa 41:11–13, 21–24; 43:8–13, 25–28; 45:20–25; 46:13; 50:4–11; 51:1–8; 53:6, 11–12; 55:3–5, 17 (Rom 8:33–34).[5]

Intertextual Analysis of Romans 8:31–34

The first two strophes of Rom 8:31–34 contains several intertextual echoes that evoke fundamental attributes of Israel's God and seminal moments from its past. The interplay between these echoes and the text generate multiple points of resonance which I will discuss below.

Romans 8:31 and Echoes of God's Help for the Trusting

Paul's rhetorical quesiton "If God is for us (εἰ ὁ θεὸς ὑπὲρ ἡμῶν), who is against us (τίς καθ᾽ ἡμῶν)?" evokes statements of trust in the psalms:

> I have hoped in God, I will not fear; what will man do to me (τί ποιήσει μοι ἄνθρωπος)? (Ps 55:12 LXX).[6]

> The Lord is my helper, I will not fear what man will do to me (τί ποιήσει μοι ἄνθρωπος). The Lord is my helper, and I will look upon my enemies (Ps 117:6–7 LXX).

---

3. Hübner, *Vetus Testamentum in Novo*, 2:136–44. See also the parallels with Wis 3:9; 4:15; Sir 47:22.
4. NA 28th ed. 497–98.
5. Seifrid, *Romans*, 633–37.
6. See also Ps 55:5 LXX.

The wider contexts of both psalms are *consistent* with Paul's thought. The psalmist experiences a tension between affliction at the hands of enemies and trust/hope that God will deliver. Therefore, we find complaints such as "My enemies trampled me all day long" (Ps 55:2a LXX) juxtaposed with statements of trust such as "I have hoped in God, I will not fear; what will man do to me (τί ποιήσει μοι ἄνθρωπος)? (Ps 55:12 LXX).[7] Such trust is predicated on God's prior saving actions, "For you delivered (ἐρρύσω) my soul from death" (Ps 55:14 LXX).[8] If God answered the prior cry for deliverance, he will do so again "My enemies turn back, in the day in which I call on you (ἐπικαλέσωμαι σε); behold I have known that you are my God" (Ps 55:10 LXX). The psalmist knows that God hears his cries and recognizes his pain, "You set my tears before you as it is in your promise" (Ps 55:9 LXX).[9]

Paul's text reflects the same tension between affliction and trust/hope that God will deliver. The Romans face unrelenting enemies which I will disuss below; however, their hope/trust for deliverance is grounded in the crucified, risen, exalted, and interceding Jesus Christ. Even more so than the psalmist, Paul and his recipients can confidently cry for deliverance and be certain that God has and will answer them in Christ. As Seifrid puts it, "The confidence of the psalmist ('What can human beings do to me?') now takes on even larger dimensions."[10] The "larger dimensions" of the psalmist's confidence for Paul and believers in Rome are grounded in the crucifixion, resurrection, and exaltation of Christ.

Romans 8:32 and Echoes of Genesis 22

Paul's second rhetorical question in Rom 8:32 echoes Gen 22.[11] Paul asks, "He who did not spare his own son (τοῦ ἰδίου υἱοῦ οὐκ ἐφείσατο) but handed him over for us all, how will he not also with him graciously give to us all things?" The phrase τοῦ ἰδίου υἱοῦ οὐκ ἐφείσατο evokes the voice of the angel of the Lord just as Abraham is about to slay his son, "And he said, 'Do not lay your hand upon the child nor do anything to him; for now I know that you fear God and you did not spare your beloved son (οὐκ ἐφείσω τοῦ υἱοῦ σου τοῦ ἀγαπητοῦ) because of me" (Gen 22:12).[12] The *volume* of the echo is high based on the correspondence between οὐκ ἐφείσω τοῦ υἱοῦ σου τοῦ ἀγαπητοῦ in Gen 22:12 and τοῦ ἰδίου υἱοῦ οὐκ ἐφείσατο in Rom 8:32. There are

7. Cf. Ps 117:10–16 LXX.

8. Cf. Ps 117:5, 10–16, 21, 28 LXX.

9. Ps 56:9 MT has a more vivid description of the way God recognizes the psalmist's pain, "You have taken account of my wanderings; you put my tears in your bottle; are they not in your book?"

10. Seifrid, *Romans*, 634.

11. I am helped here in my analysis of the Gen 22 echo by discussions with a former student, Ethan Taylor.

12. The phrase οὐκ ἐφείσω τοῦ υἱοῦ σου τοῦ ἀγαπητοῦ is repeated in Gen 22:16 as God promises to bless Abraham and his offspring, because he did not intend to spare (φείδομαι) Isaac's life. The verb φείδομαι is the translaton of חשׂך in the MT.

minor differences between the phrases. For example, the pre-text qualifies son with "beloved" (τοῦ ἀγαπητοῦ) while the text qualifies son with "his own" (τοῦ ἰδίου).

With respect to *contextual consistency*, the death of the son in both the pre-text and text is sacrificial in nature. God tests Abraham by commanding him to offer Isaac "for a whole burnt offering" (εἰς ὁλοκάρπωσιν) (Gen 22:2). Paul informs the Romans that God handed Jesus over to death "for us all" (ὑπὲρ ἡμῶν πάντων), a prepositional phrase that signals a sacrificial, even atoning, death.[13] However, Paul recontextualizes the Gen 22 pre-text by placing God in the role of Abraham and Jesus in the role of Isaac. He then escalates the pre-text by going through with the son's sacrificial death. Although Abraham is ultimately able to spare Isaac's life through the divine provision of a sacrificial ram entangled in the thicket, God the Father does not spare Jesus the Son.[14] It follows that God not sparing Jesus had an even greater effect than Abraham not sparing Isaac.

We should also note that the phrase οὐκ ἐφείσατο occurs in a handful of LXX pre-texts where such action indicates the severity of God's wrath.[15] For example, in Ps 77 LXX, the psalmist recounts how God's "did not spare" the firstborn sons of Egypt when he delivered his people from bondage:

> He made a path for his anger, he did not spare (οὐκ ἐφείσατο) their souls from death and he confined their cattle to death and he struck every first-born in Egypt, the first-fruits of their labors in the tents of Ham. And he lifted up his people like sheep, and he led them like a shepherd in the wilderness (Ps 77:49–51 LXX).

In some instances, God's own people are "not spared" by him "The Lord has done the things which he planned, he completed his words, the things which he commanded from the days of old, he torn down and he did not spare (οὐκ ἐφείσατο), and he has caused the enemy to rejoice over you, he lifted up the horn of the one who afflicts you" (Lam 2:17). It follows that when Paul takes up the phrase οὐκ ἐφείσατο he employs an idiom that signals the severity of God wrath against his enemies. This makes his reconfiguration of the idiom surprising. God "did not spare his own son" (τοῦ ἰδίου υἱοῦ οὐκ ἐφείσατο) thereby treating Jesus as an enemy in the vein of ancient Egyptians or rebellious Israel for the sake of Paul and the Romans.

---

13. See Hultgren, *Romans*, 209–10.
14. See Gen 22:13–14.
15. See the use of οὐκ ἐφείσατο in 2 Sam 12:6; 2 Chr 36:17; Isa 14:6; Lam 2:17. See also Sir 16:8; PssSol 17.12.

Romans 8:31–34 and the Echo of Isaiah's Suffering Servant

A third intertextual feature in Rom 8:31–34 involves the suffering servant in Isa 53.[16] When Paul states that God "handed him over for us all" (ὑπὲρ ἡμῶν πάντων παρέδωκεν αὐτόν), it evokes two similar expressions from Isa 53:

> We have all gone astray like sheep, everyone has gone astray in his way; and the Lord handed him over for our sins (παρέδωκεν αὐτὸν ταῖς ἁμαρτίαις ἡμῶν) (Isa 53:6).

> Therefore, he will inherit many and he will divide the spoils of the mighty, because his soul was handed over to death (παρεδόθη εἰς θάνατον ἡ ψυχὴ αὐτοῦ), and he was reckoned with the lawless; and he bore the sins of many and he was handed over because of their sins (διὰ τὰς ἁμαρτίας αὐτῶν παρεδόθη) (Isa 53:12).

The *volume* of the echo is moderate based on the semantic and syntactical overlap involving παραδίδωμι.

Contextually, God handed over the servant and the son because of the sin of ancient Israel and the Romans respectively. The pre-text explicitly states this cause (διὰ τὰς ἁμαρτίας αὐτῶν παρεδόθη, Isa 53:12) while Paul's use of the prepositional phrase "for us all" (ὑπὲρ ἡμῶν πάντων) assumes it.[17] Paul reconfigures Isaiah's servant by identifying this figure as Jesus and by expanding the soteriological effect of the servant's work to include himself and his recipients. Within the *history of interpretation*, some commentators have suggested that the phrase "he handed him for us all" is a pre-Pauline formula which "echoes the language of Isa 53:6, 12."[18] Even if the phrase is a pre-Pauline formula, the Isaianic echo remains. Moreover, in Rom 8:32, Paul combines the ʿAqedah tradition from Gen 22 with the suffering servant tradition from Isa 53.[19] We will explore the implications of this intertextual combination below.

Romans 8:31–34 and Echoes of God's Elect

Paul evokes multiple pre-texts in Rom 8:33–34 with his rhetorical questions "Who will bring a charge against God's elect (τίς ἐγκαλέσει κατὰ ἐκλεκτῶν θεοῦ)?" and "Who is the one condemns (τίς ὁ κατακρινῶν)?" When Paul refers to the Romans as "God's elect" (ἐκλεκτῶν θεοῦ), it evokes descriptions of God's people in Israel's Scriptures.[20]

---

16. Cf. the echoes of Isa 53 in Rom 4:25; 10:16.

17. The atoning associations of the prepositional phrase ὑπὲρ ἡμῶν πάντων are reflected in pre-texts such as Exod 32:30–32. For a discussion of the atoning connotations associated with the phrase, see Wallace, *Beyond the Basics*, 383–89.

18. Jewett, *Romans*, 538.

19. See Seifrid, *Romans*, 634; Witherington, *Romans*, 231–32.

20. Within the Pauline corpus, the adjective ἐκλεκτός only occurs in Rom 8:33; 16:13; Col 3:12 1

God's election (בחר/ἐκλέγομαι) of Israel is one of the nation's defining characteristics in both the OT and Second Temple literature.[21] Some of the most informative descriptions in this regard can be found in Deuteronomy, Psalms, and Isaiah:

> Because he loved your fathers and chose (ἐξελέξατο) you their seed after them and he brought you out from Egypt by his great strength (Deut 4:37).[22]

> For the Lord chose (ἐξελέξατο) Jacob for himself, Israel for his treasure (Ps 134:4 LXX).[23]

> Because of Jacob my servant and Israel my elect (Ισραηλ τοῦ ἐκλεκτοῦ μου) I will call you by your name and I will receive you, but you have not known me (Isa 45:4).[24]

God's election of Israel reaches as far back as Abraham as noted in Nehemiah's prayer, "You are the Lord God; you chose Abram (ἐξελέξω ἐν Αβραμ) and brought him out from the lands of the Chaldeans and you gave him the name Abraham" (Neh 9:7). He elected Abraham and his descendants for the ultimate purpose of blessing them and blessing the nations through them, that is redeeming them from the Adamic fall.[25] Israel's God elected them for this redemptive purpose by means of his love and through the election of individuals, or individual groups, within the nation such as priests and kings.[26] With resepct to the latter, God elected Judah and the house of David.[27] As noted in one of the storytelling psalms, "I made a covenant with my elect ones (τοῖς ἐκλεκτοῖς μου), I swore to David my servant, 'I will establish your seed forever, and I will build up your throne to all generations'" (Ps 88:4–5 LXX).[28] Overall, the scriptural motif of Israel's divine election had as its inception the choice of Abraham and his seed, its ultimate purpose the redemptive blessing to the nations, and God's love and power as the means by which those elective purposes are carried out.

Tim 5:21; 2 Tim 2:10; Titus 1:1.

21. For descriptions of Israel's as God's elect in Second Temple literature, see e.g, 2 Macc 1:25; Wis 3:9; Sir 46:1; 47:22.

22. See also Deut 7:7; 10:15; 1 Kgs 3:8; 1 Chr 16:13. Although not containing ἐκλέγομαι/ἐκλεκτός, see Exod 19:5–16.

23. See also Pss LXX 32:12; 46:5; 104:6, 43; 105:5.

24. See also Isa 14:1; 41:8–9; 42:1; 43:10, 20; 44:1–2; 45:4; 49:7; 65:9, 23.

25. See Gen 12:1–3; 18:18; 22:18; 26:4; 28:14; Acts 3:25; Gal 3:8.

26. As ancient Israel was reminded in Deut 7:7–8, "It is not because you were more numerous than all the nations that the Lord preferred you and chose you (ἐξελέξατο ὑμᾶς)–for you are smaller than all the other nations–but because the Lord loves you and keeps the oath, which he swore to your fathers, the Lord brought you out by a mighty hand and an uplifted arm and he ransomed you from the house of slavery from the hand of Pharaoh the king of Egypt."

27. See, e.g., 1 Sam 16:8–10; Pss LXX 77:68, 70.

28. Ps 89:4 MT contains the singular בחיר.

This same motif informs Paul's reference to "God's elect" (ἐκλεκτῶν θεοῦ) in Rom 8:33. Paul expands the motif ecclesiastically, christologically, and soteriologically. He includes both Jew and Gentile in the elect seed of Abraham.[29] Moreover, he identifies Jesus as the elect Davidic son through whom God accomplishes his saving purposes. Paul makes this clear from the opening of the letter, and we will return to this line of thought below as we consider Jesus' intercessory work.[30] Paul also expands the link between the election and redemption of God's people. This link in the OT often stresses the earthly, temporal, and political redemption of the elect, though not to the total exclusion of soteriological and eschatological considerations.[31] OT prophets envision a time of eschatological blessing for God's elect, "I will bring out a seed from Jacob and from Judah, and he will inherit my holy mountain, and my elect (οἱ ἐκλεκτοί μου) and my servants will inherit and they will dwell there" (Isa 65:9). For Paul, God's elect receive their eschatological blessing and protection in Christ. In this way, there is an individual and corporate dimension to Paul's understanding of God's elect just as we find in Isaiah's servant songs. As Seifrid notes, "The description of believers as 'chosen ones,' implicitly identifies them with Christ, the Son and with the figure of the Servant, which in the Servants Songs is simultaneously corporate and individual."[32] To be sure, Paul infuses the langague of election with an explicit soteriological sense that is unequaled in Israel's Scriptures. Nevertheless, Paul's move is not without at least some scriptural warrant.

Romans 8:31–34 and Echoes of Isaiah 50

This brings us to the intertextual echoes related to the condemnation (τίς ἐγκαλέσει) and judgment (τίς ὁ κατακρινῶν) of God's elect. Paul's questions evoke one of Isaiah's servant songs where the speaker utters rhetorical questions of their own, "For the one who justifies me (ὁ δικαιώσας με) is near; who is the one who contends with me (τίς ὁ κρινόμενός μοι)? Let him rise together with me; and who is the one who contends

---

29. As Longenecker notes in his analysis of ἐκλεκτῶν θεοῦ, "The title was, of course, used in the Jewish (OT) Scriptures for those who had been chosen by God as his special people, that is, the people of Israel. In his letter to Rome, however, Paul begins to use 'the elect/chosen ones of God' or 'God's elect' as applicable to all believers in Jesus, whatever the ethnicity." Longenecker, *Romans*, 756.

30. Rom 1:2–4. For a discussion of the Davidic echoes in these verses, see volume 1.

31. As Witherington notes, "The language about God's Elect comes right from OT language abou the people of God as a group. A careful reading of these texts will show that most do not entail the notion that elect individuals have some sort of advance guarantee of salvation. The concept of the 'elect' applies to the group, and individuals within the group can, and indeed often are said to, commit apostasy." Witherington, *Romans*, 232. Witherington points to the following OT and Second Temple texts: 1 Chr 6:13; Pss 89:3; 105:6; Isa 42:1; 43:20; 45:4; 65:9–22; Sir 46:1; 47:22; Wis 3:9; 4:15; Jub. 1:29; 1QS 8:6; CD 4:3–4.

32. Seifrid points to several references at this point. See Isa 49:1–6; 51:1–3; 55:3–5. He also points to the impact of these Isaianic texts in 1 QH 2:13; 1 QPHab 9:12; 4QFlor 1:19; 4QpIsa 1:19; 4QpPs2:5; 4 Q534 1:10. See Seifrid, *Romans*, 634.

with me (τίς ὁ κρινόμενος μοι)? Let him come near to me. Behold the Lord helps me; who is the one who will do evil to me (τίς κακώσει με)? Behold all of you will decay like a garment, and a moth will consume you" (Isa 50:8–9).[33] The *volume* of the echo is moderate to high. The pre-text contains the phrase τίς ὁ κρινόμενος while the text in Rom 8:33 has τίς ἐγκαλέσει and τίς ὁ κατακρινῶν.[34] Additionally, the pre-text describes God as "the one justifies me" (ὁ δικαιώσας, Isa 50:8) while the text contains "God is the one who justifies" (θεὸς ὁ δικαιῶν, Rom 8:33).

Contextual consistency occurs at the point of the suffering experienced by Isaiah's suffering servant and the divinely elected Romans. The former figure maintains his trust in God while suffering violent affliction and accusations perpetrated by his enemies:

> I gave my back to scourgings, my cheeks to strikes, I did not turn my face away from the shame of spitting. And the Lord has been my helper, for this reason I was not ashamed, but I set my face like solid rock, and I know that I certainly shall not be ashamed. For the one who justifies me (ὁ δικαιώσας με) is near; who is the one who contends with me (τίς ὁ κρινόμενος μοι)? Let him rise together with me; and who is the one who contends with me (τίς ὁ κρινόμενος μοι)? Let him come near to me. Behold the Lord helps me; who is the one who will do evil to me (τίς κακώσει με)? Behold all of you will decay like a garment, and a moth will consume you (Isa 50:6–9).

The physical afflictions are clear while the false accusations are implied by the servant's references to enemies contending (ὁ κρινόμενος) with him and God justifying (ὁ δικαιώσας) him. Such suffering is typical of OT prophets and righteous figures. Although the servant is beaten and falsely accussed, he maintains his trust that God will justify him and thereby rescue him from enemies. Similarly, Paul describes God's elect as those who could be falsely accused by enemies but still justified by God. He does not elaborate on the nature of the false accusations or identify the enemies who could utter them which has prompted various suggestions. Related to questions about the identity of the accusers is the setting of the experience. Longenecker sums up the exegetical condundrum nicely:

> A major issue about the focus of 8:33–34 has been whether the questions and answers of this passage have to do with (1) a future, eschatological judgment scenario, where Satan–as well as, perhaps, one's own sins–makes accusations against believers in Jesus and God defends them, or (2) the present opposition and oppression by nonbelievers against Christians vis-à-vis God's defense of his own people on the basis of the past and present work of Christ Jesus.[35]

---

33. For the rendering of κρίνω here, see LEH 355.

34. With respect to the verb ἐγκαλέω in Rom 8:33 and the echo from Isa 50:9, Seifrid suggests "The language of Paul's allusion (*egkalesei*: 'bring a charge') comes closer to the Hebrew text than does the LXX (*ho krinomenos*: 'one who condemns')." Seifrid, *Romans*, 634.

35. Longenecker, *Romans*, 754.

Paul here does not separate present and future justification. God's justification of the Romans over and against present accusations by Satan, sin, and nonbelievers proleptically anticipates the same eschatological experience. This is precisely what the Romans need to hear as Paul already signaled in Rom 5:1–10. Present suffering should not be interpretered as God's condemnation of the Romans now or on the last day. God's justifying work in Christ and Christ's intercessory work provide certainty of the Romans' position before God now and eschatologically. If God justifies the Romans, no one and nothing can effectively accuse them in a way that would result in their condemnation by God.[36]

Within the *history of interpretation*, the echo of Isa 50:8 in Rom 8:33–34 is widely accepted. Dodd includes the echo in his seminal discussion on early Christian usage of Isaiah's "Servant of the Lord" and "Righteous Sufferer" motifs.[37] As Sanday and Headlam confidently state, "The Apostle clearly has in his mind Is. l.8,9."[38]

Romans 8:31–34 and Echoes of Psalm 109 LXX

As Paul reassures the Romans of their justification before God, their suffering notwithstanding, his description of Christ's intercessory work evokes Ps 109 LXX. He describes Christ Jesus as "the one who died, but rather was raised, who is also at the right hand of God (ἐν δεξιᾷ τοῦ θεοῦ), who also intercedes/pleads for us (ἐντυγχάνει ὑπὲρ ἡμῶν)" (Rom 8:34). The phrase "at the right hand of God" (ἐν δεξιᾷ τοῦ θεοῦ) evokes the divine command in Ps 109:1 LXX, "The Lord said to my Lord, 'Sit at might right hand (ἐκ δεξιῶν μου), until I should make your enemies a footstool for your feet.'"[39] The *volume* of the echo is moderate due to the variation between ἐκ δεξιῶν μου in the pre-text and ἐν δεξιᾷ τοῦ θεοῦ in the text.[40] Interpreters often recognize this echo. As Hultgren notes, "That Christ is at the right hand of God (δεξιᾷ τοῦ θεοῦ)

---

36. As Hultgren puts it, "The only part that would have the legal competence to bring charges against the elect would be God. But, Paul declares, God is the one who justifies. If God is for us in the act of justification, it is impossible to think ultimately of God as a prosecutor at the final judgment." Hultgren, *Romans*, 339.

37. See Dodd, *According to the Scriptures*, 91.

38. Sanday and Headlam, *Romans*, 220.

39. Cf. the use of ἐκ δεξιῶν μου in Ps LXX 15:8.

40. Paul is also likely relying upon early Christian tradition/kerygma in which Ps 109:1 LXX featured prominently in christological reflection. As Dodd notes, "It seems clear, therefore, that this particular verse was one of the fundamental texts of the kerygma, underlying almost all the various developments of it, and cited independently in Mark, Acts, Paul, Hebrews, and 1 Peter." Dodd, *According to the Scriptures*, 35. See also Hay, *Glory at the Right Hand*. See the use of this verse in Matt 22:24; 26:64; Mark 12:36; 14:62; 16:19; Luke 20:42; 22:69; Acts 2:34; 1 Cor 15:25; Eph 1:20; Heb 1:3, 13; 8:1; 10:12. Nevertheless, even if Paul is influenced by early Christian tradition related to this one verse, it does not follow that he would be unfamiliar and uninfluenced by the verse's wider context.

recalls the opening line of Ps 110, at which the Lord addresses the king: 'Sit at my right hand (κάθου ἐκ δεξιῶν μου) until I make your enemies your footstool.'"[41]

Contextual consistency is evident in multiple ways. For example, in the both the pre-text and text, the defeat of enemies is linked to God's "right hand." The pre-text portays God as defeating enemies for the "Lord" but also empowering him to do so.[42] On the one hand, he is commanded to sit at the Lord's right hand while the Lord sudues his enemies (Ps 109:1 LXX). On the other hand, the Lord is at his right hand in battle "The Lord at your right hand (ἐκ δειξῶν σου) has crushed kings in the day of his wrath" (Ps 109:5 LXX). Similarly, in our text, God raised Jesus from the dead to his right hand, but Jesus also actively pleads (ἐντυγχάνω) at God's right hand for the Romans as they suffer.[43] The latter action points to another commonality between the pre-text and text, namely the work of intercession. In the psalm, the Lord appoints the Lord as a priest "The Lord swore and he will not regret it, 'You are a priest (ἱερεύς) forever according to the order of Melchizedek" (Ps 109:4 LXX). The position implies that ancient Israel not only needed help in battle against their enemies but also forgiveness before God.

This raises the question as to whether Paul has in view the psalmist's priestly emphasis when he describes the crucified Jesus as interceding for the Romans at God's right hand or only the emphasis on the risen Jesus' position of authority. Paul undoubtedly draws on the psalm's motif of a figure exalted to a position of power where he reigns over his enemies. As Keener notes, "Jesus's location at God's right hand indicates his exaltation (Ps 110:1), presumably including over hostile powers (Rom 8:38–39), and emphasizes his complete access to the one with whom he intercedes."[44] In this way, intercessory work in this context includes the risen Christ pleading to God for the lives of the Romans as they are bombarded with all sorts of deadly afflictions which Paul lists in Rom 8:35–39. However, does the intercessory work in this context also include pleading for the forgiveness of the Romans? To put it another way, does Christ "plead his death" before God for the forgiveness of the Romans?[45] Ultimately, it is probably unwise to separate these two strands of Christ's intercessory work. His priestly plea of forgiveness on behalf of the Romans as the crucified Christ is indissolubly linked to his authoritative plea for their protection as the risen Christ.[46] The full intercessory work of Christ, informed by Ps 109 LXX, ensures the Romans

---

41. Hultgren adds, "By using the phrase Paul attributes to the risen Christ a status not only of honor but also of authority." Hultgren, *Romans*, 339.

42. For a recent discussion on Ps 110 in relation to early Christianity, see Compton, *Psalm 110*.

43. The verb ἐντυγχάνω in Rom 8:34 bears the sense of an "earnest request," or pleading. See BDAG, 341.

44. Keener, *Romans*, 111.

45. See Dunn, *Romans*, 1:511.

46. Contra Fitzmyer who insists that "Christ's priesthood" is a "notion not found in Pauline writings." Fitzmyer, *Romans*, 533.

that "it is utterly preposterous to fear that anyone can impeach their status."[47] Even more assurance stems from the way Paul links the intercessory work of the exalted Christ to the Spirit through the use of ἐντυγχάνω in Rom 8:27 and 8:34. As Seifrid puts it, "The intercession of the Spirit for us in our hearts has its counterpart in the intercession of Christ for us at God's right hand."[48]

Romans 8:35–39

(8:35–39) Who will separate us from the love of Christ? Will tribulation or distress or persecution or famine or nakedness or danger or sword? Just as it is written, "On account of you we face death all day long, we have been reckoned as sheep for slaughter." But in all these things we overwhelmingly conquer through the one who loved us. For I am convinced that neither death nor life nor angels nor rulers nor present things nor things to come nor powers nor height nor depth nor anything other created thing will be able to separate us from the love of God which is in Christ Jesus our Lord.

Paul's final rhetorical question in Rom 8:35 echoes afflictions usually associated with divine condemnation. Paul asks, "Who will separate us from the love of Christ? Will tribulation (θλῖψις) or distress (στενοχωρία) or persecution (διωγμός) or famine (λιμός) or nakedness (γυμνότης) or danger (κίνδυνος) or sword (μάχαιρα)?" Some interpreters have associated Paul's list of afflictions here with Stoic *Peristasenkatalogs* found in the writings of Epictetus and Seneca.[49] While Rom 8:35 certainly parallels *Peristasenkatalogs*, as we shall see, Israel's Scriptures are also a conceptual influence.

Suggested Pre-texts in Romans 8:35–39

Hübner lists the following pre-texts: Ps 43:23 LXX; Zech 11:4, 7; Isa 53:7 (Rom 8:36); Ps 138:7–8 LXX (Rom 8:39).[50] Nestle-Aland 28th ed. lists the following pre-texts in its margins: Ps 43:23 LXX; Zech 11:4 (Rom 8:36).[51]

Hays devotes most of his attention to Rom 8:36 and Paul's citation of Ps 43:23 LXX.[52] He attempts to correct the interpretive tendency to downplay the implications of Paul citing a psalm of lament at this point in the letter.[53] Hays explains:

---

47. Jewett, *Romans*, 542–43.
48. Seifrid, *Romans*, 635.
49. See, e.g., Fitzgerald, *Cracks in an Earthen Vessel*, 11.
50. Hübner, *Vetus Testamentum in Novo*, 2:136–44.
51. NA 28th ed. 498.
52. See Hays, *Echoes of Scripture*, 57–63.
53. See, e.g., Cranfield, *Romans*, 1:440; Moo, *Romans*, 543–44.

It would be more accurate to say, however, that Paul reads the Psalm as a prophetic prefiguration of the experience of the Christian church, so that the texts finds it true primary meaning in Paul's own present time. The point is not that "righteous people have always suffered like this,"; rather, Paul's point in Rom. 8:35-36 is that Scripture prophesies suffering as the lot of those (i.e., himself and his readers) who live in the eschatological interval between Christ's resurrection and the ultimate redemption of the world.[54]

He also identifies Gen 22:12 as an echo in Rom 8:32 and Isa 53:7 in Rom 8:36.[55]

Seifrid discusses the following pre-texts: Deut 32:23-25; Psalms MT 43:2; 44:9, 23; 60:1; 77:7; 88:5, 14; 108:11; 139:7-12; Job 5:17-35; Isa 51:19; Jer 27:8; 38:2; Lam 3:54; Ezek 5:17; 14:21 (Rom 8:35); Ps 43:23 LXX; Pss MT 25:5; 38:6; 73:14; 74:10, 22; 79:5; 86:3; 89:38-52; 102:8 (Rom 8:36).[56]

Intertextual Analysis of Romans 8:35-39

The dominate intertextual feature here is of course the citation of Ps 43:23 LXX in Rom 8:36. As we shall see, Paul once again draws from the languge of OT lament to articulate the tension in the believer's life between the hope of glorification in Christ and suffering with him. Paul also evokes the scriptural motif of divine condemnation via the kinds of afflictions listed in Rom 8:35. Additionally, the pairs in the final strophe (Rom 8:37-39) evoke various OT motifs.

Romans 8:35 and the Echo of Divine Condemnation

The combination of "tribulation" (θλῖψις) and "distress" (στενοχωρία) only occurs in a handful of OT pre-texts:

> And you will eat the young of your womb, the meat of your sons and daughters, as much as the Lord your God gave to you, in your tribulation (στενοχωριᾳ) and in your distress (θλίψει), with which your enemy will afflict (θλίψει) you (Deut 28:53).[57]

> And they will look downwards to the earth, and behold tribulation (θλῖψις) and distress (στενοχωρία) and darkness, constricting discomfort and darkness so as not to see (Isa 8:22).

The wider contexts of both these pre-texts feature God's warning to Israel that he will judge their disobedience through "tribulation" and "distress" which will be

---

54. Moo, *Romans*, 58.
55. Moo, *Romans*, 61-63. See also Hays, *Conversion of the Imagination*, 35.
56. Seifrid, *Romans*, 633-37.
57. See also Deut 28:55, 57.

experienced at the hands of their enemies. As the preface to the covenant curses in Deut 28 states it, "And it will be if you shall not obey the voice of the Lord your God to keep and to do all his commandments, as much as I am commanding you today, all these curses will come upon you and they will overatke you" (Deut 28:15).

Paul lists several experiences in Rom 8:35 that are curse-like, specifically "persecution" (διωγμός), "famine" (λιμός), "nakedness" (γυμνότης), "danger" (κίνδυνος), and "sword" (μάχαιρα). Two of these experiences, λιμός and γυμνότης, appear in the conclusion of Deut 28, "And you shall serve your enemies, whom the Lord will send upon you, in famine (λιμῷ) and in thirst and in nakedness (γυμνότητι) and in abandonment of all things; and he will place an iron yoke upon your neck, until he should destroy you" (Deut 28:48). Additionally, Isa 8:21 links λιμός with divine condemnation "And a harsh famine (λιμός) will come upon them." What we find then is that the wider contexts of Deut 28 and Isa 8 not only contain the rare combination of "tribulation (θλῖψις) and distress (στενοχωρία)" but also "famine" (λιμός) and "nakedness" (γυμνότης). The semantic overlap between these terms in our pre-text and text are not coincidental. Instead, Paul injects experiences of divine condemnation from Israel's Scriptures into his *Peristasenkatalog*.

These experiences appear in other OT pre-texts besides Deuteronmoy 28 and Isa 8. Some OT laments decry these forms of divine condemnation:

> They have fallen asleep in the street, young and old; my virgins and young men went into captivity; with sword (ῥομφαίᾳ) and famine (λιμῷ) you killed them, in the day of your wrath you mangled them, you did not spare (Lam 2:21).

> They lied to their own Lord and said, "These things are not; calamities will not come upon us, and we will not see sword and famine (μάχαιραν καὶ λιμόν) (Jer 5:12)."

> Behold I will visit them; their young men will be killed by the sword (μάχαιρα), both their sons and daughters will die by famine (λιμῷ) (Jer 11:22).

> I will send famine (λιμόν) to them and death and the sword (μάχαιραν) until they should cease from the earth (Jer 24:10).[58]

In Israel's Scriptures, these experiences fall upon disobedient Israel and or the ungodly. Therefore, it is all the more jarring that Paul applies these experiences to the Romans whom he has just described as God's elect and justified before him through Christ. As Seifrid notes, "In these early Jewish contexts the judgments once visited upon disobedient Israel becomes punishments reserved for the ungodly (Deut. 32:23–25; Isa. 51:19; Jer. 27:8; 38:2; Ezek. 5:17; 14:21). According to their trials, therefore,

---

58. See also Jer 14:12, 16; 16:4; 18:21. For a helpful discussion of lament in Jeremiah, see Baumgartner, *Jeremiah's Poems of Lament*.

believers in Christ appear outwardly to be ungodly; the hidden Jew is the true Jew (Rom. 2:25–29)."[59]

Romans 8:36 and the Citation of Psalm 43:23 LXX

This brings us Paul's citation of a classic psalm of lament.[60] His citation brings into sharper focus the echoes of divine condemnation from the *Peristasenkatalog* in Rom 8:35. Paul follows his list of curse-like experiences by citing Ps 43:23 LXX:

ἕνεκεν σοῦ θανατούμεθα ὅλην τὴν ἡμέραν
ἐλογίσθημεν ὡς πρόβατα σφαγῆς (Rom 8:36).

כי עליך הרגנו כל יום נחשבנו כצאן טבחו
(Ps 44:23 MT)

ὅτι ἕνεκα σοῦ θανατούμεθα ὅλην τὴν ἡμέραν,
ἐλογίσθημεν ὡς πρόβατα σφαγης

(Ps 43:23 LXX)

Commentators agree that Paul's citation is an almost exact match with the LXX version which closely follows the MT.[61] As Jewett notes, "This verse suits Paul's needs so exactly that it is cited verbatim, yet its function needs to be clarified."[62] To Jewett's latter point, some interpreters argue that the wider context of Ps 43 LXX and Rom 8:31–39 are contextually incompatible. For example, Kujanpää contends "In Psalm 8:36 Paul uses a psalm verse to express Christ-believers' experience of persecution and to link it so scriptural experience. However, he only takes the words of the psalm, whereas little of their original literary context is transferred into Romans."[63]

This kind of suggestion fails in multiple ways. First, it does not take seriously how Paul underscores suffering throughout Rom 5:1—8:39. His description throughout this section of the letter maps onto the wider context of Ps 43 LXX which I will discuss momentarily. Second, the notion that Paul only "takes the words of the psalm" and not the wider thrust of Ps 43 LXX fails to recognize the intertextual subxtext of the immediate context. As I noted above, Rom 8:31–35 contains a rich intertextual subtext which collectively raises the kinds of questions expressed by the wider context of Ps 43

---

59. Seifrid, *Romans*, 636.

60. For helpful analyses of Ps 44 (43 LXX), see Basson, *Divine Metaphors*, 161–86; Melancthon, *Rejection by God*; Waltke, *The Psalms as Christian Lament*, 175–215.

61. Kujanpää observes, "The only minute deviation from the critical text of the Septuagint is that Paul reads ἕνεκεν in place of ἕνεκα, and even this deviation goes in all probability back to pre-Pauline variance in the textual tradition." Kujanpää, *The Rhetorical Quotations in Romans*, 321.

62. Jewett, *Romans*, 548.

63. Kujanpää, *The Rhetorical Quotations in Romans*, 329.

LXX. In short, just as the psalmist laments the nation's inexplicable rejection by God, Paul wrestles with afflictions that bear a striking resemblance to divine condemnation which is inexplicable if in fact the Romans are justified before God through faith in Christ.

When we turn our attention to the wider context of Ps 43 LXX, we find a lamenter torn between trust in God's faithfulness and God's inexplicable rejection of the nation.[64] Verses 2–9 recount the way God had faithfully delivered Israel from its enemies in the past. The psalmist confidently asserts, "For you saved (ἔσωσας) us from those whose afflict us and you put to shame those who hate us" (Ps 43:8 LXX). God's previous deliverance of the nations propels the psalmist's faith that the same kind of deliverance will occur in the future. However, in typical lament fashion, the lamenter's mood takes a drastic turn "But now you have rejected (ἀπώσω) us and you put us to shame and you did not go out with our armies" (Ps 43:10 LXX). This lamenter proceeds to question this inexplicable rejection on behalf of the nation. Much of what follows is the lamenter's complaint/protest on behalf of the community against God's actions which resulted in defeat and shame before their enemies.[65] The lamenter maintains the nation's innocence arguing, "If we have forgotten the name of our God and if we spread out our hands to another God, will God not seek these things? For he knows the hidden things of the heart" (Ps 43:21–23 LXX).

The lamenter follows this observation with the complaint cited by Paul, "For because of you we face death all day long, we have been reckoned as sheep for slaughter" (Ps 43:23 LXX). The lamenter lays the onus for the nation's death and its shame on God alone (ἕνεκα σοῦ θανατούμεθα). Israel's God, not the nation's guilt, is the reason for their affliction. Their enemies afflict them, but, unlike many other times in Israel's history, this affliction is not the result of God judging the nation for its sins by handing them over to their enemies. Nevertheless, the whole ordeal bears that appearance. It looks like the very kind of divine condemnation that God warned about for breaking the Mosaic covenant.[66] Yet, the lamenter insists such a transgression has not taken place.[67] God's inexplicable abandonment of the people in battle leaves them like sheep who have only been nurtured and then scattered to be slaughtered by their enemies.[68] Nevertheless, as the lamenter's closing requests indicate, his hope and trust remain

---

64. Interpreters of Ps 44 (43 LXX) do not agree on the cause behind God's rejection of the community at this in their history. Samuel Terrien suggests that the community's suffering here is "a total enigma." Terrien, *The Psalms*, 360. Contrastively, Hans-Joachim Kraus suggests "Suffering comes to the community because it belongs to Yahweh. It is experiencing martyrdom." Kraus, *Psalms*, 448.

65. See, e.g., Ps 43:11–17 LXX.

66. See, e.g., Deut 31:17–18.

67. See Ps 43:18 LXX.

68. As Grogan notes, "The nation's armies have been defeated and the psalmist sees this as rejection by God. Employing familiar pastoral imagery, he likens them to sheep reared only for slaughter. They have also been scattered." Grogan, *Psalms*, 98.

that God will deliver "Rise, O Lord, help us and ransom us because of your name" (Ps 43:27 LXX).[69]

When the wider context of Ps 43 LXX is brought to bear on the interpretation of Paul's citation in Rom 8:36, it becomes apparent that in suffering with Christ (Rom 8:17) one experiences what appears to be inexplicable rejection by God just as the psalmist and Christ did.[70] Just as God treated Israel like sheep for the slaughter, and just as he abandoned Christ at the cross, he does something similar with the Romans. Therefore, Paul maintains the tension felt by the psalmist, a tension between hope in God's faithfulness and suffering. He expands the psalmist's hope by underscoring the intercessory work of Christ (Rom 8:34) and the proximity of his love for the Romans. Paul asks, "Who will separate us from the love of Christ (ἀπὸ τῆς ἀγάπης τοῦ Χριστοῦ)?" What seems to be divine rejection in the vein of covenant curses (Deut 28) and the complaints of Ps 43 LXX cannot separate the elect from Christ's love.

Romans 8:37–39 and Echoes of God's Authority Over Inimical Forces

Paul draws on various OT pre-texts when he contrasts (ἀλλά) divine rejection in Rom 8:36 with "super-triumph" (ὑπερνικάω) in Christ in 8:37–39.[71] The various forces that Paul describes here are all created (κτίσις) by God. If these forces overcome the Romans, it follows that God has rejected them. That is because as the creator of such forces he ultimately controls them. Therefore, Paul emphatically drives home the point that these forces are overcome through Christ "But in all these things we overwhelmingly conquer (ὑπερνικῶμεν) through the one who loved us" (Rom 8:37). Paul lists these forces in four pairs. Each pair evokes OT pre-texts that describe Israel's God has having control over such forces.

The first pair in the list is death and life: "For I am convinced that neither death (θάνατος) nor life (ζωή) . . . will be able to separate us from the love of God which is in Chrisrt Jesus our Lord." While death is the "fiercest enemy of God" from Paul's perspective, life is also riddled with pain.[72] Israel's Scriptures, of course, portray God has having power over both:

> Behold, behold because I am, and there is no God beside me; I will kill (ἀποκτενῶ) and I will give life (ζῆν ποίησω), I will strike and I will also heal, and there is no one who will deliver from my hands (Deut 32:39).

---

69. See also the complaints and requests in Ps 43:24–26 LXX.

70. For a discussion of inexplicable suffering in Paul's thought as it relates to the citation in Rom 8:36, see Starling, "For Your Sake," 112–21.

71. Seifrid glosses ὑπερνικῶμεν in Rom 8:37 as "we super-triumph." See Seifrid, *Romans*, 637. Jewett renders the verb as "supervictors" and notes that similar language in Greek literature bears the sense of "crushing one's enemies completely." See Jewett, *Romans*, 548.

72. Stuhlmacher notes, "In making this list, Paul refers to death as the fiercest enemy of God." Stuhlmacher, *Romans*, 141. Cf. 1 Cor 15:26, 54–57.

The Lord kills (θανατοῖ) and makes alive (ζωογονεῖ), he brings down to Hades and brings up (1 Sam 2:6).[73]

Paul's confidence that neither death nor life can separate the Romans from God's love stems, at least in part, from these kinds of scriptural assertions. He reconfigures his intertextually charged assertion in light of God's love that is demonstrated and present in the person of Christ. For Paul, God lovingly and definitively rules over death and life through the death and resurrection of Christ the Lord.

Paul's second pair is "neither angels nor rulers" (ἄγγελοι οὔτε ἀρχαί). The referent of this pair is not immediately clear. Paul sometimes employs ἄγγελος as a referent to both godly and demonic agents.[74] He also uses ἀρχή to designate hostile spiritual forces.[75] Stuhlmacher suggests that the pair may refer to "fallen angels and principalities."[76] Cranfield allows for a reference to "benevolent or malevolent" forces.[77] In this reading, Paul's point would simply be that "no spiritual cosmic power" can separate the Romans from God's love in Christ.[78] Jewett suggests that the "rulers in view are political."[79] Regardless of the precise referent, angels and rulers in this context are part of a larger pantheon of cosmic forces that God has at his disposal to reject his enemies. Once again, if the Romans are overcome by such forces, it signals that God has rejected them. This brings us to the intertextual echoes stemming from the pair.

Israel's Scritprues portray God as one who has power over all angelic and political forces, as well as spirits, whether they be benevolent or malevolent. Israel's God sometimes sends ἄγγελοι and or ἀρχαί to dole out judgment against enemies in various scenarios. For example, he sends ἄγγελοι to destroy Sodom, "And the two messengers (ἄγγελοι) went to Sodom in the evening (Gen 19:1)."[80] The psalmist portrays God's power by referring to the angels as his servants, "The one who makes his angels (τοὺς ἀγγέλους αὐτοῦ) spirits, and his servants (τοὺς λειτουργοὺς αὐτοῦ) a flaming fire" (Ps 103:4 LXX).[81] Angels do divine work, and they are called to worship Israel's

---

73. See also Ps 67:21 LXX.

74. See, e.g., 2 Cor 11:13; 12:17; Gal 1:8; 3:19; 4:14.

75. See, e.g., Eph 3:10; 6:12; Col 1:16, 18; 2:15.

76. Stuhlmacher, *Romans*, 141. Contrastively, some interpreters suggest that Paul has in view both good and bad angels. See, e.g., Weiss, *Der Brief an der Römer*, 388. However, as Jewett notes, "Others insist that both good and bad angels are in view here, but it seems more likely in the context of this passage that Paul has only fallen angels in mind." Jewett, *Romans*, 552.

77. Cranfield, *Romans*, 1:442.

78. Cranfield, *Romans*, 1:442.

79. Jewett, *Romans*, 552.

80. The same two ἄγγελοι from Gen 19:1 are referred to as οἱ ἄνδρες in Gen 19:12–13, "And the men said to Lord, "Who is there to you here, whether sons-in-law or sons or daughters? Or if there is any other in the city, bring them out from this place; because we are destroying (ἀπόλλυμεν) this place, because their cry has been lifted up before the Lord, the Lord sent us to ruin it."

81. Cf. the use of Ps 103:4 LXX in Heb 1:7.

God "Praise him, all his angels (ἄγγελλοι); praise him; all his powers (δυνάμεις)" (Ps 148:2 LXX).[82]

Paul recontextualizes the intertextually charged pair ἄγγελοι and ἀρχαί, along with δυνάμεις at the end of Rom 8:38, by assuring the Romans that, despite all appearances, these entities cannot separate them from God's love in Christ. In keeping with God's power over these forces in Israel's Scriptures, Paul escalates that power based on what God has done in Christ. These forces have already failed given Christ's resurrection and exaltation. Therefore, those who are in Christ cannot ultimately be harmed by the forces he already conquered.

Interpreters have identified the referent of the pair ἐνεστῶτα and μέλλοντα in various ways.[83] Given Paul's use of lament language throughout Rom 8, it is likely that the referent of the pair is enemies, both political and spiritual, who, like enemies from OT lament, perpetually attempt to snuff out the lives of lamenters through flattery, false testimony, deception, betrayal, and violence.[84] Such affliction never ceases. Instead, it defines one's entire existence. As one lamenter puts it, "Many times they have battled against me from my youth (ἐκ νεότητός μου)" (Ps 128:1 LXX). Paul abstracts this constant affliction by referring to these enemies as "things present" and "things to come." Nevertheless, the very things that could presently, or in the future, separate the elect from God have been overcome in Christ.

The final pair, οὔτε ὕψμα οὔτε βάθος, compares the threat of separation to diametrically opposed spatial dimensions, and the comparison evokes spatial imagery from Israel's Scriptures.[85] Once again, given the impact of lament language on Paul's thought in Rom 8:31–39, it follows that this pair likely reflects complaints about separation from God in the Psalms of Lament:

> Look, Lord, do not be silent, Lord, do not draw away (ἀποστῇς) from me (Ps 34:22 LXX).

> Do not abandon (ἐγκαταλίπῃς) me, Lord; my God, do not draw away from me (ἀποστῇς) (Ps 37:22 LXX).

Paul's pairing of οὔτε ὕψμα οὔτε βάθος not only evokes these kinds of spatially charged complaints but also statements of trust which are also spatially charged such as, "If I

---

82. See Deut 32:43 LXX.

83. Suggestions include astrological powers and the power of the present age in comparison to a future one. See, e.g., Barrett, *1 Corinthians*, 174; Jewett, *Romans*, 553; Schlier, *Der Römerbrief*, 280. Cf. the use of ἐνεστῶτα and μέλλοντα in 1 Cor 3:22–23.

84. Cf. the description of sin in Rom 7:7–25 as discussed above. See also the intertextual analysis of enemies described in Rom 3:10–18 in volume 1.

85. Cf. the use of spatial dimensions in Eph 3:18 where he also includes "width and height." Arnold suggests that the four dimensions could indicate a concern with supernatural powers connected to the practice of magic. However, this does not seem to be applicable to Rom 8:39. See Arnold, *Ephesians*, 216.

should go up to heaven (εἰς τὸν οὐρανόν), you are there; if I should go down to Hades (εἰς τὸν ᾅδην), you are present" (Ps 138:8 LXX). Paul recontextualizes this kind of spatially charaged language to make the point that there is no location in the cosmos where inimical forces can separate belivers from God's love in the Lord Jesus Christ.

Paul closes his lists of pairs with the singular οὔτε τις κτίσις ἑτέρα.[86] In this way, Paul both accounts for anything that might not be accounted for in his list, and he drives home the point that God, as creator, is sovereign over all iminical forces.[87] This point evokes a scriptural motif wherein God's power over all things, especially forces which threaten his people, is grounded in his identity as creator.[88] As one psalmist describes it:

> The heavens are yours, and the earth is yours; you founded (ἐθεμελίωσας) the world and its fullness. You created (ἔκτισας) the north and the west; Tabor and Hermon will praise your name. Your arm is with power (μετὰ δυναστείας); let your hand be strengthened, let your right hand be exalted (Ps 88:12–14 LXX).[89]

As creator, God is enthroned high above everything he creates; therefore, he ultimately controls what is made, whether it be benevolent or malevolent.[90] Paul recontextualizes the creator's authority so that the Lord Jesus Christ shares in it. His involvement in fact guaranţees the inseparability of God's people from the creator's love. After all, it is the love of God "which is in Christ Jesus our Lord" (τῆς ἐν Χριστῷ Ἰησοῦ τῷ κυρίῳ ἡμῶν).

Interpretive Impact of Pre-texts in Romans 8:31–39

While Paul's citation of Ps 43:23 LXX stands out as the main intertextual feature in Rom 8:31–39, it obviously is not the only intertextual feature. Rather than merely recap the many intertextual features of these verses, I ultimately want to consider how the interplay between these pre-texts and text works together.

To begin, Paul characterizes himself and his recipients in the vein of OT figures whose trust in God's future protection was grounded in his past saving actions. This characterization is reflected in Paul's rhetorical question "If God is for us, who is

---

86. The use of κτίσις in Rom 8:39 bears a different sense than the uses of the same noun in Rom 8:19–22 where it refers to the entirety of creation. BDAG 573.

87. Hultgren observes, "The final line concerning 'any other creature' serves to close the list, lest anything else be left out." Hultgren, *Romans*, 342.

88. The noun κτίσις does not occur in the canonical LXX. However, see the uses of the noun in Jdt 9:12; 16;14; Tob 8:5; Wis 2:6; 5:17; 16:24; 19:6; Sir 16:17; 43:25; 49:16. In these examples, κτίσις refers to either the entirety of creation and or created things. LEH 358.

89. This psalm, like Paul's last pairing of οὔτε ὕψμα οὔτε βάθος, stresses God's authority over spatial dimensions.

90. As Abraham describes Israel's God to the king of Sodom, "I will stretch out my hand to the most high God (τὸν θεὸν τὸν ὕψιστον), who created (ἔκτισεν) heaven and earth" (Gen 14:22).

against us?" The loudest echo in Paul's question emanates from Ps 55:12 LXX which contains its own rhetorical question, "I have hoped in God, I will not fear; what will man do to me?" As the wider context of the psalm indicates, the psalmist's trust stems from God's past saving actions. Such actions give the psalmist confidence in facing present and future dangers. For Paul, these present and future dangers are eschatologically charged as the wider context of Rom 8:31–39 indicates. The definitive saving action is found in the death, resurrection, and exaltation of Jesus Christ. Paul narrates this saving action through echoes of other pre-texts.

One of these additional pre-texts is from Gen 22. When Paul describes God saving action as "not sparing" (οὐκ ἐφείσατο) his only son (τοῦ ἰδίου υἱοῦ), it evokes Gen 22:16 "Because you did this matter and you did not spare (οὐκ ἐφείσω) your beloved son (τοῦ υἱοῦ σου τοῦ ἀγαπητοῦ) because of me." In short, Paul narrates God's saving action, which gives the believer eschatological confidence, through the prism of the 'Aqedah tradition (יעקד). Paul places God the Father in the role of Abraham and God's son in the role of Isaac.[91] The interplay between these roles produce the unstated point that God did with his son Jesus what Abraham did not have to do with his son Isaac, namely hand him over to a sacrificial death. To put it another way, Abraham was ultimately allowed to "spare" his son, but God the Father did not make this allowance for himself.

The escalation between these sacrificial deaths resides in their efficacy. The result of Abraham's action towards his son results in the promise of future blessing:

> I will certainly bless you (εὐλογῶν εὐλογήσω), and I will certainly multiply your seed like the stars of heaven and like the sand which is beside the shore of the sea, and your seed will inherit the cities of its enemies; and in your seed all the nations of the earth will be blessed, because you have obeyed my voice (Gen 22:17–18).

The blessing in question is the multiplication of Abraham's seed and the sound defeat of his descendants' enemies based on the patriarch's willingness to not spare his son. The interplay of this blessing with Paul's text produces the unstated point that, based on God's willingness to not spare his son Jesus, those who trust in God receive the blessings promised to Abraham. In this way, it is God's gift of Christ, not Abraham's obedience, that ultimately leads to the fulfillment of the promise. In Christ, one receives "everything" (τὰ πάντα) that God promised to Abraham.[92] As Paul puts it, "He who did not spare his own but handed him over for us all, how will he not also with him graciously give to us all things (τὰ πάντα)?" (Rom 8:32). The referent of τὰ πάντα from Paul's intertextual perspective is the world and an existence in that world that

---

91. Although Paul does not explicitly use the divine title πατήρ in this text, it is obviously assumed given his use of υἱός to describe Jesus. See the use of υἱός in Rom 8:32.

92. Of course, as we have already seen in Rom 4, Paul reconfigures the blessings of Abraham. The promise of a land to dwell in is reconfigured as the promise to inherit the world (κόσμος) (Rom 4:13). See the intertextual analysis of Rom 4:13 in volume 1.

reverses its divinely ordained futility (Rom 8:19–22). In other words, a resurrected existence (Rom 8:23–27). Such an inheritance is guaranteed by a sacrifice even greater than what Abraham was willing to do with Isaac.[93]

Paul also narrates God's saving work in Christ, which functions as the basis for the believer's eschatological confidence, through the prism of the suffering servant in Isa 53. Once again, the phrase ὑπὲρ ἡμῶν πάντων παρέδωκεν αὐτόν in Rom 8:32 echoes the phrase κύριος παρέδωκεν αὐτὸν ταῖς ἁμαρτίαις ἡμῶν in Isa 53:6.[94] The unstated point of resonance is that Jesus is the suffering servant whom God handed over to death in the place of and on behalf of the believers in Rome. Given the wider context of Isa 53, God handed Jesus over to heal the ungodly from sin and justify sinners.[95] In this way, within the same verse, Paul combines the 'Aqedah tradition with the tradition of Isaiah's suffering servant. Jesus plays the role of both Isaac and the suffering servant, only in a greater way. God's work in the Isaac-like son whom he would not spare but handed over like Isaiah's suffering servant makes certain that God will give to the Romans everything he has ever promised his people.

No one presently, or eschatologically, can bring the kind of charge against God's "elect" (κατὰ ἐκλεκτῶν θεοῦ) that would result in their rejection before God. As noted above, Paul's description of the Romans as God's ἐκλεκτός evokes three interrelated motifs from Israel's Scriptures: (1) God's election of Abraham and his descendants; (2) God's election of David and his royal descendant; and (3) power and love as the means God uses to carry out his electing purposes. Paul recontextualizes these motifs of divine election from an ecclesiastical, christological, and soteriological perspective. The unstated point of resonance that emerges from this recontextualization and interplay is three-fold: (1) God's election of Abraham and his descendants includes both Jews and Gentiles; (2) Jesus is the Davidic king whose rule is established in the cosmos through his sacrificial death, glorious resurrection, and exaltation to the right hand of God (Ps 109 LXX); and (3) this reigning Davidic king is included in the identity of Israel's God and his saving work which extends beyond the geo-political realm.

However, the protection of God's elect does not preclude them from afflictions of all kinds which Paul highlights in this text. He evokes scriptural afflictions such as false accusations against God's people (Isa 50) and experiences such as famine and persecution which, from an intertextual perspective, could be interpreted as divine condemnation. The former affliction is signaled through the rhetorical question, "Who will bring a charge against God's elect?" (Rom 8:33). As noted above, the question evokes the description of the suffering servant in Isa 50:6–9 who faces violence

---

93. Within the *history of interpretation*, Schoeps noted some time ago that many early Christian interpreters detected the echo of Gen 22 in Rom 8:32. Schoeps explains, "This proposed interpretation is supported by Origen, Ambrosiaster, John Chrysostome, and later writers like Oekumenius and Theophylactus." Schoeps, "The Sacrifice of Isaac in Paul," 390–91.

94. See also the phrases παρεδόθη εἰς θάνατον ἡ ψυχὴ αὐτοῦ and διὰ τὰς ἁμαρτίας αὐτῶν παρεδόθη in Isa 53:12.

95. See, e.g., Isa 53:5–6, 10, 11.

and judgment from his enemies. The servant trusts in God while facing this affliction asserting, "the one who justifies me (ὁ δικαιώσας με) is near" (Isa 50:8). While facing similar affliction, namely violence and judgmental accusations, Paul confidently asserts "God is the one justifies" (θεὸς ὁ δικαιῶν) (Rom 8:33).

The interplay between *Peristasenkatalog* in Rom 8:35 and the pre-texts it echoes generates the unstated point that God's elect in Christ face afflictions which resemble the divine condemnation prescribed in Israel's Scriptures. From an intertextual perspective, the seven sources of affliction (θλῖψις, στενοχωρία, διωγμός, λιμός, γυμνότης, κίνδυνος, μάχαιρα) listed by Paul evoke the various means God uses to condemn his people, or enemies, in the OT.[96] The essence of that condemnation is the absence of, or separation from, God. However, Paul reconfigures these afflictions with the result that they should not be interpreted as divine condemnation. Nor do they signal God's absence. Divine condemnation has been removed in Christ (Rom 8:1). Inimical forces are overcome through him. Therefore, nothing can separate the Christians in Rome from God's love in Christ.

Paul's citation of Ps 43:23 LXX in Rom 8:36 confirms my interpretation of the *Peristasenkatalog* in the preceding verse. These afflictions give the appearance of divine condemnation which is inexplicable given the Romans' justification before God through faith in Christ. That inexplicability defines the larger context of Ps 43 LXX as noted above. Therefore, Paul's citation of the psalm is quite telling. God's elect in Christ cannot ultimately explain why they constantly (ὅλην τὴν ἡμέραν) suffer what looks like divine condemnation. They are like sheep for the slaughter (πρόβατα σφαγῆς).[97] However, Paul makes two points clear here: (1) the Christians in Rome should not interpret their affliction as divine condemnation; and (2) their affliction, whatever the ultimate reason for it, does not signal God's absence.

God's presence in Christ means that he is for his people and not against them. Therefore, they overwhelmingly conquer (ὑπερνικῶμεν) the inimical forces marshalled against them. After all, the forces marshalled against them are created entities, and the creator is on their side. In this way, Paul leans upon the identity of Israel's God as the creator, but he reconfigures that identity to include Christ. The Davidic figure seated at God's right hand in the vein of Ps 109 LXX, who intercedes for them, is at the same time included in the identity of Yahweh the creator as the Lord Jesus Christ. Here is the hopeful locus of the Roman's boast in their tribualtions which Paul mentions at the outset of this entire entire epistolary section (Rom 5:1–5).

---

96. See once again Deut 28:48; Isa 8:21; Lam 2:21; Jer 5:12; 24:10.

97. Perhaps a partial reason for the affliction is offered by God's eternal purpose to conform belivers to the image of the son which Paul mentions in Rom 8:29. However, it does not explain the affliction entirely. Otherwise, Paul would have followed Rom 8:35 with a restatement of God's eternal purpose rather than a citation from a classic communal lament in which the speaker questions God's inexplicable treatment of his people.

Bibliography

Ahearne-Kroll, Stephen. *The Psalms of Lament in Mark's Passion in Mark's Passion: Jesus' Davidic Suffering*. Cambridge: Cambridge University Press, 2007.
Allen, Leslie C. "The Old Testament Background of (προ)ὁρίζειν in the New Testament." *NTS* 17 (1971) 104–8.
Anderson, Bernhard W. *Out of the Depths: The Psalms Speak for Us Today*. Philadelphia: Westminster John Knox, 1983.
Arnold, Clinton E. *Ephesians*. Grand Rapids: Zondervan, 2010.
Barclay, John M. G. *Paul and the Gift*. Grand Rapids: Eerdmans, 2015.
Barr, "'Abba' Isn't Daddy." *JBL* 39 (1988) 28–47.
Barrett, C. K. *A Commentary on the First Epistle to the Corinthians*. 2nd ed. London: Continuum, 1994.
———. *The Epistle to the Romans*. Peabody, MA: Hendrickson, 1987.
Bates, Matthew W. *The Hermeneutics of the Apostolic Proclamation: The Center of Paul's Method of Scriptural Interpretation*. Waco, TX: Baylor University Press, 2012.
———. "The Old Testament in the New Testament." In *The State of New Testament Research: A Survey of Recent Research*, edited by Scot McKnight and Nijay K. Gupta, 83–102. Grand Rapids: Baker, 2019.
Batey, Richard A. *New Testament Nuptial Imagery*. Leiden: Brill, 1971.
Bauckham, Richard. *Jesus and the God of Israel: God Crucified and Other Studies on the New Testament's Christology of Divine Identity*. Grand Rapids: Eerdmans, 2008.
Baumgartner, Walter. *Jeremiah's Poems of Lament*. Decatur: Almond, 1988.
Beale, G. K. *Handbook on the New Testament Use of the Old Testament: Exegesis and Interpretation*. Grand Rapids: Baker, 2012.
Bertone, John A. *"The Law of the Spirit": The Experience of the Spirit and Displacement of the Law in Romans 8:1–16*. Berlin: Peter Lang, 2005.
Best, Ernest. *The Letter of Paul to the Romans*. Cambridge: Cambridge University Press, 1967.
Betz, Hans Dieter. *Galatians*. Minneapolis: Fortress, 1989.
Black, Matthew. "The Pauline Doctrine of the Second Adam." *SJT* 7 (1954) 170–79.
Bornkamm, Günther. "Sin, Law, and Death: An Exegetical Study of Romans 7." In *Early Christian Experience*, 87–104. New York: Harper & Row, 1969.
Bousset, Wilhelm. *Kyrios Christos: A History of the Belief in Christ from the Beginning of Christianity to Irenaeus*. Waco, TX: Baylor University Press, 2013.
Braaten, Laurie J. "All Creation Groans: Romans 8:22 in Light of the Biblical Sources." *HBTH* 28 (2006) 131–59.
Brandenburger, Egon. *Adam und Christus. Exegetisch-religionsgeschichtliche Untersuchungen zu Römer 5, 12–21 (1. Kor. 15)*. Neukirchen-Vluyn: Neukirchener, 1962.

Bray, Gerald L. "Adam and Christ (Romans 5:12–21)." *Evangel* 18 (2000) 4–8.

Bruckner, James K. "The Creational Context of Law before Sinai: Law and Liberty in Pre-Sinai Narratives and Romans 7." *ExAud* 11 (1995) 91–110.

Burge, Gary. *Jesus and the Land: The New Testament Challenge to "Holy Land" Theology*. Grand Rapids: Baker, 2010.

Burke, Trevor J. *Adopted into God's Family: Exploring a Pauline Metaphor*. Downers Grove, IL: InterVarsity, 2006.

Burns, J. Patount, Jr. *Romans: Interpreted by Early Christian Commentators*. Grand Rapids: Eedrmans, 2012.

Busch, Austin. "The Figure of Eve in Romans 7:5–25." *BibInt* 12 (2004) 1–36.

Byrne, Brendan, SJ. *Romans*. Collegeville: Liturgical, 1996.

———. *Sons of God-Seed of Abraham: A Study of the Idea of the Sonship of God of All Christians in Paul Against the Jewish Background*. Rome: Gregorian University Press, 1979.

———. "The Type of the One to Come (Rom 5:14): Fate and Responsibility in Romans 5:12–21." *ABR* 36 (1988) 19–30.

Byron, John. *Slavery Metaphors in Early Judaism and Pauline Christianity: A Traditio-Historical and Exegetical Examination*. WUNT 2/162. Tübingen: Mohr Siebeck, 2003.

Calvin, John. *Romans*. Grand Rapids: Baker, 2003.

Campbell, Constantine R. *Paul and the Hope of Glory: An Exegetical and Theological Study*. Grand Rapids: Zondervan, 2020.

———. *Paul and Union with Christ: An Exegetical and Theological Study*. Grand Rapids: Zondervan, 2012.

Campbell, Douglas A. *Pauline Dogmatics: The Triumph of God's Love*. Grand Rapids: Eerdmans, 2020.

Campbell, Keith D. *Of Heroes and Villains: The Influence of the Psalmic Lament on Synoptic Characterization*. Eugene, OR: Wipf & Stock, 2013.

Caneday, Ardel. "Already Reigning in Life through One Man: Recovery of Adam's Abandoned Dominion (Romans 5:12–21)." In *Studies in the Pauline Epistles: Essays in Honor of Douglas Moo*, edited by Matthew S. Harmon and Jay E. Smith, 27–43. Grand Rapids: Zondervan, 2014.

Capes, *Old Testament Yahweh Texts in Paul's Christology*. Waco, TX: Baylor University Press, 2017.

Casson, Sarah H. *Textual Signposts in the Argument of Romans: A Relevance-Theory Approach*. Atlanta: SBL, 2019.

Christofferson, Olle. *The Earnest Expectation of the Creature: The Flood-Tradition as Matrix of Romans 8,18–17*. Stockholm: Almqvist & Wiskell, 1990.

Compton, Jared. *Psalm 110 and the Logic of Hebrews*. LNTS 537. London: T. & T. Clark, 2015.

Cranfield, C. E. B. "The Creation's Promised Liberation: Some of Observation on Romans 8.19–21." In *Reconciliation and Hope: New Testament Essays on Atonement and Eschatology Presented to L. L. Morris on His 60th Birthday*, edited by Robert J. Banks, 224–30. Exeter: Paternoster, 1974.

———. *The Epistle to the Romans*. 2 vols. Edinburgh: T. & T. Clark, 1975.

Crisler, Channing L. *Echoes of Lament and the Christology of Luke*. Sheffield: Sheffield Phoenix, 2020.

———. "The 'I' Who Laments: Echoes of Old Testament Lament in Romans 7:7–25 and the Identity of the ἐγώ." *CBQ* 82 (2020) 64–83.

———. "Luther's Tentatio as the Center of Paul's Theology." In *Always Reforming: Reflections on Martin Luther and Biblical Studies*, edited by Channing L. Crisler and Robert L. Plummer, 31–49. Bellingham: Lexham, 2021.

———. *Pauline Theology as Agonizing Struggle*. Bellingham: Lexham, forthcoming.

———. *Reading Romans as Lament: Paul's Use of Old Testament Lament in His Most Famous Letter*. Eugene, OR: Pickwick, 2016.

Cuddon, J. A. "Echo." In *A Dictionary of Literary Terms and Literary Theory*, edited by J. A. Cuddon, 223. Chichester: Wiley-Blackwell, 2013.

Danker, Fredrick W. "Romans v.12: Sin Under Law." *NTS* 14 (1968) 424–39.

Davies, W. D. *Christian Engagements with Judaism*. Harrisburg: Trinity, 1999.

de Boer, Martinus C. "Paul's Mythologizing Program in Romans 5–8." In *Apocalyptic Paul: Cosmos and Anthorpos in Romans 5–8*, edited by Beverly Roberts Gaventa, 1–20. Waco, TX: Baylor University Press, 2013.

de Jesús Legarreta-Castillo, Felipe. *The Figure of Adam in Romans 5 and 1 Corinthians 15: The New Creation and Its Ethical and Social Reconfiguration*. Minneapolis: Fortress, 2014.

Dhanaraj, Dharmakkan. *Theological Significance of the Motif of Enemies in Selected Psalms of Individual Lament*. Glückstadt: J. J. Augustin, 1992.

Dillard, Raymond Bryan. "Joel." In *The Minor Prophets: An Exegetical and Expository Commentary*, edited by Thomas Edward McComiskey, 239–313. Grand Rapids: Baker, 2009.

Docherty, Susan. "'Do you Understand what you are Reading,' (Acts 8:30): Current Trends and Future Perspectives in the Study of the Use of the Old Testament in the New." *JSNT* 38 (2015) 112–25.

Dochorn, Jan. "Röm 7,7 und das zehnte Gebot. Ein Beitrag zur Schriftauslegung und zur jüdischen Vorgeschichte des Paulus." *ZNW* 100 (2009) 59–77.

Dodd, C. H. *According to the Scriptures: The Substructure of New Testament Theology*. London: Fontana, 1965.

———. *The Epistle of Paul to the Romans*. London: Fontana, 1959.

Dodson, Joseph R. *The Powers of Personification: Rhetorical Purposes in the Book of Wisdom and the Letter to the Romans*. Berlin: de Gruyter, 2008.

Dunn, James D. G. *Romans 1–8*. Dallas: Word, 1988.

Earnshaw, J. D. "Reconsidering Paul's Marriage Metaphor in Romans 7.1–4." *NTS* 40 (1994) 68–88.

Eklund, Rebekah. *Jesus Wept: The Significance of Jesus' Lament in the NT*. LNTS 515. London: T. & T. Clark, 2015.

Elder, Nicholas. "'Wretch I Am!' Eve's Tragic Speech-in-Character in Romans 7:7–25." *JBL* 137 (2018) 743–64.

Ellis, E. Earle. *The Old Testament in Early Christianity: Canon and Interpretation in Light of Modern Research*. Repr. Eugene, OR: Wipf & Stock, 2003.

———. *Paul's Use of the Old Testament*. Repr. Eugene, OR: Wipf & Stock, 2003.

Emerson, Matthew Y. *"He Descended to the Dead": An Evangelical Theology of Holy Saturday*. Downers Grove, IL: InterVarsity, 2019.

Erickson, Richard J. "The Damned and the Justified in Romans 5.12–21: An Analysis of Semantic Structure." In *Discourse Analysis and the New Testament: Approaches and Results*, edited by Stanley Porter, 282–315. Sheffield: Sheffield Academic, 1999.

Ferris, Paul Wayne, Jr. *The Genre of the Communal Lament in the Bible and the Ancient Near East*. Atlanta: Scholars, 1992.

Fitzmyer, Joseph A. *Romans*. New York: Doubleday, 1992.
Fitzgerald, John T. *Cracks in an Earthen Vessel: An Examination of Hardships in the Corinthian Correspondence*. SBLDS 99. Atlanta: Scholars, 1988.
Forbes, Christopher. "Paul and Rheotircal Comparison." In *Paul in the Greco-Roman World: A Handbook*, edited by J. Paul Sampley, 134–71. Harrisburg: Trinity, 2003.
Fowler, Paul B. *The Structure of Romans: The Argument of Paul's Letter*. Minneapolis: Fortress, 2016.
Friedrich, Gerhard. "ἁμαρτία οὐκ ἐλλογεῖται Röm 5,13." *TLZ* 77 (1952) 523–28.
Freitheim, Terrence E. *The Suffering of God: An Old Testament Perspective*. Philadelphia: Fortress, 1984.
Gagnon, Robert A. J. "Heart of Wax and a Teaching That Stamps: τύπος διδαχῆς (Rom 6:17b) Once More." *JBL* 112 (1993) 667–87.
Gale, Herbert Morrison. *The Use of Analogy in the Letters of Paul*. Philadelphia: Westminster, 1964.
Gathercole, Simon J. *Where is Boasting? Early Jewish Soteriology and Paul's Response in Romans 1–5*. Grand Rapids: Eerdmans, 2002.
Gaventa, Beverly Roberts. "The Shape of the 'I': The Psalter, the Gospel, and the Speaker in Romans 7." In *Apocalyptic Paul: Cosmos and Anthropos in Romans 5–8*, edited by Beverly Roberts Gaventa, 77–92. Waco, TX: Baylor University Press, 2013.
Gieniusz, Andrzej. "Rom 7,1–6: Lack of Imagination? Function of the Passage in the Argumentation of Rom 6,1–7,6." *Bib* 74 (1993) 389–98.
Goodrich, John K. "From Slaves of Sin to Slaves of God: Reconsidering the Origin of Paul's Slavery Metaphor in Romans 6." *BBR* 23 (2013) 509–30.
———. "Sold Under Sin: Echoes of Exile in Romans 7.14–25." *NTS* 59 (2013) 476–95.
Goppelt, Leonard. *Typos: The Typological Interpretation of the Old Testament in the New*. Grand Rapids: Eerdmans, 1982.
Grogan, Geoffrey W. *Psalms*. Grand Rapids: Eerdmans, 2008.
Gunkel, Hermann. *Introduction to the Psalms: The Genres of the Religious Lyric of Israel*. Atlanta: Mercer University Press, 1988.
Haacker, Klaus. *Der Brief des Paulus an die Römer*. Leipzig: Evangelische Verlagsanstalt, 2012.
Hahne, Harry Alan. *The Corruption and Redemption of Creation: Nature in Romans 8:19–22 and Jewish Apocalyptic Literature*. LNTS 336. London: T. & T. Clark, 2006.
Harris, J. Rendel. *Testimonies*. Eugene, OR: Wipf & Stock, 2009.
Hartley, John E. *The Book of Job*. Grand Rapids: Eerdmans, 1988.
———. *Leviticus*. Nashville: Thomas Nelson, 1992.
Hay, David M. *Glory at the Right Hand: Psalm 110 in Early Christianity*. Atlanta: Scholars, 1973.
Hayes, Katherine M. "When None Repents, Earth Laments: The Chorus of Lament in Jeremiah and Joel." In *Seeking the Favor of God, Vol. 1: The Origins of Penitential Prayer in Second Temple Judaism*, edited by Mark J. Boda et al., 119–43. Atlanta: SBL, 2006.
Hays, Richard B. *Conversion of the Imagination: Paul as Interpreter of Israel's Scripture*. Grand Rapids: Eerdmans, 2005.
———. *Echoes of Scriptures in the Letters of Paul*. New Haven, CT: Yale University Press, 1989.
Heckel, Theo K. *Der Innere Mensch*. WUNT 2/53. Tübingen: Mohr Siebeck, 1992.
Hengel, Martin. *Judaism and Hellenism*. 2 vols. Philadelphia: Fortress, 1974.

Hofius, Otfried. "The Adam-Christ Antithesis and the Law: Reflections on Romans 5:12–21." In *Paul and the Mosaic Law*, edited by James D. G. Dunn, 165–205. Grand Rapids: Eerdmans, 2002.

Hollander, John. *The Figure of Echo: A Mode of Allusion in Milton and After*. Berkeley: University of California Press, 1981.

Hübner, Hans. *Vetus Testamentum in Novo: Corpus Paulinum*. Göttingen: Vandenhoeck & Ruprecht, 1997.

Hultgren, Arland J. *Paul's Letter to the Romans: A Commentary*. Grand Rapids: Eerdmans, 2011.

Jensen, Robin. *Living Water: Images, Symbols, and Settings of Early Christian Baptism*. Leiden: Brill, 2010.

Jeremias, Joachim. *Abba: Studien zur neutestamentlichen Theologie und Zeitgeschichte*. Göttingen: Vandenhoeck & Ruprecht, 1966.

Jervis, Ann. "The Commandment Which Is for Life (Romans 7:10): Sin's Use of the Obedience of Faith." *JSNT* 27 (2004) 193–216.

Jewett, Paul. *Romans*. Minneapolis: Fortress, 2007.

Käsemann, Ernst. *Commentary on Romans*. Translted by Geoffrey Bromiley. Grand Rapids: Eerdmans, 1980.

Karlberg, Mark W. "Israel's History Personified: Romans 7:7–13 in Relation to Paul's Teaching on the Old Man." *Trinity Journal* 7 (1986) 65–74.

Keck, Leander E. "The Law and 'the Law of Sin and Death' (Rom 8:1–4): Reflections on the Spirit and Ethics in Paul. In *The Divine Helmsman: Studies on God's Control of Human Events, Presented to Lou H. Silberman*, edited by J. L. Crenshaw and Samuel Sandmel, 51–57. New York Ktav, 1980.

Keener, Craig S. *Romans*. Eugene, OR: Cascade, 2009.

Keesmaat, Sylvia C. Exodus and the Intertextual Transformation of Tradition in Romans 8.14–30. JSNT 54 (1994) 29–56.

———. *Paul and His Story: (Re)-Interpreting the Exodus Tradition*. Sheffield: Sheffield Academic, 1999.

Kirk, J. R. Daniel. *Unlocking Romans: Resurrection and the Justification of God*. Grand Rapids: Eerdmans, 2008.

Kister, Menahem. "Romans 5:12–21 Against the Background of Torah-Theology and Hebrew Usage." *HTR* 100 (2007) 391–424.

Kline, Meredith G. "Gospel Until the Law: Rom 5:13–14 and the Old Covenant." *JETS* 34 (1991) 433–46.

Kister, Menahem. "Romans 5:12–21 Against the Background of Torah-Theology and Hebrew Usage." *HTR* 100 (2007) 391–424.

Kraus, Hans-Joachim. *Psalms 1–59: A Commentary*. Translated by Hilton C. Oswald. Minneapolis: Fortress, 1988.

Kujanpää, Katja. *The Rhetorical Functions of Scriptural Quotations in Romans: Paul's Argumentation by Quotations*. NovTSup 172. Leiden: Brill, 2019.

Kümmel, Werner Georg. *Introduction to the New Testament*. Translated by Howard Clark Kee. Nashville: Abingdon, 1975.

Ladd. G. E. *A Theology of the New Testament*. Grand Rapids: Eerdmans, 1993.

Leithart, Peter J. "Adam, Moses, and Jesus: A Reading of Romans 5:12–14." *CTJ* 43 (2008) 257–73.

Lichtenberger, Hermann. *Das Ich Adams und das Ich der Menscheit*. WUNT 164. Tübingen: Mohr Siebeck, 2004.

Lohse, Eduard. *Der Brief an die Römer*. Göttingen: Vandenhoeck & Ruprecht. 2003.

Longenecker, Richard. *The Epistle to the Romans: A Commentary on the Greek Text*. Grand Rapids: Eerdmans, 2016.

Luther, Martin. *Commentary on Romans*. Translated by J. Theodore Mueller. Grand Rapids: Kregel, 1976.

Lyall, Francis. "Roman Law in the Writings of Paul–Adoption." *JBL* 88 (1969) 458–66.

Mandolfo, Carleen. *God in the Dock: Dialogic Tension in the Psalms of Lament*. JSOTSup 357: Sheffield: Sheffield Academic, 2002.

Markschies, Christoph. "Innerer Mensch." *RAC* 18 (1997) 266–312.

Martin, Dale B. *Slavery as Salvation: The Metaphor of Slavery in Pauline Christianity*. New Haven, CT: Yale University Press, 1990.

Maston, Jason. "Sirach and Romans 7:1–25: The Human, the Law, and Sin." In *Reading Romans in Context*, edited by Ben C. Blackwell et al., 93–99. Grand Rapids: Zonderan, 2015.

Matera, Frank J. *Romans*. Grand Rapids: Baker, 2010.

McFadden, Kevin W. "The Fulfillment of the Law's Dikaioma: Another Look at Romans 8:1–4." *JETS* 52 (2009) 483–97.

Meyer, Paul W. "The Worm at the Core of the Apple: Exegetical Reflections on Romans 7." In *The Conversation Continues: Studies in Paul and John in Honor of J. Louis Martyn*, edited by Robert T. Fortna and Beverly R. Gaventa, 62–97. Nashville: Abingdon, 1990.

McKnight, Scot, and B. J. Oropeza, eds. *Perspectives on Paul: Five Views*. Grand Rapids: Baker,

Michel, Otto. *Der Brief an die Römer*. Göttingen: Vandenhoeck & Ruprecht, 1978.

Miller, Patrick D. *They Cried to the Lord: The Form and Theology of Biblical Prayer*. Minneapolis: Fortress, 1994.

Moo, Douglas J. *The Epistle to the Romans*. Grand Rapids: Eerdmans, 1996.

———. "Israel and Paul in Romans 7.7–12." *NTS* 32 (1986) 122–35.

Moo, Jonathan. "Romans 8.19–22 and Isaiah's Cosmic Covenant." *NTS* 54 (2008) 74–89.

Mounce, Robert H. *Romans*. Nashville: Broadman & Holman, 1995.

Moyise, Steve. *Evoking Scripture: Seeing the Old Testament in the New*. London: T. & T. Clark, 2008.

Murray, John. *The Epistle to the Romans*. Grand Rapids: Eerdmans, 1959.

Nickelsburg, George W. E. *Resurrection, Immortality, and Eternal Life in Intertestamental Judaism and Early Christianity*. HTS 56. Cambridge: Harvard University Press, 2006.

Ogden, Graham S. "Joel 4 and Prophetic Responses to National Laments." *JSOT* 26 (1983) 97–106.

Packer, J. I. "The 'Wretched Man' Revisited: Another Look at Romans 7:14–25." In *Romans and the People of God: Essay in Honor of Gordon D. Fee on the Occasion of His 65th Birthday*, edited by S. K. Soderlund and N. T. Wright, 70–81. Grand Rapids: Eerdmans, 1999.

Parsons, Mikeal C., and Michael Wade Martin. *Ancient Rhetoric and the New Testament: The Influence of Elementary Greek Composition*. Waco, TX: Baylor University Press, 2018.

Philonenko, Marc. "Sur l'expression 'vendu au péché' dans l' Épître aux Romains." *RHR* 203 (1986) 41–52.

Porter, Stan. "The Argument of Romans 5: Can a Rhetorical Question Make a Difference?" *JBL* 110 (1991) 655–77.

Räisänen, Heikki. *Paul and the Law*. WUNT 29. Tübingen: Mohr Siebeck, 1983.

———. "The Pauline Concept of Original Sin, In Light of Rabbinical Background." *TynBul* 41 (1990) 3–30.

Reid, Marty L. *Augustinian and Pauline Rhetoric in Romans Five: A Study of Early Christian Rhetoric*. Lewiston: Mellen, 1996.

Sanday, William, and Arthur C. Headlam. *A Critical and Exegetical Commentary on the Epistle to the Romans*. Edinburgh: T. & T. Clark, 1895.

Sanders, E. P. *Paul, the Law, and the Jewish People*. Philadelphia: Fortress, 1983.

Sandnes, Karl Olav. "Abraham, The Friend of God, in Rom 5: A Short Notice." *ZNW* 99 (2008) 124–28.

Schlatter, Adolf. *Romans: The Righteousness of God*. Translated by Siegfried S. Schatzmann. Peabody, MA: Hendrickson, 1995.

Schlier, Heinrich. *Der Römerbrief*. Frieburg: Herder, 1977.

Schottroff, Luise. "Die Schreckensherrschaft der Sünde und die Befreiung durch Christus nach dem Römerbrief des Paulus." *EvTh* 39 (1979) 497–510.

Schreiner, Thomas R. *The Law and Its Fulfillment*. Grand Rapids: Baker, 1993.

Scott, James M. *Adoption as Sons of God: An Exegetical Investigation into the Background of Yiothesia in the Pauline Corpus*. WUNT 48. Tübingen: Mohr Siebeck, 1992.

Seifrid, Mark A. *Christ Our Righteousness Paul's Theology of Justification*. Downers Grove, IL: InterVarsity, 2000.

———. "Paul's Turn to Christ in Romans." *Concordia Journal* (2018) 15–24.

———. "Romans." In *Commentary on the New Testament Use of the Old Testament*, edited by D. A. Carson and G. K. Beale, 607–94. Grand Rapids: Baker, 2007.

———. "The Voice of the Law, the Cry of Lament, and the Shout of Thanksgiving." In *Perspectives on Our Struggle with Sin: Three Views of Romans 7*, edited by Terry L. Wilder, 1–51. Nashville: Broadman & Holman, 2011.

Shum, Shiu-Lin. *Paul's Use of Isaiah in Romans: A Contemporary Study of Paul's Letter to the Romans and the Sibylline and Qumran Sectarian Texts*. Tübingen: Mohr Siebeck, 2002.

Stanley, Christopher D. "'Pearls Before Swine': Did Paul's Audiences Understand his Biblical Quotations?" *NovT* 41 (1999) 122–44.

Starling, David. "For Your Sake We Are Being Killed All Day Long: Romans 8:36 and the Hermeneutics of Unexplained Suffering." *Themelios* 42 (2017), 112–21.

Stauffer, Ethelbert. *New Testament Theology*. New York: MacMillan, 1955.

Stendahl, Krister. "Paul at Prayer." *Int* 34 (1980) 240–49.

Stuhlmacher, Peter. *Paul's Letter to the Romans: A Commentary*. Translated by Scott J. Hafemann. Louisville: Westminster, 1994.

Still, Todd D. "Placing Pain in a Pauline Frame: Considering Suffering in Romans 5 and 8." In *Interpretation and Claims of the Text: Resourcing New Testament Theology*, edited by Jason A. Whitlark et al., 73–86. Waco, TX: Baylor University Press, 2014.

Stowers, Stanley. *A Rereading of Romans: Justice, Jews, and Gentiles*. New Haven, CT: Yale University, Press, 1994.

———. "Romans 7.7–25 as a Speech-in-Character (προσωποποιΐα)." In *Paul in His Hellenistic Context*, edited by Troels Engberg-Pedersen, 180–202. Minneapolis: Fortress, 1995.

Sutherland, John. *How Literature Works: 50 Keys Concepts*. Oxford: Oxford University Press, 2011.

Terrien, Samuel. *The Psalms: Strophic Structure and Theological Commentary*. Grand Rapids: Eedrmans, 2003.

Theobald, Michael. *Römerbrief*. 2 vols. Stuggart: Katholisches Biblewerk, 1993.

Thiselton, Anthony C. *Discovering Romans: Content, Interpretation, Reception*. Grand Rapids: Eerdmans, 2016.

———. *New Horizons in Hermeneutics: The Theory and Practice of Transforming Bible Reading*. Grand Rapids: Zondervan, 1992.

Timmins, Will N. *Romans 7 and Christian Identity: A Study of the "I" in its Literary Context*. Cambridge: Cambridge University Press, 2017.

———. "Romans 7 and the Resurrection of Lament in Christ: The Wretched "I" and His Biblical Doppelgänger." *NovT* 61 (2019) 386–408.

Tobin, Thomas H. *Paul's Rhetoric in Its Contexts: The Argument of Romans*. Grand Rapids: Baker, 2005.

Tomson, Peter J. "What Did Paul Mean by 'Those Who Know the Law' (Rom 7.1)." *NTS* 49 (2003) 573–81.

Tsmura, David-Toshio. "An OT Background to Rom 8.22." *NTS* 40 (1994) 620–21.

Villaneuva, Federico G. *The Uncertainty of a Hearing: A Study of the Sudden Change of Mood in the Psalms of Lament*. Leiden: Brill, 2008.

Vollmer, Thomas A. *'The Spirit Helps Our Weakness:' Rom 8,26A in Light of Paul's Missiological Purpose for Writing the Letter to the Romans*. BTS 36. Levuen: Peeters, 2018.

Waaler, Eric. "Multidimensional Intertextuality." In *Exploring Intertextuality: Diverse Strategies for New Testament Interpretation of Texts*, edited by B. J. Oropeza and Steve Moyise, 222–41. Eugene, OR: Cascade, 2016.

Wagner, Gunter. *Pauline Baptism and the Pagan Mysteries: The Problem of the Pauline Doctrineof Romans VI. 1–11, in the Light of Its Religio-Historical "Parallels."* Edinburgh: Burns & Oates, 1967.

Watts, Rikk E. "The Psalms in Mark's Gospel." In *The Psalms in the New Testament*, edited by Steve Moyise and Maarten J. J. Menken, 25–46. London: T. & T. Clark, 2004.

Watson, Francis. *Paul and the Hermeneutics of Faith*. London: T. & T. Clark, 2004.

Wedderburn, A. J. M. *Baptism and Resurrection: Studies in Pauline Theology Against Graeco-Roman Background*. WUNT 44. Tübingen: Mohr Siebeck, 1987.

Westerholm, Stephen. "Righteousness, Cosmic and Microcosmic." In *Apocalyptic Paul: Cosmos and Anthropos in Romans 5–8*, edited by Beverly Roberts Gaventa, 21–38. Waco, TX: Baylor University Press, 2013.

———. *Understanding Paul: The Early Christian Worldview of the Letter to the Romans*. Grand Rapids: Baker, 2004.

Westermann, Claus. *Praise and Lament in the Psalms*. Atlanta: John Knox, 1981.

———. "The Role of Lament in the Theology of the Old Testament." *Int* 28 (1974) 20–38.

Widmer, Michael. *Moses, God, and the Dynamics of Intercessory Prayer*. FAT 2/8. Tübingen: Mohr Siebeck, 2004.

Wilckens, Ulrich. *Der Brief an die Römer*. 3 vols. Zurich: Benziger, 1978–82.

Williams, Jarvis J. *Maccabean Martyr Tradition in Paul's Theology of Atonement: Did Martyr Theology Shape Paul's Conception of Jesus's Death?* Eugene, OR: Wipf & Stock, 2010.

Winger, Joseph Michael. *By What Law? The Meaning of Νόμος in the Letters of Paul*. Atlanta: Scholars, 1992.

Witherington, Ben, III. *Paul's Letter to the Romans: A Socio-Rhetorical Commentary*. Grand Rapids: Eerdmans, 2004.

Wolter, Michael. *Der Brief an Die Römer (Telband 1: Röm 1–8)*. Göttingen: Neukirchener, 2014.

Wright, N. T. *Climax of Covenant: Christ and the Law in Pauline Theology*. Minneapolis: Fortress, 1993.

———. *Justification: God's Plan and Vision*. Downers Grove, IL: InterVarsity, 2009.

———. "New Exodus, New Inheritance: The Narrative Substructure of Romans 3–8." In *Romans and the People of God: Essays in Honor of Gordon D. Fee on the Occasion of His 65th Birthday*, edited by Sven K. Soderlund and N. T. Wright, 26–35. Grand Rapids: Eerdmans, 1999.

———. *Romans*. In *The New Interpreter's Bible Commentary*, edited by Leander E. Keck, 10:395–770. Nashville: Abindgon, 2002.

Wu, Siu Fung, ed. *Suffering in Paul: Perspectives and Implications*. Eugene, OR: Pickwick, 2019.

Ziesler, John A. "The Role of the Tenth Commandment in Romans 7." *JSNT* 33 (1988) 41–56.

Ancient Documents Index

OLD TESTAMENT

Genesis

1:2	162, 163
1:3	222
1:26–27	211, 218, 219, 220
2:16–17	41, 42, 45, 75, 78, 112, 115, 117, 119, 124, 127, 159, 226
2:17	40, 45, 49, 51, 52, 54, 55, 58, 59, 60, 81, 93, 112
2:24	98
3:1	42, 49, 115
3:1–6	115
3:1–7	42, 48, 54, 55, 75
3:1–24	59
3:3	97
3:4–5	115
3:5–7	112
3:6	42, 75, 113, 115
3:8–10	58
3:12–13	58
3:13	42, 112, 113, 114, 118, 119
3:13–19	172
3:14–19	41, 52, 190
3:14–24	53
3:15	47
3:17–19	190, 191, 192, 207
3:19	40, 41, 43
3:22	112
3:22–24	41, 52, 53
3:22–25	21
4:1–17	43, 45, 51
5:1	218
5:1–32	43, 51
5:1—11:32	43
5:3	218
5:5	43
5:22	161
5:22–24	70
5:24	161
6:1—8:22	43, 45, 51
6:3	163
6:5–7	67
6:9	70, 161
7:1–24	67
8:1–22	68
9:6	218
11:10–32	43
12:1–3	67, 182, 233
12:3	17, 18
12:7	185
15:6	15, 222
15:7	185
17:1	70
17:8	185
18:18	18, 233
18:19	217
19:1	244
19:12–13	244
22:2	231
22:12	1, 149, 229, 230
22:13–14	231
22:16	1, 149, 229, 230, 247
22:17–18	247
22:18	185, 233
26:3–4	185
26:4	233
27:19	219
27:32	219
28:4	185
28:13	185
28:14	185, 233
28:20	70
35:12	185
37:24	136
38:26	72

Ancient Documents Index

Genesis (*continued*)

41:38	162, 163
48:15	161
50:20	214, 215, 225
50:24	185

Exodus

2:1–10	68
2:23	204
2:23–25	127, 131, 198, 206, 208
2:24	204
3:9	131
4:22	171, 175
4:22–23	219
6:5	204
6:6	173
11:5	219
12:39	65
13:13	173
13:14	173
13:17	177
13:21–22	179
14:19	179
14:24	179
15:1	65, 127
15:1–21	204
15:6–7	65
15:11	65
15:13	177
15:21	65
15:23–27	204
15:26	161
17:7	24
18:22	205
19:15–16	233
20:2	173
20:5	77
20:6	211, 212, 225
20:13	97
20:17	1, 76, 111, 112, 113, 115, 119, 124
22:12	239
22:28	196
22:29	196
23:10–11	194
23:19	196
23:24	77
24:12	106, 109
25:2–3	196
29:4	20, 29
29:8	20
29:10	20
31:3	162, 163
31:18	106
32:8	77
32:11–14	229
32:15	106
32:30	148
32:30–32	229, 232
32:32	106, 221
32:34	177
34:1	106
34:14	77
34:27	106
34:28	106
35:21	162
35:31	163
40:12	20
40:38	179

Leviticus

1:2	20
1:3	20
1:10	20
1:17	89
2:12	196
3:1	20
3:3	20
3:7	20
3:12	20
4:1–35	149
4:3	20, 148, 150
4:4	20
4:14	20, 148, 150
4:21	150
4:28	148
4:35	148
5:1–17	149
5:3	88
5:6	144, 148, 150
5:7	148, 150
5:8	20, 148, 150
5:9	148
5:10	148
5:11	148
5:13	148
6:7	20
6:18	148
6:23	148
7:7	148
7:8	20
7:14	20
7:16	20
7:20	88
7:21	88
7:25	20

Ancient Documents Index

7:35	20
7:37	148
8:2	148
8:13	20
8:14	20, 148
8:18	20
8:22	20
8:24	20
9:2	148
9:3	148
9:5	21, 29
9:7	148
9:8	148
9:9	148
9:10	148
9:13	148
9:15	148
9:22	148
10:16	148
10:17	148
10:19	20, 148
11:44	81
11:45	81, 112
12:6	148
12:8	148
14:2	20
14:12	20
14:13	148
14:19	148
14:31	148
15:3	88, 89
15:15	148
15:24	88
15:25	88
15:26	88
15:30	88, 148
15:31	88
16:1	20
16:3	144, 148, 149
16:5	148, 149
16:6	20, 29, 148, 149
16:9	20, 148, 149
16:11	20, 148, 149
16:15	148, 149
16:16	88
16:19	88
16:20	20
16:22	20
16:24	20
16:27	148, 149
18:1–5	118, 119
18:4–5	70, 153
18:5	70, 112, 113, 118, 119, 127, 146, 153, 155
18:6–30	118
18:19	88
18:26–30	119
19:2	81
19:19	194
19:22	148
19:23	88
20:1	89
20:21	88
20:25	88
22:3	88
22:4	88
22:5	88
23:2–4	215
23:8	20
23:10	196
23:18	20
23:19	148
23:25	20
23:27	20
23:36	20
26:1	77
26:22–46	70, 153
26:25	87
27:26	219

Numbers

5:11–31	99
5:16	20
5:20	99
6:11	148
6:12	20
6:14	20
6:16	148
7:3	20
7:16	148
7:22	148
7:28	148
7:34	148
7:40	148
7:46	148
7:52	148
7:58	148
7:64	148
7:70	148
7:82	148
7:87	148
8:8	148
8:9	20
8:10	20
8:12	148
9:15–23	179
10:34	179

Ancient Documents Index

Numbers (continued)

11:2	229
11:11–15	204
11:11–17	208
11:13–19	229
11:17	196, 205
14:14	179
15:20–21	196
15:21	196
15:24	148
15:25	148
15:27	20, 148
15:33	20
16:5	20
16:9	20
16:10	20
16:17	20
18:2	20
18:20	185
18:23	185
20:13	24
20:24	24
23:24	161
23:27	158, 161
24:2	162, 163
24:8	177
25:2	77
25:6	20
27:5	20
27:14	24
28:3	20
28:9	20
28:11	20
28:15	148
28:19	20
28:22	148
28:27	20
28:30	148
29:5	148
29:11	148
29:13	20
29:16	148
29:19	148
29:22	148
29:25	148
29:28	148
29:31	148
29:34	148
29:36	20
29:38	148
31:29	196

Deuteronomy

1:33	177, 179
4:1	122
4:5–8	113
4:8	122
4:13	106, 109
4:16	218
4:19	77
4:20	171
4:29	84
4:37	213, 233
5:6	173
5:9	77
5:10	211, 212
5:16	113
5:17	97
5:21	1, 76, 111, 112, 113, 115, 119, 124
5:22	106
5:29	113
5:33	70, 153
6:3	113
6:5	84, 211, 213
6:5–14	213
6:6–9	97
6:12	173
6:18	113, 161, 167
6:24	112, 113, 118
7:2	87
7:7	233
7:7–8	233
7:8	173
7:9	211, 212, 225
7:10–12	113
7:12–14	213
7:23	87
7:24	87, 113
7:25	113
8:2	176
8:5	175
8:6–7	70, 153
8:14	173
8:15	176
8:19	77
9:10	106
9:25–26	229
9:26	171
9:29	171
10:2	106
10:4	106
10:8	77, 88
10:12	84
10:12–13	70, 153
10:13	113

10:15	233
11:1	213
11:16	77
12:6	196
12:8	161
12:11	196
12:14–15	213
12:25	113, 161
12:28	113, 161
13:6	173
13:11	173
13:19	161
14:1	171, 175
17:3	77
17:12	77
18:4	196
18:5	77
21:5	77
21:9	161
22:7	113
24:1	100
24:1–4	97, 100, 101, 102, 108,
24:2	100
24:3	100, 101
24:4	101, 108
24:16	33, 82, 93
26:2	196
26:5–10	197, 208
26:10	196
26:16	84
26:17–19	153
27:17–19	70
28:9	63
28:11	214
28:15	240
28:48	240, 249
28:53	239
28:55	239
28:57	239
28:68	130
29:4	176
29:26	77
30:1–6	83, 94
30:2	84
30:6	84
30:9	214
30:10	84
30:12	152
30:12–13	84
30:15	112, 113, 120, 121
30:15–18	171
30:15–20	81, 113, 121, 127, 152, 155
30:16	70, 152, 153
30:16–18	112
30:17	77
30:19	119, 121
31:17–18	242
31:24	106
32:5	175
32:9	171, 186
32:10–12	177
32:23–25	239, 240
32:39	243
32:43	245
33:8	24

Joshua

1:8	107
1:15	185
4:21–24	67
7:1	48
7:4–5	48
7:6–9	131
7:16–26	48
13:14	185
18:7	185
22:20	81, 82, 93
23:6	107, 109
23:16	77
24:3	177

Judges

3:7–11	131
3:10	162, 163
5:27	135
6:34	162, 163, 164
11:29	162, 163
13:25	162, 163
14:6	162, 163
14:19	162, 163
15:14	162, 163

1 Samuel

2:6	244
2:30	224
4:1–17	22
10:6	162
10:10	162, 163
11:6	162
12:22	218
16:6	206
16:7	203, 206
16:8–10	233
16:13	162
16:14	162

1 Samuel (continued)

19:20	162, 163
23:2	162, 163

2 Samuel

7:1-17	183
7:11-14	188
7:12-13	183
7:12-14	148, 184
7:23	177
12:6	231
15:11	215
23:2	162

1 Kings

2:3	107, 109
3:8	233
3:10	158, 161
8:39	203, 206
8:51	171, 186
8:53	69, 107, 171, 186
9:9	173
16:14	171
17:1	77, 88
18:12	162
18:15	77
19:9	125
21:20	130
22:24	162
25:1-13	102
25:14-31	102
25:32-35	102
25:36-38	102
25:39-42	102
25:40	102

2 Kings

2:16	162
3:3	63
3:14	77
5:16	77
8:19	77
10:31	63
11:16	77
12:17	148
14:6	81, 82
15:14	64
17:17	130
21:14	171

1 Chronicles

6:13	234
16:13	229, 233
17:21	177

2 Chronicles

5:1	163
10:7	214
15:1	162
18:7	214
18:23	162
20:14	162
24:20	162, 163
25:4	81, 82
29:11	21, 29
29:21	148
29:23	148
29:24	148
36:17	231

Ezra

3:2	107, 109
6:17	148
7:18	161
8:22	214
8:35	148
9:7	131
9:8	173
9:9	173
10:11	161

Nehemiah

1:5	212
2:18	214
5:19	214
9:6-38	131
9:7	233
9:12	177, 179
9:17	173
9:19	177, 179
10:34	148
10:38	196

Esther (LXX)

7:4	130

Esther (MT)

7:4	130

Job

1:5	148
1:6	77, 88
2:1	77
3:18	200
3:24	198
5:17–35	239
24:12	198
27:3	162, 163
30:3	136
30:25	198
31:38–40	193
33:4	162, 163
42:8	229

Psalms (LXX)

1:1	32
1:2	125
1:4	32
1:5	32
1:6	32
2:1–6	183
2:7–12	183
2:8	183
3:5	180
4:2	23
4:4	180
4:6	200
5:3	32
5:4	77
5:7–8	128
5:8	32
5:9	32, 177
5:10	129
5:12	14, 23, 200, 213
5:12–13	139
6:7	198
6:8	32
6:11	32, 139
7:2	137, 200
7:3	132
7:5	32
7:6	32
7:7	32
7:10	32
7:18	139
8:3	32
8:6	196
9:4	32
9:6	32
9:7	32
9:10	23
9:11	200
9:14	44, 137
9:17	32
9:14	32
9:18	32
9:19	14
9:22	23, 138
9:23	32
9:25	32
9:34	32
9:36	32
10:2	32
10:5	32
10:6	32
10:7	139
11:6	136, 198
11:9	32
12:2	138
12:2–3	126
12:3	32
12:5	32, 127
12:5–6	128
12:6	127, 139
13:1	159
13:3	136
13:3–4	125
13:6	200
13:7	138
15:1	200
15:5	186
15:8	236
16:3	203, 206
16:6	180
16:7	200, 201
16:8–9	136
16:9	32
16:12	132
16:13	32
16:15	139
17:1	32
17:2–3	213
17:3	200
17:4	32
17:5	44
17:6	44
17:7	180
17:17	68
17:18	32, 137
17:20	32, 137
17:31	200
17:38	32
17:41	32
17:42	180
17:49	32
18:1	223

Psalms (*continued*)

19:2	23
20:8	200
20:9	32
21:2	25, 126
21:2–3	25
21:3	180
21:4–6	25
21:5	14, 200
21:5–6	26, 201
21:6	25, 26, 180, 200
21:7–11	25
21:9	200
21:10	200
21:12	23, 25, 26
21:13–14	25
21:13–19	25
21:20–22	25
21:22	137
21:25	180
21:23–32	25
21:30	63
21:31–32	25
22:3	177
22:4	44, 229
23:3–4	21, 29
24:2	32
24:2–3	14
24:3	26
24:5	177
24:9	177
24:13	185
24:17	23
24:19	32
24:20	26, 200, 201
24:22	23
25:1	200
25:2	24
25:5	32
25:9	32
25:10–11	128
26:2	32
26:7	180
26:11	32
27:1	136, 177, 180
27:3	32
27:7	200
29:2	32
29:3	180
29:9	180
30:2	200, 201
30:4	177
30:7	128, 200
30:9	32
30:11	198
30:12	32
30:13	125
30:14–15	128
30:15	200
30:16	32, 137
30:20	200
30:23	180
30:24	213
30:25	200
31:3	132, 180
31:4	136
31:6	68
31:7	23
31:10	32, 200
31:32	26
32:6	222, 225, 227
32:11	23, 29
32:12	171, 186, 233
32:18	200
32:18–19	137
32:19	137
32:21	200
32:22	200
33:7	23, 180
33:9	200
33:18	23, 180
33:20	22, 23, 137
33:22	32
33:23	200
34:12–13	128
34:22	245
34:25	125
34:27	19
35:2	159, 167
35:4–5	129
35:8	200
35:12	32
35:13	229
36:3	200
36:5	200
36:9	185
36:10	32
36:11	185
36:12	32
36:14	32
36:16	32
36:17	32
36:20	32
36:21	32
36:22	185
36:28	32
36:32	32
36:34	32

36:35	32
36:38	32
36:39	23
36:40	32, 137, 200, 201
37:2–4	134, 141
37:4	71, 134
37:5	136
37:6	134
37:7	132, 134, 135
37:8	134
37:10	198
37:11	134
37:13–15	128
37:16	135, 200
37:17	32
37:19–20	134
37:20	32, 134
37:22	245
37:22–23	135
38:2	32
38:8	23, 29
38:9	137
39:3	136
39:4	200
39:5	200
39:7	148
39:13	136
39:17	213
40:3	32
40:6	32
40:8	32
40:10	201
40:12	32
41:6	181, 200, 201
41:10	32, 138
41:12	138, 181, 200, 201
42:2	32, 138
42:3	177
42:5	138, 181, 200, 201
43:4	185
43:6	32
43:7	201
43:8	242
43:10	242
43:11	32
43:11–17	242
43:17	32
43:18	242
43:20	44
43:21–23	242
43:22	203, 206
43:23	1, 8, 143, 228, 238, 239, 241, 242, 246, 249
43:24–25	138
43:24–26	243
43:25	23, 138
43:27	243
44:5	177
44:6	32
45:2	23
46:5	186, 233
48:15	44
49:1	215
49:15	23
49:16	32
50:15	32
51:9–10	128
53:7	32
53:9	23, 32
54:4	23, 32
54:5	44
54:16	44
54:16–17	128
54:17	180
54:22	129
54:24	32, 128, 200
55:2	230
55:3	32, 132
55:3–4	128
55:4	200
55:5	200, 229
55:6–7	132
55:9	230
55:10	32, 230
55:12	200, 229, 230, 247
55:14	44, 138, 230
56:3	180
57:3	125
57:4	32
57:11	32
58:2	32
58:2–3	137
58:3–4	132
58:11	32
58:16–17	128
58:17	23
59:11	177
59:13	23
60:3	180
60:4	32, 177, 200
61:6	24
61:9	200
61:10	190
61:11	201
63:2	32
63:11	200, 201
64:6	200
64:14	180

Psalms (*continued*)

65:3	32
65:6	65
65:10	24
65:11	23
65:14	23
65:17	180
66:5	177
67:2	32
67:3	32
67:21	44, 244
67:22	32
67:24	32
68:2	68
68:4	180, 200, 201
68:5	32
68:9	186
68:13–14	128
68:15	68
68:19	32
68:21	136
68:32	158, 161, 168
68:36	185
68:37	213
69:5	213
70:1	14, 200
70:4	32, 137,
70:5	14, 24
70:10	32
70:12–14	167
70:13	167
70:13–14	128
70:14	200
70:20	23, 167, 169
71:1–3	17
71:1–4	17
71:1–17	17
71:3	18, 19
71:5	17
71:7	17, 18
71:8–9	17
71:8–11	18
71:9	32
71:11	17
71:12–14	17, 18
71:13	14
71:15	17, 18
71:17	17, 18
72:3	32
72:12	32
72:24	177
73:1	138
73:2	186
73:3	32
73:10	32, 138
73:11	138
73:13	65
73:18	32
73:22	132
74:9	32
74:11	32
76:2	180
76:3	23
76:20–21	65
76:21	177
77:10	125
77:12–13	65
77:14	177
77:36	129
77:49	23
77:49–51	231
77:50	44
77:52–53	65
77:53	32, 177
77:61	32
77:62	186
77:66	32
77:68	233
77:70	233
77:71	186
77:72	177
78:5	138
78:11	198
79:2	177
79:5	138
79:7	32
80:8	23, 24
80:15	32
80:16	32
81:2	32
81:3	72
81:4	32
82:3	32
83:11	32
83:13	200, 201
84:4	18, 19
84:5	18
84:6	18
84:7–8	18
84:9	19
84:10	19
84:11	18, 19
84:12–14	19
85:2	200, 201
85:3	180
85:7	23, 180
85:11	63, 177
85:17	214

Reference	Page(s)
87:2	180
87:7	44
87:10	180
87:14	180
87:15	138
87:18	132
87:19	136
87:27–28	219, 220, 226
88:4	219
88:4–5	219, 229, 233
88:11	32
88:12–14	246
88:20–21	219
88:21	219
88:22	205
88:23	332
88:24	32
88:27	219
88:29–30	220
88:30	219
88:36	219
88:36–37	219
88:39–52	219
88:43	32
88:47	138
88:49	44, 137
88:50	219
88:52	32
89:13	138
89:16	177
90:1–13	224
90:2	200
90:3	137
90:8	32
90:9	200
90:14	200, 201
90:14–16	224
90:15	23, 223, 224, 227
90:15–20	211
91:8	32
91:10	32
91:12	32
93:3	32, 138
93:5	186
93:13	32
93:14	186, 218
96:3	32
96:10	32, 137, 213
97:2	222
98:6	229
100:8	32
101:6	198
101:9	32, 132
101:21	198
102:13	176
103:4	244
103:35	32
104:6	176, 229, 233
104:11	185
104:16	215
104:24	32
104:36	196
104:43	233
105:5	233
105:7–12	65
105:9	177
105:10	32
105:18	32
105:21–22	65
105:23	229
105:40	186
105:41	79
105:42	32
105:40–45	132
106:2	32
106:6	180
106:7	177
106:10	44
106:13	180
106:14	44
106:18	44
106:19	180
106:28	180
106:30	177
106:39	23
107:11	177
107:13	23
107:14	32
108:2	32
108:3–4	128
108:6	32
109:1	32, 229, 236, 237
109:2	32
109:4	229, 237
109:5	237
110:10	32
111:7	200
111:8	32
111:10	74
113:17	200
113:18	200
113:19	200
114:3	23, 44
114:8	44, 138
117:5	23, 230
117:6–7	229
117:7	32
117:9	201

Ancient Documents Index

Psalms (continued)

117:10–16	230
117:18	44
117:21	230
117:28	230
118:8–9	122
118:16	125
118:35	177
118:45	180
118:46	180
118:47	213
118:48	213
118:53	32
118:61	32
118:69–70	128
118:78	128
118:87	128
118:95	32
118:97	213
118:98	32
118:110	32
118:113	213
118:116	14
118:119	32, 213
118:122	214
118:127	213
118:132	213
118:139	32
118:140	213
118:143	23
118:147	180
118:155	32
118:159	213
118:165	213
118:167	213
119:1	180
121:6	212
123:4	68
124:3	32
126:5	32
128:1	245
128:3	32
128:4	32
129:1	180
129:5–6	202
129:6	200
129:8	85
130:3	200
131:18	32
134:4	233
135:11–15	65
135:24	32
136:8	135
137:7	23, 32
138:1	24
138:1–5	203, 206
138:1–6	217, 225
138:3	217
138:7–8	238
138:8	246
138:10	177
138:16	221
138:19	32
138:21	32
138:22	32
138:23	24
138:24	177
139:3	132
139:5	32
139:9	32
139:11	136
139:16	221
140:1	180
140:5	32
140:8	200, 201
140:10	32
141:2	180
141:3	23
141:6	180, 200
141:7	137
142:2	222
142:2–3	179
142:2–10	23
142:3	32
142:4	179
142:8	200
142:9	32, 137
142:10	177, 179
142:11	23
142:11–12	23
142:12	32
143:2	200
143:7	68
143:11	137
144:15	200
144:20	32, 213
145:9	32
148:2	245
149:5	23

Psalms (MT)

1:1	70, 153
5:10	32
13:2–3	126
13:5	127
13:6	127
15:2	70, 153

22:1	126
22:6	14
22:22	140
22:23	140
25:5	239
25:20	14
26:1	70
26:11	70, 153
38:4	134
38:6	239
38:8	134
38:14	128
43:2	239
44:9	239
44:23	239, 241
51:7	125
56:9	230
60:1	239
69:30	140
69:31	140
72:17	18
73:14	239
74:10	239
74:22	239
77:7	239
78:10	70, 153
78:14	179
79:5	239
81:8	24
81:13	70, 153
82:5	70, 153
84:11	70, 153
85:11	19
85:14	70, 153
86:3	239
86:11	70, 153
88:5	239
88:6	99
88:14	239
89:3	234
89:4	233
89:31	70, 153
89:38–52	239
101:2	70, 153
101:6	70, 153
102:8	239
102:15–16	21
105:6	234
105:39	179
108:11	239
110:1	237
116:9	70, 153
118:6	229
119:1	70, 153
119:3	70, 153
128:1	70, 153
139:7–12	239

Proverbs

3:2	160
4:2	122
6:20	99
6:20–35	99
6:23	112
6:23–24	97
6:24	97, 99
6:27–28	99
6:28	70
6:29	97, 99, 108
6:29–35	99
8:20	70
8:20–21	212
11:31	31, 35, 36
12:20	125
21:3	161
24:9	81, 82
24:18	161

Ecclesiastes

1:2	190, 192
1:2–7	207
1:3–7	192
1:14	192
2:1	192
2:11	192
2:15	192
2:17	192
2:19	192
2:21	192
2:23	192
2:26	192
3:19	192
4:4	192
4:7	192
4:8	192
4:16	192
5:6	192
5:9	192
6:2	192
6:4	192
6:9	192
6:11	192
6:12	192
7:6	192
7:15	192
8:10	192
8:14	192

Ancient Documents Index

Ecclesiastes (continued)

9:2	192
9:9	192
11:8	192
11:9	70
11:10	192
12:8	192

Isaiah

1:2	175, 176
1:17	72
5:24	125
8:21	249
8:22	239
9:5	16
9:6–7	19
9:7	19
11:2	162, 163, 171
11:4	171
11:10	201
14:1	233
14:6	231
14:21	185
14:27	221
19:25	186
21:4	64
22:12	215
24:4–6	193
24:23	21
25:8	44, 49
25:9	201
26:1	194
26:3	16
26:8	201
26:11–12	194
26:12	16
26:16–18	196
26:17–19	195
27:5	16
27:6	104, 109
28:15	201
28:16	14, 26, 27
28:17	201
28:18	201
29:8	201
30:1	163
30:12	201
31:2	201
32:1	16, 19
32:2–8	16
32:9–14	16
32:15	27
32:15–17	14
32:15–18	168
32:15–20	16
32:17	14, 15, 16, 17
33:1	135
37:30	104
38:3	161
40:1–11	229
40:13	162
40:26	215
41:8–9	215, 233
41:11–13	229
41:21–24	229
42:1	163, 229, 233, 234
42:4	201
42:6	215
42:6–10	69
43:1	216
43:1–17	229
43:2	68
43:8–12	229
43:10	233
43:16	65, 68
43:19	69
43:20	233, 234
43:25–28	229
43:20	229
44:1–2	233
44:3	154, 163
44:3–4	147
45:4	216, 229, 233, 234
45:7	16
45:20–25	229
46:11	215
46:13	229
47:6	186
47:10	201
47:11	136
48:6	69
48:12	216
48:15	216
48:16–17	154
48:17–18	17
48:18	16, 19
49:1	216
49:1–6	234
49:7	233
49:8	185
49:14–23	229
50:1	125, 130
50:2	65, 68
50:4–11	229
50:6–9	235, 248
50:8	72, 235, 236, 249
50:8–9	229, 235

50:9	235
51:1–3	234
51:1–8	229
51:2	216
51:5	201
51:10	65, 68
51:19	239, 240
52:3	130
52:5	7
52:7	16
52:13	184
52:13—53:7	229
52:13—53:12	150, 156
52:14—53:11	184
52:15	4
53:1–12	188
53:4–6	33
53:5	16
53:5–6	248
53:6	33, 156, 229, 232, 248
53:7	238, 239
53:8	33
53:10	148, 150, 156, 248
53:11	1, 12, 50, 56, 57, 60, 156, 248
53:11–12	33, 229
53:12	151, 183, 184, 229, 232, 248
54:1–14	17
54:1–17	229
54:5	103
54:6	216
54:8	15
54:9	68
54:10	16, 19
55:3–5	229, 234
55:9–10	225
55:10–11	222, 227
55:17	229
57:2	16
57:19	16
59:1–15	84
59:7	136
59:8	16
59:15	161
59:20	84
59:21	163
60:8–17	17
60:17	16, 19
60:18	136
61:1	162, 163, 164
62:5	103, 109
63:7	177
63:7–10	159
63:7–14	177
63:8	176, 177
63:9	177
63:10	159, 167, 177
63:11–14	177, 178
63:12	68
63:14	154, 162
63:15–19	177
63:17	186
64:5	89
65:9	229, 233
65:9–22	234
65:12	216
65:15	229
65:17	69
65:23	229, 233
66:4	216
66:12	16
66:22	69

Jeremiah (LXX)

1:4–5	217, 225
1:5	217
1:10	217
1:11–19	217
3:19	171, 175
3:19–20	206
3:21	175
3:22	175
4:30–31	195
14:11	214
15:8	137
15:11	214
15:21	214
21:10	214
24:5	214
24:6	214
28:19	186
30:16	195
36:28	105
38:12	105
38:20	176, 206
38:30	82
38:31–34	69
38:39	81
39:9	214
41:13	173
45:6	136
46:16	214

Jeremiah (MT)

1:5	211
3:1	100

Ancient Documents Index

Jeremiah (continued)

4:13	135
4:17–22	193
4:19–31	195
4:20	135, 136
4:27	193, 195
4:27–29	196
4:28	193
4:31	195
5:4	125
5:12	240, 249
6:7	136
6:26	136
9:18	135
10:16	186
10:20	135
11:22	240
12:3	203, 206
12:7	186
12:8	186
12:9	186
12:12	135
12:15	186
14:12	240
14:16	240
15:8	136
16:4	240
16:18	186
17:10	203, 206
18:21	240
20:8	136
24:1–10	94
24:7	85
24:10	84, 240, 249
27:8	239, 240
29:28	105
31:12	105
31:20	176, 206
31:30	81, 82
31:31	148
31:31–34	69, 110
34:13	173
38:2	239, 240
38:6	136
39:16	214
49:22	195
51:19	186

Lamentations

2:4–5	158, 167
2:17	231
2:21	240, 249
3:39	148
3:54	239

Ezekiel

3:20	82
5:17	239, 240
9:9	89
11:5	162
11:19–20	154, 157
11:24	162, 163
14:21	239, 240
16:8	103
22:5	89
22:10	89
31:3	164
34:25	14
34:25–31	19
36:16–38	89, 90, 94, 107, 108, 110
36:17	89
36:18–19	90
36:20	90
36:21–25	90
36:25–27	90
36:26	125
36:26–27	107, 108, 154, 157
36:26–29	147, 155
36:27	91, 147, 148, 163
36:29	90, 147, 215
36:29–30	108
36:30	90, 91, 105
36:31–33	89
36:32	91
36:33	90
36:34–35	90
36:36–38	91
37:1	162
37:1–14	147, 154, 157, 165, 166, 168
37:3	165
37:5	169
37:5–6	165
37:7–8	165
37:8	165
37:9	166
37:10	166
37:11	166
37:12-14	166
37:13–14	163, 164
37:14	147, 155, 157, 163
37:26	14, 19
38:21	215
39:9	214
39:24	89
39:29	163

42:13	148	4:14	27
42:19	148		
42:21	148	**Amos**	
44:28	186	3:10	136
44:30	196	5:9	136
47:12	69, 107	7:4	215
47:17	105	9:4	214
		9:14	105, 109

Daniel

6:18	136	**Jonah**	
7:13–14	183, 188	2:1–10	68
7:22	50		
7:27	50	**Micah**	
9:11	107, 109	1:12	214
9:13	107	2:4	135
12:1	92	3:8	162, 163
12:2	63, 92, 93, 95	4:10	195
12:3	92	5:4	19
12:4	92	6:4	173
12:5–13	92		
12:5–7	92	**Habakkuk**	
12:8	92	1:3	136
12:10	93	2:4	23, 160, 168, 222
		2:17	136
Hosea		3:10	195
1:2	103	3:17	104
1:10–11	171		
2:1	31	**Zephaniah**	
2:16	103, 109	1:15	35
2:25	31	1:18	35
3:1	31, 97	2:3	35
3:3	97, 100		
6:6	168	**Zechariah**	
6:17	40	4:6	163
10:9	63	4:14	77
11:1	175	6:5	77, 88
11:1–9	31	6:8	163
11:8	206	8:12	104, 109
11:10–11	206	11:2	135
13:14	44, 49	11:3	135
		11:4	238
Joel		11:7	238
1:5	27		
1:10	135	**Haggai**	
1:15	136, 137	2:5	163
2:1	27	2:9	19
2:11	27		
2:22	105	**Malachi**	
3:1	27	2:5	160
3:1–2	14, 163		
3:4	27		
3:5	27		

ANCIENT DOCUMENTS INDEX

Malachi (*continued*)

3:4	158, 161
3:8	196
3:11	105

NEW TESTAMENT

Matthew

1:21	84
2:15	175
9:13	168
11:3	46
12:7	168
13:23	104
13:46	129
18:25	129
19:16	92
19:29	92
22:24	236
25:46	92
26:9	129
26:36–46	180
26:64	236

Mark

4:20	104
4:28	104
10:17	92
10:30	92
12:36	236
14:5	129
14:34	181
14:36	179, 180
14:39	180
14:41	180
14:62	236
16:19	236

Luke

4:18	162
7:20	46
8:15	104
10:40	205
10:25	92
18:18	92
18:30	92
20:42	236
22:69	236

John

3:15	92
3:16	92
4:14	92
4:36	92
5:24	92
5:39	92
6:27	92
6:40	92
6:47	92
6:54	92
6:68	92
8:46	148
10:28	92
12:5	129
12:25	92
12:50	92
15:22	148
16:8	148
16:9	148
17:2	92
17:3	92

Acts

2:17	30
2:34	236
2:45	129
3:25	233
4:3	129
5:4	129
5:9	162
7:51	177
8:39	162
10:45	30
13:46	92
13:48	92
14:18	34
16:7	162
27:7	34
27:8	34
27:16	34

Romans

1:1	14, 215
1:1–15	14
1:1—4:25	1, 12, 14, 15
1:2	199
1:2–4	4, 220, 234
1:4	14, 160, 220
1:5	54, 55
1:6	14, 215
1:7	14, 160, 215
1:8	14

Ancient Documents Index

1:9	160
1:11	94
1:12	3
1:13	104
1:16	26, 225
1:16–17	3, 9, 28, 197, 208
1:16—4:25	13, 28, 30, 39
1:17	23, 39, 160, 168, 222
1:18	18, 35, 36, 39
1:18–32	89
1:18—3:20	30, 79
1:19	39
1:21	39
1:23	39, 79
1:24	39, 86, 88, 130
1:24–32	94
1:25	39
1:26	39, 86, 130
1:27	23, 116
1:28	39, 86, 130, 139
1:29–31	151
1:31	28
1:32	39, 49, 53, 151
2:1–11	39
2:1–16	28, 35
2:2	39
2:3	39
2:4	39
2:5	39, 84, 168
2:7	91, 92, 160
2:9	23, 116
2:10	160
2:11	39
2:12–16	222
2:13	39, 59, 222
2:15	84, 168, 182
2:16	14, 39
2:17	39
2:17–24	89
2:23	39
2:24	7, 39
2:25	39
2:25–29	241
2:26	39, 53, 151
2:27–29	105
2:28	39
2:29	39, 84, 91, 107, 160, 168
3:1–8	35
3:2	39
3:3	39
3:4	39, 63, 222
3:5	31
3:6	39, 63
3:7	39
3:9	39, 66, 75, 79, 88, 166
3:10–18	22, 32, 129, 159, 160, 166, 245
3:11	39
3:13	32, 129
3:16	136
3:17	160
3:18	39
3:19	39, 58, 109
3:19–20	22, 39, 113
3:20	124, 222
3:21	39
3:21–22	208
3:21–26	20, 21, 149, 156
3:22	14, 39
3:23	39
3:24	14, 39, 91, 198, 222
3:25	29, 34, 39, 148, 149
3:26	14, 39, 156, 222
3:27	146
3:28	222
3:29	39
3:30	39, 222
3:31	63
4:1–8	15
4:1–25	18, 28, 222
4:2	39, 222
4:3	15, 39
4:4	78, 96
4:5	222
4:6	39
4:6–8	15
4:9	15
4:11	54
4:12	15
4:13	15, 182, 184, 247
4:13–14	182
4:15	23, 35, 39, 58, 116
4:16	78
4:17	39, 215
4:17–18	15
4:18–22	15
4:20	39
4:22	15
4:23	15
4:23–25	12, 14
4:24	14
4:25	33, 86
4:25	39, 87, 94, 232
4:25—8:18	50
5:1	14, 16, 18, 19, 20, 26, 63, 147, 160, 170, 222
5:1–2	13, 21, 54

279

Romans (*continued*)

5:1–5	9, 13, 15, 16, 24, 28, 30, 169, 199, 228, 249
5:1–10	10, 18, 21, 236
5:1–11	12, 13, 15, 30, 37, 39
5:1–21	54
5:1—7:25	14
5:1—8:17	36
5:1—8:39	1, 12, 13, 14, 18, 21, 28, 30, 37, 49, 55, 228, 241
5:2	20, 21, 22, 29, 61, 199, 223
5:2–3	15
5:3	22, 26, 37, 116
5:3–4	22, 23, 29
5:3–5	37, 157
5:4	24, 199
5:5	14, 16, 23, 25, 26, 27, 30, 91, 160, 168, 199, 201, 208, 213
5:6	31, 34
5:6–8	32
5:6–10	18, 26, 27, 28, 29, 30, 31, 32, 33, 34, 35
5:6–11	35
5:7	34, 35, 36, 96
5:8	31, 34, 149, 213
5:9	19, 31, 34, 149, 222
5:9–10	28, 91
5:9–11	35
5:10	31, 32, 49, 160
5:10–11	35, 36, 45
5:11	14, 39, 54
5:12	38, 39, 40, 41, 42, 43, 47, 48, 49, 52, 58, 59, 60, 88, 158
5:12–14	38, 39, 40, 41, 42, 44, 47, 48, 49, 66, 75, 120, 158
5:12–19	5, 7, 47, 58, 79, 81, 115, 142, 155, 187, 219
5:12–21	7, 38, 51, 144, 158
5:12—7:25	76, 164
5:13	44, 45, 88
5:13–14	44, 45, 48
5:14	7, 40, 45, 46, 47, 49, 51, 57, 60, 79, 159
5:15	14, 50, 52, 57, 59, 60, 94
5:15–16	51
5:15–17	52, 59
5:15–19	41, 47, 71, 76, 78
5:15–21	47, 50, 52, 59, 60
5:16	52, 57, 59, 94, 144, 145, 151
5:17	14, 18, 49, 53, 59, 78, 79, 159, 160
5:17–19	53
5:18	52, 55, 144, 145, 151, 160
5:18–19	54, 60
5:19	12, 50, 56, 57
5:20	58, 88
5:20–21	57, 60, 63, 74
5:20—6:1	80
5:21	13, 14, 18, 42, 49, 60, 79, 88, 91, 92, 159, 160
6:1	63, 64, 65, 66, 74, 88
6:1–4	64
6:1–11	62, 63, 66, 67, 68, 69, 72, 74, 75
6:1–14	96
6:1–23	63, 108
6:1—8:39	39
6:2	75, 88, 160
6:3	14, 49, 66, 69
6:3–4	64, 67
6:4	49, 55, 69, 70, 73, 160, 184, 223
6:5	28, 49, 55, 67
6:5–7	67
6:6	42, 66, 71, 73, 75, 88
6:6–7	71
6:7	42, 66, 69, 74, 75, 222
6:7–18	84
6:9	49, 66, 79, 98, 120, 159
6:10	63, 160
6:10–11	75
6:11	14, 69, 160
6:12	42, 53, 66, 74, 75, 76, 79, 88, 159
6:12–14	74, 78, 79, 80, 81
6:12–23	24, 87, 165
6:13	76, 88, 160
6:14	66, 78, 80, 88, 98, 144, 159
6:14–15	85
6:15	63
6:15–16	81
6:15–23	80, 81, 82, 88, 91, 93, 96
6:16	42, 49, 55, 79, 81, 84, 85, 88, 120
6:16–17	83
6:17	42, 85, 86, 88, 94, 138, 168
6:17–18	85, 86, 87
6:18	18, 66, 86, 87, 88, 91
6:19	81, 87, 88, 89, 91
6:19–23	87, 90, 91, 93, 94

Ancient Documents Index

6:20	42, 88	7:10–12	112
6:21	49, 91, 93, 120	7:11	42, 54, 88, 112, 114, 118, 129
6:21–22	81	7:12	98, 107, 121, 122, 123, 139
6:22	42, 88, 91, 92, 93, 160	7:13	23, 42, 49, 63, 88, 116, 120, 122, 123
6:22–23	92	7:14	42, 88, 98, 111, 125, 128, 129, 130, 139, 145, 135, 139
6:23	14, 49, 81, 88, 92, 94, 95, 96, 120, 160	7:14–24	
7:1	79, 96, 97, 98, 99, 101, 160	7:14–25	122, 123, 124, 125, 134, 135, 141, 142
7:1–6	7, 96, 97, 98, 101, 102, 103, 104, 105, 108, 112, 139, 144	7:15	23, 54, 116, 123
		7:15–16	125
7:1–16	76	7:17	23, 88, 111, 116, 123
7:2	97, 99, 160	7:17–20	125
7:2–3	96, 100, 101, 102	7:17–23	133
7:3	97, 100, 160	7:18	23, 116, 123, 134
7:4	49, 96, 101, 105, 108, 109	7:20	23, 42, 88, 111, 116, 123
7:4–5	104	7:21	132
7:5	42, 49, 88, 97, 101, 105	7:22	125, 133
7:6	71, 91, 105, 107, 109, 110, 160	7:23	42, 88, 125, 131, 132, 139
7:7	1, 42, 63, 78, 88, 111, 112, 113, 124, 139	7:24	49, 111, 120, 134, 135, 136, 137, 138, 140, 141, 145, 151
7:7–8	75		
7:7–12	114, 115, 116, 117, 119, 120, 122, 129, 132	7:24–25	18
7:7–9	112	7:25	14, 42, 88, 111, 138, 139, 140, 141, 155
7:7–11	122, 123	8:1	14, 137, 141, 144, 145, 146, 154, 155
7:7–13	112, 113, 114, 118, 119, 120, 121, 123, 125, 127, 135	8:1–2	145
		8:1–4	26, 29, 139, 141, 143, 144, 145, 146, 154, 155, 157
7:7–23	141		
7:7–24	139, 140	8:1–11	143, 169
7:7–25	3, 8, 30, 58, 66, 71, 73, 76, 98, 105, 111, 112, 117, 127, 128, 133, 137, 140, 141, 142, 144, 151, 155, 158, 164, 171, 197, 245	8:2	14, 49, 88, 91, 140, 146, 148, 151, 155, 160
		8:2–4	155
		8:2–7	148
		8:3	1, 88, 144, 148, 149, 150
7:7–8:4	158	8:3–4	151, 156
7:7–8:17	207	8:4	1, 53, 70, 91, 144, 148, 151, 152, 153, 157, 158, 160, 164
7:7–8:39	187		
7:8	23, 42, 54, 88, 116, 123, 124, 129		
7:8–11	124	8:5	91, 153, 158, 160
7:8–13	116	8:5–8	158, 161
7:9	42, 88, 111, 116, 128, 160	8:5–11	144, 157, 158, 167
		8:5–17	157
7:9–10	116, 128	8:5–27	153
7:9–13	117	8:6	91, 159, 160, 161, 168, 207
7:10	49, 88, 111, 112, 117, 118, 120, 128, 141, 146, 160	8:6–7	158
		8:7	159, 167, 207

281

Romans (continued)

8:7–8	162
8:8	158, 161, 167
8:9	91, 148, 160, 162, 165
8:9–11	30, 162, 164, 165, 166, 168
8:10	88, 91, 146, 155, 160, 164, 165, 168, 169, 199
8:11	14, 28, 55, 91, 148, 154, 160, 165, 166
8:12	153, 160
8:12–13	172
8:12–17	170, 171, 172, 174, 178, 179, 182, 187, 188, 205
8:12–39	3
8:13	49, 91, 153, 160, 170, 171, 172
8:14	91, 160, 162, 170, 176, 177, 178, 179, 188
8:14–15	171
8:14–17	176
8:15	91, 160, 172, 173, 174, 179, 180, 181, 198
8:15–17	170
8:16	91, 160
8:17	4, 9, 164, 169, 171, 178, 182, 183, 184, 185, 189, 207, 222, 226, 243
8:18	63, 171, 189, 190
8:18–22	190
8:18–24	16
8:18–25	28, 184
8:18–27	7, 9, 23, 205, 207
8:18–39	26, 30, 73, 199, 222, 224
8:19	198
8:19–20	190
8:19–22	158, 190, 191, 193, 195, 207, 246, 248
8:20	190, 193
8:20–21	190
8:21	172, 184
8:22	192, 193, 194, 197, 207
8:23	16, 91, 160, 174, 196, 198, 199, 207
8:23–25	146, 196, 197, 199, 208, 223
8:23–27	248
8:24	22, 55, 199, 202
8:24–25	199, 201, 202
8:25	202
8:26	91, 160, 197, 203, 205
8:26–27	203, 204, 205, 206, 208
8:27	91, 160, 205, 238
8:28	210, 212, 213, 214, 215, 216
8:28–30	24, 186, 210, 211, 216, 224, 228
8:29	211, 216, 217, 218, 219, 220, 226
8:29–30	213, 216, 220, 224, 225
8:30	211, 215, 220, 221, 222, 223, 224, 227
8:31	228, 229
8:31–34	9, 29, 227, 228, 229, 232, 234, 236
8:31–39	18, 144, 147, 158, 169, 171, 183, 190, 210, 211, 215, 228, 241, 245, 246, 247
8:32	1, 87, 149, 182, 229, 230, 239, 247, 248
8:33	222, 232, 234, 235, 248, 249
8:33–34	229, 232, 235, 236
8:34	14, 21, 236, 237, 238
8:35	213, 238, 239, 249
8:35–36	239
8:35–39	237, 238
8:36	1, 7, 49, 143, 228, 238, 239, 241, 243
8:37	213, 243
8:37–39	239, 243
8:38	49, 120, 160, 245
8:38–39	237
8:39	14, 213, 238, 245, 246
9:1	160, 182
9:1–5	3
9:3	153
9:4	174, 176
9:5	153
9:7	215
9:12	215
9:13	213
9:14	63
9:20–24	96
9:24	215
9:25	213, 215
9:25–26	31
9:26	215
9:33	26, 208
10:5	70, 153, 160
10:7–8	84
10:8	168
10:9–10	85
10:11	26, 208
10:13	103
10:16	85, 152, 232

10:17	225
11:2	218
11:8	160
11:1	63
11:15	36, 160
11:16	160
11:16–24	96
11:17–24	97
11:22	65
11:23	65
11:26	160
11:26–27	84
11:27	88, 160
11:29	94
11:34	139
12:1	160
12:1—16:27	1
12:2	78, 139
12:6	94
12:9	213
12:10	213
12:11	91, 160
12:18	160
13:2	54
13:11–14	28
13:13	70
14:1—15:6	3
14:5	139
14:7	160
14:8	160
14:9	79, 160
14:10–11	28
14:11	160
14:15	28, 70, 213
14:17	91, 160
14:19	160
14:23	168
15:1	162
15:3	162
15:12	201
15:13	91, 160
15:4	4, 9, 199
15:16	8, 91, 160
15:18	23, 55, 85, 116
15:18–21	8
15:19	91, 160, 162
15:20–21	4
15:24	4
15:30	91, 160, 213
15:30–33	3
15:33	160
16:7	65
16:8	65
16:13	232
16:17–20	3
16:18	114
16:19	55, 85
16:20	160
16:26	55, 85, 199

1 Corinthians

1:7	198
1:10	139
1:13	64
1:14	64
1:15	64
1:16	64
1:17	64
1:26	153
2:10	206
2:11	162
2:14	162
2:16	139
3:3	70
3:16	165
3:21–23	183
3:22–23	245
4:4	223
6:9	182
6:11	223
6:12–20	102
6:15	63
7:10	101
7:11	36
7:14	88
7:17	70
7:32–34	162
7:40	162
10:1–2	64
10:1–13	64, 205
10:6	8, 46
10:11	46, 51, 64, 66
10:18	153
11:23	86
11:25	69
11:27	69
12:3	162
12:13	64
12:31	123
14:14	139
14:15	139
14:19	139
15:1–11	86
15:3	86
15:20	197
15:22	219
15:23	197

Ancient Documents Index

1 Corinthians (*continued*)

15:25	236
15:26	243
15:29	64
15:40	184
15:40–43	223
15:41	184
15:43	184
15:45	219
15:49	226
15:50	182
15:54–55	44, 49
15:54–57	243
15:57	138

2 Corinthians

1:8	123
1:17	153
2:9	24
2:14	138
3:3	69
3:6–7	106
3:17	162
4:2	70
4:4	226
4:17	123
5:7	70
5:14–15	33
5:16	153
5:18–20	36
5:21	33
6:17	88
8:2	24
9:13	24
9:15	138
9:16	138
10:2	153
10:2–3	70
10:3	153
11:2	103
11:3	42, 114
11:13	244
11:18	153
12:6–10	227
12:17	244
12:18	70
12:21	88
13:3	24

Galatians

1:4	156
1:8	244
1:10	162
1:13	123
1:18	65
2:16	223
2:17	63, 223
2:19	108
3:2	225
3:5	225
3:8	217, 223, 233
3:11	223
3:12	70, 153
3:13	33
3:18	182
3:19	244
3:21	63, 98
3:23–29	109
3:24	58, 223
3:27	64
3:29	182
4:1	182
4:5	173
4:6	180
4:7	182
4:8–11	109
4:9	172
4:14	134, 244
4:23	153
4:24	172
4:29	153
4:30	182
5:1	172
5:2–6	109
5:4	223
5:5	198
5:16	70
5:18	178
5:19	88
5:21	105, 182
5:22–23	105
6:8	91, 92
6:14	63

Ephesians

1:5	173
1:14	182
1:20	236
2:1–3	43
2:6	227
3:6	185
3:10	244
3:18	245
4:5	64
4:11	8
4:17	139

4:19	88
4:23	139
4:30	162, 177
5:3	88
5:5	88, 182
5:21–33	102
5:25–33	103
6:5	153
6:12	244

Philippians

1:19	162
1:24	65
1:29	227
2:8	60
2:22	24
3:3	162
3:10	218
3:20	198
3:21	184, 218, 223
4:7	139

Colossians

1:6	104
1:10	104
1:16	244
1:18	244
1:23	65
1:24	134
2:15	244
2:18	139
3:4	184
3:5	88, 124
3:12	232
3:22	153
3:24	182

1 Thessalonians

2:3	88
2:4	162
2:15	162
4:1	162
4:7	88

2 Thessalonians

1:4–5	227
2:2	139
2:3	114
2:13	197
2:14	184

1 Timothy

1:1	200
1:16	91, 92
2:13	42
2:14	114
3:16	223
4:16	65
5:21	233
6:5	139
6:12	91, 92

2 Timothy

2:4	162
2:10	233
3:8	139

Titus

1:1	233
1:2	91
1:15	139
2:3	200
3:7	91, 92, 223

Philemon

18	45

Hebrews

1:3	21, 236
1:7	244
1:13	21, 236
5:6	21
5:8	60
6:20	21
7:3	21
8:1	21, 236
10:6	148
10:8	148
10:12	21, 236
10:13	148
11:5–6	161
11:9	185
13:11	148

James

1:18	197
4:9	135
5:1	136

1 Peter

1:11	162

1 Peter (continued)

3:7	185
3:18–22	68
3:20	68
3:21	68
4:18	34

1 John

1:2	92
2:25	92
3:15	92
322	162
5:11	92
5:13	92
5:20	92

Jude

1:21	92

Revelation

3:17	135
14:4	197
7:17	177

APOCRYPHA

Judith

4:15	214
7:25	130
9:6	216
9:12	246
11:19	216
12:7	64
12:14	161
16:14	246

Tobit

4:21	161
6:13	100
8:5	246
13:12	135

2 Maccabees

1:25	233
2:11	148
4:47	135
5:22	135
6:23	122
6:28	122
7:9	33, 93
8:21	33
12:43	148

3 Maccabees

1:23	34
5:15	34
5:47	135

4 Maccabees

1:8	33
1:10	33
2:5	112, 113
2:6	114
5:13	93
16:7	135
18:8	112

Wisdom of Solomon

2:6	246
2:12–20	30
2:23	218
2:24	40
3:9	229, 233, 234
3:11	135
4:14	161
4:15	229, 234
5:17	246
6:13	216
7:26	218
8:8	216
9:9	161
9:11	177
9:16	34
9:18	161
10:7	104
10:10	177
10:17	177
13:10	135
16:24	246
18:6	216
19:6	246

Sirach

1:10	212
7:13	214
9:9	99
16:8	231
16:17	246
17:3	218

21:20	34	54:15	40
26:29	34	56:6	43
32:7	34		
34:25	64	**4 Ezra**	
39:25	214	3:7	43
39:27	214	3:20–27	40
41:23	99	3:21	40
43:25	246	4:30–32	40
45:5	112	7:18–20	43
46:1	233, 234	8:60	43
47:22	229, 233, 234	10:9	190
48:22	161	23:26	190
49:16	246		

Psalms of Solomon

2:15	72	**Testament of Abraham**	
3:5	72	18:11	166
4:8	72		
4:25	212	**Testament of Joseph**	
6:6	212	13:4	65
8:7	72		
10:3	212	**Testament of Solomon**	
14:1	212	12:3	220
14:2	112		
17:12	231	**Jubilees**	
		1:29	234

Baruch

1:10	148
3:9	112
4:1	112, 117
4:6	130

OT PSEUDEPIGRAPHA

1 Enoch

5:7	19
5:9	19
10:17	19
11:2	19

3 Enoch

11	122

2 Bar

15:8	190
19:8	40
23:4	40, 43
48:42–43	40

DEAD SEA SCROLLS

CD

4:3–4	234

1QH

2:13	234
12:20–26	20

1QHab

9:12	234
10:14	21

1QM

4:6	21
4:8	21

1QPHab

9:12	234
19:9–10	130

Ancient Documents Index

1QS
4:7	93
8:6	34

4Q504
2:15	130

4Q534
1:10	234

4QFLor
1:19	234

4QpIsa
9:12	234

4QpPs
2:5	234

JOSEPHUS

Antiquities
4:295	122
13:5–6	33
14:135	65
15:281	65
18:109–36	102

PHILO

De decalogo
142	114
150	114
173	114

Legum allegoriae
3:94	65

De vita Mosis
2:3	122
2:14	122

De specialibus legibus
4:48	65
4:85	114

RABBINICAL WRITINGS

m.Abot
3:14	117

TACITUS

Annals
11:12–38	102

EURIPIDES

Alcestis
295	117

AESCHYLUS

Agamemnon
1260	140

OVID

Metamorphoses
9:474	140

www.ingramcontent.com/pod-product-compliance
Lightning Source LLC
Chambersburg PA
CBHW080730300426
44114CB00019B/2536